Praise for *The Battle* [barcode: T0153974] *...tine*

"Every community that stands fast, loving its people and its land, its customs and its ways, will be seen, eventually, as worthy of saving. This is because it is our own humanity we are learning from, our own value. There will also arise a special voice to champion us, one that is brave, trustworthy, and true. In *The Battle for Justice in Palestine* it is the voice of Ali Abunimah, fierce, wise—a warrior for justice and peace—someone whose large heart, one senses, beyond his calm, is constantly on fire. A pragmatist but also a poet. This is the book to read to understand the present bizarre and ongoing complexity of the Palestine/Israel tragedy. And though it is filled with the grim reality of this long and deadly, ugly and dehumanizing conflict, it also offers hope: that as more people awaken to the shocking reality of what has for decades been going on, we can bring understanding and restitution to the Palestinian people. Their struggle to exist in dignity and peace in their own homeland—and this may be the biggest surprise of Abunimah's book—is mirrored in the struggles for survival and autonomy of more than a few of us."

—Alice Walker, author of *The Color Purple* and many other works, winner of the Pulitzer Prize and National Book Award

"A crucially needed dose of educated hope. This is what hits me from this fascinating amalgam of incisive journalism, analytic prose, and intellectually compelling vision that emanates from many years of brilliant activism. Sailing effortlessly from the domestic to the global, from Johannesburg to Belfast and from Chicago to Tel Aviv, Ali Abunimah paints a lucid, accessible picture out of a complex web of racism, racialized oppression, and creative resistance. Ali does not give us hope; he helps us dig for it within us by meticulously laying out before us the facts, the trends, the challenges, and the inspiring resistance to them."

—Omar Barghouti, Palestinian human rights activist, co-founder of the BDS movement, author of *Boycott, Divestment, Sanctions: The Global Struggle for Palestinian Rights*

"With incisive style and scrupulous attention to documentation and detail, Ali Abunimah's new book offers a complex portrait, from every angle, of the Palestinian struggle for justice today."

—Rebecca Vilkomerson, Executive Director, Jewish Voice for Peace

"This is the best book on Palestine in the last decade. No existing book presents the staggering details and sophistication of analysis that Abunimah's book offers. Abunimah's scope includes an analysis of the politics, economics, environmental policies, identity politics, international relations, academic scholarship and activism, global solidarity, and official and unofficial lobbies that have come to bear on Palestine and the Palestinians. *The Battle for Justice in Palestine* is the most comprehensive treatment of Palestinian suffering under Israeli control and offers the only possible way to end it. It is a must read for anyone seeking to understand the current situation of the Palestinians and Israel."

—Joseph Massad, Columbia University

"In *The Battle for Justice in Palestine*, Ali Abunimah—the most astute commentator writing on Palestine today—bursts the leaky myths of Israeli exceptionalism while carefully examining where the battle for Palestine is currently being waged. Forget the endless "peace process," which has ushered in little more than massive economic exploitation, tragic environmental degradation, and servile and destructive politics. Focus instead, Abunimah tells us, on the many civil society and campus initiatives around the world that are bravely ushering in a new era of global grassroots organizing for justice. Rich in information and deep in analysis, *The Battle for Justice in Palestine* will inspire readers that Palestinian self-determination is not only possible but absolutely necessary."

—Moustafa Bayoumi, author, *How Does It Feel to Be a Problem?:*
Being Young and Arab in America

The Battle for Justice
in Palestine

Ali Abunimah

Haymarket Books
Chicago, Illinois

First published by Haymarket Books in 2014
© 2014 Ali Abunimah

Haymarket Books
P.O. Box 180165
Chicago, IL 60618
773-583-7884
info@haymarketbooks.org
www.haymarketbooks.org

ISBN: 978-1-60846-324-4

Distributed to the trade in the US through Consortium Book Sales and Distribution
(www.cbsd.com) and internationally through Ingram Publisher Services
International (www.ingramcontent.com).

This book was published with the generous support of Lannan Foundation and
Wallace Action Fund.

Special discounts are available for bulk purchases by organizations and institutions.
Please call 773-583-7884 or email info@haymarketbooks.org for more information.

Cover design by Eric Ruder. Cover image of a celebration in Gaza in November
2012 by Majdi Fathi, APAimages.

Printed in the United States.

Library of Congress CIP data is available.

Entered into digital printing February 2021.

Contents

List of Abbreviations

ADL	Anti-Defamation League
AIPAC	American Israel Public Affairs Committee
ANC	African National Congress
ANSWER	Act Now to Stop War and End Racism
BDS	Boycott, divestment, and sanctions
BMIP	Bethlehem Multidisciplinary Industrial Park
BNC	Boycott National Committee
CSUN	California State University, Northridge
DUP	Democratic Unionist Party
GATT	General Agreement on Tariffs and Trade
HIDTA	High Intensity Drug Trafficking Area
IACP	International Association of Chiefs of Police
IMF	International Monetary Fund
IPCC	Israeli-Palestinian Chamber of Commerce
IPO	Initial public offering
IRA	Irish Republican Army
JINSA	Jewish Institute of National Security Affairs
JNF	Jewish National Fund
JTA	Jewish Telegraphic Agency
LGBTQ	Lesbian, gay, bisexual, transgender, and queer
MSA	Muslim Student Association
NCLR	National Council of La Raza
NUG	National unity government
NYPD	New York Police Department
OCR	Office of Civil Rights
OECD	Organisation for Economic Co-operation and Development
OFC	Olympia Food Co-op
OPIC	Overseas Private Investment Corporation
PADICO	Palestinian Development and Investment Company

PCRF	Palestine Children's Relief Fund
PIEFZA	Palestinian Industrial Estate and Free Zone Authority
PA	Palestinian Authority
PRC	Palestinian Return Centre
SJP	Students for Justice in Palestine
SOAS	School of Oriental and African Studies
TSA	Transportation Security Administration
UCSA	University of California Student Association
UNRWA	United Nations Relief and Works Agency
WTO	World Trade Organization

Acknowledgments

It would be impossible to thank everyone who played a role in helping me write this book individually. The ideas and experiences I describe were shaped by countless interactions over several years, from conversations in cars with students who came to pick me up at airports for events to articles and conversations shared on Twitter. I would especially like to mention my visit to the Gaza Strip in May 2013 at the invitation of the Palestine Festival of Literature. For a week I barely slept as I visited almost every corner of the territory and heard from so many people who were unstintingly generous with their time and insights. Just a few weeks after that visit, the Egyptian military coup regime tightened the closure of Gaza, meaning that a similar trip would be all but impossible today.

From conception to completion, my editor Anthony Arnove provided invaluable advice and reassurance that enabled me to finish the book. And as I told Sarah Grey, the copy editor, "I like my writing much better after you've edited it." Her skillful pen greatly improved the quality of my prose. Everyone at Haymarket Books has made me feel that they are as excited about this book as I am.

Several individuals were exceptionally generous with their time, commenting on chapters or sections. Although the shortcomings are entirely my responsibility, this book is much better thanks to Nora Barrows-Friedman, David Boodell, Michael Brown, Benjamin Doherty, Joseph Massad, Maureen Murphy, and Alaa Tartir. Dena Shunra was always ready to help me find and analyze Hebrew sources and Maath Musleh helped me answer questions that required on-the-ground research in the occupied West Bank. I'm grateful to others—too numerous to name individually—who answered queries or helped me find references along the way.

Chapter 3 is adapted from an essay that appeared in *Pretending Democracy: Israel, an Ethnocratic State,* edited by Na'eem Jeenah (Johannesburg: AMEC, 2012), and chapter 7 is adapted from an essay first published by Al-Shabaka.

I was honored and fortunate to be awarded the Lannan Foundation's 2013 Cultural Freedom Fellowship which provided me with the time and space to work on this book, including two months in Marfa, Texas, where significant portions were written. I'm grateful to everyone at the Lannan Foundation who make me feel that my work matters. As important, my amazing colleagues at the *Electronic Intifada* stepped up so that I could take the time I needed to write the book.

I am as ever grateful for the friendship and support of Benjamin Doherty. In writing this book, and in all I do, my parents and family have given unlimited love and encouragement.

Preface

The Palestinians are winning. That might seem like hubris or even insensitivity. After all, in so many ways things have never looked worse. As I write these words, 1.7 million people in the Gaza Strip face their darkest days. After years of Israeli siege and war, electricity is out for most people for up to eighteen hours a day. With no pumps to take it away, sewage floods the streets. The water supply is undrinkable and there's no escape as Israel and its ally, the Egyptian military regime, keep Gaza's borders under near-permanent closure.

A short distance away in the occupied West Bank, things are hardly better, as Israel—ruled by a triumphant and seemingly unassailable far right—relentlessly presses ahead with violent colonization aimed at "Judaizing" what remains of Palestinian land. In the past two decades, Israeli military occupation has been complemented by something even more insidious: the Palestinian Authority's collaborationist neoliberal regime, which robs its people of economic self-sufficiency and control even before "statehood" is achieved.

Meanwhile, Palestinian citizens in present-day Israel face escalating incitement from Israeli leaders who consider them an unwanted fifth column in a "Jewish state." For Palestinian refugees who have languished in exile since 1948, life has rarely been more desperate. Among the millions displaced in Syria's horrifying civil war are more than two hundred thousand Palestinians, half of the Palestinian refugee population living in that country. In Egypt, the revolutionary expressions of support for Palestinian rights that threatened to up-end the Egyptian-Israeli peace treaty after the 2011 overthrow of Hosni Mubarak have been drowned out by the coup regime and private media's scapegoating Palestinians. Once again, Palestinians, prevented from returning to their homeland, are at the mercy of violent geopolitics over which they exercise no control. Burdened with at-best-ineffectual leaders lacking in vision, the Palestinians seem to many to be adrift.

Yet for all these undeniable truths, it is not the Palestinians, as a people seeking self-determination and liberation, who face constant doubt and anxiety about the legitimacy and longevity of their political project. "Israel's current state of relative security and prosperity does not change the fact that today's status quo will not be tomorrow's or the future's," US Secretary of State John Kerry has warned.[1] His solution to Israel's existential crisis remains as unimaginative and unlikely as that of his predecessors: the so-called two-state solution whose desired outcome is "an independent, viable Palestinian state, and . . . recognition of Israel as the homeland of the Jewish people."

Those who believe that this vision can ever be fulfilled are a dwindling band—nor can such a formula ever lead to peace or justice. The mantra-like repetition of "solutions" like Kerry's has too often replaced thinking about and challenging dominant definitions of the "problem" in Palestine and how it can be resolved. If we were to invest our hopes or any more effort in pursuing this dead end, then the future of the Palestinians would indeed be as bleak as the present circumstances so many are living. I cannot count the number of times I've been told that "the only solution is two states" and without that nothing will ever change. Yet our obsession with states and borders has often obscured just how much everything is changing.

Today, the very claim that Israel has a "right to exist as a Jewish state" has become a central controversy in a way that seemed unthinkable even a decade ago. Today, Palestinian youths in Israel are not waiting for permission to return to the lands from which their parents and grandparents were expelled. They are actually returning to villages such as Kufr Birim and Iqrit in the Galilee. This "grassroots, youth-led movement unprecedented in the history of activism for the right to return," as Nadim Nashef, director of the Haifa-based Association for Arab Youth–Baladna, calls it, directly challenges the racist, anti-Palestinian foundations of the Israeli state.[2] Palestinians can take on Israel's might and prevail. As I write, news has come that in the face of determined, organized opposition, Israel's government has withdrawn the "Prawer Plan" to forcibly displace tens of thousands of Palestinian Bedouins from their lands.[3] Whether this is a temporary reprieve or a lasting victory is an open question, to be determined in the course of an ongoing struggle.

Today, Israel is mobilizing unprecedented resources in an effort to fight a global boycott, divestment, and sanctions (BDS) movement that wins new adherents and chalks up new achievements every week. In a way unimaginable just a few years ago, academic associations, trade unions, churches and pension funds are debating and adopting policies to isolate Israeli institutions and foreign companies that are complicit in crimes against the Palestinian people.

Prominent American Jewish philosopher Judith Butler, who overcame her own opposition to an academic boycott, writes that "within the last two years I have seen how individuals and groups have emerged from their state of mute fear and anxiety into a tentative desire to talk."[4] Rather than shutting down dialogue—as critics claim BDS does—it is generating more discussion and action than ever. This movement is finding new support—small but growing—even among Israeli Jews. Ronnie Barkan, an Israeli activist who helped found Boycott From Within, a group that fully supports the Palestinian BDS campaign, explains: "In a country founded on the basis of ethnic cleansing and ethnic segregation, whose main concern up to this day is the maintaining of an artificially-created Jewish majority, the only response to this type of thinking is to negate it in its totality." For Barkan, opposition to Zionism is inseparable from the "struggle towards democracy in this region."[5]

As one consequence of these efforts, the question of Palestine is being redefined not as the "Palestinian problem," but as the settler-colonial problem and the problem of Zionism's attempt to deny the rights, the history, and even the existence of the Palestinian people. Amid this transformation, Palestinians are rediscovering the necessity of waging a joint struggle with others, in the United States and around the world, who face systematic violence rooted in ideologies of racial and cultural supremacy. None of this is happening because governments or politicians have suddenly found the courage to confront Israel, but despite their persistent refusal to do so. In South Africa, where he was attending the memorial for Nelson Mandela, Palestinian Authority leader Mahmoud Abbas declared, "No, we do not support the boycott of Israel."[6] But millions of people disagree with him. The change is happening because people all over the world—responding to the resistance and steadfastness of Palestinians in their villages, fields, and fishing boats, in their refugee camps, and in Israel's prisons—are organizing to hold Israel accountable.

While Palestinians have always enjoyed broad global public support, this support has been too easily neutralized as long as it was limited to periodic street demonstrations—important though those can be—or channeled through unrepresentative governments. What is different now is that Palestinians and the global solidarity movement are mobilizing this support in a sustained campaign that Israel has defined as an "existential threat" to its dominance.

So now let me qualify my opening claim: the Palestinians are winning the *argument* and Zionists are losing it. Israel's panicked but formidable counterattack—

a key topic of this book—underscores that the battle for justice in Palestine is and has always been, first and foremost, a battle of ideas: that Zionism has a right to colonize Palestine, expel its indigenous people, and deny rights to those who remain; that Jews form a collective that has a right to claim Palestine for itself; that resisting Zionism's violent takeover of Palestine is "extremism" and "terrorism" while acquiescing to it is "moderation" and "peace"; that there is no future except through partition and segregation; that decolonization and a just future for all who live in historic Palestine remains within reach.

Our notions of the possible and impossible, the just and the unjust, the desirable and the undesirable are bounded by such ideas and how legitimate and "realistic" they are seen to be. It is precisely to prevent us from breaking out of the strictly enforced limits of current thinking that Israel and its lobbies are investing so much in efforts to stop mere discussion—especially in the United States, Israel's indispensible sponsor.

There can never be a guarantee about what will happen in the future, and it would be easy enough to submit to despair about the catastrophes facing so many people in the region around Palestine today. But for the reasons I explore in this book, I believe that the possibilities for fundamental transformation in the next few years remain open, promising, and exciting.

The victory against Israeli apartheid, colonialism, and racism that I am convinced Palestinians and their allies have it in their power to make will not be theirs alone. It will belong to everyone who believes in, and fights for, equality and justice.

Ali Abunimah
December 2013

Chapter 1

Shared Values, Shared Struggle

Israel, European and US leaders often insist, is a shining beacon for the world. François Hollande, the Socialist candidate elected France's president in 2012, observed that Israel faced so much criticism precisely because it is a "great democracy."[1] In a similar vein, Matthew Gould, the British ambassador in Tel Aviv, wrote that his country's close cooperation with Israel stemmed from the "principles of freedom, democracy and the rule of law that we work together to protect. These shared principles are the bedrock of our relationship."[2] American leaders, however, are second to none in the intensity of their ardor. In 2008, Senator Barack Obama insisted that "the establishment of Israel was just and necessary" and that "the bond between Israel and the United States is rooted in more than our shared national interests—it's rooted in the shared values and shared stories of our people."[3] It is a theme he has returned to often as president, enumerating, for instance, some of the "shared values" in a 2012 speech to the American Israel Public Affairs Committee (AIPAC): "A commitment to human dignity. A belief that freedom is a right that is given to all of God's children. An experience that shows us that democracy is the one and only form of government that can truly respond to the aspirations of citizens."[4] Among the "shared stories" is the fact that both the United States and Israel were established by European settler colonists who usurped lands inhabited by indigenous peoples, though this is something Obama did not mention to his AIPAC audience.[5] Another contemporary "shared value" that went unacknowledged is that Israel's practice of "targeted killings"—extrajudicial executions of "terrorist" suspects and bystanders, once condemned by the United States—has become the signature policy of Obama, the only president in history known to keep a "kill list" of US

1

citizens and others.[6] But despite these incongruities, it would appear at first blush that, at least when it comes to officially sanctioned racism and discrimination at home, the United States and Israel diverge sharply.

In his second inaugural address President Obama harked back to the iconic ideas shaping America's view of itself as a beacon for the world. He stood before a crowd of thousands as the living embodiment of the progress and opportunity he now sought to extend even further in a society more willing than ever to embrace multiple cultures. "We affirm the promise of our democracy," the president said. "We recall that what binds this nation together is not the colors of our skin or the tenets of our faith or the origins of our names. What makes us exceptional, what makes us America, is our allegiance to an idea articulated in a declaration made more than two centuries ago. 'We hold these truths to be self-evident, that all men are created equal.'" Yet even Obama conceded that "while these truths may be self-evident, they've never been self-executing." The history of the United States is one of conflict, sometimes at great cost and bloodshed, to make these ideals real for ever more Americans, whether brought in bondage, born at home, or hopeful immigrants coming to seek a better life. It is a familiar story: the time when official white supremacy was the natural and seemingly unassailable order—enforced by a system of juridical and customary violence known as Jim Crow—has passed forever. The abolition of slavery; the civil rights movement and the end of segregation; comprehensive civil rights legislation ending discrimination in education, housing, and employment; and voting rights are celebrated as milestones toward realizing the promise that all are "created equal." Few deny that significant disparities have yet to be eliminated. Few deny that racial gaps in health, wealth, and education are vast in the United States, just as they are between Jews and Arabs in Israel. But these are often talked about as "legacies." Even the most conservative opponents of social programs intended to remedy these disparities do not claim—as Prime Minister Benjamin Netanyahu has in Israel—that too much integration in and of itself would constitute an existential threat to the United States. Contrast this optimistic and liberal vision to Israel's record of state-sponsored racism and inequality, which, as we shall see, is broadly supported by Israeli Jewish opinion and justified as necessary for the state's survival.

On its face, then, the American system—and the liberal narrative that Obama offers—would appear to share everything in common with the "state of all its citizens" that Palestinian parties in Israel demand, and nothing at all with a discriminatory and demographics-obsessed "Jewish and democratic state." Sadly, however, despite Obama's colorblind rhetoric, Palestinians under Israeli rule and people of color in the

United States increasingly find themselves facing similar racist ideologies—even if they sometimes take veiled forms—and systems of physical and social control that are interconnected. These may be the real "shared values" of Israel and the United States—and they demand of us a shared understanding and a shared struggle to change them. While abolishing the racism and violence Zionism practices against Palestinians is the key to justice and peace in historic Palestine, no less than the abolition of slavery and Jim Crow in the United States were absolutely necessary, recent American history demonstrates that systems of racial control and the ideologies underpinning them remain robust and adaptable. A formally liberal and rights-based order can allow a system just as oppressive as Jim Crow to hide and flourish in plain sight. Understanding the present-day experience of African Americans and other non-European groups in the United States offers critically important lessons to Palestinians and underscores that the struggle for Palestinian human rights must be closely linked to the struggle for human rights in the United States and around the world.

On the eve of Barack Obama's 2012 re-election, 51 percent of Americans expressed "explicit anti-black attitudes, compared with 48 percent in 2008," an Associated Press survey found. The number of Americans with implicit "anti-black sentiments" jumped from 49 to 56 percent from 2008, while "the share of Americans expressing pro-black attitudes fell."[7] In 2008, 55 percent of whites voted for Obama's Republican opponent, Senator John McCain, while in 2012, 59 percent of whites voted for Republican Mitt Romney. Obama lost every white age group and white women.[8] These are signs that even as legal forms of discrimination have been abolished, the United States has in many ways become more racially polarized; Obama's re-election was secured only because he won majorities of every nonwhite demographic group. These facts—and the incessant cable news and Internet propaganda depicting Obama variously as foreign and Muslim—run counter to the warm narrative that Obama's 2008 election was historic proof that America had overcome its troubled racial past. These attitudes challenge the comforting assertion that, though there is still much work to be done, the history of the United States is one of steady progress. Indeed, in important respects, things are moving backward.

Becky Pettit, professor of sociology at the University of Washington and author of the 2012 book *Invisible Men: Mass Incarceration and the Myth of Black Progress*, found that the exclusion of millions of incarcerated Black men from national statistics on voting, wages, employment, and education has for years grossly exaggerated "progress" in virtually all indicators of achievement. When the population of incarcerated Black men is included in the statistics, the status of African Americans overall has, shockingly, actually deteriorated in the decades since the great civil rights victories.[9] How could this be?

In her influential 2010 book *The New Jim Crow: Mass Incarceration in the Age of Colorblindness*, civil rights lawyer and Ohio State University law professor Michelle Alexander challenges the optimistic liberal narrative "that emphasizes the death of slavery and Jim Crow and celebrates the nation's 'triumphs over race' with the election of Barack Obama" as "dangerously misguided."[10] Alexander argues that, after enacting formal civil rights, the United States took a wrong turn and reversed much of what had been achieved, despite the increasingly common sight of prominent African Americans in high office. As Jim Crow once replaced slavery, so mass incarceration, brought about with the drug war, has "emerged as a stunningly comprehensive and well-designed system of racialized social control that functions in a manner strikingly similar to Jim Crow"[11]:

> What has changed since the collapse of Jim Crow has less to do with the basic structure of our society than the language we use to justify it. In the era of color-blindness it is no longer socially permissible to use race, explicitly, as a justification for discrimination, exclusion and social contempt. So we don't. Rather than rely on race, we use our criminal justice system to label people of color "criminals" and then engage in all the practices we supposedly left behind. Today it is perfectly legal to discriminate against criminals in nearly all the ways in which it was once legal to discriminate against African Americans. Once you're labeled a felon, the old forms of discrimination—employment discrimination, housing discrimination, denial of the right to vote, denial of educational opportunity, denial of food stamps and other public benefits, and exclusion from jury service—are suddenly legal. As a criminal you have scarcely more rights, and arguably less respect, than a black man living in Alabama at the height of Jim Crow. We have not ended racial caste in America; we have merely redesigned it.[12]

Alexander describes a system in which children, overwhelmingly Black, are shuttled from decrepit and underfunded schools and neighborhoods where unemployment far exceeds even the levels during the era of formal segregation to brand-new, high-tech, and well-funded prisons, often owned and operated by the multibillion-dollar private prison industry. Within a span of thirty years, "for reasons unrelated to crime rates," incarceration rates quintupled in the United States and the prison population exploded from three hundred thousand to more than two million, as the country created a penal system on a scale unprecedented in world history. US incarceration rates far surpass those of Russia, China, and Iran, countries regularly portrayed as particularly repressive.[13] By the mid-2000s, thirty-one million Americans, roughly the population of Canada, had been arrested in the war on drugs; seven million are currently behind bars, on probation, or on parole.[14] These millions are in many cases juridically "locked out" of voting, work, jury service, housing, and other basic needs by the "criminal" label they will carry all their lives. The devastation affects not only the individuals themselves, but millions more people in their families and communities.

But it is the racial dimension that Alexander finds most striking: "No other country in the world imprisons so many of its racial or ethnic minorities."[15] In many urban communities, three out of four young Black men can expect to serve time in prison.[16] More African American adults are in prison or under correctional supervision, probation, or control than were enslaved in 1850 in the United States. In 2004, more African American men were denied the right to vote due to felon disenfranchisement laws than in 1870 due to formal racial discrimination, poll taxes, and literacy tests. In jurisdictions across the United States, Black men are admitted to prison on drug charges at a rate ranging from twenty to fifty-seven times greater than white men.[17] In 2006, one in every fourteen Black men was in prison, compared with one in every 106 white men. The systematic removal of Black men from their communities has produced such a significant gender gap that the difficulty many Black women face in finding life partners is a widely discussed phenomenon.[18]

Drawing on meticulous research, Alexander demonstrates that no crime statistics can explain the dramatic rise in incarceration—or its disproportionate impact on people of color. Rates of crime and incarceration have moved independently of each other. Government statistics show that people of all races use and sell drugs at roughly the same rates. Among students, for example, whites and Blacks use marijuana at nearly identical rates, although white students use crack and cocaine at more than seven times the rate of Black students.[19] And like much else in American life, drug markets are segmented by race and class: whites sell drugs to whites, Blacks to Blacks, students to students, rural people to rural people.[20] Alexander explodes the myth that the focus on people of color is justified because hardcore violent criminals are concentrated in their neighborhoods, and that the war on drugs is aimed at "kingpins" and big-time dealers. The vast majority of arrests—four out of five in 2005—were for possession; only one out of five was for selling. Arrests for marijuana possession accounted for 80 percent of the growth in drug arrests during the 1990s.[21] Nor can violent crime explain the shocking numbers. Violent crime rates have been falling; only a minuscule proportion of the astronomical increase in incarcerations is due to convictions for homicide. It is the way that the war on drugs has been waged, in communities already devastated by economic neglect, decline, and mass incarceration, that has proved to be one of the great engines for generating crime and violence.[22]

In major cities, homicides are heavily concentrated in the poorest, most economically disenfranchised, and most heavily policed communities. In 2013, Chicago mayor Rahm Emanuel received press accolades for bringing down the city's homicide rate by "saturating" specific neighborhoods with hundreds of police officers (at a massive and unsustainable cost to the city's budget of tens of millions of dollars in extra overtime pay).[23] Meanwhile, Emanuel has overseen the largest mass shutdown of public schools in the country's history. The children in the fifty schools Emanuel announced he would close in 2013 were 88 percent Black, 94 percent low-income, and overwhelmingly concentrated in economically deprived areas. It is difficult to see how such slash-and-burn tactics can do anything but speed up what many in Chicago call the "rail to jail" for children and their parents. As Glenn Greenwald observes, "growing up with a parent in prison is itself a predictor of later criminality."[24] Thus the very mass incarceration policies that target the poorest and most powerless, while political and economic elites enjoy ever-greater immunity from the law, actually perpetuate the crime they are supposedly intended to fight.

Racializing Crime

The "enemy" in the drug war, Alexander argues, has been racially defined; the war has been waged almost exclusively in poor communities of color. Draconian sentencing laws give prosecutors immense power to coerce people, often with little evidence, to accept plea bargains that send them to prison because losing the gamble of a trial with inadequate legal resources could result in a sentence lasting decades. Nonetheless, going to prison at all is enough to mark one as a "felon," with all of that label's lifelong consequences. This system "locks people not only behind actual bars in actual prisons, but also behind virtual bars and virtual walls that are invisible to the naked eye but function nearly as effectively as Jim Crow."[25]

It has become common to associate the post–September 11, 2001, PATRIOT Act with the dramatic erosion of civil liberties and individual rights and the increase in intrusive government surveillance in the United States and other Western societies. In fact, this gutting of constitutional protections began much earlier. In cities across the United States and along the highways connecting them, hundreds of thousands, perhaps millions of people, overwhelmingly brown and Black, are subjected annually to intrusive "stop-and-frisk" searches or traffic stops used as a pretext for such searches.

Several years ago, while driving with a friend toward Chicago through northwest Indiana, I was pulled over by an Indiana state trooper for what was ostensibly a routine traffic stop. But the officer subjected me to frightening and intimidating treatment. I was made to get out of the car and stand in the cold rain in the glaring headlights of his squad car as he questioned me aggressively. He wanted to know where I was coming from, where I was going, and where I lived. My voice shaking, I asked him if I was required to answer his questions. He said I wasn't, but if I refused he would issue me all sorts of citations.

I remember thinking, "This is one of those moments when things could go badly wrong if I am not very careful about what I say and do." It was shortly after a spate of police shootings in which unarmed motorists had been shot because police claimed to have mistaken ordinary objects in their hands for weapons. I did my best to stay calm as the officer kept badgering me and accusing me of giving "suspicious" answers. In reality I was freezing and scared, but I think I understood at the time that he was trying to provoke me into reacting to create a pretext to search the car without my consent—the legal term is "probable cause." I did my best not to give it to him. But when he started to ask me about my friend, I said I didn't think I should have to answer questions about any passengers in my car. The officer said he would go and speak to my friend himself and ordered me to remain standing with my hands on my head and face the headlights of his car, which was stopped behind mine. "If you turn around I will arrest you for assault," he warned. My friend was not legally obliged to speak to the police officer either, but managed to convince him that we were simply two people driving in a car. The officer returned with a completely changed demeanor and offered me his hand. He explained that police were monitoring the highway for people driving suspiciously slowly, who they suspected might be drug couriers trying to avoid detection. What had made me a target of suspicion, apparently, was obeying the speed limit on that stretch of the Indiana Toll Road. It is outrageous that he thought this explanation would make me feel better or justify his behavior, but I was too shaken and relieved to offer any more resistance. He let me go with no citation. It was an experience I will never forget.

Only after I read Alexander's book did I recognize that what happened exactly fit a pattern used hundreds of thousands of times by local police departments all over the country as part of a federal Drug Enforcement Agency program called Operation Pipeline. This program has trained tens of thousands of officers "how to use a minor traffic violation as a pretext to stop someone, how to lengthen a routine traffic stop and leverage it into a search for drugs, how to obtain consent from a reluctant motorist, and how to use drug-sniffing dogs to obtain probable cause."[26] Blessed by the Supreme Court, such stops, which rarely turn up any drugs, eviscerate constitutional protections against unreasonable search and seizure. They allow police to use arbitrary and nonsensical profiling criteria including "traveling with luggage, traveling without luggage, driving an expensive car, driving a car that needs repairs, driving a rental car, driving with out-of-state license places," and driving with "mismatched occupants." In some states—clearly, in my experience, in Indiana—officers are even told to watch out for "scrupulous obedience to traffic laws."[27] The effect of such scattershot criteria is to give police the power to stop anyone at any time for any reason and bully them into cooperating.

While, fortunately, I have rarely been subjected to such special attention (at least outside of airports), it is daily routine for many young people in American cities. "The militarized nature of law enforcement in ghetto communities has inspired rap artists and Black youth to refer to the police presence in Black communities as 'The Occupation,'" observes Alexander. "In these occupied territories, many Black youth automatically 'assume the position' when a patrol car pulls up, knowing full well that they will be detained and frisked no matter what."[28] These tactics, ubiquitous in American inner cities, are unknown in predominantly white suburban areas or on college campuses, where drugs are just as prevalent. But as narrated through the lyrics of Tupac Shakur and of Public Enemy's *Fear of a Black Planet*, this "occupation" was immediately recognizable to three young men in Lydd, near Tel Aviv, who were inspired to form the pioneering and now world-acclaimed Palestinian hip-hop group DAM.

From the Old to the New Jim Crow

What is devastating about Alexander's thesis is her explanation of how racial targeting was not just the outcome of this project but integral to its design. She traces the origins of this "human rights nightmare" to the lingering resentments and racial fears that accompanied the civil rights era. Among whites, the end of formal segregation had its greatest impact not on the liberal elites who were pushing the reforms, but on poor working-class whites, scarcely better educated on average than Black people. These whites faced what many saw as a social demotion. Poor whites were the ones expected to "bear the burden of this profound social adjustment even though many of them were as desperate for upward social mobility and quality education as African Americans." Affirmative action, moreover, created the impression that Blacks were leapfrogging over whites. In the absence of a narrative, social investments, and a movement that could have given everyone a stake in the "nascent integrated racial order," the situation was ripe for political exploitation.[29]

Civil rights had made overt racial fearmongering unavailable as a political discourse in the new era of colorblindness, but conservative, especially Republican, politicians "found they could mobilize white racial resentment by vowing to crack down on crime."[30] An ostensibly race-neutral but highly racialized discourse preyed on fears about social disorder, explicitly linking crime to the kinds of civil disobedience that had been practiced during the struggle to end Jim Crow. This was the essence of Richard Nixon's "Southern Strategy" to lure white voters away from the then-dominant Democratic Party. Nixon himself had explained to an advisor "that you have to face the fact that the whole problem is really the Blacks. The key is to devise a system that recognizes this without appearing to." Nixon's 1968 campaign strategy, as presidential advisor John Ehrlichman explained, was to "go after the racists" and so a "subliminal appeal to the anti-Black voter was always present in Nixon's statements and speeches."[31]

But it was Ronald Reagan who perfected this method by announcing the "war on drugs" in 1982 as a convenient vehicle to advance a racialized discourse on crime without having to use any explicitly racial language. Reagan's "war on drugs" was never intended to be about drugs or crime, so the initial resistance from law enforcement agencies that couldn't see the need for it was eventually broken by massive federal financial incentives, including the transfer of vast quantities of military weaponry to police forces across the country. When the "epidemic" of crack-cocaine use emerged in 1985, years after the drug war had been declared, the Reagan administration launched a massive propaganda effort, assisted by the media, effectively associating drugs and crime with people of color. Deeply entrenched stereotypes of "crack whores," "crack babies," and young Black men as feral "predators" took on the forms that shape perceptions and policies to this day.[32] Israeli politicians, too, have aggressively portrayed Black African migrants and asylum seekers as a criminal class, despite the fact that their crime rate is lower than that of the general Israeli population—but without taking the care Reagan did to avoid explicitly racial language.[33] In America, racialized yet overtly colorblind language has also found a use in international relations. As Joseph Massad observes, Israeli and American politicians, including Obama, frequently describe Israel as "living in a tough neighborhood" where Iranians and Arabs "are the 'violent blacks' of the Middle East and Jews are the 'peaceful white folks.'"[34]

The triumph of Reagan's strategy was how quickly and thoroughly it was adopted by ostensibly liberal Democrats eager not to be seen as "soft on crime." Under the Clinton and Obama administrations, the war on drugs, the militarization of policing, mass incarceration, and the number of rights and benefits formally denied to people labeled "felons" reached ever-more-astounding heights. The war on drugs, "cloaked in race-neutral language, offered whites opposed to racial reform a unique opportunity to express their hostility toward blacks and black progress without being exposed to the charge of racism," Alexander writes.[35] And so it is little surprise that "mass incarceration tends to be categorized as a criminal justice issue as opposed to a racial justice or civil rights issue."[36] The system now runs on autopilot, with no need for the major campaigns of the 1980s to convince the public of the need for the war on drugs. It requires no overt or conscious bigotry to produce these grossly disproportionate racial outcomes. The "war propaganda" has moved on to new ground: "Crack is out; terrorism is in."[37] The "colorblind" parallel should be clear: there was no need to call the "War on Terror" a "war on Muslims." Everyone understood this—those fighting it as well as its victims at home and abroad—despite the constant assurances by public officials to the contrary.[38]

Israel as Warning and Model

As America's wars spread domestically and internationally, Israel and its occupation of the Palestinians have emerged as direct inspirations, not just as metaphor in the rhymes of hip-hop artists. In *The Shock Doctrine,* Naomi Klein offered Israel as a cautionary example for the rest of the world. The assumption in the early days of the "peace process" was that Israel needed peace in order to foster and sustain economic growth and prosperity. But in the post–9/11 environment, Klein shows how Israel transformed its economy into one "that expands in direct response to escalating violence" and has become the world's "shopping mall for homeland security technologies," reaping billions.[39] In 2012, Israel's "security" and "defense" industries, including conventional arms sales, saw record exports worth $7.5 billion, with much of the recent growth coming from the Asia-Pacific region. Israel's arms exports have more than doubled from $3.5 billion in 2003, making it the world's sixth largest arms exporter. Israel's global sales of unmanned aerial vehicles—more commonly known as drones—are second only to those of the United States.[40]

Klein says Israel has offered the "West" a simple pitch: "'The War on Terror you are just embarking on is one we have been fighting since our birth. Let our high-tech firms and privatized spy companies show you how it's done.'"[41] "From a corporate perspective, this development has made Israel a model to be emulated in the post-9/11 market," but from a social and political perspective, Israel should serve as a "stark warning." The fact that "Israel continues to enjoy booming prosperity, even as it wages war against its neighbors and escalates the brutality in the occupied territories, demonstrates just how perilous it is to build an economy based on the premise of continual war and deepening disasters."[42] As Klein shows, the United States has been a major market for Israeli technologies of surveillance and control that were frequently developed and tested on captive Palestinian populations. Indeed, four million Palestinians in the West Bank and Gaza Strip "have become little more than guinea pigs in military experiments designed to enrich a new elite of arms dealers and former generals," according to a 2013 investigative Franco-Belgian–produced documentary by Israeli director Yotam Feldman.[43] Jeff Halper, founder of the Israeli Committee Against House Demolitions, argues that this gives Israel even more reason to want to hold onto the West Bank. "The occupied territories are crucial as a laboratory not just in terms of Israel's internal security, but because they have allowed Israel to become pivotal to the global homeland security industry," Halper has observed.[44]

Since 9/11, pro-Israel lobbying groups have created a veritable industry of shuttling police chiefs from major US cities to Israel to "learn" from the "best." These missions function as important marketing opportunities for Israel's "security" industry as well as to shore up ideological support for, and identification with, Israel among US elites. In 2010, the Jewish United Fund, in cooperation with the Israeli government and Israel's notoriously abusive Shin Bet secret police, sponsored a high-level delegation of Chicago law enforcement officials to Israel, where they were treated to an "intensive seminar" on "intelligence-led policing techniques and responses to critical events."[45] Among the sites they visited were occupied East Jerusalem and "checkpoints for people, vehicles and cargo." Israel's oppressive and internationally condemned occupation regime was being openly touted as a model for Chicago, a city that Michelle Alexander identifies as already one of the worst places to see the devastating effects of racial segregation, militarized policing, and mass incarceration.[46] This trip was the second of its kind; between the two delegations, commanders of every major division of the Chicago police had been to Israel, including Counter-Terrorism and Intelligence, Bureau of Investigative Services, Organized Crime Division, Mobile Strike Force, SWAT, and the city's Office of Emergency Management. The Chicago Police Department "is today more effective operationally and tactically as a result of these two trips and the enduring partnership with our Israeli institutional and individual counterparts," said department chief of staff Michael Masters.

A 2008 ADL-sponsored delegation with police officials from fourteen cities, including Miami; Philadelphia; Lexington, Kentucky; Mobile, Alabama; and Salt Lake City, Utah, featured tours of checkpoints in the occupied West Bank and a visit to Hebron, where one hundred thousand Palestinians have lived for years under lockdown so that a few thousand of the most extreme Israeli settlers can have the run of their city. Hebron is where some of the worst abuses by Israeli occupation forces have been consistently documented by Palestinian and international human-rights organizations. The Israeli organization Breaking the Silence collected testimonies from former Israeli soldiers stationed throughout the occupied territories between 2005 and 2011.[47] One soldier from the Kfir Brigade, stationed in Hebron in 2006 and 2007, explained what he and his colleagues would do for amusement: "We'd be on patrol, walking in the village, bored, so we'd trash shops, find a detonator, beat someone to a pulp, you know how it is. Search, mess it all up. Say we'd want a riot? We'd go up to the windows of a mosque, smash the panes, throw in a stun grenade, make a big boom, then we'd get a riot." It is no wonder that soldiers and settlers attack Palestinians with complete impunity, whether for fun or to take their land. Yesh Din, an Israeli legal advocacy group, examined 781 cases of criminal complaints filed by Palestinians for alleged criminal acts by Israeli civilians against people or property from 2005 to 2011. It found that 84 percent of cases were closed due to "investigational failures" and observed that the "failure to maintain an effective law enforcement mechanism in the West Bank indicates that the State of Israel is failing to meet its obligation to protect Palestinian civilians in areas subject to its military occupation."[48]

One recent victim of this lawlessness was Muhammad al-Salaymeh, who was shot dead by an Israeli Border Police officer at a checkpoint only feet from his home in Hebron on December 12, 2012, his seventeenth birthday, as he went out to buy a cake. The officer, Nofar Mizrahi, told Israeli media that Salaymeh, a talented athlete who attended acrobatics school, had seized her colleague by the neck and was holding a gun to his temple, even after she fired the first shot. A video released days later disproved the officer's account. Salaymeh never pulled out a gun and held it to anyone's temple. Although the video showed a brief altercation with one of the occupation soldiers, when Muhammad was shot he was not in contact with anyone and presented no danger.[49]

Why did Muhammad die? What really happened? His case, like those of thousands of other shootings and killings of Palestinians by Israeli "security" forces and settlers, has never been credibly investigated. When it comes to the lives, limbs, and property of Palestinians, the advanced evidence-gathering techniques Israel showcases for its American guests are nowhere in sight. But in cases where investigations do take place, Yesh Din found that 94 percent of criminal investigations by the Military Police Criminal Investigations Division against soldiers suspected of criminal violent attacks against Palestinians and their property were closed without indictments. Almost any Palestinian child knows he is without protection, including Atta Muhammad Atta Sabah, a twelve-year-old boy who was shot and paralyzed by an Israeli soldier in the Jalazoun refugee camp in the West Bank in May 2013, as he approached a checkpoint to retrieve a school bag soldiers had confiscated the day before.[50] "I'm not expecting anything to happen to [the soldier who shot me]," Atta said in an interview with Defence for Children International.[51] In the minority of cases where there were indictments, conviction resulted in very light sentences.[52] Nevertheless, Chief Alan Rodbell of the Scottsdale, Arizona, police department came away from his tour of the occupied West Bank struck by the "Israeli people's amazing capacity for compassion."[53]

An October 2012 delegation to Israel, the tenth of its kind, organized by the American Jewish Committee's Project Interchange, included officers from New York; Los Angeles; Oakland, California; Maryland; and Austin and Houston, Texas.[54] On their itinerary was a visit to Megiddo Prison, near Haifa, notoriously one of the sites where Israel holds hundreds of Palestinian political prisoners. These include "administrative detainees" held without charge or trial, a practice Amnesty International has frequently demanded Israel end.[55] These calls became more urgent as thousands of Palestinian prisoners, among them hundreds held without charge or trial, emulated Khader Adnan, an administrative detainee at Megiddo Prison who waged an epic sixty-six-day hunger strike in early 2012 to secure his release. These hunger strikes gained global attention, especially after calls on Israel from international football stars and Sepp Blatter, president of the global soccer federation FIFA, to release Mahmoud Sarsak. Sarsak, a twenty-two-year-old member of the Palestinian national football squad, was arrested on his way to a match and held for more than two years without charge or trial at Ramleh Prison. By the time Israel agreed to free Sarsak, he had been on a hunger strike for three months and was on the brink of death.[56] Israel's detention practices came under renewed scrutiny in February 2013, when Arafat Jaradat, a thirty-year-old father of two young children, died at Megiddo Prison after an interrogation by the Shin Bet. Palestinian human-rights groups and Physicians for Human Rights Israel observed that Jaradat's death was "symptomatic of the utter disregard with which Israel holds the lives of Palestinian prisoners" after an autopsy found evidence that he had been tortured.[57]

Megiddo Prison is also where Israel detains Palestinian children who are subjected to abuses amounting to torture. In 2011, sixty-eight of more than two hundred Palestinian children detained from the occupied territories were held there.[58] In one case documented by Defense for Children International's Palestine Section, in the same month as one of the visits by US police chiefs, Adham D., a sixteen-year-old from Nablus in the occupied West Bank, went with a friend to the Israeli military coordination office to apply for permits that would allow them to work in Israel. Instead, the boys were detained, cuffed, blindfolded, and marched on foot to the Huwwara detention center.[59] Adham was then transferred from the occupied territories to the Al-Jalame interrogation center inside Israel, a breach of the Fourth Geneva Convention, where he was held for twelve days in solitary confinement in a filthy, tiny cell and subjected to frequent harsh interrogation. Adham said:

> The mattress was very dirty. The toilet had a horrible smell and there were two holes in the ceiling that allowed freezing cold air in. The lights were dim yellow and left on the whole time. I spent 12 days in this cell. I could not tell day from night. I could not tell what time it was. I did not even see the prison guard who brought me food and passed it through a gap in the door. I did not sleep at all on the first night because I was so scared.[60]

Adham described being bound to a small chair in a painful position (a frequent Israeli torture technique) and interrogated without access to a lawyer or his family. He denied accusations, typically leveled against Palestinian youths, that he had thrown stones or Molotov cocktails. But suffering from the cold, pain, and fear, he broke. "On the third day a doctor came to see me and asked me a few questions about my health but did not examine me physically. I was in bad shape. . . . It was really hard to spend days and nights in the cell, not to mention that the interrogator told me all my friends had provided confessions against me. This is why I decided to confess," Adham recalled. "Even though I confessed on the fourth day, I was interrogated for 11 days. The interrogator wanted information about other people in my town but I did not cooperate." After that Adham was transferred to Megiddo Prison, where he remained as of early 2013.

Jamal S., sixteen, a Nablus teen who was snatched from his bed during a night raid on his family home by Israeli soldiers, also ended up at Megiddo that month. Like Adham, he was first taken to Al Jalame, where he was forced to confess to accusations he denied, with no lawyer or family present; the interrogator threatened him with prolonged solitary confinement. "I actually believed him when he said this," Jamal recalled. "My body started shaking and I felt really dizzy. I begged him not to put me back in the cell and I confessed to throwing stones, Molotov cocktails and grenades at military jeeps, even though I never did it."[61] Adham and Jamal bear witness to just two examples of what Defence for Children International terms the "systematic and institutionalized ill-treatment and torture of Palestinian children by Israeli authorities."[62] The abuse of children at Israeli facilities is so pervasive that the British–Danish multinational security company G4S has become a major target of international boycott, divestment, and sanctions (BDS) campaigns for providing security equipment to Al Jalame and Megiddo.[63] G4S also describes itself as "the leading security company in the United States," where it is a major contractor to federal, state, and local police agencies and runs numerous prisons and juvenile detention centers nationwide.[64] Palestinians such as Jamal and Adham, if they ever face "trial," would go before the military court reserved for Palestinians in the occupied West Bank; the conviction rate in these kangaroo courts is 99.74 percent.[65]

It is instructive to contrast this with the treatment received by Israeli settlers and their children, who, unlike Palestinians, go before Israeli civilian courts. Jamila Hassan, her husband Ayman, and their children, Iman, four, and Muhammad, six, were riding in a taxi in the occupied West Bank south of Bethlehem in August 2012, along with another passenger and the driver, when their vehicle was hit by a Molotov cocktail. Ayman and the two children were badly injured, with Muhammad suffering severe burns on his back, hands, legs, and face. "We are lost, our life has turned upside down, the father, son and daughter are each in different worlds, our life is difficult and we're miserable," Jamila told Ma'an News Agency two weeks after the attack, just as Muhammad emerged in agony from another surgery. "He screams from the pain a lot," the child's mother said.[66]

Israeli police arrested three minors from a nearby Jewish settlement in the attack and told the judge who remanded the boys in custody that they had found fingerprints linking the suspects to the crime. According to *Haaretz*, Judge Yaron Mintkevich "said he rules to keep the boys in police custody with a heavy heart, due to their age," which was reported to be between twelve and thirteen.[67] But in January 2013, Israeli prosecutors dropped the case, citing a "lack of evidence," even though the DNA of one of the suspects was found on a glove at the scene of the crime.[68] Certainly, there was no question of the settler boys being kept in solitary confinement, shackled in painful positions, deprived of family contact and legal counsel, and otherwise abused until they confessed. It is unknown whether any children jailed at Megiddo, such as Adham D. or Jamal S., might have caught a glimpse of the visiting American police officials. But following the familiar script, Los Angeles Police Department commander Richard Webb praised the Israeli officials he had met as "world leaders and innovators in counterterrorism and security" who "do their duties while vigilantly protecting human rights." Webb vowed to "take many lessons I learned back to Los Angeles."[69]

How widespread is the Israeli-American cooperation in policing? No comprehensive studies appear to have been done, but the claims made by Israel lobby groups alone are impressive. The Jewish Institute of National Security Affairs (JINSA), a neoconservative Washington think tank that advocates for Israeli interests, says it has brought more than one hundred federal, state, and local law enforcement officials to Israel as part of its Law Enforcement Exchange Program and has trained eleven thousand more law enforcement officers across the United States since 2002. JINSA has worked closely with the US-based International Association of Chiefs of Police (IACP), the world's largest organization of police executives. In 2008, an IACP luncheon hosted by JINSA honored the Israel National Police.[70] One JINSA delegation to Israel that year included officers from the New York and Los Angeles police departments, the Major County Sheriffs' Association, the New York Port Authority, and the New York Metropolitan Transportation Authority. The American Jewish Committee's Project Interchange, which claims to have taken six thousand influential figures from dozens of countries to Israel since 1982, doesn't only target law enforcement agencies in the United States. Recent delegations have included city, county, and state elected officials, "Latino leaders," and a "civil rights" delegation. The American Israel Education Foundation, an arm of AIPAC, also frequently brings US law enforcement leaders on visits to Israel and the occupied territories.

It is also clear that the Israeli government is itself directly invested in promoting relations with US law enforcement agencies in order to boost Israel's lucrative "homeland security" export industry. The Consulate General of Israel to the Midwest in Chicago, for example, sponsored two visits by Israeli police officials in 2012 to address hundreds of US law enforcement officials in St. Louis, Chicago, Detroit, Minneapolis–St. Paul, Kansas City, Milwaukee, and Indianapolis. The participants "were encouraged to attend the HLS2012 Conference, Israel's premier Homeland Security Seminar and Exhibition."[71] Ofer Sachs, chief executive officer of the Israeli Export Institute, one of the conference sponsors, explained that a key goal was to increase Israel's "market share" of the estimated two-hundred-billion-dollar global homeland security sector.[72] This weapons and security technology fair, held in Tel Aviv in November 2012, was addressed by much of Israel's top military and security echelon, including former leaders of the Shin Bet secret police, Atlanta chief of police George Turner, and Tom Ridge, former governor of Pennsylvania and US Secretary of Homeland Security (and now a homeland security profiteer).[73] Turner is also chair of the High Intensity Drug Trafficking Area (HIDTA) program, created by Congress at the height of the drug war to promote exactly the kinds of practices that have led to mass incarceration.[74]

Journalist Max Blumenthal believes that examples such as these are only the tip of the iceberg. What he calls the "Israelification" of American policing came into full view with attacks on Occupy Wall Street movement protestors in 2011, but, he asserts, it has taken place "at every level of law enforcement, and in areas that have yet to be exposed. The phenomenon has been documented in bits and pieces, through occasional news reports that typically highlight Israel's national security prowess without examining the problematic nature of working with a country accused of grave human rights abuses" or the quality of what is being sold. Also unexamined is the fact that "former Israeli military officers have been hired to spearhead security operations at American airports and suburban shopping malls, leading to a wave of disturbing incidents of racial profiling, intimidation, and FBI interrogations of innocent, unsuspecting people."[75]

The Israeli Connection

There were few consequences when Associated Press investigative reporters Matt Apuzzo and Adam Goldman began to reveal in 2011 that the New York Police Department (NYPD) had systematically spied on and infiltrated Muslim communities, organizations, and mosques; mapped Muslim-owned restaurants and businesses; and kept tabs on ordinary citizens for more than six years. The specially formed "Demographics Unit" focused on people from twenty-eight "ancestries of interest," nearly all of which were from predominantly Muslim countries. One of those ancestries was "American Black Muslim."[76] This systematic spying included filing reports on conversations overheard between private individuals just because they spoke Urdu and building a database of New York Muslims "who adopted new, Americanized surnames."[77] The NYPD even paid informants to "bait" Muslims into saying inflammatory things as part of a strategy they called "create and capture," which involved "creating a conversation about jihad or terrorism, then capturing the response to send to the NYPD." In recompense, one informant, whose story was corroborated by the Associated Press, received payments of one thousand dollars a month and "goodwill" from the police regarding several arrests for marijuana.[78] Although the focus of NYPD spying was on Muslims and their opinions, surveillance was soon expanded to include political and social groups, such as a women's group organizing a boycott to protest undercover NYPD officers' 2006 killing of Sean Bell, an unarmed Black man, on his wedding day.[79] In all its years of existence, the Demographics Unit never built a single case against any of the thousands of people on whom it spied merely because of their ethnicity, religion, or political views. "It was a bunch of bullshit," concluded Hector Berdecia, an NYPD lieutenant who at one time supervised the program, but later criticized it publicly.[80]

How much of this activity was a consequence of the NYPD's work with Israel is difficult to say, especially since, historically, American government institutions have needed little outside encouragement to spy on their own citizens. But there are important clues. Tellingly, Larry Sanchez, a CIA agent seconded to the NYPD to spearhead the creation of the Demographics Unit, "told colleagues he had borrowed the idea from Israeli methods of controlling the military-occupied West Bank."[81] In 2007, New York City police commissioner Raymond Kelly told a Jewish community breakfast in Brooklyn that his department had set up a post in Israel as "an early warning system on terrorism."[82] The department even set up a branch in Tel Aviv "headed by a former Israeli and veteran NYPD detective."[83] Despite all the revelations about NYPD spying and gross violations of First Amendment rights, the program continued without any effective supervision or oversight.[84]

The admiration ran in both directions. Israel's police chief Yochanan Danino visited New York in April 2013 on a fact-finding mission, hoping to make his force more like the NYPD. The Israeli police had already copied the NYPD's uniforms, but now Danino was interested in learning about its "ring of steel" camera surveillance system as well as its "community relations" strategy. Israel's police would be showing an "incredible lack of concern for community relations" if it emulated New York's "out of control stop-and-frisk practices," said Donna Lieberman, executive director of the New York Civil Liberties Union.[85] Danino, who signed an agreement with Kelly creating several joint task forces, commented that "the challenges of modern crime in the field of terror demand tightened cooperation and maximum real-time transfer of information between the police forces."[86]

Israel's airport "security" is perhaps the signature product that has been relentlessly marketed since the September 11, 2001, attacks, but the evidence is that its practices rely much less on sophisticated techniques than on crude racial profiling. In 2012, more than two dozen Transportation Security Administration (TSA) officers at Boston's Logan International Airport complained "that passengers who fit certain profiles—Hispanics traveling to Miami, for instance, or Blacks wearing baseball caps backward—are much more likely to be stopped, searched and questioned for 'suspicious' behavior." One officer, whom the *New York Times* identified as white, alleged, "They just pull aside anyone who they don't like the way they look—if they are Black and have expensive clothes or jewelry, or if they are Hispanic."[87] The profiling extended into matters that seemed to have nothing to do with aircraft safety. In written complaints, officers said "managers' demands for high numbers of stops, searches and criminal referrals had led co-workers to target minorities in the belief that those stops were more likely to yield drugs, outstanding arrest warrants or immigration problems."

What the *New York Times* did not reveal was that, several years prior to the scandal, Boston airport had hired Rafi Ron, the former security chief of Ben-Gurion Airport, and his firm New Age Security Solutions as its security consultants. AIPAC had boasted of the deal in 2009, explaining that the firm used "behavior pattern recognition," a technique "modeled after the system used at Israel's Ben-Gurion Airport" to identify "subconscious mannerisms indicating nervousness, stress, or fear." Asked if Israeli airport security relied on racial profiling, Ron told National Public Radio in 2010, "We use profiling. It is not the racial profiling. It is profiling that takes into consideration where somebody comes from and if somebody's home address is Gaza we should be paying more attention to details compared, for example, to a Holocaust survivor from Tel Aviv."[88] One Boston airport TSA officer was rather more blunt, telling the *New York Times*, "The behavior detection program is no longer a behavior-based program, but it is a racial profiling program."[89] Ominously, the newspaper described Boston as the "testing ground for an expanded use of behavioral detection methods at airports around the country." Similar programs have been implemented in Miami, San Francisco, and Minneapolis.[90] A year after the Boston TSA officers' revelations, a report from the Department of Homeland Security's inspector general concluded that there was no evidence that the billion-dollar behavioral detection program screened passengers objectively. The TSA cannot "show that the program is cost-effective, or reasonably justify the program's expansion," the report added.[91]

Another revealing glimpse into the Israeli methods being sold around the world came to light in 2009, when Jonathan Garb, a former security official with the Israeli airline El Al, told the South African investigative television program *Carte Blanche* that the airline's security had been a front for the Shin Bet for years and that it used explicitly racist tactics against Black and Muslim travelers at Johannesburg's international airport. "What we are trained is to look for the immediate threat—the Muslim guy," Garb claimed. "The crazy thing is that we are profiling people racially, ethnically and even on religious grounds. . . . This is what we do."[92] After *Carte Blanche* sent in an undercover reporter whose experience corroborated the discriminatory and unconstitutional treatment of Muslims, South Africa protested to Israel and deported an El Al security official.[93] Although the Israeli connection is clear in the Boston airport case, it would be foolhardy to conclude that Israeli influence is causing American security and law enforcement to adopt racist practices they might otherwise eschew. The arbitrary and clearly racist profiling tactics and dragnet approach in use at Boston's airport have long been mainstays all over America's cities and highways in the drug war; they rely on precisely the same stereotypes.[94] Rather, by repackaging racial profiling as the clever-sounding "behavior pattern recognition," Israel gives American law enforcement an opportunity to spin discrimination as a sophisticated technical "solution" forged through Israeli high-tech prowess in the "tough neighborhood" of the Middle East. It also makes many Israeli companies rich.

In *Global Palestine,* John Collins speaks about a "Palestine that is becoming globalized and a globe that is becoming Palestinized."[95] He observes that "colonized territories have long served as laboratories for new forms of violence and social control and should thus be viewed, in an important sense, as ahead of their time."[96] In "an emerging world of pervasive securitization," the technologies of control and repression Israel is constantly refining, in Palestine in particular, have proven to be a "prophetic index" of what is to come for disempowered communities all over the world.[97] Even if its full extent and impact have yet to be exposed and understood, there is no other country in the world that is making a more deliberate, sustained, and broad effort to gain a foothold in the business of US law enforcement than Israel. As the United States expands its various wars within its own territory and around the world, this is bound to have dire consequences for Palestinians, Americans, and others, especially those already targeted by mass incarceration and the escalating brutality of militarized and racist policing.

Chapter 2

Does Israel Have a Right to Exist as a Jewish State?

> If the plaintiff has a right, he must of necessity have a means to vindicate and main-
> tain it, and a remedy if he is injured in the exercise or enjoyment of it, and, indeed
> it is a vain thing to imagine a right without a remedy; for want of right and want of
> remedy are reciprocal.
>
> —Lord Chief Justice Holt, *Ashby vs. White,* 1703

On September 9, 1993, Yasser Arafat met one of Israel's longest-standing demands. In a letter to then–Israeli prime minister Yitzhak Rabin, the PLO chairman wrote, "The PLO recognizes the right of the State of Israel to exist in
peace and security." Rabin responded the same day with a single sentence informing
Arafat that, in light of his letter, "the Government of Israel has decided to recognize
the PLO as the representative of the Palestinian people and commence negotiations
with the PLO within the Middle East peace process."[1] This exchange of letters was
hardly reciprocal. Arafat had recognized Israel's "right to exist," promised to amend
founding PLO documents, "renounce[d] the use of terrorism and other acts of violence," and pledged to "discipline violators." Rabin, by contrast, offered no recognition of any Palestinian rights whatsoever, only that Israel would talk to the PLO.
Four days later, the two men signed the Oslo Declaration of Principles on the White
House lawn.

Arafat, once Israel's nemesis, had granted legitimacy and a *right* to exist to the
state that had expelled his people from their homeland and refused to allow them

to return. He thereby transformed the Palestine Liberation Organization into a sub-contractor and enforcer for the occupying power from which Palestinians were seeking liberation. But Israel was dissatisfied with its gains and began to set the bar even higher with the demand that Palestinians recognize it as an explicitly "Jewish state," meaning, in practice, a state with an overwhelming Jewish majority in which Jews could always monopolize political power. Arafat obliged, effectively conceding this demand in a *New York Times* op-ed in 2002: "We understand Israel's demographic concerns and understand that the right of return of Palestinian refugees, a right guaranteed under international law and United Nations Resolution 194, must be implemented in a way that takes into account such concerns."[2] In other words, Arafat was all too ready to subordinate Palestinian refugee rights to Israel's demand for Jewish supremacy.

Still, this was not enough. In its official response laying out its objections to President George W. Bush's "Roadmap" peace plan in 2003, Israel demanded that "declared references must be made to Israel's right to exist as a Jewish state and to the waiver of any right of return for Palestinian refugees to the State of Israel."[3] And standing next to the new American president, Barack Obama, at the White House in May 2009, Prime Minister Benjamin Netanyahu insisted that in order for negotiations to resume, "the Palestinians will have to recognize Israel as a Jewish state."[4] While almost no state has yet explicitly endorsed this Israeli demand, its key international sponsors and allies have. Obama, adopting Israeli language almost verbatim, told the pro-Israel lobbying group AIPAC in 2011 that "the ultimate goal is two states for two people: Israel as a Jewish state and the homeland for the Jewish people and the State of Palestine as the homeland for the Palestinian people."[5] Similarly, Canadian prime minister Stephen Harper promised Netanyahu that his country "will continue to uphold Israel's right to exist, as a Jewish state, in peace and security."[6] It is no coincidence that Israel has pressed this demand with increasing fervor as Palestinians become the majority population once again in historic Palestine—Israel, the West Bank, and the Gaza Strip combined—and Israel has rendered the already remote possibility of a two-state solution even more implausible.

Given the centrality of Israel's claim, the question of whether Israel does indeed have a "right to exist as a Jewish state" deserves serious consideration. A useful lens through which to examine this proposition is the foundational legal maxim I cited at the beginning of this chapter. Put in simple terms, if a person bears a right, then there must be some venue—usually a court of law—where she can seek to have that right enforced, to have a penalty imposed on the violator, or to obtain some other form of legal relief.[7] In the formulation of the eighteenth-century jurist William

Blackstone, "It is a settled and invariable principle in the laws of England, that every right when with-held must have a remedy, and every injury its proper redress." His insertion of the word *proper* reminds us that a remedy must be lawful and equitable. If my neighbor cuts down my tree, a proper remedy might include paying damages to me, replacing the tree, and perhaps some restraining order to prevent him from felling other trees. It would not be a proper remedy for me to vengefully cut down my neighbor's trees, demolish his house, or kill his children.

Let us accept, for the sake of argument, that Israel has a "right to exist as a Jewish state"—or to maintain its "Jewish character" or "Jewish and democratic character," to use other common formulations—and that this means in practice that Israel has a right to maintain a Jewish demographic majority. Let us also leave aside for now the fact that the Jewish majority within Israel's pre-1967 boundaries was created when Zionist militias, and later Israel, expelled most of the indigenous Palestinian population in 1947 and 1948 and then prevented their return.

First, how can Israel's right to maintain a Jewish majority be violated and by whom, and by what means can Israel enforce it? There are three groups of Palestinians, broadly speaking, who represent a threat to Israel's right to exist as a Jewish state: Palestinian refugees in exile, Palestinian citizens of Israel, and Palestinians in the occupied West Bank and Gaza Strip. (There are also citizens of Syria still living in the occupied Golan Heights.) Palestinian refugees could violate the right by returning home in sufficient numbers that the Jewish majority disappeared. The straightforward remedy Israel constantly demands is that the right of return be abrogated. But even if Palestinian refugees waived their rights and not a single one returned, this would be insufficient to protect Israel's right to exist as a Jewish state for very long against an even more imminent threat from Palestinians already living in territories controlled by Israel. Palestinian citizens of Israel and Palestinians in the occupied territories together comprise half the population living under Israeli rule. Simply put, Palestinian parents are trampling all over Israel's right to maintain a Jewish majority by having children, and their babies, by virtue of not being born to Jewish parents, are violating Israel's right merely by living and breathing. Israelis themselves see the births of non-Jewish babies—whether to Palestinian citizens of the state or in the occupied territories —as an assault on their rights and on the very existence of Israel. The routine use by politicians and media of the term "demographic threat" to describe these babies attests to this phenomenon.[8] "The most pungent expression of this fear," David Hirst reminds us, came from Golda Meir, who was Israeli prime minister in the 1970s. "The Palestinians' birth-rate was so much higher than the Jews' that her sleep was often disturbed, she would say, at the thought of how many Arab babies had been born in the night."[9] But the threat comes not only from Arab babies. Non-Jewish African refugees, asylum seekers, and other migrants are also violating Israel's right to be Jewish by living in the country and reproducing.

Now that we have identified the principal violators of Israel's right to exist as a Jewish state and the injury they are causing to Israel merely by procreating, we must ask what remedies Israel could seek and whether any of them is proper. As noted, the "threat" from Palestinian refugees is dealt with by abrogating their right of return. But what about Palestinian citizens of Israel and Palestinians in the West Bank and Gaza Strip, who would remain uncontrolled violators? The remedies at Israel's disposal would have to include physical and/or political measures to reverse and prevent further violations of its right to exist as a Jewish state. In theory, these could include the expulsion of Palestinians, a step that would serve the dual purpose of reducing their existing numbers and eliminating the risk of future violations by Palestinian babies who might be born to those expelled. Failing that, Israel could issue restraining orders against Palestinian parents to limit the number of children they are permitted to have or engage in other practices designed to deter the births of Palestinians and encourage those of Jews. Similar measures could be used against other non-Jewish violators as well. Among political or legal measures, Israel could punish and prevent violations by stripping Palestinian citizens of Israel of their right to vote or by maintaining a separate regime for Palestinians in Israel and in the occupied territories that allows Jews to get on with running the country without any challenge to their power and control of resources. These are measures that flow naturally from the assertion that Israel has a right to exist as a Jewish state, yet it is impossible to think of one that does not do outrageous violence to basic principles of human rights, equality, and antiracism. Yet many of these noxious ideas are already in place or being advocated in Israel.

In the last decade, Israel has stepped up measures to curtail non-Jews' right to family life in order to keep their numbers down. In 2003, Israel introduced "temporary" emergency amendments to its Nationality and Entry into Israel Law—renewed every year since by the Knesset—that deny residency or citizenship to Palestinians from the occupied West Bank or Gaza Strip who marry Israeli citizens. The law was broadened in 2007 to include citizens of Iran, Iraq, Syria, and Lebanon, so-called enemy states.[10] Adalah, a legal advocacy group for the rights of Palestinian citizens of Israel, observed that the law was unlike any that existed "in any democratic state in the world, depriving citizens from maintaining a family life in Israel only on the basis of the ethnicity or national belonging of their spouse."[11] Israel justified the law nominally on the grounds of "security," an excuse dismissed by Human Rights Watch, which said the "sweeping ban" without "any individual assessments of whether the person in question could threaten security, is unjustified" and "imposes severely disproportionate harm on the right of Palestinians and Israeli citizens to live with their families." The discrimination in the law could be measured "by its effects on Palestinian citizens of Israel as opposed to Jewish citizens," it noted.[12] Then–prime minister Ariel Sharon admitted the true purpose of the law in 2005 when its renewal was under debate. "There is no need to hide behind security arguments," Sharon said. "There is a need for the existence of a Jewish state."[13]

The demographic purpose of the law was reaffirmed in 2012 when the Israeli Supreme Court threw out Adalah's challenge. "Human rights are not a prescription for national suicide," wrote Judge Asher Grunis for the 6–5 majority. Effectively endorsing demographic gerrymandering, the court's ruling added that "the right to a family life does not necessarily have to be realized within the borders of Israel."[14] I'm reminded of a young man I met in South Africa in 2010 who was born in Transkei— one of the now-defunct, nominally independent Black "homelands" set up by the former apartheid government—because his parents had to move there from Johannesburg for violating South Africa's prohibition on mixed marriages. Those policies were justified by South African rulers in the same terms used by Israel's highest court today, as when Prime Minister Daniel Malan said in 1953 that "equality . . . must inevitably mean to white South Africa nothing less than national suicide."[15]

With this and another ruling legitimizing the pillage of natural resources from the occupied West Bank by Israeli companies, "Israel's highest court has veered seriously off course in serving as a final bastion for upholding human rights," admonished Sarah Leah Whitson, Middle East director of Human Rights Watch.[16] But Whitson was mistaken. The court was very much steering an intentional path. In lieu of a written constitution, Israel has fourteen "basic laws" that establish various state institutions, upholding the privileges of Jews and some rights of non-Jews while violating the rights of others. An important example is the 1980 Basic Law: Jerusalem, Capital of Israel, which purports to annex eastern occupied Jerusalem in direct violation of international law and against the will of Jerusalem's legitimate residents.[17] None of Israel's basic laws is a bill of rights, but in 1992 the Knesset passed the Basic Law: Human Dignity and Liberty.[18] This law "appears on its surface to offer protection for all Israeli citizens, but in reality, the text is quite troubling for the Palestinian minority," observes Ben White, author of *Palestinians in Israel: Segregation, Discrimination and Democracy*.[19] Section Eight of the Basic Law reads, "There shall be no violation of the rights under this Basic Law except by a law befitting the values of the State of

Israel, enacted for a proper purpose, and to an extent no greater than required." These "values" can be found right at the beginning of the law, which begins: "The purpose of this Basic Law is to protect human dignity and liberty, in order to establish in a Basic Law the values of the State of Israel as a Jewish and democratic state." The inclusion of the words "Jewish and democratic" open the door to all the forms of legal discrimination that the Israeli government has long practiced, often with the court's blessing. The Basic Law is rendered hollower by its final clause, which allows for the rights it protects to be denied or restricted "when a state of emergency exists." A declared "state of emergency," renewed annually by the Knesset, has existed since 1948. Under this pretext, Israeli authorities have systematically violated the rights of Palestinian citizens of Israel, including banning individuals from travel and seizing vast tracts of land, without compensation, for the exclusive use of Jews.

These policies must not be seen as aberrations—or "veering off"—but as part of the foundational logic that Israel has a right to exist as a Jewish state. Whereas in most countries—and certainly in any that claim to be democratic—rights accrue to citizens without discrimination, Israel makes a fundamental distinction between citizenship and nationality. Rights are allocated on the basis of latter, not the former, with "Jewish" nationality enjoying privileged status. Over the years, several Israeli citizens have petitioned the high court unsuccessfully to have the official registration of their nationalities changed from "Jewish" to "Israeli." But the court ruled in the 1970s that "there is no Israeli nation separate from the Jewish nation."[20] In 2013, the Israeli Supreme Court rejected the latest attempt by a group of Jewish citizens to have their nationality recorded in the population registry as "Israeli." The court ruled that such a change would undermine Israel's "Jewish character."[21]

From its earliest years, Israel's laws have disenfranchised Palestinians and privileged Jews in a variety of ways. The 1953 nationality law, for instance, deprived 750,000 Palestinian refugees of citizenship in the state that had been established on the ruins of their homeland and canceled their Palestinian citizenship, which had been recognized by the British mandatory authorities in 1925.[22] But even many of the Palestinians who remained behind in what became Israel had to seek "naturalization" actively and swear an oath of loyalty to the Jewish state. Many were denied citizenship and expelled. The Absentees' Property Law was used to confiscate the land and real property not only of refugees but also of Palestinian citizens of Israel, who were given the Orwellian designation of "present absentees."[23] Much of their land was handed over to the quasi-official Jewish National Fund, which administers and allocates it on an openly discriminatory basis not to Israeli citizens, but specifically to Jews.[24] Meanwhile, as Palestinians were being denationalized and dispossessed, Jews from anywhere could claim Israeli citizenship the moment they set foot in the country under the discriminatory Law of Return.

Even though the law is plainly designed to exclude indigenous Palestinians and prevent the return of refugees while attracting Jewish settlers, Zionists sometimes defend the Law of Return on the grounds that other countries, such as Ireland, grant citizenship through descent to persons born abroad.[25] Such arguments take for granted that a transhistorical entity called "the Jewish people" is the indisputable natural owner and claimant of the country, analogous to that of continuously present, stable populations in other countries (except of course for Palestinians, whose continuous presence is denied or dismissed as irrelevant).[26] But even if we accept that claim, for the sake of argument, there are fundamental differences. The Republic of Ireland grants citizenship to any person born abroad if that person has at least one grandparent who was born anywhere on the island of Ireland, whether in the Republic or in the British-ruled north.[27] This certainly means that many persons in the global diaspora who identify with an Irish Celtic or Irish Catholic cultural heritage are eligible to "return" to Ireland. But this is no analogy to Israel's Law of Return. The Irish law, unlike Israel's Law of Return, contains no conditions that beneficiaries must belong to a specific cultural, ethno-national, or religious group. The law applies the same way for persons of Irish Catholic descent as it does to those descended from Protestants whose ancestors arrived with English-Scottish colonialism, as well as to people whose ancestors might have immigrated to Ireland from anywhere else in the world. A better analogy for the Law of Return would be the White Australia policy that operated until the 1970s, favoring immigration from Europe while non-European immigrants and Aborigines faced appalling official racism and the continuing legacy of colonialism and land loss.

Some liberal Zionists have argued that the discrimination that pervades every aspect of the lives of Palestinian citizens of Israel consists of unfortunate and rectifiable abuses that are not inherently necessary to defend Israel's "right to exist as a Jewish state." As Tikva Honig-Parnass observes, "Most Zionist Left intellectuals share the conviction that Palestinians in Israel should be denied the rights that embody and sustain the national identity and existence of Jews. The intellectuals agree that Palestinians should instead be granted 'civic equality'—namely, equal access to funds from local Palestinian municipalities or public institutions, and equal funding for religious, educational and welfare services."[28] But in practice it has proven utterly futile to make a distinction between privileged "national" rights belonging to Jews collectively, on the one hand, and, on the other, "civic" rights to be enjoyed equally by every citizen, including Arabs. In reality, many individual rights in Israel are directly tied to ethno-religious identity. Israeli leaders have consequently always viewed restricting the basic rights and spatial existence of Palestinian citizens within the state as a fundamental necessity to extend and maintain Jewish political and territorial control.

Since Israel's founding, no Arab party has ever been invited to join a government, a near-total exclusion from political decision-making that is still supported by two-thirds of Israeli Jews.[29] Israeli politicians frequently talk about various decisions, especially those related to the "peace process" or Israel's "Jewish character," as requiring a parliamentary majority among Zionist (read Jewish) parties if they are to have political and social legitimacy. There have, moreover, been repeated attempts to ban parties representing Palestinian citizens of Israel from even being in the Knesset. In 2009, for instance, the Knesset Central Elections Committee voted to ban two Arab parties from running in that year's elections, a decision later overturned by the high court. But the reason for the ban, according to its sponsors, was that the parties—and representatives such as Haneen Zoabi—had displayed "disloyalty" to the state.[30]

From 1948 until 1966 Palestinian citizens of Israel lived under military government, and in these years vast tracts of land were taken from them. Israeli leaders did not hide the fact that military rule was a mechanism for dispossessing Palestinian citizens of their land so that it could be given to Jews. Shimon Peres, deputy defense minister in 1962, explained that it was only thanks to the military government's repressive powers that "we can directly continue the struggle for Jewish settlement and Jewish immigration."[31] Israel's first prime minister, David Ben-Gurion, stated that "the military government came into existence to protect the right of Jewish settlement in all parts of the state."[32] The rights of non-Jews were simply not a factor. Even after military rule was formally ended, land expropriations without compensation from Palestinians did not stop. In 1976, major land confiscations in the Galilee sparked marches and a general strike that Israeli authorities met with lethal violence. Those protests, and the police killing of six Palestinian citizens of Israel, are commemorated annually on March 30 by Palestinians everywhere as Land Day.[33]

Little seems to have changed in the outlook of Israeli and Zionist officials charged with implementing policies designed to transfer land from Palestinians to Jews. "David Ben-Gurion once said that if we fail to settle the Negev, we will lose Tel Aviv," Efi Stenzler, chair of the Jewish National Fund, which actively assists the government's forced removal of Palestinian Bedouins, told donors at a 2012 fundraiser in Florida. "Today, we know how right he was."[34] Similarly, in 2009, housing minister Ariel Atias declared that it was "a national duty to prevent the spread of a population that, to say the least, does not love the state of Israel." He was speaking about Palestinian citizens of Israel. "If we go on like we have until now, we will lose the Galilee," Atias warned, adding, "Populations that should not mix are spreading there. I don't think that it is appropriate [for them] to live together."[35] If we follow Atias's logic, then legislation equivalent to the US Fair Housing Act (1968), part of the civil rights–era reforms ending racial segregation, would lead to the disintegration of Israel. This passionate commitment to Jewish domination of the land and ethnic segregation of the population was further entrenched in 2011 when the Knesset passed a law formalizing "admissions committees" in hundreds of Jewish towns with the right to exclude potential residents who do not meet vague suitability criteria. Human Rights Watch denounced the committees, with seats reserved for officials from the Jewish Agency or World Zionist Organization, as a form of "officially sanctioned discrimination" intended to keep Arabs out.[36]

Prominent local officials have argued that leaving Palestinians to live their lives could be a major threat to the territorial integrity of the Jewish state. Shimon Gapso, the mayor of Upper Nazareth, angrily rejected a request to open the first school for the 1,900 children of the city's Arab population—one-fifth of its fifty-two thousand residents—as a "provocative nationalist statement." Explaining his refusal, Gapso insisted, "Upper Nazareth was founded to make the Galilee Jewish and must preserve this role."[37] Gapso could argue with some justification that he was only fulfilling the vision of Israel's founders. His town was built on heights overlooking the Palestinian city of Nazareth on the orders of Ben-Gurion and Peres. Ben-Gurion was "outraged by the presence of so many 'Arabs' in the Galilee when he toured the region in 1953." In 1948, he had already warned, "We have liberated the Galilee and the Negev. It is not enough to expel the foreign invader"—his description of the indigenous Palestinians—"we have to replace him with the Hebrew settlers."[38] But over the decades, as the predominantly Palestinian town of Nazareth has been allocated little space to grow, Arab families have moved to Upper Nazareth. Gapso seized on protests by Palestinian citizens during Israel's November 2012 air bombardment of Gaza to urge the government to declare neighboring Nazareth a "hostile" city. "If it was in my hands, I would evacuate from this city its residents, the haters of Israel whose rightful place is in Gaza and not here," Gapso wrote in a letter to the interior minister.[39] As he ran for re-election in 2013, Gapso defended his policies in a *Haaretz* op-ed with the refreshingly honest headline "If You Think I'm Racist, Then Israel Is a Racist State." Gapso made the case that in a country with "racially pure kibbutzim without a single Arab member and an army that protects a certain racial strain" as well as "political parties that proudly bear racist names" and "even our racist national anthem [that] ignores the existence of the Arab minority," it was sheer "hypocrisy and bleeding-heart sanctimoniousness" for liberals in Tel Aviv to pick on his city as racist. The mayor cited the Bible, in which, he said, "the God of Israel told Moses how to act upon conquering the land: he must cleanse the land of its current inhabitants."[40] Gapso was re-elected by a landslide.

Gapso was perhaps being unfair to Tel Aviv, however, where he has his fair share of emulators. Tel Aviv deputy mayor Arnon Giladi, for instance, led his Likud party's 2013 municipal election campaign with a promise to "silence" the remaining mosques in Jaffa. Once the Palestinian cultural and commercial capital, the vast majority of Jaffa's population was forced to flee by sea as Zionist militias invaded and occupied the city in April 1948. Alarmed by the fact that a few thousand Palestinians were hanging onto their way of life and their religious practices in the city—now annexed to the Tel Aviv municipality—Giladi warned, "It is not possible that only a few kilometers from the center of town there will be a Palestinian nationalist autonomy that alienates itself from the values of the State of Israel." He promised that his party would "act to correct this situation and crystallize a national plan that will guarantee that Jaffa will remain a part of the State of Israel and also have a Jewish character."[41] In recent years Jaffa's remaining Palestinians have struggled against gentrification calculated to displace them for the benefit of wealthier Jewish newcomers.[42]

The close connection between the need to repress the political aspirations and rights of Palestinian citizens, on the one hand, and Israel's "right to exist as a Jewish state," on the other, was expressed by *Haaretz* columnist Israel Harel in 2008 when he warned Israeli leaders against recognizing Kosovo, the province of Serbia that seceded under NATO tutelage in 2008. Harel, a founder and influential leader of the council representing Israeli settlers in the West Bank and Gaza, was worried about the precedent. "Kosovo's declaration of independence has sparked concern in certain circles in Israel," he wrote.[43] "The day may not be far off when the Arabs of Galilee start clamoring for political independence too." Comparing the two cases, Harel asserted that "the Muslims of Kosovo constitute an absolute majority of the population, and the same is true for the Galilee Arabs," his term for Palestinian citizens of Israel. "Quite a few Jews have been leaving the Galilee . . . and not many are joining the sparse Jewish population there, despite an array of financial incentives." The consequence of allowing Palestinian citizens to exercise rights or express their cultural and political identity freely would be to put the very existence of Israel at risk: "Unlike the Kosovars in the Balkans, who are satisfied with their separatist province and do not claim ownership over all Serbian territory, the Arabs of the Galilee, and certainly the northern wing of the Islamic Movement, claim ownership—political and territorial—over all of Israel." Harel compared each additional right that might be granted to Palestinian citizens to allowing them to cut off another slice of salami. Soon, before Israel knew it, he warned, the Arabs would have swallowed the whole Zionist state.

Even the grossly inadequate budgets for education and public services allocated to Arab communities in Israel are closely tied to the effort to preserve the "Jewishness" of the state. Benjamin Netanyahu expressed the dilemma best when he observed in 2003, "If there is a demographic problem, and there is, it is with the Israeli Arabs who will remain Israeli citizens."[44] If they were to "become well integrated and reach 35–40 percent of the population, there will no longer be a Jewish state but a bi-national one," Netanyahu, who was then finance minister, explained, according to *Haaretz*. "But, if Arabs remain at 20 percent but relations are tense and violent, this will also harm the state's democratic fabric." Therefore, Netanyahu concluded, "a policy is needed that will balance the two." He also praised the separation wall Israel built in the West Bank, saying it would prevent a "demographic spillover." From the record of every Israeli government, including those headed by Netanyahu, it would appear that decent schools for Palestinian citizens, sufficient land for housing and development, a fair shot at employment, a role in government and national decision-making, and national symbols that foster inclusion could all cause too much integration and therefore present an existential threat to the Jewish character of Israel.

The cumulative impact of Israeli policies deemed necessary to protect Israel's right to exist as a Jewish state can be seen in the yawning gulf that exists between Jewish and Palestinian citizens. Sikkuy, an Israeli organization that monitors inequality, found that in four of the five areas it surveys for its periodic Equality Index—health, housing, education, employment, and social welfare—there had been a "distressing increase" in inequality between Jewish and Arab citizens from 2006 to 2009.[45] The only exception was in education, where there was a slight decrease in inequality, although gaps remained large.[46] Jews live on average four years longer than Palestinian citizens of Israel; that gap had widened. Infant mortality among Palestinian citizens, at 7.7 per thousand live births, is two and half times the rate for Jewish babies. Among one- to four-year-olds, the mortality rate among Arab boys is three and a half times higher than for Jewish boys.[47]

Palestinian citizens of Israel not only live shorter lives on average than Jews and have considerably worse education and employment prospects, they struggle with much greater poverty throughout their lives as well. The numbers are stark: the official poverty rate in 2009 in Israel stood at 17 percent for Jews, but 54 percent for

Arab citizens. Among children the poverty rate was a shameful 24 percent for Jews, but a shocking 63 percent for Arabs.[48] The "accelerated poverty" among Arab citizens was the result of cutbacks in social programs (annual per-capita social welfare spending was 551 Israeli shekels for Jews and 375 shekels for Arabs) and "the policy of exclusion and the absence of a supportive policy for fair representation of Arabs in the various branches of the job market."[49]

Education disparities start at the earliest age and go up through secondary school in resources, class size, dropout rates, and achievement scores, all of which favor Jews. Though there has been an increase in the proportion of Palestinian citizens of Israel who attend university since the 1990s, these students must overcome high hurdles. Israel has never permitted the establishment of an Arabic-language university, fearing it would become a "hot-bed of anti-state activity and radicalism" and presumably another source of danger to Israel's territorial integrity and right to exist as a Jewish state, so Palestinian citizens of Israel must attend Jewish-dominated universities if they want to study in their own country.[50] They are often hindered by entrance standards that require knowledge of Hebrew and English. For many Arab students, Sikkuy observes, English is a fourth language, after spoken Arabic, standard literary Arabic, and Hebrew. A result is that many students go abroad for their studies. In 2009, an estimated five thousand Palestinian citizens of Israel were studying in Jordanian universities alone.[51]

After receiving a separate and unequal education, it is no surprise to find that "Arabs are overrepresented in low-wage labor-intensive industries, unskilled industry, construction and agriculture," while being "almost entirely absent from prestigious branches of the economy that offer high salaries," such as technology, banking, insurance and finance, electricity, and water—the kinds of industries Israel uses to burnish its image abroad.[52] Many jobs are advertised as requiring the applicant to have completed military service, which acts as an effective bar to Palestinian citizens of Israel who, with a few minor exceptions, do not serve in the Israeli army. Jews hold 93 percent of civil service posts, while Arabs, who comprise 20 percent of Israel's citizenry, hold just 7 percent.[53] The labor force participation rate for Jewish women stood at 56 percent in 2009, but was just 19 percent for Arab women in Israel.[54] This is ironic since Israel frequently boasts that Arab women are far better off under its rule than women in any Arab or Muslim-majority country. But it might help explain why Israel ranked a lowly thirty-fifth out of thirty-six countries in the Organisation for Economic Co-operation and Development's (OECD's) index on gender equality.[55]

One exception to these gross employment disparities has been the medical profession, "the only environment where relative integration occurred" and where by the mid-1990s Palestinian citizens had achieved leadership positions even in Jewish hospitals.[56] Although the government health services offered lower wages than other highly skilled professions such as the high-tech sector, medicine was one of the few such fields open to Palestinian citizens, as Israel faced a chronic shortage of doctors. Even though Arabs faced increasing competition from immigrants from the former Soviet Union, by 2011 one-quarter of medical students in Israel were Palestinian citizens of the state. A country aiming to eliminate persistent and widening social gaps ought to have celebrated and built on this achievement. But that isn't what has happened. "In 2008 the Israeli universities [medical schools] unashamedly decided to raise the age of acceptance from eighteen to twenty," historian Ilan Pappé explains. "The Palestinian students, since they do not serve in the army, could join the Israeli universities at the age of eighteen. However, now they cannot be admitted or even apply until two years after they have graduated from high school; they are more likely to try abroad or maybe pursue an alternative career."[57] Israeli educational discrimination has the effect of encouraging thousands of the best and brightest Palestinian citizens to go abroad, from where, many Israelis undoubtedly hope, they will never return. All of this occurs as Israel makes strenuous efforts to stop and reverse the brain drain of its most educated Jewish citizens, who have found better opportunities overseas.[58]

The concern Netanyahu expressed in 2003 about the number of Palestinian citizens of Israel rising too high, and his fear that these citizens might integrate too well, raises the question of whether the unspoken but intended effect of this comprehensive system of legal and de facto discrimination is to create conditions so dire that Palestinian citizens of Israel will find no option but to leave—not only if they want to marry the person of their choice, gain a higher education in their native language, or put their hard-earned skills to work in a fitting profession, but in order to gain the possibility of any sort of dignified life. Talk of expulsion or "transfer" of the Palestinians from Israel and the occupied West Bank and Gaza Strip has been gaining ground for a long time, but it has taken a much more subtle form in recent years.[59] Few Israeli public figures now talk about forcing Palestinians onto trucks and buses at gunpoint and dumping them in Jordan. This may be to avoid falling afoul of laws that prevent Israeli parties from explicitly advocating forced expulsion, but it may also be from a realization that these nasty ideas need better marketing, especially in the international arena.

Nowadays exclusivist schemes are designed to give Palestinians a "choice." Moshe Feiglin, elected to the Israeli parliament from Netanyahu's Likud party in 2013, has proposed paying Palestinian families five hundred thousand dollars each to leave the West Bank for good.[60] It does not take much imagination to see Feiglin, who has declared his intention to seek the leadership of Likud, extending this idea to Palestinian citizens of Israel, whom he has accused of a "creeping Arab conquest inside" Israel.[61] In offering to pay Palestinians to leave, Feiglin was taking into the mainstream an idea pushed for years by Jerusalem Summit, a far-right-wing organization that touts what it calls a "humanitarian" solution to the Palestinian "problem." The group boasts of endorsements from former US senator and current Kansas governor Sam Brownback and Baroness Caroline Cox, a member of the British House of Lords, and makes no effort to disguise the virulent Islamophobia scattered all over its website. "This is a problem that can conceivably be dealt with by means of money—specifically generous sums paid to the Palestinians to relocate and resettle elsewhere in the Arab/Moslem world," it argues, proposing "a grant of US $100,000–150,000 to each family unit."[62] In 2007 polls found that "half the Jewish population of Israel believe the state should encourage Arab emigration."[63] Now, elected members of Israel's ruling party are unabashedly championing these ideas in public.

There are also credible allegations that Israel may have engaged in the most noxious methods of ethno-racial population control. In 2012, a number of Ethiopian women said that they had been forced to take the long-acting injectable birth control drug Depo-Provera before they were allowed to emigrate to Israel. The matter came to light when an Israeli journalist began to investigate an astonishing 50-percent drop in births among Ethiopian women over a mere ten-year period, a decline unexplainable by social factors. Some of the Ethiopian women said they had been threatened and forced to take the drug while still in transit camps awaiting permission to emigrate to Israel and told that, if they didn't take it, they wouldn't be allowed to leave or would be denied medical care. "They told us they are inoculations," said one of the women interviewed by *Haaretz*. "They told us people who frequently give birth suffer. We took it every three months. We said we didn't want to."[64] The government denied the practice but ordered clinics not to renew prescriptions for the contraceptive "for women of Ethiopian or any other origin, if there is the slightest doubt that they have not understood the implications of the treatment."[65] Several months after the allegations came to light, Israel's state comptroller announced an independent investigation.[66] While the women affected were entering Israel under the Jews-only Law of Return, Israeli officials and state rabbis have long delayed or denied entry to tens of thousands of Ethiopians whose Jewishness did not conform to official criteria. In the early 1990s, for instance, Prime Minister Yitzhak Shamir accused thousands of Ethiopians of secretly being Christians.[67] The contraception program was administered by the Netanyahu government, in which

Netanyahu also acted as health minister. Netanyahu had also vocally claimed that immigrants and refugees from Africa "threaten our existence as a Jewish and democratic state."[68] Even more striking, at the height of the fearmongering against immigrants, Interior Minister Eli Yishai had declared, "Muslims that arrive here do not even believe that this country belongs to us, to the *white* man."[69] Ethiopians could perhaps, grudgingly, be recognized as Jews, but they could never pass as white.

The Two-State Problem

If Israel's approach to preventing its Palestinian citizens from violating its right to be Jewish is now clear, what about the threat from Palestinians in the occupied West Bank and Gaza Strip? For a generation, the more mainstream approach has been the "two-state solution." From a Zionist perspective, the logic is straightforward: creating a nominally independent Palestinian state would allow Israel to take millions of Palestinians in the West Bank and Gaza off its population rolls, thus shoring up a Jewish majority without having to shed its self-description as a "democratic state." Since Israel withdrew its settlers from Gaza in 2005 and moved its occupation forces to the periphery to enforce a blockade, many Israelis already believe the "problem" of Gaza has been solved. Still, Zionist supporters of a two-state solution often repeat portentous warnings that if Israel does not end its occupation of the West Bank and allow a Palestinian state to emerge, Israel will *become* an "apartheid" state, as Palestinians outnumber Jews. Israel, they fear, would forfeit its right to be viewed as a liberal democracy.

Yet even some enthusiastic proponents of this approach have recognized its severe limitations and inherent contradictions. If we accept, for the sake of argument, that the creation of a Palestinian state roughly along the 1967 lines remains realistic and achievable, there would still be 1.5 million Palestinian citizens of Israel within Israel, a prospect that causes Zionists considerable anxiety. "There is a basic tension between Arab and Jewish Israelis," Peter Beinart notes in *The Crisis of Zionism*. "The Jewish Israelis want Israel to be a Jewish state; the Arab Israelis don't." Beinart hopes that a two-state solution would nonetheless produce a virtuous circle that would obscure this fundamental conflict: "But when the occupation recedes, Arab Israelis grow less hostile to the Jewish state, Jewish Israelis grow less hostile to Arab Israelis, and reconciling liberal democracy and Zionism becomes easier."[70] Beinart's rosy predictions pay little more than lip service to the history of Israeli state violence and dogged discrimination against Palestinian citizens, always justified in the name of protecting Israel's Jewishness. Nor does he consider that present and future trends portend a rather more vicious cycle should the kind of two-state solution Beinart hopes for ever come about.

The fears Netanyahu expressed, that too much integration for Palestinian citizens risks turning Israel into a "binational state," would likely only intensify. "It's as if someone sells you a flat and then demands that his mother-in-law continues living there," Avigdor Lieberman, Israeli foreign minister and leader of the Yisrael Beitenu party, explained. For Lieberman there is simply no point in a two-state solution that does not result in an overwhelming and permanent Jewish majority in Israel.[71] Rather, Lieberman has argued, a solution to "the conflict must be based on an agreement to exchange territories and populations, and the creation of a reality of two homogenous nation-states, so as not to create a situation in which the Palestinians have a state and a half and the Jews have half a state."[72] In other words, Lieberman proposes that Palestinian citizens be stripped of their citizenship and that areas heavily populated by them be transferred to the Palestinian state, while Israel annexes the land it has settled in the West Bank.[73] Lieberman's version of a two-state solution is not aimed at "ending the occupation" and reviving Israel's liberal soul. It is about ethno-racial gerrymandering of the crudest kind.

Expunging Palestinians politically or physically from Israel's body politic is an idea with broad support within the admittedly narrow Zionist political spectrum. The Palestine Papers, leaked confidential records of peace negotiations between Israel and the Palestinian Authority, revealed that in 2008 then–foreign minister Tzipi Livni proposed annexing Arab villages in Israel to the future Palestinian state, which would, according to one assessment, force "tens of thousands of Israeli Arabs to choose between their citizenship and their land."[74] In one session Livni, often portrayed as a "dovish" figure (including by some Palestinian Authority leaders) explained to her Palestinian counterparts, "Our idea is to refer to two states for two peoples. Or two nation-states, Palestine and Israel, living side by side in peace and security with each state constituting the homeland for its people and the fulfillment of their national aspirations and self-determination." Livni stressed, "Israel [is] the state of the Jewish people—and I would like to emphasize the meaning of 'its people' is the Jewish people—with Jerusalem the united and undivided capital of Israel and of the Jewish people for 3,007 years."[75] For Livni, who was appointed as justice minister in the Israeli government formed in 2013 and put in charge of negotiations with the Palestinian Authority, just as for Lieberman, a Palestinian citizen of Israel is a contradiction in terms. Livni's formula—code for ethnic segregation—was adopted as official US policy. "Negotiations will be necessary," President Obama stated during his presidential visit to Israel in

March 2013, "but there's little secret about where they must lead—two states for two peoples."[76]

Just how likely is Beinart's utopian vision of rifts healing and conflicts receding after a new partition of historic Palestine? How likely would a shrunken, ultranationalist Israeli Jewish state nursing wounds from "giving up" territories and perhaps relocating thousands of settlers be to prioritize reversing the deepening inequalities inflicted on its Palestinian citizens? One telling sign is that, as objective measures of inequality and discrimination against Palestinian citizens of Israel surge, along with anti-Arab incitement and laws targeting their rights, Israeli Jews are less able even to perceive these realities. Over the past decade, the number of Jews agreeing with the statement "Arab citizens of Israel are discriminated against as compared with Jews" has fallen steadily from over half to just 38 percent in 2012. Moreover, just 0.7 percent of Israeli Jews felt that "improving the situation of the Arab sector" deserved to be a spending priority for the government.[77] The prevailing attitude was summed by journalist Shmuel Rosner in a column deploring the high birth rates of both Arabs and religious Haredi Jews, both communities often accused of absorbing a disproportionate share of state welfare. "I must admit that, like many other Jewish Israelis, I have come to feel alienated from and impatient with Haredis and Arabs," Rosner wrote. "As a result I see less the needs of their children than the burdens they've placed on Israel."[78]

In other places, the kinds of upheavals and repartitions it would take to create any sort of "two-state solution" that would satisfy Israel's insistence on Jewish supremacy have historically not led to harmony but to more conflict, violence, and outright ethnic cleansing. Any attempt to create a two-state solution would place Palestinian citizens of Israel at immediate risk, because all the ingredients that have existed in other countries for a reviled and rejected minority to be subjected to additional persecution or outright expulsion are present in Israel.[79]

An indicator of the current climate is that even mere talk of full equal rights for Palestinian citizens of Israel can be considered by the authorities as a violation of the right to exist as a Jewish state. In the mid-2000s, elected officials, intellectuals, and activists from the Palestinian community in Israel published several widely discussed proposals for transforming Israel into a liberal democratic state. Capturing the spirit of these efforts, one of the documents advanced the hardly radical notion that "the relation between the Palestinians and Jews in Israel should be based on attainment of equal human and citizen rights based on international conventions and the international relative treaties and declarations."[80] But the head of Israel's Shin Bet domestic intelligence agency reacted swiftly to the proposals, vowing that his agency would "foil the activity of anyone seeking to harm Israel's Jewish or democratic character, even if that activity was carried out by legal means."[81] From its founding, Israel has worked hard to keep Palestinian citizens separated in distinct and often competing sectarian subgroups—Druze, Christian, Muslim, Bedouin—in a policy of "divide and rule" aimed at preventing them from forming a collective national identity and uniting to demand equal rights.[82] The Shin Bet certainly wasn't going to sit by and watch all that hard work be undone. Even Beinart has been forced to concede that a two-state solution acceptable to Zionists depends on the continued violation of fundamental Palestinian rights. "I'm not asking Israel to be Utopian. I'm not asking it to allow Palestinians who were forced out (or fled) in 1948 to return to their homes. I'm not even asking it to allow full, equal citizenship to Arab Israelis, since that would require Israel no longer being a Jewish state," he told the *Atlantic's* Jeffrey Goldberg. "I'm actually pretty willing to compromise my liberalism for Israel's security and for its status as a Jewish state."[83]

He is not alone. Beinart's commitment to Jewish supremacy is widely shared among American liberal elites, who seldom question Israel's claim that it has a "right to exist as a Jewish state." A striking example of how far some establishment intellectuals will go to accommodate demands for Jewish privileges came from Anne-Marie Slaughter, former professor of politics and international affairs at Princeton University and, as of 2013, president of the New America Foundation, an influential liberal think tank. Slaughter, also former director of policy planning at the State Department during Obama's first presidential term, proposed what she called a "new conception of statehood" for Palestinians and Israelis.[84] In her vision, Palestinians and Israelis could live wherever they wanted within historic Palestine, "forming a single, binational community," but they would have citizenship in separate Jewish and Palestinian states whose borders would fall roughly along the 1967 lines. So far this does not sound like a great deviation from the elite consensus around the "two-state solution." But here's the rub: "Israeli Arabs would then be required to transfer their citizenship, national identity and national voting rights—but not their residence—to the new Palestinian state." Using the considerable prestige of her institutional affiliations, Slaughter had taken Lieberman's and Livni's dream of stripping Palestinians in Israel of their citizenship and laundered it into an exciting "new" and even progressive idea. Under Slaughter's proposal, a Palestinian born in Nazareth and living in Nazareth would now suddenly be a citizen of a foreign state solely based on her religion and ethnonational identity. Given the actions and statements of Israeli politicians like Netanyahu, Lieberman, and Livni and officials like Upper Nazareth's mayor Shimon Gapso, how long would it be before these Palestinian "permanent residents" in the country of their birth might be forced to leave the "Jewish state" for good, like so many Palestinians before them? Nor does Slaughter explain what sort of state apparatus would be needed to classify citizens in such ethnic terms, given the inevitability of humans miscegenating. To which "state" would the offspring of mixed partnerships and marriages, should they be allowed, belong, and what sort of odious apartheid-like bureaucracy would decide?

Despite her pretensions, there is really little new about this. Slaughter's proposal has strong echoes of the Bantustan system set up by apartheid South Africa. Blacks born and raised in cities like Johannesburg or Pretoria were told that they were suddenly citizens of nominally independent states such as Transkei and Ciskei, areas of South Africa in which they might have never have set foot. If Black people wanted to vote and have national belonging, the white supremacist regime told them, it would be in those remote "homelands"—impoverished puppet states that no country in the world formally recognized—but not in white-run South Africa itself. Slaughter's proposal also has echoes of the separate parliaments South Africa introduced for Indians and those it classified as Coloureds during the 1980s, as a "liberal" reform intended to forestall the eventual collapse of the racist regime. Morally and juridically, Slaughter's idea is no different than if the United States had responded to the struggle for African American civil rights by designating, say, Mississippi or Alabama as the "State of the Negroes" and declaring that no matter where they lived in the United States, African Americans could have citizenship and vote only in the Negro State. Her disturbing suggestion is a reminder that ideas that are appropriately deemed repugnant in any other situation are often perfectly acceptable to liberal intellectuals as long as the goal is the preservation, legitimization, or concealment of Israeli Jewish supremacy over Palestinians.

So What If It's Apartheid?

"If the day comes when the two-state solution collapses, and we face a South African-style struggle for equal voting rights" for Palestinians in the West Bank and Gaza Strip, "then, as soon as that happens, the State of Israel is finished," Prime Minister Ehud Olmert famously warned in 2007.[85] It was this fear that had transformed him from a staunch proponent of "Greater Israel" into an evangelist for a two-state solution and, if necessary, "unilateral separation" from the Palestinians. The most brutal manifestations of this separation have been the walls constructed in the West Bank and the reconfiguration of the occupation of Gaza into a permanent siege and blockade. Olmert's warning has been echoed countless times by Israeli commentators and American liberal Zionists hoping to instill urgency in Israeli leaders and American administrations that a Palestinian state should be created before the "demographic clock" runs out. Two-staters take comfort in poll after poll showing that an overwhelming majority of Israeli Jews—three-quarters in 2012— prioritized maintaining a Jewish majority within the Israeli state over retaining all the land Israel currently controls.[86] Three-fifths of Israelis even considered it "urgent" that Israel reach peace with the Palestinians.[87]

But a curious thing happened in Israel's January 2013 election. Netanyahu's coalition, which had brazenly accelerated settlement construction in the occupied West Bank, retained office. Some took comfort in the rise of Yesh Atid, a supposedly centrist party headed by former TV personality Yair Lapid, which gained some seats at the expense of Netanyahu's bloc. But the shift was illusory. The "centrists" offered no challenge to the Zionist consensus in favor maintaining the status quo of occupation, colonization in the West Bank, the siege of Gaza, and political exclusion of Palestinian citizens.[88] Indeed, one of the first pronouncements Lapid made was to rule out including Arab parties in the governing coalition.[89] Invoking his late father Yosef Lapid, a Holocaust survivor who chaired Israel's Yad Vashem Holocaust memorial, Yair Lapid insisted, "My father didn't come here from the ghetto in order to live in a country that is half Arab, half Jewish. He came here to live in a Jewish state."[90]

The 2013 election also marked the rise of Habeyit Hayehudi (the Jewish Home), a party whose youthful leader, Naftali Bennett, accuses Netanyahu of betraying Zionism by agreeing in principle to a demilitarized Palestinian state. Bennett's party won twelve of the Knesset's 120 seats, gaining him a portfolio in the new cabinet alongside Netanyahu and Lapid. In his campaign, Bennett declared that the 1967 boundary between the West Bank and pre-1967 Israel "has no meaning" and vowed, "I will do everything in my power to make sure they [the Palestinians] never get a state." For Bennett, a successful Internet entrepreneur and former soldier in an elite unit, it is a simple matter: "The land is ours."[91] Under his plan, Israel would annex what the Oslo Accords designated as Area C of the occupied West Bank—that is, more than 60 percent of the territory—while millions of Palestinians would be allowed to have autonomy in Areas A and B, ghettoes comprised of the major cities and their nearby villages. In practice this is not very different from the situation that has existed for years, except the pretense that a Palestinian state might someday be created would be dropped forever.[92] The Palestinian population of Area C—estimated to be one hundred fifty thousand, though Bennett put it at only fifty thousand—would receive Israeli residency or citizenship, in order, bizarrely, to "counter any claims of apartheid."[93] But that would be a small concession for the great prize of permanently locking millions more Palestinians out of citizenship rights.

In contrast to various other "two-state solution" proposals, Bennett would not permit Palestinian refugees to return even to the West Bank. "Descendants of the refugees should be absorbed into the countries where they currently reside," the Bennett plan says, "and will not be allowed to move west of the Jordan River." There would also be no "safe passage" between the West Bank and Gaza Strip. Instead, Gaza would be completely cut off from the rest of Palestine and Palestinians would not be allowed to move between the territories—much the situation that has prevailed for years, but under Bennett's proposal the "burden" of Gaza would be "passed to Egypt" permanently.

As for the millions of Palestinians corralled into Areas A and B, they would be allowed a measure of "self-rule" under the watch of the Israeli army, which would maintain "a strong presence in, and complete security control over, Judea and Samaria." What Bennett meant came into clearer focus when he told the cabinet that Israel should carry out summary executions of people it captured as "terrorists." When a cabinet colleague suggested that this might be illegal, Bennett retorted, "I have killed lots of Arabs in my life—and there is no problem with that."[94] This brutal regime would foreclose any Palestinian hope of ever achieving freedom in their own land and would, Israeli right-wingers hope, lead to "a potential exodus of dispirited Palestinians eastward into Jordan, where Palestinians are already a majority."[95] "The world will not recognize our claim to sovereignty, as it does not recognize our sovereignty over the Western Wall, the Ramot and Gilo neighborhoods of Jerusalem, and the Golan Heights," Bennett admits. "Yet eventually the world will adjust to the de facto reality."[96] Though Habayit Hayehudi's performance was impressive, with only twelve of the Knesset's 120 seats, it would still seem to be a relatively marginal party. But Bennett articulates thinking that has much broader resonance among Israelis. And by doing so, he has forced Netanyahu to back away from even his hollow commitment to a Palestinian state.[97]

How could the Israeli Jewish public—ostensibly deeply concerned about maintaining a Jewish majority—be so relaxed about formalizing permanent rule over a Palestinian majority? The answer, it would seem, is that the Israeli Jewish public doesn't care about democracy as much as those warning about demographic doom claim. True, three-quarters of Israeli Jews preferred "that Israel remain a country with a Jewish majority, with one-quarter preferring that Israel continue to rule all of the Land of Israel west of the Jordan," the Israel Democracy Institute found in 2012. And two-thirds said they would oppose continued Israeli rule of the West

Bank if they knew that it would "lead to one state for Jews and Arabs in the entire Land of Israel that would not have a Jewish majority." Those findings—replicated in poll after poll—would seem to support the two-staters' case that the Israeli public will eventually accept the creation of a Palestinian state in order to guarantee a durable Jewish majority. But what the survey found next tells a different story that has rarely been emphasized:

> The majority (54 percent) did not agree with the claim that continued rule in the territories will result in a country without a Jewish majority. Some 54 percent believe that continued rule in the territories will not prevent Israel from remaining a Jewish and democratic state. In other words, the [Jewish] public indeed prefers that Israel be a Jewish state over continued rule over the whole Land of Israel, but most of it does not believe there is a contradiction between the two objectives.[98]

More evidence that Habeyit Hayehudi was tapping into the Israeli Jewish public's zeitgeist came from a *Haaretz* survey months before the election which found that 69 percent of Israeli Jews objected to giving Palestinians the right to vote if Israel annexed the West Bank. Three in five wanted preference for Jews over Arabs in government jobs and half wanted "the state to treat Jewish citizens better than Arab ones." A full third of Israeli Jews wanted a law barring Palestinian citizens of Israel from having the vote and almost half wanted "part of Israel's Arab population to be transferred to the Palestinian Authority." The most anti-Arab group were ultra-Orthodox Jews, 95 percent of whom favored open employment discrimination. Among the least racist group, secular Israeli Jews, only 50 percent believed Arabs should not be discriminated against.[99] Like Naftali Bennett, whose wife is a noted pastry chef, most Israeli Jews think they can have their West Bank cake and eat it, too.

Months into the new government, and with news that Secretary of State Kerry had engineered a resumption of peace talks between Israel and the Palestinian Authority, even the longstanding nominal support for a two-state solution appeared to be evaporating. In July 2013, the Israel Democracy Institute found that Israeli Jews overwhelmingly rejected key elements of a permanent peace agreement "that includes security arrangements for Israel, a demilitarized Palestinian state, international guarantees, and a Palestinian declaration of the end of the conflict." Seventy-seven percent of Israeli Jews opposed "Israeli recognition in principle of the right of return, with a small number of Palestinian refugees being allowed to return and financial compensation for others." Almost two-thirds opposed withdrawal to the 1967 border, even with "land swaps," and three in five opposed evacuating even the smaller settlements.[100] What these consistent trends demonstrate is that the vast majority of Israeli Jews are comfortable with deepening colonization of the West Bank, and, contrary to the claims of liberal Zionists, see no urgent or existential need to end the occupation.

There Is No Right to Be Racist

Even in the most "liberal" versions of Zionism, the rights of the vast majority of Palestinians suffer irreparable injury. Refugees would be forever banished from their homeland solely because they are not Jews. Palestinian citizens of Israel would remain second-class citizens of a state whose Jewish nationalism can never include them, and would likely face rising calls for their expulsion. Palestinians in a truncated state in the West Bank and Gaza would live, at best, under restrictions and conditions that would render statehood, sovereignty, and independence meaningless. In practice, Israel's "right to exist as a Jewish state" translates, as Joseph Massad puts it, into a right "to colonize Palestinian land, to occupy it, and to discriminate against the non-Jewish Palestinian people."[101]

Israel's assertion of a "right to exist as a Jewish state" has, moreover, never been recognized anywhere in international law, whereas all the Palestinian rights Israel seeks to deny have been repeatedly and specifically recognized by large majorities in the United Nations. These rights derive directly from the Universal Declaration of Human Rights, the UN Charter, and the whole body of law that developed in the latter half of the twentieth century to protect the rights of colonized and indigenous peoples. Zionists will often claim legitimacy from the 1947 UN partition plan that contemplated a "Jewish state" and an "Arab state." But that plan, never implemented in practice, would have seen the creation of a "Jewish state" half the population of which would have been Palestinians. The partition resolution stipulated that in each state, "No discrimination of any kind shall be made between the inhabitants on the ground of race, religion, language or sex."[102] Israel's routine practices, justified as necessary to protect its Jewish character, patently violate this principle.

Israel was created as a "Jewish state" by expelling Palestinians and preventing their return. It can only survive in this form by maintaining current and committing future violations of the rights of Palestinians. To deny the rights of Palestinians wherever they are so that Israel can maintain a Jewish majority created through violence and discrimination flouts every contemporary principle of human rights and international law. It flouts the will of the Palestinian people, the vast majority of whom, after almost seven decades, show no sign of being ready to give up on their rights. Respecting all the rights of Palestinians, by contrast, requires no violation whatsoever of any legitimate rights of Israelis, an issue I will discuss in chapter 7. Israel's "right to exist as a Jewish state" is one with no proper legal or moral remedy and one whose enforcement necessitates perpetuating terrible wrongs. Therefore it is no right at all.

This leaves open the question of whether Israel has a "right to exist" at all. Here the answer is straightforward. States either exist or do not exist and other states either recognize them or do not, but no other state has claimed an abstract "right to exist." If Israel is indeed a normal state among the nations, as its Zionist founders wished it to be, then it has no greater "right to exist" than East Germany, Czechoslovakia, South Vietnam, or the Soviet Union. All of those states dissolved, and there is no one with any standing to bring a case in any forum demanding that they be resurrected based on any abstract "right to exist" separate from their legitimate residents' right to self-determination. Israel, even if its legitimacy were universally accepted, would have no more "right to exist" than the United Kingdom, which would cease to exist in the form it has taken for more than three centuries if the people of Scotland were to vote for independence. Similarly, Belgium has no inherent "right to exist" if its people decide to break it up into separate Flemish and Walloon states. Israel has no greater right to exist than its chief sponsor, the United States, whose own Declaration of Independence affirms that "whenever any Form of Government becomes destructive of" the inalienable rights of those who live under it, "it is the Right of the People to alter or to abolish it, and to institute new Government."

Chapter 3

Israeli Jews and the One-State Solution

Anyone who rejects the two-state solution won't bring a one-state solution. They will instead bring one war, not one state. A bloody war with no end.
—President Shimon Peres, November 7, 2009[1]

The ANC [African National Congress] is a typical terrorist organization. . . . Anyone who thinks it is going to run the government in South Africa is living in cloud-cuckoo land.
—Prime Minister Margaret Thatcher, 1987[2]

American Jews can be very critical of Israeli policy, and even convinced that it must grant equal rights to the Palestinian Israeli minority, but it is inconceivable that American Jews can be won over en masse, now or in the foreseeable future, to the dismantlement of Israel. When you make such predictions, you have crossed over, not into the Promised, but to La-La Land.
—Norman Finkelstein on prospects for a one-state solution, June 6, 2012[3]

There's no such thing as a one-state solution. You cannot have peace on any one side with the concept of a one-state solution. It just won't happen. You can't subsume other people into one state against their will. . . . So you'll have a perpetual state of conflict if somebody tries to achieve that.
—Secretary of State John Kerry, November 7, 2013[4]

One of the most commonly voiced objections to a one-state solution stems from the accurate observation that the vast majority of Israeli Jews reject it and fear being "swamped" by a Palestinian majority if a single democratic state were ever established in historic Palestine, or what is today known as Israel, the West Bank, and the Gaza Strip.[5] This fact, perhaps more than any other, sustains residual support among Zionists—in principle, if not in practice—for a two-state solution. Yet South Africa's experience suggests that this Israeli Jewish opposition may be quite malleable and need not stand in the way of a peaceful transition to a democratic and decolonized state that offers citizenship and equal rights to all who live between the Jordan River and the Mediterranean Sea.

The End of the "Peace Process" and the Two-State Paradigm

The 2008 election of President Barack Obama generated hyperinflated hopes in many quarters that the United States would, at last, take the necessary positions and apply the required pressure on Israel to bring about a repartition of historic Palestine into separate Jewish and Palestinian states. The euphoria received a further boost when Obama's special envoy, former US senator George Mitchell, who had brokered the 1998 Belfast Agreement in Northern Ireland, managed to secure a ten-month partial (though ultimately illusory) "freeze" on Israeli settlement construction in the West Bank, except for Jerusalem. Yet even the optimists were quickly disappointed after the United States asked Israel to renew the freeze to give peace talks a chance—but then quickly folded in the face of Israeli intransigence. After this brief and ineffectual departure, US efforts quickly lapsed back into the long-established pattern of substituting endless process for substance and investing all efforts into renewing "peace negotiations" without preconditions while Israel busily gobbled up Palestinian land.

Meanwhile, the United States has actively aided and abetted Israel in intensifying its violence, colonization, and other practices that negate the possibility of the partition that successive administrations have claimed to want to achieve. Obama has boasted, correctly, that US military aid to Israel has reached unprecedented levels under his administration. The Obama administration, moreover, has arguably been more active than any of its predecessors in using its international clout to shield Israel from any consequences for its actions. Obama has offered Israel unstinting support when it has used US-supplied weapons to carry out brutal massacres of Palestinians, most notoriously refusing to condemn the 2008–2009 assault on Gaza that killed 1,400 Palestinians. When she was appointed US ambassador to the

United Nations in 2009, Obama advisor Susan Rice proclaimed that one of her chief priorities, especially in the United Nations Human Rights Council, would be to battle the "anti-Israel crap."[6] The administration deployed all of its diplomatic resources to undermine, discredit, and sabotage the UN-commissioned Goldstone Report, which called for perpetrators of war crimes in Gaza to be brought to justice. The "crap" that the US has valiantly fought has also included every effort to hold Israel accountable for the very settlement construction that ensures that there will never be a two-state solution.

In February 2013, for instance, the UN Human Rights Council published the results of an independent investigation of Israel's settlements on occupied Palestinian land. Some saw the report as opening the door for third-party states to take practical measures, including legal cases against Israel and its leaders under universal jurisdiction, banning international trade in settlement products, or other steps designed to raise the cost to Israel of its actions. When the report came up for debate, several EU countries successfully pressured the Palestinian Authority to put forward a weak resolution that would effectively see the report shelved.[7] The Obama administration, however, signaled its anger that Israeli settlements should be debated at all by boycotting the Human Rights Council and condemning the UN body's attention to Israel's decades of unchallenged violations as "disproportionate."[8]

When Secretary of State Kerry said, shortly after he took office, that "the window for a two-state solution is shutting," it could have sounded like one of the countless similar warnings from international officials. What made Kerry's warning notable was that, for the first time, a US secretary of state had put an actual expiry date on decades of US policy. "I think we have some period of time—a year to year and a half to two years, or it's over," Kerry told the House Committee on Foreign Affairs in April 2013.[9] The ever-more-threadbare "peace process" can no longer conceal reality from even the most stalwart supporters of this charade, including those such as Kerry charged with keeping it going. The already-present reality is a de facto binational state, albeit with apartheid conditions, throughout historic Palestine.[10]

The ideological collapse of the two-state solution leaves no alternative but to shift our discourse and practice toward democratic and decolonizing alternatives. I have long argued that the transitions in South Africa and Northern Ireland offer instructive experiences. In neither place did the end of one political regime and the beginning of another result in a utopia. Both countries demonstrate that decolonization is a very lengthy, difficult, uneven, and contentious process that occurs within an internal context of "post-conflict" politics that must balance healing and "putting the past behind" with the need for justice and radical redistribution of material resources and power. These goals are often at odds. Any new regime must also contend with an international neoliberal economic and geopolitical order that constrains every state's sovereignty and scope for action and hinders economic democracy in favor of an unrestrained capitalism that only exacerbates inequalities. Changing the political regime to one that is legitimate and formally democratic is an essential but insufficient condition. But only in such a context can the kinds of decisions on transitional justice, social reform, restitution, land reform, affirmative action, or planning needed to advance "ethical decolonization," as Omar Barghouti has termed it, take place.[11]

Could we even get as far as South Africa or Northern Ireland in Palestine, given that, across the political spectrum, Israeli Jews insist on maintaining a separate Jewish-majority state? Does solid Israeli Jewish opposition to a one-state solution mean that a peaceful one-state outcome is so unlikely that Palestinians should not pursue it and should instead focus only on "pragmatic" solutions—however imperfect and short of justice they fall—in the hope that they might meet less fierce resistance from Israeli Jews? The experiences of South Africa and Northern Ireland strongly suggest otherwise.

White South Africans and the Prospect of Democratic Transition

On April 27, 1994, tens of millions of South Africans went to the polls in the country's first-ever nonracial democratic election, bringing the African National Congress (ANC) to power and Nelson Mandela to the presidency in a landslide. Hailed as a triumph around the world, the election was the culmination of years of negotiations that had brought political apartheid to an end and ushered in (after a transitional period of power-sharing) a unitary democratic state with a one-person, one-vote system. This was the fulfillment of the political vision set out in the ANC's 1955 Freedom Charter, the manifesto of the liberation movement. Before this historic transition occurred, just how likely did this outcome look? Was there any significant constituency of whites prepared to contemplate it? And what if the ANC and other South African liberation organizations had only advanced political demands that whites told pollsters they would accept?

In fact, until close to the end of apartheid, the vast majority of whites—including many of the system's liberal critics—overwhelmingly rejected a one-person, one-vote system, predicting that any attempt to impose it would lead to a bloodbath. As late as 1989, shortly before assuming office as South Africa's last apartheid president, F. W. de Klerk, described the ANC's demand for a one-person, one-vote system as "totally unacceptable."[12] His position wasn't surprising. "At present, a majority of whites will not countenance this demand for blacks—and will turn out any leader who dares sponsor it," Anthony Heard, the former editor of the *Cape Times*, a liberal antiapartheid newspaper, observed.[13] A 1988 study by political scientist Pierre Hugo documented the widespread fear among South African whites that a transition to majority rule would not only entail an inevitable loss of political power and socioeconomic status, but engender "physical dread" and fear of "violence, total collapse, expulsion and flight."[14] Successive surveys, Hugo found, showed that four out of five whites thought that majority rule would threaten their "physical safety."

Fears of apocalyptic collapse if whites loosened their grip on power were heightened by frequent reporting in Afrikaans media of atrocities in other parts of Africa, infused with common racist tropes that Africans were inherently savage and violent. The Mau Mau rebellion in Kenya in the early 1950s, in particular, had an indelible impact on the white South African collective psyche, conjuring up "nightmare images of mutilated bodies and bloodied pangas [machetes], of remote clearings in the forest . . . peopled by shadowy forms engaging in obscene and bestial rituals" as whites' farmhouses stood exposed and vulnerable.[15] After the Congo gained independence in 1960, South African media again became obsessed with the alleged lot of whites now shorn of protection from the colonial regime; unverified reports of mass rapes of white women and other atrocities filled the pages of the dominant Afrikaner newspapers, *Die Burger, Die Vaderland,* and *Die Transvaler*. Headlines typical of the era included: "The Lot of White Women in the Congo," "Shocking Stories about Black Violence against Whites," "Chaos, Pitiful Scenes as Whites Flee," and "Rule of Terror in Congo: Whites Dead."[16]

Newspapers offered several standard interpretations of these atrocity stories that confirmed whites' belief that apartheid was not a choice but a necessity forced on them by the undeniable realities of Africa:

> (i) The Congo had finally exposed the folly of liberalism and integration as solutions to the problem of white and black relations in Africa, and especially in South Africa; (ii) the West did not understand the problems and realities of Africa, and could not be depended on to see the white man's side of the matter; and (iii) Communist influences were poised to take advantage of the West's capitulation to black nationalists who were unqualified to be given independence.[17]

The message *Die Burger* drove home in July 1960 was "that black nationalism was not prepared to tolerate any form of partnership with whites" and that the forces driving decolonization across Africa were determined to expel whites completely, no matter what.[18] *Die Transvaler* echoed the consensus that since "white South Africans could not flee to Belgium or to Britain like other whites who had been expelled from Africa, they would realize once and for all that the answer to South Africa's racial problem lay in whites remaining master in their land while blacks should be allowed to do the same in their [separate] areas."[19] This "Congo reflex," as Hugo dubs it, was to shape white South African opinion until almost the end of the regime. No less than the earlier cases, the departures of more than a million white *colons* from Algeria after the 1954–62 war of independence against France and the 1975 airlift of three hundred thousand Europeans from Angola as Portugal withdrew from its colony set terrifying and palpable precedents of what the physical collapse, "meltdown," and outright destruction of white society in South Africa would entail if Black people were allowed to rule.

As South Africa became more isolated throughout the 1980s, polls showed that whites increasingly understood that apartheid could not last, but only a small minority ever supported majority rule and a one-person, one-vote system. In a March 1986 survey, for example, 47 percent of whites said they would favor some form of "mixed-race" government, but 83 percent said they would opt for continued white domination of the government if they had the choice.[20] A 1990 nationwide survey of Afrikaner whites (native speakers of Afrikaans, as opposed to English, who traditionally formed the backbone of the apartheid state) found that just 2.2 percent were willing to accept a "universal franchise with majority rule."[21]

How could such solid opposition to a universal franchise be cracked within just a few years? Perhaps an enlightened white elite was able to lead the white masses to higher ground? This appears not to have been the case, at least not until the final stages. A 1988 survey of more than four hundred white politicians, business and media leaders, top civil servants, academics, and clergy found that just 4.8 percent were prepared to accept a unitary state with a universal voting franchise; two-thirds considered such an outcome "unacceptable."[22] According to the authors of the study, Kate Manzo and Pat McGowan, white elites mirrored the sentiments and biases of the rest of the society, which overwhelmingly considered whites inherently more civilized than and culturally superior to Black Africans.

Just more than half of the elite whites were, however, prepared to accept "a federal state in which power is shared between white and non-white groups and areas so that no one group dominates."[23] Reflecting this emerging consensus, the *Washington Post* reported in 1989 that de Klerk had "made clear that whatever new political order evolves from negotiations, power in South Africa would be shared on the basis of racially defined groups and not according to the principle of majority rule."[24] In March

1990, the month following the unbanning of the ANC and the release of Nelson Mandela from prison, South Africa's minister for constitutional development, Gerrit Viljoen, told the *Independent* that one-person, one-vote in a unitary state would be "suicidal."[25] Viljoen predicted gradual change that would end Black exclusion from political power, but leave whites with an effective veto. "If we accept a new constitution in which there is a simple majority on a common voters' register, well, that would be the end. But we won't accept that," Viljoen asserted confidently. In 1988 another South African cabinet minister put forward the stark—and, to most whites, commonsense—logic behind such thinking: "Everywhere in Africa, coups, insurrections and political violence have been endemic as ethnic groups have struggled for supremacy. . . .Why would majority rule be any different in South Africa?"[26] The same year, former *Cape Times* editor Anthony Heard predicted that whites would eventually come around to accepting majority rule. "They haven't yet. It might take twenty years."[27]

Not only did whites not appear to be moving toward such acceptance, but significant numbers seemed to be drifting away. With their backs against the wall, the white electorate in South Africa moved to the right during the 1980s, just as Israel's Jewish electorate has done dramatically in recent years. In 1986, it was estimated that membership in the Afrikaner Weerstandsbeweging—the Afrikaner Resistance Movement led by Eugene Terreblanche, notorious for his khaki uniform and the swastika-like symbol on his armband—had tripled within a year and stood somewhere between fifty and a hundred thousand members.[28] More broadly, support seeped from the ruling National Party, which had formally established apartheid in 1948, to the even more extreme Conservative Party, led by Dr. Andries Treurnicht, who warned voters that the National Party was leading South Africa "on the broad road to a hell of white destruction and racial conflict."[29]

Yet "on the issue of majority rule," Hugo observes, "supporters of the National Party and the Conservative Party, as well as most white voters to the 'left' of these organizations, ha[d] little quarrel with each other."[30] The vast majority of whites, wracked with existential fears, were simply unable to contemplate relinquishing effective control over political decision-making in South Africa. Similarly, Israelis today, whether "left" Zionists or right-wingers, agree that Israel's top priority must be maintaining a Jewish majority and thus Jewish political control of a "Jewish state." Observing the rightward lurch at the polls, Allister Sparks, editor of the liberal *Rand Daily Mail,* lamented that whites had "demolished the hope that [South Africa's] racial conflict might be resolved by peaceful constitutional change." With liberals isolated and viewed as "aberrant and treasonous," Sparks concluded that "white politics has shifted irrevocably to a struggle between the right and the far right."[31]

Because of whites' staunch opposition to a unitary democratic state, the ANC heard no shortage of advice from abroad that it should seek a "realistic" political accommodation with the apartheid regime and that no amount of pressure could force whites to succumb. As township protests, strikes, and international pressure mounted, the *Economist* observed in an extensive 1986 survey of South Africa that many "enlightened" whites "still fondly argue that a dramatic improvement in the quality of black life may take the revolutionary sting out of the black townships—and persuade 'responsible' blacks, led by the emergent black middle class, to accept some power-sharing formula."[32] Schemes to stabilize or reform the apartheid system abounded, and bore a strong resemblance to the Israeli government's current vision of an "economic peace" in which a collaborationist ("moderate") Palestinian Authority leadership would manage a still-subjugated Palestinian population anesthetized by consumer goods and shopping malls without Israel having to make any fundamental concessions (see chapter 4).

The ANC was warned that insistence on majority rule would force Afrikaners to retreat into a militarized garrison state and siege economy, preferring death before surrender. William Raspberry, the noted African American columnist at the *Washington Post*, dismissed as "rosy-eyed optimists" the African American activists who believed that "the white minority government can, by the prospect of some combination of economic pressure and international embarrassment, be nudged in the direction of racial justice."[33] Despairing of any path to ending apartheid peacefully, Raspberry declared that "expecting white Afrikaners to relinquish their awesome power to the black aborigines is no more realistic than expecting white Americans to hand control of this country to the American Indians." Even the Soviet Union, which supported the ANC's armed struggle, urged the liberation movement to show more "flexibility." One Soviet bloc diplomat told the *Los Angeles Times* that the ANC's "focus must be what it can do itself . . . to make such a settlement much more attractive to whites." Gleb Starushenko, a leading Soviet academic at the Africa Institute in Moscow, even proposed a federal system made up of "autonomous components" and a parliamentary system "that would give the white minority an effective veto within a majority-rule government." ANC officials bristled at this advice. "We can't go back to our people, particularly the youth, and say, 'Please accept this quarter loaf—we'll have to get the rest later.' We get very strong negative reactions whenever there is a hint of compromise on the fundamental issues," one said in response to the Soviet proposals.[34] But, as the *Economist* observed, the view that whites would prefer "collective suicide" was something of a caricature. The vast majority of Afrikaners were "no longer Bible-thumping Boers." They were "part of a spoilt, affluent suburban society, whose economic pain threshold may prove to be rather low." The *Economist* concluded that if whites would only come so far voluntarily, then it was perfectly reasonable for the antiapartheid movement to bring them the rest of the way through "coercion" in the form of boycott, divestment, and sanctions (BDS) tactics and other types of pressure. "The quicker the white tribe submits," the magazine wrote, "the better its chance of a bearable future in a black-ruled South Africa."

Despite the ominous warnings, the ANC and its allies insisted firmly on a one-person, one-vote system with no white veto. And ultimately, the combination of internal resistance, military pressure on South Africa from the Cuban-supported liberation movement in Angola, and international isolation did force whites to abandon political apartheid and accept the one thing they overwhelmingly said they would never accept: majority rule. As scholars Na'eem Jeenah and Salim Vally, both veterans of the antiapartheid struggle, recall,

> In the period between the unbanning of the various liberation movements in February 1990 and the election in April 1994, South Africa witnessed the worst ever political violence with just under 15,000 people being killed—more than in the rest of the apartheid period from 1948. In those tense four years nothing was certain and many South Africans cringed as we lived through negotiations that could easily have led to massive compromises with the potential to undermine the South African people and our struggle. Nevertheless, the 1994 civil war—that thousands of journalists from around the world descended on South Africa to report upon—did not happen.[35]

It is essential to note that, for all the mass mobilizations and tumultuous change, the combined strength of the antiapartheid movement never seriously threatened the physical integrity of the white regime. Even after the massive township uprisings of 1985 and 1986, the South African regime was physically secure. "So far there is no real physical threat to white power," the *Economist* noted, and "little threat to white lives. . . . The white state is mighty, and well-equipped. It has the capacity to repress the township revolts far more bloodily. The blacks have virtually no urban or rural guerrilla capacity, practically no guns, few safe havens within South Africa or without." This balance never changed, and a similar equation could be written today about the relative power of a massively armed and much more ruthless Israeli state and lightly armed Palestinian resistance factions.

What did change for South Africa, and what all the government's weapons could not prevent, was the complete loss of the legitimacy of the apartheid regime and its practices. Once this legitimacy was gone, whites lost the will to maintain a system that relied on repression and violence and rendered them international pariahs. They negotiated a way out and lived to tell the tale. It all happened much more quickly and with considerably less violence than even the most optimistic predictions of the time. But, crucially, this outcome could not have been predicted based on what whites said they were willing to accept—and it would not have occurred had the ANC been guided by opinion polls rather than the democratic principles of the Freedom Charter.

Catalyzing Change among Israeli Jews

Zionism, as many Israelis openly worry, could suffer a fatal loss of legitimacy similar to that of South Africa's apartheid regime. As discussed in chapter 5, Israel's influential Reut Institute warned that the state faces a gathering threat from a growing global Palestine-solidarity movement that seeks to "delegitimize" it. This threat, Reut predicted, "possesses strategic significance, and may develop into a comprehensive existential threat within a few years." It further warns that a "harbinger of such a threat would be the collapse of the two-state solution as an agreed framework for resolving the Israeli-Palestinian conflict, and the coalescence behind a 'one-state solution' as a new alternative framework."[36]

This analysis reflects an understanding that no regime can survive if its only resource is brute force; it must have internal and external legitimacy. Israel's self-image as a liberal "Jewish and democratic state" is proving impossible to maintain and market internationally against the reality of a militarized, ultranationalist Jewish sectarian settler colony that denies equal rights to its non-Jewish citizens and must carry out periodic massacres of "enemy" civilians in order to check the resistance of the region's indigenous people, a practice Israeli military and political leaders frequently call "restoring deterrence." Already difficult to disguise, the loss of legitimacy may become impossible to conceal once Palestinians are a demographic majority ruled by a Jewish minority, a transition that is already under way.[37] Israel's demand that Palestinians recognize Israel's "right to exist as a Jewish state" is in effect an acknowledgement of failure: without Palestinian consent, something unlikely ever to be granted, the Zionist project of a Jewish ethnocracy in Palestine has fading long-term prospects.

The core Zionist assumption, observes South African political scientist Steven Friedman, "is that Jewish survival hinges on Jews maintaining a specifically Jewish state" in Israel. "Without this, it is claimed, Jews face the constant threat of the genocidal violence unleashed by Nazism—or, at least, of constant persecution."[38] The parallels to the fears of white South Africans in an earlier era are obvious. Friedman argues that such claims do not just lead the majority of Israeli Jews to reject a single democratic polity shared by Palestinians and Jews: they also place any sort of accommodation beyond reach "by constantly reinforcing a sense of threat within the Jewish Israeli mainstream." He explains how the emphasis on "existential" fears and threats has created a vicious circle that

> has enabled successive Israeli governments to pass off virtually any measure inimical to Palestinian interests as a "security" precaution, which may at least explain the continuing rightward shift in Jewish Israeli politics. Continued Palestinian resistance is portrayed as an existential threat. . . .As long as Jewish survival is equated with the maintenance of an ethnic state, no resolution that might win sustained Palestinian loyalty is possible. The rigidity of the Jewish Israeli equation of ethnic statehood with safety, often cited as an eternal obstacle to a single state, is in reality also a powerful argument against the viability of a "two-state solution." As long as this equation persists, it seems highly implausible that a separate Palestinian state will appear to mainstream Israeli opinion as a viable guarantor of the security of the Israeli state. And if the view that ethnic statehood is integral to Jewish survival begins to erode, then so does much of the rationale for two separate states. The insistence that without a state of their own Jews are in constant peril is thus an obstacle to any settlement . . . [and] means that accepting the principle of Jewish ethnic statehood on pragmatic grounds . . . is a strategy doomed to fail. Prospects for justice and peace rest, then, on a positive future in which Jewish statehood will no longer be seen as essential to Jewish survival and in which minority status in a democratic state will be seen as an appropriate means of achieving Jewish security.[39]

This is a powerful challenge to "liberal" Zionism and "pragmatic" logic, but how realistic is the kind of transformation in mainstream Israeli thinking that Friedman lays out? From the perspective of today, it seems at least as unlikely as white South Africans accepting a one-person, one-vote system in, say, 1987. But Friedman believes that, just as happened with whites in South Africa, "a reassessment of Jewish statehood, which makes minority status in a democratic state acceptable, is plausible and may even be inevitable."[40] It is important to stress here that Israeli Jews do not have a choice about their minority status within historic Palestine. Unless they resort to mass expulsions of Palestinians—something sizable minorities of Israelis nonetheless support—the demographic facts are given. Their choice is about how to deal with this reality, whether through building higher walls to shore up an ethnic state or seeking a radically different form of security without walls.

South African beneficiaries of apartheid typically did not justify their opposition to democracy in terms of a desire to preserve their privileges and power, or even always in terms of survival. They also deployed liberal arguments about protecting distinctive cultural differences. Hendrik Verwoerd Jr., the son of assassinated prime minister and apartheid founder Hendrik Verwoerd, expressed the problem in these terms in 1986: "These two people, the Afrikaner and the black, are not capable of becoming one nation. Our differences are unique, cultural and deep. The only way a man can be happy, can live in peace, is really when he is among his own people, when he shares cultural values."[41] The younger Verwoerd was on the far right of South African politics, leading a quixotic effort to carve out a whites-only homeland in the heart of South Africa. But his reasoning sounds remarkably similar to liberal Zionist defenses of the "two states for two peoples solution" today. The *Economist* clarified the use of such language at the time: "One of the weirder products of apartheid is the crippling of language in a maw of hypocrisy, euphemism and sociologese. You talk about the Afrikaner 'right to self-determination'—meaning power over everybody else."[42]

Similarly, Zionism's claim for "Jewish self-determination" of a settler-colonial group amid an intermixed population is in effect a demand to preserve and legitimize a status quo in which Israeli Jews exercise power in perpetuity, a quest that generates constant insecurity since it requires the active and violent suppression of the rights of millions of non-Jews. Yet there is little reason to expect that Israeli Jews would abandon this path voluntarily any more than South African whites did, as long as they feel that pursuing it is less costly than any alternative. As in South Africa, considerable pressure is necessary to steer Israeli Jews toward a different calculus. Given the overwhelming military superiority of the Israeli state, Palestinian resistance alone, including BDS and military resistance, is unlikely to bring about the collapse of Israel's system of domination over Palestinians, just as the repressive apparatus of the South African apartheid state remained intact until the end. Rather, the goal of such pressure must be to increase the cost of the status quo, isolating Israel and thus, as Friedman puts it, "to force those who preside over [this system] to reconsider their options and to negotiate a settlement with the Palestinian leadership."[43] The growing BDS movement is one of the most powerful and proven tools of pressure that Palestinians possess; its potential, along with other kinds of discourse, mobilization, and resistance, to fatally undermine Israel's system has been recognized by the Reut Institute, the Israeli government, and Zionist organizations around the world.

Some critics of the BDS movement, however, have argued that Israel may be less susceptible to the kinds of international pressure and internal resistance brought to bear on South African apartheid because South Africa was dependent on Black labor to a much greater extent than Israel is on Palestinian labor. As I show in chapter

4, Israel relies on Palestinian labor to a greater extent than is commonly acknowledged, but let us concede that this Palestinian labor is neither sufficient in quantity
nor organized enough such that its withdrawal can prove a decisive factor in changing Israeli calculations. This means that Palestinians must employ different strategies
and, as Friedman argues, Israel may suffer from "weaknesses that apartheid [in South
Africa] did not face, such as dependence on a diaspora which may prove less committed to resisting change than the Israeli state."[44] Israel's panic about the growing
BDS movement is an important piece of evidence that this campaign is already
working. In Friedman's assessment, sustained diplomatic, political, social, and economic pressure can, with time, "ensure a change in Zionist strategic calculations
which will, as in South Africa, ensure that a common democratic polity in which
Jews may be a minority becomes an acceptable strategic option."[45]

This shift, moreover, can be supported and legitimated by what Friedman calls
a "usable tradition" within Judaism and within the Jewish history of alternatives to
ethnocracy. Zionism is a relatively recent development and was until the middle of
the twentieth century a minority position. It is not a given that Israeli Jews will forever see themselves as victims or potential victims and Arabs as the successors to the
Nazis. As pressure increases, Israelis may begin to recognize that ethnic statehood
has done little to ensure their security and in fact has made Jews more prominent
targets, to the extent that they are associated by Israel and Zionism with Israel's in-
justices toward the Palestinians.

The contradiction in the claim that Israel is vital to Jewish security can be seen
in Israel's own propaganda, which holds simultaneously that Israel's existence as a
Jewish state is necessary to ensure the survival of Jews, but that all Jews in Israel face
mounting dangers in their "tough neighborhood," most ominously the shadow of
nuclear holocaust from Iran. On its current path, it is impossible to foresee a day
when Zionism will not be plagued by existential fears and nightmare scenarios of one
kind or another. Indeed, the only mainstream narrative that would ostensibly normalize Zionism and "peacefully" integrate Israel into the region is the "two-state solution," to which Israel pays lip service but which it fatally undermines in practice.

Friedman points out that "democracies that survive protect Jews who live in
them better than the Jewish state." Democracies are not guaranteed to survive, he
concedes; therefore

> a single-minded concern for Jewish safety would most effectively be expressed
> in vigorous efforts to defend democracy, which protects Jews as well as others,
> rather than to defend ethnic statehood which . . . promises only continued vio-
> lence. Lest this seem like yet another fanciful intellectual construct unlikely to

make any impact on real-life calculations of Jewish security, it is worth noting that . . . millions of Jews who live in democracies and could therefore freely leave their countries for the Jewish state, choose to stay where they are. More importantly, significant numbers of Jewish Israelis emigrate, clearly signaling that they do not need the protection of ethnic statehood.[46]

By this logic, Jews can find security in a single democratic and decolonized state in Palestine where they will be the minority. The predictable objection that Palestinians—unlike Canadians, Americans, or Britons—are inherently incapable of democracy should be viewed with no more seriousness than the relentless claims of apartheid supporters in South Africa that, unleashed from colonial rule, Black Africans would immediately resort to savagery against whites. The prospects for a successful democratic transition and decolonization in Palestine will depend on what happens there between Palestinians and Israelis, not on some supposedly immutable "cultural" traits attributed to Arabs, Muslims, or, for that matter, Jews.

This leaves the notion of a Jewish ethnic state as an "insurance policy" for Jews should they face persecution elsewhere. Indeed, a key premise of Zionism is that, by creating Israel, Jews ensured that they would never again have to depend on the goodwill of others for their safety and survival. Aside from the dubious morality of keeping on hand a spare country at the expense of that country's indigenous people, Israel's existence and security are only guaranteed by constant promises of support from the United States and other international sponsors. But "the political shifts in the major democracies required to place anti-Semitism on the agenda are surely far greater than those required to withdraw support from the Israeli state," observes Friedman, thus rendering the insurance policy "invalid."[47]

Indeed, this has been tacitly acknowledged in the disproportionate emphasis major Zionist groups place on defending US support for Israel as opposed to warding off anti-Semitism, which thankfully remains a marginal phenomenon and certainly no bar to the full integration of Jews in every aspect of US life. In 2012, the century-old American Jewish Committee announced that henceforth it would focus its resources on advocacy for Israel, abandoning much of its traditional domestic agenda.[48] That was an example of how diaspora organizations are working to save Israel, rather than Israel saving Jews around the world. Israel's dependence on diaspora support is why, when Peter Beinart declared that there was a "crisis of Zionism," that crisis was in the United States, where young Jews overwhelmingly feel themselves to be integrated, liberal, and mainstream Americans. These young people are indifferent or even antipathetic toward Israel and its appeals for their ethnic and tribal loyalties. Without the renewal of support for Israel in the United States, Beinart and other liberal Zionists see dim prospects for its future. Israel's and Zionism's reliance on diaspora support is therefore an advantage and an opportunity for Palestinians seeking to build a solidarity movement that taps into the universal values binding young Jews to their US homeland. Israel's vulnerabilities may be different from those of apartheid South Africa, but Israel is not invulnerable to pressure.

The strong similarities between Zionism and Afrikaner nationalism in their claims to be indigenous to the land they colonized, including assertions of biblical legitimacy, have been explored elsewhere, including in my earlier book *One Country*. Both Zionists and Afrikaner nationalists, moreover, have appealed to real histories of persecution to legitimate their claims that statehood and perpetual domination over natives were a matter of survival. But when the power balance begins to shift, as it did in South Africa, dominant narratives begin to change as well, and "seemingly abstract alternatives developed by intellectuals can be deployed to justify revised strategic retreats by dominant groups." In other words, when the story the dominant group has been telling itself to justify past and present actions is no longer suitable, it can be changed with remarkable ease. A narrative that once seemed like a formidable obstacle to compromise melts away.

So it was that the vast majority of South Africans could shift from a belief that white rule was essential for survival to embracing the idea of South Africa as a "rainbow nation" in which they had a stake and a future but no veto on political decisions. Such "alternative understandings," observes Friedman, "cannot change power relations, but they can enable members of dominant groups to make sense of, and adapt to, those changes when they are confronted by mounting pressures on their dominance."[49] In practice, this means that it is unlikely that very many committed Zionists will be persuaded to adopt a different approach merely, say, by reading this book or hearing other compelling expositions. The argument is that, in combination with pressure from the growing Palestinian-led solidarity movement, Israeli Jews will start to hear and formulate new narratives that accompany and facilitate what seem today like unimaginably radical changes. Another striking example of such a shift comes from Northern Ireland.

Changing the Story in Northern Ireland

I was in Dublin on March 26, 2007, and I recall the widespread consternation when a smiling Gerry Adams, leader of the nationalist party Sinn Féin, appeared on television sitting next to Ian Paisley, founder and leader of the Democratic Unionist Party (DUP). The DUP had bitterly opposed the 1998 Belfast Agreement, which created a power-sharing government in Northern Ireland between predominantly Catholic Irish nationalists and mostly Protestant British-backed unionists. Nationalists, particularly those known as republicans, are committed to ending the partition of Ireland by placing the whole of the island under a single republic. Unionists, especially the militias known as loyalists, view Northern Ireland's existence as part of the United Kingdom as a matter of survival for their community. In the years after the agreement was signed, people in all parts of Ireland became accustomed to the "peace process" and talk of "power-sharing," and had heard much about a "shared future." In its actual implementation, however, the agreement faced many obstacles, including fierce obstructionism by the likes of Paisley, opposition from anti-agreement republicans, state and militia violence, and repeated suspensions of the power-sharing authority by the British.

Still, nothing had prepared people for the strange and carefully stage-managed sight of Adams and Paisley sitting together. Each man was the leader of the largest and also the most "extreme" party in his respective community. In recent elections, Sinn Féin and the DUP had each overtaken the respective nationalist and unionist "moderate" parties that had signed the agreement. Sinn Féin had long been described as the "political wing of the IRA [Irish Republican Army]"; Paisley called it "a filthy nest of murderous Irish nationalism."[50] After Adams suffered multiple gunshot wounds in an assassination attempt by the loyalist Ulster Freedom Fighters in Belfast in 1984, Paisley declared, "All I can say is that my lord and master the lord Jesus Christ said that those that take the sword shall perish by the sword. . . . I don't think that anybody during the war would have shed many tears of grief if Hitler had been assassinated."[51] For Paisley, even the republic to the south with its capital in Dublin was "a foreign enemy state" and its leader the "Saddam Hussein of Ireland."[52] Paisley's enmity was not merely directed at Sinn Féin and the Irish state. A fiery evangelical preacher, he frequently engaged in overtly sectarian anti-Catholic rhetoric, calling the pope the "anti-Christ."[53] He even castigated fellow Protestant clergymen who participated in ecumenical efforts to combat sectarianism as a "Fifth Column" whose aim was "to eradicate Protestantism" and facilitate a "takeover by Rome."[54]

Having led or participated in every effort to wreck previous attempts at power-sharing, Paisley had vowed repeatedly that he would never sit in government with the likes of Sinn Féin, nor permit any such government to rule over Northern Ireland. So when he appeared with Adams to seal a deal to do exactly that, it was no less shocking or surreal for many observers than a coalition between Israeli prime minister Benjamin Netanyahu and Hamas leader Khaled Mishal would look today. Two months after their meeting, it was Gerry Adams himself who rose from his seat in the Northern Ireland Assembly to propose the motion for Paisley to become first minister, with Sinn

Féin's Martin McGuinness, a former IRA commander, as his deputy. The DUP and Sinn Féin would now be jointly responsible for implementing the Belfast Agreement, which left the status of Northern Ireland to be determined by referendum at some unspecified future time. In the meantime, they would have to run the government according to the democratic principles enshrined in the agreement:

> Whatever choice is freely exercised by a majority of the people of Northern Ireland, the power of the sovereign government with jurisdiction there shall be exercised with rigorous impartiality on behalf of all the people in the diversity of their identities and traditions and shall be founded on the principles of full respect for, and equality of, civil, political, social and cultural rights, of freedom from discrimination for all citizens, and of parity of esteem and of just and equal treatment for the identity, ethos, and aspirations of both communities.

This commitment would mark a radical break from how Northern Ireland had been governed up to that point; it was the culmination of decades of nationalist struggle against fierce unionist and British intransigence and repression. Once they took office, Paisley and McGuinness got on so jovially that the media dubbed them the "Chuckle Brothers," after a television comedy duo. Although Paisley, already in his early eighties, retired after just one year as first minister, the DUP–Sinn Féin partnership in government has continued uninterrupted. The durability of the Belfast Agreement, which Paisley once opposed with all his considerable might, owes something to his ability to rewrite history creatively to help unionists get out of the impasse into which he had helped steer them.

Although Irish nationalists point to eight centuries of invasion and colonization from Britain, the modern conflict in Northern Ireland traces back directly to the colonization of the island's northeast in the early 1600s. As the British granted land to Scottish and English settlers, native Catholics were violently displaced. Britain annexed Ireland in 1801, but that failed to stem repeated rebellions; the question of "home rule" for Ireland bedeviled British politics well into the twentieth century. Unionists, comprised of the ascendant and long-settled Protestant population, adamantly opposed home rule, fearing it would threaten their privileged status as the political and economic elite of Ireland. In 1912, unionist militancy, military preparations, and threats of violence succeeded in forestalling British attempts to implement home rule. Meanwhile, Irish nationalists gained increasing support for independence, especially after the British executed the leaders of the failed 1916 Easter Rising, who had proclaimed an "Irish Republic." In the 1918 election to the British parliament, republican Sinn Féin won a landslide of Irish seats on a platform of total independence from Britain.

Following a guerilla war between British and republican forces that ended in a stalemate, the sides concluded the 1921 Anglo-Irish Treaty establishing the Irish Free State, an autonomous "dominion" of the British Empire that eventually became the Republic of Ireland. But the treaty also partitioned the island, carving out six of the country's thirty-two counties as "Northern Ireland," a self-governing entity linked to Britain and gerrymandered to have a two-thirds Protestant majority. Nationalist resistance to partition was brutally suppressed by British forces and unionist militias. In the first year of partition, hundreds of Catholics were killed in Belfast, eleven thousand were forced from their jobs, and twenty-two thousand, a quarter of the city's Catholic population, were driven from their homes.[55] For the next fifty years, Northern Ireland was run as a unionist one-party state. Catholics, a third of the population of Northern Ireland, found themselves as subjects of a state that viewed and treated them as an undesirable enemy within, just like the Palestinians left in what became Israel after 1948.

After partition, unionist political and historic narratives were quickly developed to entrench the new geopolitical division of the country. A newly invented Northern Ireland Protestant culture "defined the two parts of Ireland as different places, separate from and alien to each other"; politicians and journalists were always "careful to avoid statements that implied that North and South were part of a single, larger entity."[56] While the "new official public culture was pluralist and inclusive in respect of Protestant differences," it was "exclusionary with respect to the Catholic minority."[57]

Although unionist intellectuals attempted to create a distinct artistic, literary, and linguistic "Ulster" culture to which Protestants could lay exclusive claim and thus distance themselves from "Irishness," the "main cultural foci of the state were Protestantism and Britishness." These identities supposedly embodied such virtues as respectability, honesty, a strong work ethic, sobriety, cleanliness, order, and respect for authority.[58] Unionists generally held "an unquestioned belief in the superiority of this culture to the one emerging in the South."[59] Indeed, Catholics and the Republic (as "their" state) were commonly represented as embodying laziness, drunkenness, irrationality, lack of industry, a propensity to violence, and slavishness to theocratic dictates from Rome, while harboring an insatiable determination to destroy Protestants and their way of life. Unionists also justified their position by claiming, like Zionists and Afrikaners in South Africa, that they were a "covenant people" chosen by God for a special mission.[60] All of these themes had been reinforced over decades in the rhetoric of Paisley and other unionist leaders. Systematic and deliberate discrimination, legitimized by this official culture and enforced with state and state-sanctioned vigilante violence, kept Catholics economically, politically, and socially subordinate.

Even if not all unionists subscribed to overt bigotry and racism, the Northern Ireland state institutionalized Protestant culture—especially the virulently sectarian Protestant Orange Order fraternal organization—and violently suppressed expressions of nationalist identity.[61] Northern Ireland's first prime minister, James Craig, informed the entity's parliament at Stormont Castle near Belfast that theirs was "a Protestant Parliament and a Protestant State," despite Catholics forming a third of the population at the time Northern Ireland was established.[62] Unionists viewed any effort to create a united Ireland as a mortal threat. In 1990, James Molyneaux, leader of the then-dominant Ulster Unionist Party, described the Republic of Ireland's constitutional claim to the north as "a demand for the destruction of Northern Ireland" that was "equivalent to Hitler's claim over Czechoslovakia."[63] Again, there is a striking similarity to Zionist claims that any challenge to the status quo, especially calls for a one-state solution, are tantamount to demands for the "destruction of Israel." Just like Zionists and Afrikaner nationalists, unionists also harbored an obsession with demography, worried that a Catholic majority would erode Protestant power. "The basic fear of Protestants in Northern Ireland," a former prime minister said, "is that they will be out-bred by the Roman Catholics. It is simple as that."[64]

In short, as Williams College political scientist Michael MacDonald put it, "to be Protestant [was] to be privileged; to be privileged [was] to require that Catholics be visibly deprived; and to deprive Catholics is to build the social order on overt as well as covert domination."[65] Protestant identity and privilege were so tied together that Catholic-nationalist demands in the 1960s for civil rights within the existing Northern Ireland state were perceived "not as an enhancement of democracy . . . but as an attack on Protestant identity and on the very existence of the Northern [Ireland] state."[66] Unionist authorities responded to the civil rights movement with violent repression. We can see a similar dynamic in Israel, where recent proposals for a liberal democratic constitution published by Palestinian citizens of Israel prompted the head of the Shin Bet secret police to warn that his agency would "foil the activity of anyone seeking to harm Israel's Jewish or democratic character, even if that activity was carried out by legal means."[67] During Israel's January 2009 invasion of Gaza, Irish journalist and veteran Middle East correspondent Patrick Cockburn compared Israel to Northern Ireland, noting that unionists, like Israelis, had "a highly developed siege mentality which led them always to see themselves as victims even when they were killing other people. There were no regrets or even knowledge of what they inflicted on others and therefore any retaliation by the other side appeared as unprovoked aggression inspired by unreasoning hate."[68]

The violent unionist rejection of nationalist demands for equality inaugurated the three-decade low-level civil war known as "the Troubles," in which more than 3,500 persons were killed and fifty thousand injured, nearly 2 percent of the Northern Ireland population.[69] As violence escalated, the British abolished the Stormont government in 1972, imposed direct rule from London, and sent in the army. The unionist state had collapsed, but the unionist-dominated status quo was preserved, as the army quickly began to act and to be seen by Catholics as an occupying force. A reconstituted IRA resumed armed struggle, initially in defense of Catholic communities, but later against the police, army, and loyalist militias. The IRA and other republican armed groups also carried out bomb attacks and political assassinations that killed noncombatants, including in Britain. British tactics included curfews, internment (imprisonment without charge or trial, similar to Israel's "administrative detention"—also a legacy of British colonial rule in Palestine), assassinations, and extrajudicial executions. There was extensive (and now well-documented) collusion between state forces and the loyalist militias that killed hundreds of noncombatant Catholics in brutal sectarian attacks.

Beginning with the nationalist civil rights movement in the late 1960s, but especially after 1972, Protestant cultural, political, and economic hegemony began a long, slow decline.[70] This led some unionists to question the exclusionary premises of their politics and identity. Traditional unionist leaders even agreed to form a short-lived power-sharing administration with nationalists in 1974, but this was brought down by a paralyzing general strike organized by unionist labor leaders. But such doubts evaded a large segment of the unionist community that held fast to a Protestant identity buttressed by the pervasive sense that British betrayal was never far off. Urban working-class Protestants increasingly formed the base of Paisley's Democratic Unionist Party. While other unionist politicians offered doubt, Paisley remained the most uncompromising face of unionism.

A central ritual enactment of Protestant domination has been the annual July 12 Orange Order marches throughout Northern Ireland, which celebrate the 1690 Battle of the Boyne near Drogheda in the present-day Republic of Ireland. On that battlefield, the forces of the Protestant King William of Orange defeated Catholic King James. Unionism held this as the decisive Protestant victory over Catholicism in Ireland. The Orange Order's triumphalist, crudely sectarian celebrations were often accompanied by violence as they forced their way through nationalist areas under police and army lockdown. Paisley frequently used the marches to incite his followers against Catholics and against any form of political compromise. In his worldview, the "enemies" at the gates at the dawn of the twenty-first century were the same ones King William had humiliated three centuries earlier. In 1995, Paisley commanded thousands of Orangemen gathered in the town of Portadown to "die if necessary rather than surrender" to nationalist protestors blocking the marchers' intended route through their community.[71] At a 2004 Orange march in Rasharkin, County Antrim, Paisley railed against the peace process:

> It is back to Reformation days as far as Rome is concerned. Rome dictates to the Protestants what church they should march to. The traditional unionists have passed through a time of the most severe testing. Their self-appointed leaders have been exposed as self-appointed traitors, experts in deception, fraud and betrayal. But this 12th July 2004 is different. A change has come about, and today the traditional unionists have been revived, and have partaken of a new zeal to defeat our ancient enemies, and crush the vipers who poisoned our society. A new determination has been born, and this 12th July the traditional unionists of Ulster are on the march to another great victory.[72]

With this background, it is not difficult to understand the widespread consternation at seeing Paisley and Adams together. What is remarkable is how Paisley justified this move by deftly ditching elements of the unionist narrative he had spouted for decades. On taking office as first minister, Paisley affirmed that, "I have not changed my unionism . . . but we are making together a declaration, we're all aiming to build a Northern Ireland in which all can live together in peace, being equal under the law and equally subject to the law."[73] Even if he denied it, Paisley had changed much about his unionism, rhetorically stripping it of supremacist and sectarian elements and affirming his commitment to the equality he had long opposed. Indeed, the changes were already audible in his 2004 speech, as he hinted that Sinn Féin could enter the government provided the IRA disarmed completely. When he felt there was no choice, Paisley showed flexibility that few had expected and none could have predicted.

Twice during his year in office, Paisley appeared at the Battle of the Boyne site in Drogheda, where the Irish government was building a visitors' center. Standing next to the Irish prime minister (no longer "Saddam Hussein"), Paisley retooled the key unionist foundational myth. "The Boyne conjures up all manner of stereotypes, many of which are far from the reality of what this ground signifies," he declared. And whereas the history of the Battle of the Boyne had long been deployed as a reliable template for understanding contemporary events and struggles, Paisley now consigned it to a common past: "At last we can embrace this battle site as part of our shared history."[74] A year later, Paisley continued rewriting history, emphasizing that "the armies which faced one another were not, as many think, totally Protestant and totally Romanist. Both sides had Protestants and Romanists in their ranks." Not even the Orange tradition, the symbolic bedrock of unionism, was to be spared from Paisley's insertion into the past of elements that would justify his dramatic change of course in the present and future: "It is to be remembered that many Princes of Orange were staunch Roman Catholics and the title itself was a Roman Catholic invention."[75] This was certainly not a point that Paisley had seen fit to make in previous decades. The crystal-clear narrative of the past had served as a script for the future unionists desperately wanted but which never came: a total victory over Irish nationalism and unionist hegemony forever affirmed. With that dream gone, Paisley began tentatively writing an updated history, still recognizable but shorn of triumphalism and more suited to the messy era of power-sharing and "parity of esteem" in which, as Paisley put it, "We . . . believe . . . that we should live in peace on this island in which we find ourselves by the over-ruling providence of Almighty God."[76]

Beyond Constitutionalism and Liberal Rights

Twenty years after the historic election that brought the ANC to power, many South Africans worry that theirs is a troubled country. While civic freedoms and political democracy exist, many of the promises of the Freedom Charter remain unfulfilled. As Na'eem Jeenah and Salim Vally observe, "For ordinary working class South Africans, the development of the constitution and the process of 'reconciliation,' such as it has been, have contributed little or nothing to ending their lives of struggle, misery, poverty and racism." South Africa "has become one of the most unequal societies in the world."[77] I saw some of this depressing reality when I visited South Africa in 2010. As I traveled out of the impressive splendor of central Cape Town, I saw the shantytowns of the Cape Flats. As far as the eye could see, tiny squatter shacks made of corrugated metal, plastic sheeting, and cardboard were jammed together, barely offering shelter from the famously stormy weather of the Cape. Home to hundreds of thousands of people, these camps lacked basic services from electricity to sanitation.

During apartheid, millions of Black people were forced to resettle in the Bantustans, their internal movement restricted by "influx controls" designed to prevent them from moving to areas reserved for whites. Once these racist rules were abolished, millions left the remote and economically barren former Bantustans for Cape Town, Johannesburg, and other major cities in search of work. This partly explained the growth of the shantytowns. They were a delayed consequence of apartheid, not the result of its end. But undoubtedly South Africa's inability to cope with the needs of the population was exacerbated by the economic compromises made during and after the transition to democracy. The sharp rise in inequality and the persistence of what has come to be known as "economic apartheid," where whites, albeit joined by a small Black elite, retain control of the commanding heights and even the foothills of the economy, was not inevitable. It was, however, preordained by the way the negotiations to end white minority rule occurred. In *The Shock Doctrine*, Naomi Klein describes how, while all eyes were on the constitutional negotiations that led to the new nonracial political system, the economic negotiations to which few paid attention—including many grassroots activists in the liberation struggle—resulted in a South African democracy "born in chains."[78]

The National Party knew it had to give up political power, but pushed for and won compromises that kept key decisions in "safe" hands so that the new ANC government could implement virtually none of the promises of redistribution and economic justice at the heart of the Freedom Charter:

> Want to redistribute land? Impossible—at the last minute, the negotiators agreed to add a clause to the new constitution that protects all private property, making land reform virtually impossible. Want to create jobs for millions of unemployed workers? Can't—hundreds of factories were actually about to close because the ANC had signed on to the GATT [General Agreement on Tariffs and Trade], the precursor of the World Trade Organization [WTO], which made it illegal to subsidize the auto plants and textile factories. Want to get free AIDS drugs to the townships, where the disease is spreading with terrifying speed? That violates an intellectual property rights commitment under the WTO, which the ANC joined with no public debate as a continuation of the GATT. Need money to build more and larger houses for the poor and to bring free electricity to the township? Sorry—the budget is being eaten up servicing the massive debt, passed on quietly by the apartheid government. Print more money? Tell that to the apartheid-era head of the central bank. Free water for all? Not likely. The World Bank, with its large in-country contingent of economists, researchers and trainers (a self-proclaimed "Knowledge Bank"), is making private-sector partnerships the norm.[79]

And so on. Many of the early compromises were not necessarily the result of a deliberate betrayal, although there were class differences within the ANC that might explain some of what occurred. But the ANC, amid the risks and tensions of a never-guaranteed transition, was also outwitted and outmaneuvered. An army of officials from the International Monetary Fund (IMF), the World Bank, and Western governments were on hand to advise and warn ANC negotiators about the limits of what was economically possible. Thabo Mbeki, who led the economic negotiations, imposed economic policies that he himself termed "Thatcherite" when he became deputy president after 1996 and when he eventually succeeded Mandela as president in 1999.[80] All this was done following the usual claims that subjecting the economy to market "discipline" would attract international investors and that the trickle-down effects would bring growth for all instead of the rising inequality that has been the actual result.

Could the same happen in Palestine in a one-state solution? Michael Neumann, author of *The Case against Israel* and a strong proponent of two states, has warned that in a single state "the democratic process" would "not ensure that the will of the majority really prevails. Dominant economic groups know how to confuse, divide and conquer. They may well, through a mixture or bribery and manipulation, remain dominant."[81] All of this means that in a nominally democratic state Israeli Jews could retain and even expand their present economic advantages, just as whites have done in South Africa. This criticism is absolutely right. But a two-state solution cannot in and of itself avoid this pitfall: economic inequality can't be ended by drawing borders. A two-state solution, in whatever form it might be realized, would simply ratify and legitimize the massive inequalities between Israel, on the one hand, with its First World economy, and on the other, the destitution in Gaza and much of the West Bank that is the direct result of years of Israeli usurpation of Palestinian land, resources, and rights. And "statehood" by itself—aside from the romantic notions of flag-waving independence—is no guarantee of economic viability and sovereignty for any state. For the Palestinians, for whom statehood is always proposed with extraordinary limits on sovereignty to assure Israel's "security," there would be even less economic freedom.

When ANC leaders fell under the economic spells cast by the IMF and the World Bank, these doctrines were at the height of their influence. Two decades later, especially in the wake of the 2008 global financial crisis, no country is safe from the ravages of unrestricted capital markets. Even one-time success stories such as Greece, Cyprus, Ireland, Spain, and Italy have seen their economic and political sovereignty hijacked by supranational bodies, unfettered financial markets that can bring them to their knees, and punishing IMF-imposed austerity programs. In May 2012, as economic depression brought on by externally imposed austerity led to an alarming social breakdown, IMF director Christine Lagarde generated outrage among Greeks when she said she was saving her sympathy for people in sub-Saharan Africa who were still worse off. But less than a year after her callous remarks, malnourished children were showing up at schools across Greece in such numbers that the *New York Times* reported, "When it comes to food insecurity, Greece has now fallen to the level of some African countries."[82] As the government slashed healthcare spending in line with the demands of

Greece's creditors, the health system was ill equipped to cope with the sudden reemergence of malaria as a result of cuts to mosquito abatement programs, as well as a 200 percent spike in HIV infections as needle-exchange programs for heroin users were closed down.[83]

This is the economic environment in which South Africa exists and emerged as a democracy, and against which every country seeking economic democracy and sovereignty must struggle. Nowhere has this struggle been more intense in recent years than in Palestine's immediate region. The early promise of the popular uprising that overthrew Egypt's president Hosni Mubarak in February 2011 looked like it had been betrayed as the army overthrew Mohamed Morsi, the country's first democratically elected president in July 2013, amid jubilation by some sectors of Egyptian society. Egyptian liberals argued that this was not a coup but a continuation of the revolution against an incompetent and polarizing Muslim Brotherhood president who had, in any case, been only too happy to follow IMF directives. But the unarguable reality was that triumphant Mubarak-era elites who had long participated in pillaging the country had now retaken the commanding heights of the state.[84]

The innovation in Palestine is that the theft of all economic sovereignty from the people and the imposition of a neoliberal order, with rules written by international financial bodies to soften the country up for "investors," has been completed even before political independence or statehood. One can even say that Palestine has been a dystopian model for how international powers have reacted to the financial crisis. In Greece and Italy, elected governments were replaced for a time by unelected "technocratic" administrations that would implement IMF, EU, and European Central Bank austerity policies whether the people wanted them or not. This was not unlike the insistence of the United States and European Union that "technocratic" ex–IMF official Salam Fayyad be appointed Palestinian Authority prime minister in 2007 so he could faithfully implement their economic plans, under the guise of "institution building" and preparing Palestinians for statehood.

The question, then, is not whether an economic disaster like South Africa's could happen after a political settlement in Palestine, but how to stop and reverse the disaster already under way in which a Palestinian elite flourishes, comfortably aligned with its Israeli economic and political counterparts, while millions of Palestinians languish in refugee camps and villages with bleak futures. There is no reason to believe that this dynamic will change by itself. If the economic question is not addressed up front, then years after a political victory, in whatever form it comes, Palestinians will find themselves facing the same shattered dreams and disappointments with which South Africans are coping today.

"A central part of the South African struggle, one that's usually not talked about, is that mass forced displacement was central to the South African apartheid regime," observes Hazem Jamjoum. "Because forced removals were so rampant . . . the struggle against South African apartheid, like the Palestinian struggle, was also a struggle for return of the displaced and a struggle to get back the stolen land."[85] Jamjoum, a Palestinian researcher, was part of a study tour organized by Badil and Zochrot, two organizations that work for the Palestinian right of return. The tour went to South Africa in 2012 to learn lessons from that country's successes and failures. "Much of our discussion focused on redistribution, refugees leading the process of how we want our communities to look and operate, how we think we can make sure people can have a decent life after we return, and not just be the poor and unemployed class of a post-facelift Israel," Jamjoum said.

The tour was part of ongoing efforts to develop a vision and practical frameworks not just for the return of refugees, transitional justice, and economic redistribution, but also for the "de-Zionization of culture and education." This would include overhauling the educational system to create a new system that would promote "diversity and pluralism" and "endorse and celebrate processes of healing and reconciliation taking place in society at large." The vision recognizes that the significance of religion in many people's lives "requires that religious communities and leadership be called upon to take a role" in the process. In place of Israel's discriminatory immigration system, the new decolonizing political entity in Palestine "will offer asylum to refugees and persecuted individuals regardless of race, ethnicity, religion, gender or sexual orientation in accordance with international law."[86] There are other precedents Palestinians and Israelis can look to: in the decade following the 1995 Dayton Agreement that ended the Bosnia war, almost half a million refugees and internally displaced persons returned home with international assistance "to places that are now dominated demographically and politically by members of another ethno-national community"—an enormous achievement in a country with a total population of 3.5 million and deep traumas as a result of the recent war. In the assessment of London School of Economics comparative politics professor Sumantra Bose, this outcome provided "a vigorous affirmation of the right of all victims of 'ethnic cleansing' to return to and reclaim their homes."[87]

Without indulging Israeli racism or preserving undue privilege, the legitimate concerns of ordinary Israeli Jews can be addressed directly in any transition to ensure that the shift to a democratic and decolonized state is orderly and that essential redistributive policies are carried out fairly. Inevitably decolonization will cause some pain as Israeli Jews, particularly settlers, lose power and privilege, but there are few reasons to believe it cannot be a well-managed process or that the vast majority of Israeli Jews would not be prepared to make the adjustment for the sake of a normality and legitimacy they cannot have any other way.

It is important not to fall into the trap of thinking of Palestinians only as potential winners and Israeli Jews only as potential losers. While Palestinians in every part of historic Palestine are on average much worse off than Israeli Jews today, Israeli Jews have not been spared the consequences of neoliberalism, privatization, and privileging the interests of business elites over communities and people. Inequality, rising prices, the lack of affordable housing, and the deterioration of health and education services brought hundreds of thousands of Israeli Jews into the streets in the summer of 2011 to call for "social justice." This movement was rightly criticized for its narrow nationalism, exclusion of the Palestinians from its vision of justice, and refusal to challenge the "colonial, racist Zionist ideology" of the Israeli state.[88] In effect, Israeli Jews were simply calling for a redivision among themselves of the pie stolen—or made from ingredients stolen—from Palestinians. But the groundswell even within Israeli Jewish society suggests that an economic agenda in a democratic state of all its citizens, one that puts people's basic needs for housing, education, work, and health first, has the potential to create new political and social coalitions across boundaries that today seem unthinkable. Moreover, thinking along these lines is essential to any kind of just future.

In *The New Jim Crow,* Michelle Alexander observes that "nothing could have been more important in the 1970s and 1980s than finding a way to create a durable, interracial, bottom up coalition for social and economic justice to ensure that another caste system did not emerge from the ashes of Jim Crow."[89] But the failure to do that created the conditions for the current horrifying reality of mass incarceration of people of color to emerge—a new, formally "colorblind" caste system that has reproduced racial inequalities in the United States as stark and violent as the overt system of segregation that civil rights abolished. Alexander stresses the need for a positive vision of a society in which "all human beings of all races are treated with dignity, and have the right to food, shelter, health care, education and security."[90] Such an expansive vision, she believes, "could open the door to meaningful alliances between poor and working-class people of all colors, who could begin to see their interests as aligned, rather than in conflict—no longer in competition for scarce resources in a zero-sum game."[91] South Africa, two decades after the end of apartheid, now also stands at a critical turning point. Its people must decide if the heroic sacrifices and historic victory of the struggle to overturn political apartheid will be lost as a new economic-racial caste system takes its place, or whether there is still time to build a country that fulfills the promises of the Freedom Charter.

Similar challenges exist in Northern Ireland, where the poorest republican communities have yet to see the promises of equality and opportunity materialize in the lives of their members. Although gaps have narrowed, predominantly nationalist areas of Northern Ireland are still, on average, considerably poorer than predominantly unionist areas. But loyalists in working-class neighborhoods, shorn of the privileges and job security they long enjoyed as the foot soldiers of the "Protestant state," have also been left behind in impoverished urban enclaves as middle- and upper-class unionists have moved to leafy suburbs. Such urban ghettoes have often been the places where the most virulent expressions of defensive sectarianism persist. It will be in the fulfillment of the Belfast Agreement's promises of equality and empowerment to the poorest and most excluded that its durability and legitimacy will be tested in years to come.

The lessons are clear for Palestine, as well: we must make economic justice an integral part of the Palestinian struggle for liberation from Zionism. This includes a frank discussion of how decolonization will cost Israeli Jews economic, social, and political privileges they have unfairly enjoyed for decades at grievous expense to Palestinians. But we must also begin to explore the ways in which decolonization can be the prelude for new forms of inclusion, even for Israeli Jews at the bottom of the ladder, whose only advantage has been what in the US context has been called the "psychological wage" of belonging to the privileged group. At a time when the sovereignty of states is less of a guarantee of economic security for their populations than ever and the possibility of democracy is negated by the overwhelming power of international capital, Palestinians must also look beyond visions—whether in one state or two—that have been too focused on idealized notions of statehood. One by-product of the BDS movement is that, in preparation for specific campaigns, it has created a culture among activists of researching the economic ties between Israeli, Palestinian, and multinational corporations. This kind of research can also serve as a basis for much broader education about the economic structures that will need to be challenged and reformed as part of decolonization and transformation. Palestinians must think about their struggle not only in local terms, but in the context of a global struggle to win back economic sovereignty for people and communities from democracy-crushing transnational markets and local economic elites. Failing this, no narrow political or constitutional solution can bring Palestinians the liberation and self-determination for which they have made so many sacrifices.

Much More Is Possible

I have argued in this chapter that a public consensus that seems absolutely mono-lithic and unchangeable can crumble rapidly once power starts to shift. In 1950, the end of Jim Crow in the United States within a generation would have seemed completely unthinkable. In 1987, a one-person, one-vote system seemed a remote fantasy in South Africa. In 2004, the image of Gerry Adams and Ian Paisley sitting down together, let alone governing as partners, defied imagination. This is where the wealth of research and real-life experience about the successes, failures, difficul-ties, and opportunities of managing such transitions at the level of national and local politics, neighborhoods, schools and universities, workplaces, and state insti-tutions that is emerging from South Africa and Northern Ireland could be of enor-mous value.

Palestinians and Israelis will not follow precisely in the footsteps of those who have gone before them. In light of the serious shortcomings of the settlement in South Africa, we should very much hope they don't. Rather, the message is simply this: we don't need to allow our vision of justice to be constrained only by what seems realistic from the perspective of today, and especially not by what powerful and privileged groups deem acceptable or pragmatic. Frederick Douglass's observa-tion that "power concedes nothing without a demand" remains as true today as it did during the struggle to abolish slavery. Things change because people change them—and as situations change, so do the boundaries of what is considered achiev-able. But it starts with knowing where you want to go.

Chapter 4

Neoliberal Palestine

In August 2009, *New York Times* columnist Thomas Friedman announced that he'd discovered "the most exciting new idea in Arab governance ever."[1] The lucky recipients of this blessing were none other than the long-suffering Palestinians. Friedman dubbed his discovery "Fayyadism," for Salam Fayyad, the former IMF official appointed Palestinian "prime minister" after the 2007 US-instigated subversion of the Hamas-led "national unity government." The US-backed plot sparked a bloody and brief civil war that split the Palestinian Authority between an internationally financed and supported West Bank wing under Fatah, led by Mahmoud Abbas, and the Hamas wing, boycotted and besieged in the Gaza Strip. The bitter struggle for legitimacy and power between the two factions continues to this day.

The West—in particular the US, and in this case Thomas Friedman—portrays Abbas's West Bank regime as the exemplary model, striding toward order and development under the benign hand of "moderate" Palestinian men in business suits. According to Friedman, "Fayyadism is based on the simple but all-too-rare notion that an Arab leader's legitimacy should be based not on slogans or rejectionism or personality cults or security services, but on delivering transparent, accountable administration and services." Friedman couldn't and didn't say that legitimacy should be based on winning elections, because Fayyad had not been elected by anyone: his Third Way party came in dead last, garnering just 2.4 percent of the vote in the 2006 election. But this was a minor detail in the picture Friedman painted of a burgeoning economic and political miracle. "Things are truly getting better in the West Bank," Friedman declared, "thanks to a combination of Fayyadism, improved Palestinian security and a lifting of checkpoints by Israel." Hundreds of new companies were being registered every month, Friedman said, and the IMF—Fayyad's former employer—was predicting West Bank economic growth of 7 percent that year.

Many of the elements what would become Fayyadism were set out in the 2007 *Palestinian Reform and Development Plan*, a document aimed at winning donor backing, effectively written by international consultants but published by the Palestinian Authority. The same month as Friedman's 2009 column, Fayyad issued a new plan with the grand title *Ending the Occupation, Establishing the State*. It set out a vision of "Palestine" as "a stable democratic state with a multi-party political system" in which "transfer of governing authority is smooth, peaceful and regular in accordance with the will of the people, expressed through free and fair elections conducted in accordance with the law." Fayyad's plan would lay the foundation for this state with a "good governance" agenda based on "building effective institutions, consolidating the rule of law and serving its citizens." This, in turn, would contribute to "liberating the Palestinian national economy from external hegemony and control, and reversing its dependence on the Israeli economy."[2] Fayyad and his boosters insisted that this ambitious vision could and must happen within two years. These were big plans; they even included building an international airport in the Jordan Valley. "We look forward to welcoming President Obama there aboard Air Force One, not Marine One. In other words, on his Jumbo jet rather than his helicopter," Fayyad announced.[3]

In the press, the plan was succeeding spectacularly, even if few believed the airport would be built in time for Obama to arrive there as president. Where Friedman led, others soon followed to declare a Palestinian renaissance. Israel's *Haaretz* marveled at a new shopping mall in the northern West Bank city of Nablus, "where the city center is thriving" and "cafes are bustling." Mercedes and BMW dealerships in the city were struggling to keep up with demand for luxury cars.[4] Germany's *Der Spiegel* saw a Palestinian "tiger" economy in the making, its reporter impressed by the fact that "Ramallah now has a five-star hotel, sushi restaurants and parking meters" and that a "rotating, panoramic restaurant will soon open on the 28th floor of the Palestine Trade Tower, floating above Ramallah like a space ship."[5] Rawabi, a new Qatari-financed Palestinian "city" near Ramallah, was hailed perhaps more than any other project as the symbol of the boom; dozens of glowing media reports appeared worldwide. Back in Ramallah, *New York Times* columnist Roger Cohen stepped out of Fayyad's office to observe that "stores and restaurants are full" and "Palestinian Authority police are everywhere in their crisp uniforms."[6] Inside the government buildings, too, order and industry prevailed. "Ministries now operate much more effectively than in the past," *Der Spiegel* reported confidently, when previously they were little more than "teahouses for the minions of former Palestinian leader Yasser Arafat." Roads were being paved, schools opened, water lines laid—the infrastructure of the new Palestine. Fayyad was "building it rather than bally-hooing it," Cohen gushed.

Top government officials in Europe and the United States pushed the same line. US Secretary of State Hillary Clinton publicly praised Fayyad's "reforms" and claimed they had "fueled continued economic growth." She too lauded the opening of the five-star Mövenpick Hotel Ramallah. "New businesses are opening," she claimed, more than a hundred in a single month, "everything from venture capital funds to local hardware stores. As a result, more and more Palestinians are finding jobs."[7] From the US perspective, marketing the West Bank as an economic success story went hand in hand with continued US support for the siege of Gaza, which was still devastated from Israel's invasion in December 2008 and January 2009. This carrot-and-stick approach was meant to demonstrate to Palestinians that they would be better off opting for leaders handpicked for them by the United States and Israel than insisting on choosing their own.

Many of the loudest cheerleaders for Fayyadism were not previously known for any great sympathy toward Palestinians or their rights. Los Angeles rabbi Kenneth Chasen, for instance, found Ramallah—which he had imagined to be a "refugee camp"—instead to have "streets teeming with auto and pedestrian traffic. . . . Beautiful new buildings of stone and glass" and "government offices patrolled by polite, well-trained security personnel," all adding up to a "general atmosphere of busyness and safety." It was, Chasen said, "everything we all have hoped to see after the establishment of a Palestinian state alongside Israel—only it's all happening beforehand."[8] Chasen was delighted to find that "Israeli political leaders across the spectrum—from Shimon Peres to Ehud Barak to numerous members of Benjamin Netanyahu's Likud Party—have lauded Fayyad" and that "many of America's staunchest defenders of Israel, such as Alan Dershowitz, have declared that Fayyad is for real." A year after announcing his discovery of "Fayyadism," Friedman himself returned to Ramallah—this time to give his readers stock tips. The tiny Palestinian stock exchange was up, outperforming the stock indices of most Arab countries. And Friedman found Fayyad "upbeat too." What was happening, according to Friedman, was "the real Palestinian revolution."[9]

The crowning endorsement came from Israeli prime minister Benjamin Netanyahu in his triumphant May 2011 speech to the US Congress (where he received more standing ovations than President Obama had at his State of the Union speech a few months earlier).[10] "The Palestinian economy is booming. It's growing by more than ten percent a year," Netanyahu claimed. "And Palestinian cities—they look very different today than what they looked just . . . a few years ago. They have shopping malls, movie theaters, restaurants, banks. They even have e-businesses, but you can't see that when you visit them." Netanyahu took credit for helping "Palestinian economic growth by removing hundreds of barriers and roadblocks to the free flow of goods and people, and the results have been nothing short of remarkable."[11]

It wasn't only the e-businesses that no one could see. There was something else that all these glowing reports rarely acknowledged: reality. There was no Palestinian miracle; this was, if anything, a counterrevolution. The glittering illusions peddled by pundits and politicians concealed a dismal reality: while some Palestinians indulged in a credit-fueled consumption binge, unemployment continued to go up. Millions of Palestinians remained mired in poverty, many with not enough to eat. With the Gaza Strip under a punishing blockade, Israel's military occupation and creeping annexation of land in the West Bank continued to stifle Palestinian social and economic life as the Palestinian Authority and the population became more dependent on foreign aid and credit. Meanwhile, Palestinians have become guinea pigs for practices that the global financial crisis laid bare all over the world: neoliberal economic policies pushed by the United States, the European Union, the World Bank, and the IMF. All this has been done with the active collusion of countries that claimed to champion Palestinian aspirations, and, of course, of Israel and the Palestinian Authority.

In tandem, with the assistance of the United States and Israel, the Palestinian Authority in Ramallah built a repressive police-state apparatus that sought to suppress and disarm any resistance to Israeli occupation and to crush internal Palestinian dissent and criticism with increasing ferocity. Some Palestinians even called their condition a "double occupation"—not just by the Israeli army and settlers, but by the Palestinian Authority as well. In Gaza, under brutal siege, Hamas consolidated its rule through methods that were often no less repressive.[12] But behind a smoke-screen of "state-building" rhetoric and flag-waving, a small Palestinian elite has continued to enrich itself by deepening its political, economic, and military ties with Israel and the United States, often explicitly undermining efforts by Palestinian civil society to resist. This catastrophic assault on Palestinians has been masked with the language of "technocratic" government and marketed as nothing less than the fulfillment of the Palestinian "national project." Although Fayyad himself resigned in 2013, his basic approach remains intact.[13] If these are indeed the foundations of a future Palestinian state, then a people who have struggled for so long for liberation from Zionism's colonial assault can only look forward to new, more insidious forms of economic and political bondage.

Fayyadism: A Strategy Born in Blood

Although Fayyad, longtime finance minister in the Palestinian Authority, was presented as the paragon of "Western-style" modernity, technocracy, efficiency, and liberalism, his rise came about the old-fashioned way: through thinly veiled threats and subversion. The Bush administration pushed Palestinian Authority president Mahmoud Abbas to hold elections for the Palestinian Legislative Council in January 2006; to the surprise of the United States, Hamas won handily, taking more than half the seats. Abbas was compelled to appoint Hamas's Ismail Haniyeh as PA prime minister, but behind the scenes the furious Americans, together with Abbas, Egypt, and Israel, were working to undermine Hamas. Within days of Hamas's victory, the Quartet—an ad hoc group made up of the United States, the European Union, Russia, and the United Nations which functioned, in effect, as an "international" fig leaf for directing US and Israeli demands at the Palestinians—vowed not to provide any assistance or recognition to any government that did not commit "to the principles of nonviolence, recognition of Israel, and acceptance of previous agreements and obligations," including President Bush's 2002 Roadmap.[14] Hamas refused, its officials noting on many occasions that the demands were lopsided: Israel frequently engaged in widespread violence, had never accepted or recognized any fundamental Palestinian rights or political demands, and was in constant violation of the Roadmap, which, among other things, demanded that Israel "immediately" dismantle new settlement outposts built since 2001 and "[freeze] all settlement activity."

But Hamas, contrary to how it has been portrayed, immediately signaled its political flexibility, emphasizing its offer (first extended several years earlier) of a long-term truce or *hudna* if Israel withdrew from the West Bank and Gaza Strip. While acknowledging that the fundamental issues of the conflict were too deep to resolve in the present, the *hudna* would, as a senior advisor to Prime Minister Haniyeh explained in a *New York Times* op-ed, "bring about an immediate end to the occupation and . . . initiate a period of peaceful coexistence during which both sides would refrain from any form of military aggression or provocation." An end to violence, he argued, would "create the space and the calm necessary to resolve all outstanding issues."[15] This view reflected directives from the highest echelons. On February 8, 2006, just two weeks after the election victory, Hamas leader Khaled Mishal told the BBC, "We now say that if Israel withdraws to the 1967 borders there could be peace and security in the region and agreements between the sides."[16] Mishal's interview—especially his acceptance of the 1967 borders as a basis for a long-term agreement—reflected remarkable shifts over several years in his organization's thinking. After so much more bloodshed, it is sobering to think what might have happened if this opening had been seized. After all, just such gradual breaks with long-held positions, painstakingly reciprocated by various leaders over a period of years, were what eventually made possible the historic 1998 peace agreement in Northern Ireland brokered by Senator George Mitchell.[17]

We will never know what might have been and how many lives could have been spared; Israel, the United States, and the European Union were unwilling to test this apparent opening. Instead, they immediately suspended their subsidies and transfers to the aid-dependent PA, plunging it into crisis as the salaries of tens of thousands of workers went unpaid. Israel, meanwhile, demonstrated its respect for Palestinian democracy by rounding up dozens of elected members of the legislative council, including several government ministers. It began implementing a permanent blockade of Gaza, where Haniyeh's government was based. As the suffering of ordinary Palestinians worsened, the donors set up mechanisms to bypass the elected government and channel their funds in ways they hoped would bolster Abbas and generate a backlash against Hamas. This overt pressure was only part of the story. When cutting off aid produced no results, Condoleezza Rice traveled to Ramallah in October 2006 and demanded, behind closed doors, that Abbas dissolve the government within two weeks.[18] As it was Ramadan, Abbas stalled, and weeks later the US consul general in Jerusalem, Jacob Walles, was sent in to instruct Abbas to deliver a final ultimatum. Walles accidentally left behind a copy of his talking points, prepared by the State Department, revealing their blunt nature. "Hamas should be given a clear choice with a clear deadline," Walles's instructions stated. "They either accept a new government that meets the Quartet principles, or they reject it. . . . If Hamas does not agree within the prescribed time, you should make clear your intention to declare a state of emergency and form an emergency government explicitly committed to that platform."[19] There is no provision in the Palestinian Authority's basic law granting Abbas indefinite extraordinary powers. Any government and prime minister appointed by the Palestinian Authority president must be confirmed by the legislative council, in which Hamas, not Abbas's loyalists, held an absolute majority. But such democratic and constitutional niceties were not the concern of the US government. And, unbeknownst to all but a few Palestinians directly involved, the United States was mounting even more aggressive efforts to overturn the elected authority.

Since 2005, the year Israel withdrew its settlers from Gaza and tightened its control of the territory's perimeter, Lieutenant General Keith Dayton, the US security coordinator for the Palestinian territories, had been overseeing efforts to "reform" the PA security forces. In practice, this meant turning them into a formidable force for suppressing armed resistance to Israel as well as for internal repression. All of this was done in the name of promoting "law and order." After the Hamas election victory, Dayton's focus turned increasingly to making these forces into a subversive anti-Hamas militia loyal to Abbas. As *Vanity Fair*'s David Rose revealed, Dayton's effort became a crucial element in "a covert initiative, approved by Bush and implemented by Secretary of State Condoleezza Rice and Deputy National Security Adviser Elliott Abrams, to provoke a Palestinian civil war."[20] Bush personally identified Gaza strongman Muhammad Dahlan, the longtime head of the PA's notoriously abusive Preventive Security Force, as the Americans' Palestinian counterpart. "He's our guy," Bush told aides.[21] Dahlan, whose forces worked closely with the CIA, was already despised by Hamas—not least for torturing many of its cadres, as Dayton himself has acknowledged.[22] Although the Bush administration made lavish promises of funding to arm Dahlan's militias, members of Congress blocked the payments, fearing the guns might fall into the hands of groups that would use them to resist Israel. Rice lobbied Arab rulers to provide the money and weapons instead and the United Arab Emirates came through with an estimated thirty million dollars.[23] Jordan and Egypt provided bases and training and Israel cooperated, allowing arms shipments to pass through the borders it still controlled into Gaza. The involvement of the neoconservative Abrams, convicted and later pardoned for misleading Congress over the Reagan administration's illegal channeling of funds earned from arms sales to Iran to the Nicaraguan Contras in the 1980s, led some to dub this operation "Iran-Contra 2.0."[24] The scheme bore many similarities to the dirty wars the United States fought by proxy in Central America.

With Fatah-controlled PA security forces refusing to take orders from the elected government, Hamas set up its own "Executive Force." Dahlan waged what he called a "very clever war," which involved his men kidnapping and torturing members of the Executive Force. By the end of 2006, tensions broke out into open battles, claiming dozens of lives. With the death toll mounting amid provocations by Dahlan's militia and tit-for-tat atrocities between Fatah and Hamas forces, Abbas buckled—not to Rice and the US, but to Arab pressure. In February 2007, the parties negotiated an agreement in Mecca to form a national unity government. Hamas did not accept the Quartet's dictates and Haniyeh kept his role as prime minister, but now senior Fatah and independent figures would join the cabinet. The deal was sealed with pledges from Saudi Arabia to provide the funds to pay PA salaries. Palestinians, alarmed at the prospect of full-blown civil war, were relieved, and Hamas and Fatah members celebrated together in Gaza, firing their guns into the air.[25]

The mood in Washington was not so celebratory; an "apoplectic" Rice set in motion "Plan B," which called for Abbas to "collapse the government." Dayton's and Dahlan's role now, as the US envisioned it, was to ensure that as long as the unity government stayed in office, Hamas would not integrate into or gain control over the security forces. A State Department memo outlining the US plan stated that over the following months, "Dahlan [would oversee work] in coordination with General Dayton and Arab [nations] to train and equip [a] 15,000-man force under President Abbas's control to establish internal law and order, stop terrorism and deter extralegal forces"—a reference to Hamas's Executive Force. All of this was aimed, the memo said, at giving Abbas "the capability to take the required strategic political decisions . . . such as dismissing the cabinet [and] establishing an emergency government."[26]

In 2011, the existence of a secret "quadripartite forum" of Israeli, American, Egyptian, and Palestinian officials was revealed in the Palestine Papers, which had been leaked to Al Jazeera. Known to have met at least twice in March and April 2007, the forum's explicit goal appears to have been to undermine the national unity government. The key figures at the meetings were Dayton, Dahlan, Israeli general Amos Gilad, and one General Sharif from Egypt. The leaked minutes state that the "forum is backed by the highest political echelons of each government" and that all participants had agreed to keep its existence absolutely secret.[27] The Israelis alleged that Hamas was attempting to "emulate the Hizbullah model" of resistance and that its "main strategic goal . . . is to take over the PA and then the PLO." The Palestinians presented plans for how they would crack down on tunnels between Gaza and Egypt in order to prevent Hamas bringing in weapons; Dayton explained that the "purpose of these efforts is to prevent Hamas from using the NUG [national unity government] as a means of gaining more powers and building up more arms." The aim was also explicitly political—to build up Fatah's strength until the siege had, its backers hoped, sapped Hamas of election-winning popularity. "If you can keep Hamas from overwhelming the PLO forces, and keep Fatah together, until Hamas is no longer an attractive option," Dayton advised, "you prevent it from winning militarily until the next elections." As for Israel's General Gilad, he had high praise for Egypt's notoriously repressive police state, which was supporting the US-backed effort to undermine Hamas. "I always believed in the abilities of the Egyptian Intelligence Service," he said. "It keeps order and security among 70 millions—20 millions in one city—this is a great achievement for which you deserve a medal."

The situation in the Gaza Strip continued to deteriorate, with attacks and counterattacks by the opposing forces leaving scores dead. In all, Hamas estimated that about 250 of its fighters were killed in the first months of 2007. In April 2007, a portion of the US plan was leaked to the Jordanian newspaper *Al-Majd*, convincing Hamas leaders that "there was a plan, approved by America, to destroy the political choice."[28] A few weeks later, five hundred newly trained members of Fatah's National Security Force, equipped with expensive new equipment, marched into Gaza from Egypt. This was the last straw for Hamas. "Finally we decided to put an end to it. If we had let them stay loose in Gaza, there would have been more violence," Hamas spokesman Fawzi Barhoum explained.[29] This is the background for what happened between June 10 and 15, 2007, when Hamas, convinced that it faced an imminent, externally backed coup, moved to take over Fatah-controlled security facilities in Gaza. Senior Hamas leader Mahmoud Zahar says that the original plan was only to get rid of Dahlan's Preventive Security Force, as they "were the ones out on every crossroads, putting anyone suspected of Hamas involved at risk of being tortured or killed."[30] By all accounts, the fighting was vicious, with atrocities committed by fighters from both factions. But the US-backed Fatah forces were routed, many refusing to fight and others fleeing to safety in Israel and eventually Ramallah by land and sea. After a week, Hamas was in full control of Gaza. But Abbas, claiming that it was Hamas that had carried out a "coup," had the excuse he needed to appoint the "emergency government" Rice had demanded, with Salam Fayyad named prime minister. Although Fayyad never received confirmation by the legislative council, his Ramallah-based authority was granted full international recognition and aid, while Gaza faced an ever-tighter Israeli blockade with the tacit support of Abbas and his entourage. In the West Bank, the PA's Dayton-trained forces began an intense crackdown on Hamas and other opponents of Abbas's rule and closed down hundreds of charities and organizations suspected of affiliation or sympathy with the resistance. Fayyadism was born.

Poverty, Debt, and Dependence

Despite billions in aid, by mid-2012 the Ramallah bubble looked like it might be bursting. "The unemployment rate is rapidly increasing, and we face a high cost of living," Abbas minister and senior Fatah apparatchik Muhammad Shtayyeh said. "The PA is powerless and incapable of meeting its financial commitments."[31] Fayyad's government was broke and unable to pay its growing army of 150,000 employees. Since "Palestine" was not a recognized state, the PA could not turn to international institutions for loans and had gone a billion dollars into debt to local banks. Almost none of the money was spent on long-term development projects, but instead was used to pay day-to-day bills. Unemployment surged to 24 percent between 2007 and 2010 in the occupied territories, with rates approaching 35 percent in Gaza. Palestinians already faced "some of the highest unemployment rates in the world," the World Bank said, but even these figures "actually understate the true degree to which Palestinians lack work."[32] In the West Bank, Palestinian refugees were disproportionately hit by "falling employment growth, accelerating unemployment and lower real wages," according to the United Nations Relief and Works Agency (UNRWA).[33]

By late 2011, the official unemployment rate had fallen from its 2010 peak of 25 percent to just over 22 percent, with the vast majority of new jobs in the bubble-inflated construction sector. But the actual number of unemployed workers remained higher than in 2009 due to population growth and the lack of new jobs to absorb new workers.[34] Other figures, including a report by the UN Conference on Trade and Development, suggest employment continued to rise all along.[35] What no official estimate disputed was that mass unemployment remained a permanent feature of the Palestinian economy. If the jobs weren't there, there was also no sign of any impact from all the new businesses Friedman and Clinton had been counting by the hundreds. World Bank research found "little private investment in the productive sectors" of the economy and, from 2006 to 2010, the contribution to Palestinian economic growth from manufacturing was a cool zero percent.[36] Not only were Palestinians not investing, but there was also virtually no foreign direct investment, despite a much-ballyhooed US government–sponsored Palestine Investment Conference in Bethlehem in 2010.[37]

The fans of Fayyadism weren't imagining things, however, when they saw shops, cafés, luxury cars, and hotels in Ramallah and a few other cities. The West Bank and Gaza Strip economies did "grow" in the latter half of the 2000s. In Gaza, the "growth" was mostly a bounce-back from the extremely depressed levels of economic activity that had resulted from years of war and siege. But in the West Bank, what the boosters were confusing—or deliberately misrepresenting—as evidence of a Palestinian economic renaissance, indeed the makings of a thriving future state, was nothing more than a construction and consumption binge fueled by easy credit and foreign aid. "Need a student loan? No problem. Need a car loan? Simple. Want to get married—how much do you need? A home? Why rent when you can own? Don't have the latest iPhone? Don't sweat it, just sign here and pay NIS 5 [$1.25] for the next 200 years. While you're at it, every home needs a computer, what's the difference between a NIS

5 and NIS 7 payment?" That's how Palestinian businessman and analyst Sam Bahour satirized the frenzy of lending in the West Bank as "the banking system jumped out of its conservative straightjacket and started begging for customers to take out loans. Not one loan, not two, but as many as possible."[38]

Official figures indicate that Bahour wasn't exaggerating. Consumer credit increased sixfold, from $70 million in 2008 to $415 million in 2011; car loans almost tripled, from $40 million to $112 million.[39] The Bank of Palestine advertised consumer loans for PA employees of up to twenty-five times their monthly salaries, a package that included something called an "Easy Life Card." Most of this easy money went to pay for goods imported from or through Israel, benefitting Israeli companies and Palestinian middlemen. Already in 2007, after international aid to the Palestinian Authority was restricted as punishment for Hamas's election victory, Palestinian families ran up a debt burden of almost one billion dollars, with 40 percent reporting they had sold off personal goods such as jewelry—a traditional form of savings—furniture, and other personal items just to survive.[40] By mid-2011, half of Palestinians in the West Bank and Gaza Strip had debts and a fifth of those said that their current debts exceeded their annual income. More than a third said they routinely bought from stores on credit.[41]

Exploding consumer borrowing is only part of the story. Credit for real estate and construction tripled from $188 million in 2008 to more than half a billion dollars in 2012. Yet during this period, virtually all the "growth" recorded in the Palestinian economy was directly due to foreign aid. In 2010, according to the World Bank, foreign aid to the PA topped $1.1 billion dollars, on top of billions in previous years. Since its establishment, the World Bank observed, the PA "has become more donor dependent at an increasing rate," with "the majority of the recent donor aid" allocated "to pay PA salaries and arrears, which has pumped up consumption and imports of consumer goods."[42] Yet even this aid was insufficient to meet current expenses, which was why the PA also ran up a huge tab with local banks. Sam Bahour, himself an American citizen, observed that the devastating economic impact of Israeli control, combined with aid dependency, was "Americanizing" the Palestinian population. When "donor involvement is basically dominating and driving the economy and people are being indebted even further, people become very individualistic and are out to make the best for themselves," Bahour lamented.[43]

Paradoxically, as aid has grown, so have debt and poverty. Per-capita foreign aid to Palestinians rose from $392 in 2006 to $685 in 2008, and in the same period debts and arrears owed by the Palestinian Authority doubled to two billion dollars, a study by the Bisan Center for Research and Development found. At the same time, a staggering 40 percent of the PA budget has been allocated for "security"—the repressive forces built up by the Palestinian Authority under American supervision.[44] As the Palestinian elites in Ramallah went on their credit-induced spending binge, by 2011, half of Palestinian households in the West Bank and Gaza Strip were struggling to obtain sufficient nutrition, with one-third classified as food insecure. In Gaza, more than half already experienced food insecurity—a chronic lack of access to sufficient safe, nutritious food—and 13 percent were vulnerable.[45] Other effects of poor nutrition could be seen in high rates of stunted growth among children, which in much of Salam Fayyad's "booming" West Bank were more than double those in Gaza. More than fifteen percent of children were underweight and in some areas almost half suffered from diarrhea, the biggest killer of children under age five in the world.[46] The West Bank Palestinians facing the worst situation were the tens of thousands living in "Area C"—the 60 percent of the West Bank that remains under full Israeli military occupation under the 1993 Oslo Accords. Eight in ten communities surveyed in these areas in 2010 by the UK charity Save the Children lacked sufficient nutritious food, an even worse crisis than in besieged Gaza. Mere survival on the land—not a shortage of luxury cars, investors, or five-star hotels—was the main concern for these families, 84 percent of which relied on humanitarian assistance to survive. In East Jerusalem—already annexed by Israel in defiance of international law and the focus of intense Jewish colonization—78 percent of the city's quarter-million Palestinians and 84 percent of their children lived in poverty by 2012, increasingly cut off from the rest of the West Bank by Israel's walls, checkpoints, and settlements and thus from jobs, commerce, and any sustainable economic existence.[47]

While the poorest—especially Palestinians in refugee camps—were the hardest hit, salaried employees of the Palestinian Authority were not immune to the economic catastrophe, as researcher Haneen Ghazawneh observed.[48] These workers were especially vulnerable to political machinations and often saw their salaries delayed for months or only paid in part as the aid-dependent PA begged for donors to make good on pledges. The conspicuous consumption that Friedman and company celebrated as signs of Fayyadism's success also added to the pressures. "As many Palestinians have increasingly embraced a culture of consumption and debt, some have bought houses and cars they cannot afford," the UN's humanitarian news service noted in one report. "If salaries suddenly stop coming and people fall behind on their loan payments, the banks could have problems. And this, perhaps, could fuel a larger financial crisis that would impact food security."[49] Other economic changes weakened the resilience of Palestinian households. Many coped with food shortages by deferring payments of utility bills, lowering the quality and quantity of the food they ate, and borrowing. But electricity privatization and the installation of prepaid meters, part of Fayyad's neoliberal reforms, took the option of deferring bills away from the poorest households, leaving them even more vulnerable.[50] The stresses related to high levels of poverty and unemployment were also eroding Palestinians' social fabric and "contributed to an increase in tension, and ultimately violence within families," according to a December 2011 UN Economic and Social Council report.[51] The widening inequality gap that left millions struggling while a minority prospered was never a concern for Tom Friedman. These harsh realities, if exposed, would have shattered the illusion of the Fayyadist renaissance.

Rawabi: Shining City on a Hill

"The downtown area will be up there, with a pedestrian zone like we have in old sections of Palestinian cities, but very modern," Palestinian-American property developer Bashar Masri told an awestruck journalist during a tour of the construction site where Rawabi was rising, a few kilometers northwest of Ramallah. "There will also be a convention center, a five-star hotel and a shopping mall, all in high-tech buildings, surrounded by high-quality residential units for the middle class. I'm building a city for the Facebook generation."[52] Rawabi symbolizes, like no other project, the way the Israeli occupiers, the Palestinian Authority, and the profiteering tycoons tied to the PA are joining forces to reshape the physical, social, and economic landscape. They are doing so with the support of Israel's international allies, especially the US government, and of Gulf Arab capital. This powerful convergence is helping to mask and normalize the worst abuses of occupation, now under the guise of development, modernity, state-building, and Israel's "economic peace."

A slick campaign by Bayti, the development company, whose name means "my house" in Arabic, markets Rawabi as a Palestinian "national project," the first "new city" providing thousands of units of "affordable" housing—the very cornerstone of the coming state. It was frequently hailed as concrete evidence of the Fayyadist vision becoming reality, of a new Palestine of smartphones, business suits, and suburban nuclear families replacing the old image of the *feda'i* fighter carrying a gun. "Young, Internet-savvy, educated English-speakers" is how Rawabi's commercial manager, Ramzi Jaber, described the development's clientele.[53] Rawabi became an obligatory stop for the endless parade of international officials who posed for photo ops with Bashar Masri, reinforcing the supposed significance of the project. Yet for all the glitz, Masri insists that Rawabi is deeply in tune with Palestinian values and ways of life. "We knew that Rawabi should be structured around the traditional *hai* neighborhood system that is all across places in Palestine, where neighbors know each other and can gather," Masri told an Israeli website.[54]

Notwithstanding his emphasis on public space, Masri has acknowledged that Rawabi "was conceived as a commercial venture and not an altruistic one."[55] Rawabi is financed by Qatar, with political backing and significant direct and indirect subsidies from the United States government. Bayti is chaired by Masri and jointly owned by his own investment firm, Massar International, and Qatar's state-owned luxury real-estate developer, Qatari Diar. Qatar provided the bulk of the billion-dollar cost of the project's first phase. "His royal highness the Emir is personally aware and pushes for the investment in Rawabi," Masri boasted.[56]

Any Palestinian looking at the artist's drawings of Rawabi or at the apartment blocks that have already risen would be unlikely to see anything resembling a traditional Palestinian neighborhood or the villages that nestle against the slopes and along the valleys. They might recognize what looks like just another fortress-like Israeli settlement, replacing the cut-off mountaintop and imposing itself over the surrounding landscape.[57] This was not lost on the *Jewish Daily Forward,* which illustrated a glowing profile of Masri with an image of Rawabi captioned, "Settlement Echoes: A rendering of a planned West Bank city for Palestinians consciously copies architecture in Jewish settlements."[58] The newspaper noted that Rawabi bears "a striking resemblance to Modi'in," an Israeli city that is "a stronghold of Anglo immigrants, and built with their housing preferences in mind." Moshe Safdie himself, the famous Israeli architect who designed Modi'in, took Rawabi's architects on a tour of the Israeli city.[59] Rawabi is "a city modeled after a housing complex, like a settlement," observed Palestinian contemporary artist Shuruq Harb. But it is the most visible incarnation of forces that have the potential to transform the whole country: "It clearly represents neoliberal policies . . . a privatized city."[60]

"In this land are olive trees and memories that the bulldozers will uproot, and the scents of our fathers and grandfathers," Shahir al-Attari told the Jordanian newspaper *Al-Ghad,* against the background roar of Rawabi's construction machinery. He and dozens of other villagers were protesting the seizure of their land in January 2010.[61] Al-Attari's words underscore that Rawabi's resemblance to the settlements goes deeper than its outward appearance and layout. Masri's city is built on land taken from surrounding Palestinian villages, this time not by Israel but by his company, using the Palestinian Authority as its enforcement arm. Masri had succeeded in purchasing significant tracts from private owners, but large areas were confiscated by a November 2009 compulsory purchase decree by Mahmoud Abbas—1,500 dunams (375 acres) from the village of Ajjul, 122 dunams from Attara, and 118 dunams from Abwin.[62] Villagers like al-Attari, who owned fifteen dunams of the land, had resisted Masri's demands to sell, prompting the Fayyad cabinet initially to pass the decree in March 2009. But the order could not take effect until Abbas signed it, which he did the following November.

Meanwhile, villagers tried to save their land. In one petition published in the newspaper *Al-Quds*, villagers called on Abbas to cancel the order and "lift the aggression on their land which they inherited from their forefathers, and for whose sake they gave martyrs and prisoners who are still inside the occupier's jails."[63] In another appeal published in Palestinian media, landowners from Ajjul and Attara condemned "the confiscation and rape of our land for the benefit of a private company" and warned that the seizure "gives the Israeli occupation the excuse to confiscate and expropriate land in order to build settlements on it."[64] Villagers planned to go to court to challenge the confiscation of their land ostensibly for "public use" when it was in fact for the benefit of a private real-estate developer. They vowed to wage a campaign against the order, including one on Facebook, though they were clearly not the "Facebook generation" Masri was eager to impress. Rawhi Aqel, the mayor of Attara, told *Al-Ghad* that there had been no consultation with the three villages over the plan to build Rawabi and that construction of the city would leave no room for the development of his village, whose lands now fell within Rawabi's master plan. Many villagers who lived abroad returned home, Aqel said, and were in a "state of shock" when they learned that their land was no longer theirs.[65] It now belonged to Bayti. This might have been undemocratic and improper, but it typifies how the PA makes decisions, disregarding local communities and the views of Palestinian society at large about how best to use scarce and valuable resources.

Unbeknownst to the villagers, Masri told diplomats in a private meeting at the US Consulate General in Jerusalem in November 2009 that Abbas's expropriation order was the "last necessary step" to clear the way for Rawabi.[66] One landowner told Wattan TV that a lawyer had asked him for a retainer of $28,000 to take his case to court. Another described his frustration trying to find out what the compensation levels would be. "You go to the [PA] ministry of local government to ask them and they tell you, go and ask the Rawabi company [Bayti]. The Rawabi company is the government, the judge, and the executioner."[67] Some spoke of intimidation, alleging that Bayti's land agents spread rumors that any resistance to the confiscation would be deemed resistance to the president and sabotage of "national projects."[68] They had good reason to fear, since almost every Palestinian and international announcement pointed to Rawabi as the showpiece project of Fayyadism;

the same international sponsors rarely spoke up when the PA used its dictatorial powers to repress opposition.

Bashar Masri was unimpressed by villagers' complaints, dismissing their assertions that their land was dear to them as "nonsense." He accused them of "greed" and "blackmail," contending that the villagers, who ought to have been grateful to him that Rawabi had raised land prices in the area, were simply holding out for more money.[69] "Who would have dreamt of getting twelve or twenty thousand dinars for a dunam? The land used to be worth pennies," he declared.[70] But if that was the case, Abbas's confiscation order gave Masri the upper hand. Ahmad al-Attari, whose extended family stood to lose seventy dunams, said that before the order was announced, Bayti had offered 35,000 Jordanian dinars (US$50,000) per dunam, but dropped the price as low as JD5,000 (US$7,000) after the confiscation.[71] Many villagers feared that if they didn't sell, Bayti would take their land anyway, for much less than it was worth. The PA, meanwhile, was clearly on the side of the developers. Its spokesman Ghassan Khatib proclaimed that "the expropriation was carried out according to legal procedures, especially since the Rawabi city project is for the public good and falls in the framework of economic development."[72]

Masri also told American officials that money for the expropriated land would be set aside in an escrow account, so that "as landowners prove that they own parcels of land, they will be compensated."[73] It is worth noting that most land ownership in the West Bank is not officially registered due to a 1968 Israeli military order that halted the registration of parcels for decades. Despite the lack of registration, traditional knowledge records which tracts specific families and villages use, tend, and own, though inevitably disputes arise. Many pieces of land have dozens of owners, as with each successive generation the heirs multiply. Having created this situation, Israel used the fact that thousands of square kilometers of land remained unregistered and uncultivated to declare large tracts "state land" and seize them for Jewish settlement.[74] Masri acknowledged that this was the case with land he wanted for Rawabi—and resorted to precisely the same logic. After Attara's mayor objected to village lands being included within Rawabi's master plan, Masri scornfully laid the blame for Israeli land theft and colonization on Palestinians themselves.[75] "These are lands that have been left uncultivated. So for twenty, thirty years you did nothing to develop it, and you did not expand. And you let the Israeli settlements expand, and they took from Attara's land. And now when we come to plan for your land, you say, we took two thousand [dunams]?"[76]

Demanding that owners "prove that they own parcels of land" *after* the land had already been designated for seizure—another tactic familiar to Palestinians whose land has been taken by Israel—was at best a *fait accompli* and at worst an effective way to ensure some owners might not get compensated at all. Anyone who made it as far as a compensation claim would find that land values would be set by a committee appointed by the same Palestinian Authority that had issued the confiscation decree.[77] Any compensation, divided among numerous owners and heirs, might amount to a pittance that could never reflect the value of something irreplaceable. Yet this is how the "free-market economy" functions in the Palestinian state-in-the-making. I wrote Masri several times asking how many landowners had applied for compensation, how much had been paid out, and the average price per dunam. I never received a reply. Masri's victim-blaming and his insistence that the onus is on individuals to defend their land in a byzantine and hardly transparent legal system, when they clearly do not have the resources and wherewithal to stand up to his billion-dollar US- and Qatari-backed company and media blitz, offer a stark precedent for how vulnerable the Palestinian people are to powerful elites turning the disastrous situation created by Israel's prolonged occupation to their own advantage.

Mortgaging Palestine

In the early days of Rawabi, Masri launched a website encouraging diaspora Palestinians to make donations to plant trees in Palestine.[78] A scandal quickly followed when it emerged he planted several thousand pine trees donated by the Jewish National Fund (JNF), the Israeli Zionist agency that has for decades used tree-planting initiatives to raise funds from Jewish Americans to support the forcible "Judaization" of confiscated Palestinian land. Under pressure, Masri agreed to remove the non-native pines and replace them with local olive trees.[79] He claimed, implausibly, that he had no idea what the JNF was when Rawabi accepted the trees.[80] But mimicking and working with the JNF can have been no more accidental than Masri's turn to the Israeli settlements for architectural inspiration. The two went hand in hand: as the *Jewish Daily Forward* explained, "the tree planters of today are the second-homers of tomorrow"—a reference to well-to-do Palestinians with US, Canadian, or EU passports that would permit them to enter the Israeli-occupied territories. They would buy his apartments, Masri explained, "just like [diaspora Jews] buy second homes in Israel."[81] Now Palestinians, too, could find their piece of heaven on land taken from Palestinian villages.

"Rawabi is specifically designed for upwardly mobile families of a sort that in the United States might gravitate to places such as Reston, VA," a suburb of Washington, DC, the *Washington Post* reported.[82] But in the economically devastated and aid-dependent West Bank there was no such population, save for a privileged few. In 2010, Masri told me that he estimated units in Rawabi would sell for sixty to a hundred thousand US dollars—translating into mortgage payments of $450 to $750 per month. By US lending standards, this would require qualifying borrowers to have monthly incomes between $1,600 and $2,700. That is still far beyond the reach of the vast majority of Palestinians in the West Bank, where annual per-capita GDP hovers at $1,600 and more than a third of households reported monthly incomes below the official poverty line of NIS2,237 ($560). Half of all households reported monthly incomes of less than $750, while less than a fifth said they brought in more than a thousand dollars per month—and these were overwhelmingly concentrated in the area around Ramallah, which is flush with aid money and NGO cash.[83] Even Palestinian Authority officials told US diplomats that the new apartments would be "out of the reach of average Palestinians."[84] Wealthy diaspora Palestinians mimicking American Zionist settlers might not be able to absorb the five thousand units initially planned for Rawabi. So Masri claimed that Rawabi was going to provide "affordable housing."[85] He also told me that Rawabi did not include any low-income housing but that his company would announce plans "for limited-income housing" at an unspecified "later stage."[86] In the meantime, the magic ingredient that would turn cash-strapped and debt-laden Palestinians into home buyers would be American-style mortgages.

In 2006, a decades-long property bubble burst in the United States, triggering the global financial crisis two years later and puncturing the deeply ingrained idea that homeownership (albeit through massive debt) was the fulfillment of the American dream and the surest means to financial security. A toxic mix of bank profiteering, outright fraud enabled by lax government oversight, exploitative "subprime" lending, unregulated international financial markets, and a generation-long stagnation in real incomes for the vast majority of Americans helped turn a financial crisis into a social catastrophe. In numbers not seen since the Great Depression, millions of families who could no longer afford their monthly payments lost their homes. Across the country, "foreclosure ghost towns" appeared. Social-service agencies, themselves hit hard by recession, reported a surge in families seeking assistance from food pantries or living in the streets, homeless shelters, and their cars. Those who were already worst off were hit the hardest. From 2005 to 2009, US median household wealth fell by 28 percent, but the plunge was 66 percent for Latinos and 53 percent for African Americans against just 16 percent for whites. The ratio of white household wealth to the rest grew to an astonishing 20 to 1, as unemployment for African Americans remained stubbornly stuck at twice the national average.[87]

As all this was happening, US officials were busy working to bring a similar lethal cocktail of debt culture, financial profiteering, lax regulation, and government collusion to the West Bank. House building has always been an important part of the culture and economy, but it has been done without mortgage debt. From the experience of my extended family, I can identify with anthropologist Khalil Nakhleh's observation that building new homes for family members "always acquired a sacred aura" and often involved volunteering from relatives and neighbors and capital raised from savings and remittances, buying and selling parcels of land, and contributions from family members.[88] Not all Palestinians—especially refugees and others without access to land—would be able to build a home that way, so there is a good argument for an accountable, well-planned housing policy that prioritizes and supports truly affordable housing.

Before American-style debt could be introduced, Palestinian resistance had to be overcome. Nasser Kamal, a Palestinian tycoon with business interests in Germany, Croatia, and Dubai and chairman of Byder for Development and Real Estate, had successfully sold out a sixty-unit apartment building in Ramallah. But he had trouble selling similar apartments in Nablus. Ramallah residents "were more cosmopolitan and had been exposed to the idea of paying interest to access capital," Kamal told officials at the US consulate in Jerusalem. In Nablus, however, people were more "traditional" and "overwhelmingly rejected long-term mortgages because of the interest-to-principal ratio and fears about losing their home if they defaulted."[89] A loan of $100,000 for twenty-five years at 7 percent, for example, would accrue interest of $112,000—more than 100 percent of the principal. While such high interest-to-principal ratios are standard in the United States, Palestinians balked. Kamal told American officials that he was able to finesse this through a mechanism that, in the consulate's words, kept the interest "hidden" from borrowers. Kamal insisted that a "consumer education campaign" was needed to sell the idea of mortgages to Palestinians. In fact, the United States had already been working on this for several years.

In April 2008, a *New York Times* headline declared, "New Home-Buying Plan May Bolster Abbas." The article announced a US government scheme in the West Bank "which establishes a $500 million mortgage company [that] aims to build 10 new neighborhoods over the next five years and, in the process, create thousands of jobs in construction and real estate." The program was dubbed the Affordable Mortgage and Loan Corporation and was given the acronym AMAL—which means "hope" in Arabic. But it didn't represent the hopes of ordinary Palestinians as much as the political machinations of its sponsors. AMAL "could improve the depressed local economy and the political prospects of the Palestinian president, Mahmoud Abbas, of the relatively pro-West Fatah party," the *Times* explained. At the Ramallah launch ceremony, attended by ubiquitous Quartet representative Tony Blair, Abbas said he wished the program could apply to Gaza, but that the "coup d'état" there had made that impossible. A "secondary aim" of AMAL was "to send a message to the Gaza Strip, run by the Islamist party Hamas, that its citizens, too, could benefit from international generosity and economic progress if they restore Fatah's authority, overturned by Hamas forces" in June 2007.[90] "We believe this gives the Palestinians of Gaza a reason to try to change the status quo," said Mohammad A. Mustafa, chief executive of the Palestine Investment Fund, also an AMAL sponsor. All of this was utterly detached from reality. Palestinians in Gaza had yet to live through the nightmare of Israel's Operation Cast Lead assault, which destroyed thousands of homes in the space of three weeks, but between 2000 and 2004 Israel had systematically demolished thousands of Palestinian homes in Gaza, making more than sixteen thousand people homeless. Many lost their homes for the second or third times in their lives, especially in the border town of Rafah.[91] With much of Gaza's population surviving on humanitarian aid and knowing that they could face an Israeli assault any time, twenty-five-year mortgages would be the last thing on anyone's mind.

AMAL's American sponsors also understood the housing project to have explicitly political goals. "Our role is to deploy private capital as a soft power tool," explained Robert Mosbacher Jr., head of the Overseas Private Investment Corporation (OPIC), which provided half the financing for the scheme. OPIC describes itself as the "US Government's development finance institution," a government agency which "mobilizes private capital to help solve critical world challenges and in doing so, advances U.S. foreign policy" while "help[ing] U.S. businesses gain footholds in emerging markets." OPIC officials saw Rawabi as the "greatest market" for AMAL mortgage loans and estimated that there were in total nine housing projects throughout the West Bank that they could finance.[92] These projects were not part of any transparent public plan addressing the needs of Palestinian communities. Like Rawabi, they were the brainchildren of tycoons driven by their own assessments of where they could maximize profits. The twenty-five-year fixed- and variable-rate mortgages were to be offered through the Bank of Palestine and Cairo Amman Bank, obscuring from Palestinian borrowers the role of OPIC and its partners, including the World Bank's International Finance Corporation, USAID, the PA-controlled Palestine Investment Fund, and the UK's Department for International Development. What also gave this scheme additional cover was the involvement of UN HABITAT and various other local and international NGOs.[93] Alternatively, their involvement can be seen as evidence of the close integration between the aid and NGO industries, on the one hand, and the advance of neoliberal economics and US hegemony, on the other.

One example of this integration is CHF International—originally the Cooperative Housing Foundation—which the US government contracted to launch the Palestinian Homebuyer Education Program, effectively a marketing campaign for mortgages and American-style debt.[94] CHF (recently renamed "Global Communities") describes itself as a nonprofit development organization that "serves millions of people each year, empowering them to improve their lives and livelihoods for a better future." Its list of donors is a who's-who of international and Arab regional banks that stand to benefit from the expansion of mortgage lending, but the United States government provides two-thirds of its $260 million annual budget. OPIC head Mosbacher was also chairman of the board of CHF International. The two US government–sponsored organizations collaborate closely around the world advancing free-market policies, especially in the wake of US military interventions in places including Iraq, Kosovo, Haiti, and countries across Africa. CHF International's "development" activities in the West Bank and Gaza Strip are wide-ranging and include a program in Gaza to help families cope with food insecurity.[95] Nowhere in its marketing materials does CHF International explain that food insecurity in Gaza is primarily a consequence of the economically devastating Israeli blockade supported by the same United States government that sponsors CHF.

American officials hoped that "education" by CHF could break down the resistance to long-term mortgages, but something more heavy-handed would be needed to clear legal obstacles. In October 2008, OPIC vice president Robert Drumheller told US officials in Jerusalem that OPIC "needs to secure a Palestinian Presidential Decree invalidating an Ottoman-era law which stipulates that the total amount of interest on a loan cannot exceed the original amount of the loan, thereby making a 25-year loan impossible."[96] The law also capped the amount of interest at 9 percent, "which could prohibit banks from penalizing delinquent borrowers." The World Bank, too, urged changes to the law to make evictions easier because "political and social sensitivities of eviction make foreclosure difficult and it is employed mostly as a last resort."[97] The record shows that, as Palestinian communities struggled to maintain their presence on land and in homes threatened by Israeli settlements, the US and international agencies were working with Palestinian developers and officials to concoct new ways for economically stressed Palestinians to be thrown out of their homes. Once again, key policies and decisions that might one day affect hundreds of thousands of families were formulated behind closed doors with no transparency or democratic process.

Masri had successfully lobbied American officials to use aid money to build infrastructure exclusively for Rawabi. One US government estimate said that without donor assistance, the average price of a unit would increase by sixteen thousand dollars, echoing Masri's claim that such aid was needed to keep Rawabi "affordable."[98] The word he never used was "profitable." It was characteristic of Masri's entrepreneurialism that it could always count on preferential US government treatment, guarantees, and financing. In 2010, for example, Bayti received seven hundred thousand dollars in direct grants for Rawabi from the US Trade and Development Agency, also under the pretext of supporting "affordable housing," and USAID paid for Rawabi's roads and retaining walls.[99] And in 2012, the Siraj Palestine Fund, a private equity investment vehicle headed by Masri, was launched with an initial thirty million dollars in capital from OPIC, part of an initiative announced by President Obama.[100] The largest subsidy, of course, was the hundreds of millions of dollars in OPIC backing for the AMAL mortgage fund, which Masri hoped would be used to buy apartments in Rawabi. He also relied on American diplomatic muscle. For years Israel had refused approval for Masri to pave a crucial access road to Rawabi which ran through Area C of the West Bank. As he forged ahead with construction of Rawabi's first buildings anyway, high-level international officials, including President Obama's special envoy George Mitchell, routinely lobbied Israel to allow the road.[101]

Helping Israel Tighten Its Grip

Rawabi's marketers often took "future homeowners" on tours of the construction site, accompanied by guides wielding iPads loaded with "a Rawabi custom virtual tour application." They went through a visitors' center featuring "9-screen simulcast video wall and surround-sound" and models of the "city center and neighborhoods" to be. The last stop on the tour was a model home prototype. "As families stood on the balcony in the embrace of the fresh air and the sweeping views before them, many expressed both excitement and swell [sic] of Palestinian pride—the achievement of the first Palestinian planned city is something that belongs to every citizen," a company newsletter boasts of one group of potential customers.[102] The same newsletter affirms that "our builders and contractors hail from every major city in Palestine." This is typical of how Rawabi's marketing stresses its Palestinian national credentials and contributions. Future homeowners were definitely *not* shown a list of the Israeli companies Masri had invited to help build Rawabi.

The Boycott National Committee (BNC)—the steering group for the Palestinian BDS movement—expressed concern when it was revealed that Bayti was buying materials for Rawabi from Israeli firms, a move Masri has repeatedly justified as necessary due to the Israeli occupation's stranglehold on Palestinian economic activity. The actual construction, Masri insisted, was all being done exclusively "by Palestinian contractors and Palestinian human resources."[103] Although he did not release the names of the Israeli suppliers, he said a condition was that they had to refrain from sourcing any goods in Israeli settlements in the West Bank. The BNC has conceded that Palestinians often have to use Israeli firms where there is no other option, but called on Masri and his companies to "end all normalization activities with Israel and its complicit institutions, beyond the bare necessity that all Palestinian businesses in the occupied territory must reckon with."[104] But Masri has made clear that his work with Israel goes far beyond simply securing building materials for which there is no other viable source. He fired back at the boycott activists, telling a visiting American business delegation that Palestinian "radicals" had "attacked me because I work with Israeli companies. . . . You have to. . . . I don't do it because I have to. I do it because I like to also."[105] The numbers bear him out. Bayti's deputy managing director, Amir Dajani, told the *New York Times* that the developer spent eighty to a hundred million dollars a year in Israel on "know-how" and materials, terming this not an odious necessity imposed by occupation but rather "a true example of an economy for peace."[106]

Masri has been a formidable champion for the involvement of Israeli business in the occupied territories, for instance giving a talk to Israeli CEOs in Tel Aviv, co-hosted by the Israel-America Chamber of Commerce, titled "Prospects for Investing in the Palestinian Authority." The other co-host was the Israeli-Palestinian Chamber of Commerce (IPCC), a body headed by retired Israeli army lieutenant colonel Avi Nudelman, who spent his career in military intelligence and as military administrator of the occupied West Bank. IPCC's goal is to provide Israeli companies with up-to-date information about the "Palestinian market" for "Israeli and foreign companies who wish to find business partners in the West Bank"—in other words, explicitly undermining the boycott movement. Masri's lawyer in his Israeli business transactions, including a failed effort to buy a financially insolvent Israeli settlement in East Jerusalem, was none other than Dov Weisglass, former advisor to Prime Minister Ariel Sharon, who notoriously explained in 2006 that Israel's goal of besieging Gaza "is to put the Palestinians on a diet."[107] The BNC also condemned Masri's 2012 participation in an Israeli "high-tech" conference supported by the foreign ministry as "a shameless act of normalization of the worst type," not least because of the "symbiotic relationship between Israel's high-tech industry and military complex . . . built in part on the back of Palestinians since Israel uses its military occupation of the West Bank and the Gaza Strip to battle-test" its weapons systems.[108]

As well as undermining the boycott effort, the BNC saw Masri's actions as promoting a "business as usual" approach to Israel and noted that Qatar's involvement "in a Palestinian project where Israeli companies are also involved is certainly a form of normalization" that "uses the Palestinian side as a bridge to normalize, or a fig leaf to cover up, collusion with Israeli companies almost all of which are complicit in Israel's occupation, apartheid and denial of fundamental Palestinian rights." Also helping Israel to penetrate the Arab world commercially is Masri's own understanding of his role. "Israeli businessmen come to me time and time again seeking help in entering the Palestinian market and the Arab world," he explained to *Ynet*.[109]

In early 2012, Masri announced that Israel had at last given permission for the access road to Rawabi. Now, however, prices for apartments in Rawabi would be about 40 percent higher than he had estimated in 2010. By August 2013, Bayti announced it had sold out the first phase of six hundred apartments, whose new owners would move in by early 2014. Masri, however, expressed disappointment that only about half of the buyers had taken up the US-backed mortgages and that the bankrupt Palestinian Authority had failed to come through on $150 million in subsidies for the private development's infrastructure. Instead, "investors [had been] forced to finance the provision of power, water, sewage, schools and roads," the *Guardian* reported. "I never envisioned that we would not have this funding with all the donor money that has come to Palestine in recent years," Masri complained, underscoring the entitlement he felt to receive public subsidies even though democratic processes for planning and accountability were nonexistent. He still had not announced any plans for low-income housing for Palestinians, but was already eyeing new markets for Rawabi's apartments and their "European-crafted" kitchens. "Israelis are invited to come and visit [Rawabi] any time, and even though our target audience is Palestinian, if Israelis also want to buy apartments there, they're welcome," he told an Israeli newspaper.[110] With that offer, Rawabi's transformation into the kind of Israeli settlement that had inspired Masri—albeit with a Palestinian flavor—was almost complete.

Fayyadism and the Shock Doctrine

When Benjamin Netanyahu boasted to Congress about the supposed boom in the West Bank, he was selling his policy of "economic peace," announced when he returned to office in 2009. The idea—which echoes the approach some advocated in apartheid South Africa in the 1980s—is that a modicum of prosperity, or at least the appearance of a higher standard of living, could blunt demands for political change and deflect international criticism and pressure on Israel. "I don't delude my-self for a second that an economic peace is a substitute for political peace," Netanyahu told Quartet envoy Tony Blair, but economic peace was the only game in town as Netanyahu forged ahead with colonization of the West Bank, to the despair of those who still clung to a two-state solution. Economic growth, Netanyahu asserted, "has contributed to stability" and would contribute to "peace and security in the long term."[111] Israeli businessmen like oil-refining billionaire Idan Ofer have also wel-comed Netanyahu's approach for the opportunities it afforded them to penetrate Palestinian markets and bring normalization with Arab states. "It's no secret that big money is being poured in by Qatar and other countries to build up the West Bank," Ofer said during a Ramallah meeting with Mahmoud Abbas, Israeli businessmen, and top Israeli officials, including former heads of the army and the Mossad. "We can be involved in many projects here, in water, gas, and industry."[112]

The BNC summed up the understanding of Netanyahu's "economic peace" as "the sidelining of basic Palestinian rights, including the right to self determination of all Palestinians, in favour of economic gains for an elite minority, part of Israel's carrot-and-stick approach that rewards obedience to Israeli dictates."[113] Fayyadism and "economic peace" are in effect two sides of the same coin. For Khalil Nakhleh, both entail "normalization with continued occupation and hegemonic controls; sus-tained flows of international aid" and treating the small pockets of West Bank land under Palestinian Authority control as "an economic project for sale."[114] Both are predicated on ever-closer coordination between Israel and the Palestinian Authority within the framework of Israeli dominance and control. Both presume that eco-nomic prosperity can induce political docility in the Palestinian population.

Proponents hope that a focus on economics and "technocratic" governance can ultimately soften Palestinian resistance to a final "peace agreement" on Israeli terms. For years, US administrations have tried without success to induce Palestinians to make significant concessions, especially the rights of refugees, in order to clinch a deal. As US diplomat Robert Danin explains, "Fayyadism empowers Palestinian leaders to convince their constituents that it is worthwhile to make the painful com-promises that will be necessary for a genuine settlement to be reached."[115] The in-herently colonial approach is that the Palestinians have to prove their worthiness and competence to their dispossessors and occupiers. This was the essence of Bush's "Roadmap," which was accompanied by the demand that Palestinians choose new leaders and "reform" themselves. Weisglass famously said at the time that the new conditions meant that Israel was off the hook until the Palestinians managed to utterly transform themselves and—in his words—"turn into Finns."[116]

This logic has carried over into the era of economic peace and Fayyadism, where, Danin claims, better "Palestinian performance on the ground in the realms of security, economic growth, and administration will instill confidence among Israelis that they can hand over control of the occupied territories to a reliable Palestinian partner." But ensuring Israel's security—a priority Danin emphasizes repeatedly—is not the only goal: "Fayyadism represents, above all, a fundamental attitudinal shift. Its emphasis on self-reliance is a conscious effort to change the role of the Palestinians in their narrative from that of victims to that of agents of their own fate." In other words, to change the "narrative" from a true one, where Palestinians were and are indeed *victims* of a prolonged and brutal US-financed Israeli occupation and colonization, to a false and fraudulent one where, with some pluck and entrepreneurialism, Palestinians can pull themselves up by their bootstraps without Israel having to do much except move the occasional checkpoint here and there. Israel thus becomes the aggrieved party to whom Palestinians have to prove their good intentions and faith. "As the situation on the ground improves and the PA delivers increasing economic prosperity and security for the Palestinians and, ultimately, for Israel," Danin asserts, "the PA will provide a sense of possibility where one has been sorely lacking." This narrative takes as a given that Israel has only refused to withdraw from the occupied territories because it feels insecure. This circumvents the obvious reality that Israel is engaged in a massive, continuous, and state-directed settlement project, a necessarily violent process that itself generates Palestinian resistance. Reality has shown that it is delusional to expect that Palestinians can bring prosperity and good governance under such circumstances—even with a little help from their occupiers. It is as though Palestinians, collectively, are a prisoner lying on the ground with his hands and legs shackled and Israel is a soldier standing over him with a boot on his neck. "Stand up," the soldier says, "and *then* I will remove your shackles and take my boot off you."

This is also false in another fundamental way. Naomi Klein observes that wherever radical free-market policies have been implemented over the past three decades, "what has emerged is a powerful ruling alliance between a few very large corporations and a class of mostly wealthy politicians—with hazy and ever-shifting lines between them."[117] This has absolutely been the case in the putative Palestinian state, with the twist that the wealthy politicians and businessmen are also in cahoots with the occupiers they claim to be resisting. Klein's key insight is that wherever these policies have been forced on a country, it has been facilitated by brutal force, a usurpation of democratic rule, and torture. Chile, after Augusto Pinochet's 1973 US-backed coup against Salvador Allende, is the archetypal case. "From Chile to China to Iraq, torture has been a silent partner in the global free-market crusade. But torture is more than a tool used to enforce unwanted policies on rebellious peoples; it is also a metaphor of the shock doctrine's underlying logic."[118] A population stunned by a political crisis, invasion, coup, or natural disaster is, like a prisoner undergoing torture, vulnerable, disoriented, open to suggestion, and unable to resist the captor's will. The Roadmap and the US-Israeli demands for "reform" followed hot on the heels of Operation Defensive Shield in March 2002, when Israel invaded almost every major West Bank city. The attack, its largest in the West Bank since 1967, left not only hundreds of Palestinians dead, but much of the Palestinian Authority's infrastructure in ruins. Israeli tanks bulldozed much of Palestinian leader Yasser Arafat's Ramallah compound, with him inside, and occupied it. For much of the remaining two years of his life, Arafat holed up in what was left, sidelined by Israel and the United States. But months after the assault, Salam Fayyad was brought in as finance minister to begin implementing the "international community's" reforms. In March the following year, the Bush administration insisted that Arafat create the position of prime minister and appoint Mahmoud Abbas to fill it.

If Operation Defensive Shield was the first shock, the US-backed overthrow of the national unity government, followed by Operation Cast Lead, Israel's 2008–2009 invasion of Gaza, was the second. Contrary to the fantasies of the likes of Danin, this too has been followed by real and metaphorical torture. "Those who cite Fayyad's success at building institutions rarely cite a single institution that has been built," George Washington University political science professor Nathan Brown wrote in 2010. The reason: "There simply have been few institutions built in Ramallah since the first Fayyad cabinet was formed in 2007." But Brown found that the security services had burgeoned, routinely disregarding the rule of law, illegally detaining and abusing people, and interfering in every aspect of life, including dismissing teachers, civil servants, and municipal workers on purely political grounds. Brown, a longtime observer of the Palestinian scene, was surprised by the "degree of politically-generated fear on the West Bank."[119]

Notwithstanding some marginal improvements in administration, the entire Fayyadist program, Brown concluded, "is not simply based on de-emphasizing or postponing democracy and human rights but on actively denying them for the present." That is not to say that human-rights groups have not documented similar excesses by the Hamas-run authority in Gaza; they have. The major difference is that only the West Bank authority has been receiving billions in international support while being marketed as the showcase of modern liberal state-building. In Palestine, the shock doctrine was applied not only to force the usual neoliberal economic policies. Its practitioners also hoped to disarm Palestinians politically, rendering them vulnerable to a "peace" that leaves them shorn of their national rights.

Built-In Dependency

Although Netanyahu gave it his own novel spin, Israel's manipulation of the Palestinian economy has always been one of its most potent tools to suppress and co-opt resistance. In the first years after Israel's 1967 occupation of the West Bank and Gaza Strip, the Palestinian economy in those areas boomed for two main reasons: large numbers of Palestinians were permitted to work in Israel, and many Palestinians, lacking opportunities at home went to the Gulf Arab states and sent home remittances. But Israeli measures to improve the economy, economic researcher Shir Hever observes, were "the outcome of a premeditated and well-planned policy" by the military and political leadership "in order to improve their control over the occupied population and stifle resistance."[120] This policy was relatively successful for the first twenty years of the occupation, until the First Intifada broke out in 1987. But the relative prosperity "hid the true extent of the subjugation of the Palestinian economy to Israel" because Israeli occupation authorities had "put in place a complex system forcing Palestinians to obtain permits for nearly any economic activity, from going to work inside Israel to setting up a shop." These permits were subject to constant renewal and were routinely revoked in the case of any Palestinians accused of "dissenting political activity" by Israel's Shin Bet secret police.[121]

Over the decades—despite the initial economic boost—this setup was utterly corrosive, hollowing out the Palestinian economy and leaving Palestinians ever more vulnerable to Israel. While the occupied territories became a principal and captive "export" market for Israeli manufacturers, Israel systematically prevented Palestinian industries from exporting their products. Israel's policy, according to the World Bank, was to "encourage income growth for the Palestinian population while restricting activities that directly competed with Israeli businesses."[122] As neighboring countries' economies saw significant industrialization, the West Bank and Gaza Strip experienced almost none. By 1999, the average Palestinian industrial establishment had just four workers, the same number as in 1927.[123] The different paths followed by the West Bank and the East Bank (present-day Jordan) are telling. Until 1967, the West Bank "was one of the most developed parts of Jordan."[124] By 2008, industry had risen to 26 percent of GDP in Jordan, while agriculture had dropped to less than four percent. In the West Bank and Gaza, industry's share of GDP was just 16 percent, while agriculture remained at 6 percent.[125] Meanwhile, as Palestinian farmers left their land to work in Israel, where wages were considerably higher, Israeli authorities "often took advantage of this and confiscated land that remained uncultivated."[126]

In the mid- to late 1980s, the relative prosperity came to an end. Israel's own economic crisis and hyperinflation eroded the real wages earned by Palestinian laborers and cut the number of opportunities for them in Israel. Meanwhile, a drop in oil prices sharply reduced the demand for Palestinian workers in the Gulf states. These economic shocks contributed to the outbreak of the First Intifada.[127] Then the 1990 Iraqi invasion of Kuwait and the subsequent US-led war ended what had been relatively easy access to employment in the Gulf, as Gulf states retaliated for the PLO's support of Iraq by expelling and barring Palestinians. By the eve of the 1993 Oslo Accords between Israel and the PLO, the West Bank and Gaza Strip were almost completely dependent on Israel and economically isolated from other countries. Nearly 60 percent of the West Bank's exports and more than 90 percent of imports were to and from Israel; the trade deficit was almost 45 percent of GDP. The figures for Gaza were similar, but the trade deficit was even higher. Nearly a third of the Palestinian workforce was employed in Israel.[128]

This state of dependency was codified in the 1994 Paris Protocol on Economic Relations, part of the Oslo Accords. Like other agreements it was supposed to be "interim," pending a "final status" agreement, but instead became part of an open-ended status quo. The economic protocol gave Israel full control over customs and trade in the areas supposedly under Palestinian Authority control, including setting rates for import tariffs. The accords gave Israel an effective monopoly on supplying basic commodities, including fuel. Israel collects taxes from Palestinian workers in Israel as well as all customs revenues on behalf of the Palestinian Authority. A new Palestinian Monetary Authority, created under the agreement, had some of the functions of a central bank, but the PA was required to circulate the Israeli shekel as the de facto currency and forbidden from issuing a Palestinian currency without Israeli agreement. Crucially, given the dependence of the Palestinian economy on labor in Israel, the agreement stated that "both sides will attempt to maintain the normality of movement of labor between them," but gave "each side" complete discretion over the movement of workers. In practice, this meant Israel had full control, since the labor flow was only in one direction. Exploiting this dependence even further, Israel has deducted some two billion dollars in welfare contributions from Palestinian workers for benefits to which they are not entitled. Israel's main labor federation, the Histadrut, participated in the theft, collecting fees from Palestinian workers even though they are not allowed to join and are not represented in labor disputes.[129]

In 1991—almost three years before the first Palestinian suicide bombings—Israel began to impose regular closures and a permit regime to restrict the number of Palestinian workers who could enter Israel, a process that only accelerated after the Oslo Accords were signed. The number of workers, mostly employed in the construction industry, fell from a peak of 116,000 in 1992 to 36,000 by mid-1996. Although the number rose again to 135,000 in mid-2000, it dropped to 40,000 in June 2001, highlighting a key characteristic observed by economist Leila Farsakh: the workforce allowed into Israel "fluctuated and became erratic," generating additional unpredictability and precariousness for thousands of Palestinian families.[130] Access became more difficult as Israel tightened its grip, especially for Palestinians in Gaza. Before 1993, Farsakh notes, Israel had absorbed 35 to 40 percent of Gaza's total active labor force, but less than 15 percent by mid-2000. After 2006, when Israel imposed a tight blockade, virtually no workers were allowed out of Gaza. When I visited Gaza in 2013, it was striking how isolated young people there felt from the rest of Palestine. Few have ever been to Jenin, Ramallah, or Nazareth. It is a frequent refrain that it is more realistic for a young person in Gaza to think of traveling to Europe or America than to Jerusalem, just a few miles away. Palestinians in the West Bank, kept out of Jerusalem and restricted from travel to present-day Israel by the West Bank wall and dozens of checkpoints, have increasingly shifted from work inside Israel to work in the settlements, where they are often abused and exploited by Israeli companies and multinational firms, such as the popular home soft-drink machine manufacturer SodaStream.[131] In the 1990s, Israel also made a concerted effort to reduce its dependence on Palestinian workers by bringing in hundreds of thousands of replacement workers from abroad, particularly from Southeast Asia.

Despite cutting back on the number of permits, Israel's iron grip on Palestinian workers has remained a tool for advancing its political and demographic goals. As the mirage of Fayyad's economic miracle evaporated in mid-2012, Israel feared a collapse of the Palestinian Authority and a new uprising. In an effort to ease the pressure, Israel announced it would increase by five thousand the number of entry permits it would provide to Palestinian workers. Occupation officials also admitted that the increase "is supposed to reduce the activity of the foreign workers who stay in Israel for long periods, and might settle here." With Israeli xenophobia against foreign workers and refugees, especially from Sudan and Eritrea, at fever pitch, Palestinian workers are a handy labor reservoir to be exploited as needed to protect Israel's so-called "Jewish character." Unlike the "foreign workers," the Israeli official explained, "Palestinians arrive in Israel [during the] day and usually leave in the evening."[132] In effect, Israel has perfected the system that apartheid South Africa operated for decades, in which Black workers, regulated under the notorious "pass laws," would come into the cities by day and then travel long distances home to their segregated townships and shantytowns at night.

For workers like Hassan Khader, a fifty-two-year-old father of five, the process of trying to obtain a permit is onerous and unpredictable. Rejected four times without explanation, he nevertheless applied again. "I'm tired," he told a journalist. "It's not a good situation." But he had to keep trying, because he had no other way to put food on his family's table. For workers like Khader, a typical day may involve standing in line from three in the morning with hundreds of other workers in long cage-like tunnels, waiting to get through a series of metal turnstiles Israelis operate by remote control.[133] The laborers must often wait in crowded enclosures late into the morning, when the rising sun brings insufferable heat. Understandably, the agony of the checkpoints is too much for some to bear. In July 2012, Israeli occupation forces fired at a van carrying fourteen workers trying to enter Jerusalem without permits, killing one, Hassan Bader, and injuring three others.[134] Shawan Jabarin, the director of the Palestinian human-rights group Al-Haq, said such incidents were all too common. But desperation drives people to take risks. "Most of the people have no salaries," Jabarin explained. "They just want money to feed their families."[135] Even Israeli media drew direct comparisons with apartheid South Africa when Israel set up segregated bus lines for Palestinian laborers so they would not have to ride home on the public buses Israeli settlers use.[136]

While millions of Palestinians suffer under the Oslo economic regime, a small elite thrives. Indeed, after Oslo, there was no fundamental change in the basic reality of Israeli control. Rather, through the accords, Israel managed to co-opt Palestinian capitalists, who found that profit and occupation can coexist. The conditions that allowed them to do so were built into the occupation itself. In Edward Said's view, the Oslo Accords were a shameful and disastrous political sellout of the Palestinian national cause. Columbia professor Joseph Massad was prescient in foreseeing how the accords would open the door to foreign capital and profiteering. Mocking the Palestinian Authority, which the Oslo Accords created, as nothing more than a "municipality," Massad predicted in 1994 that the PLO

> will come down in history as the only Third World liberation movement who has sought liberation through selling the resources it expects to "liberate" to international capital before it even "liberated" them. Western countries and their global instruments of economic domination, the World Bank and the IMF, are

already devising different types of plans for investment in the Municipality of Gaza and Jericho once their projected mayor, Yasser Arafat, takes office.[137]

Sadly, the last two decades proved Massad correct when he predicted that "in the long run nothing would have changed in the economic and political realities of the Palestinians. The status of the Palestinian people as a cheap labor force for Ashkenazi Israel has been ratified, through the agreement, by the Palestinian comprador bourgeoisie, who will be the ultimate beneficiary of this arrangement."[138] But at the time, the Oslo Accords were marketed to Palestinians, Israelis, and the world as a historic political breakthrough heralding an era of economic cooperation and development that would produce peace dividends for all.

When Arafat returned to set up the Palestinian Authority, he brought an entourage of Palestinian diaspora capitalists, many of whom had made fortunes in the Gulf Arab states. They quickly established themselves at the commanding heights of the Palestinian economy and still control much of it.[139] Their ability to accumulate wealth depends on political ties to the Palestinian Authority and on maintaining a symbiotic relationship with the Israeli occupation, even as everything they do is trumpeted as building the "national" economy and preparing for independence. Undoubtedly the most powerful subset of this tiny elite is the Nablus-based Masri family. Munib Masri, an uncle of Rawabi developer Bashar Masri, made his fortune in oil and gas and contracting with Gulf regimes, especially Saudi Arabia. His cousin, Sabih Masri, reaped staggering wealth through catering and logistics contracts with the Saudi military. His biggest and most lucrative break was the 1990–91 war on Iraq, when Masri's firm ASTRA won the contract to provide supplies for more than a million soldiers in the US-led coalition.[140] Both Masris, and many of their relatives, control or are represented on the boards and executives of all the most valuable and powerful companies and financial institutions operating in the Palestinian territories.

Munib Masri was among the small group of Palestinian capitalists who in 1993 founded PADICO, a private, for-profit holding company registered in Liberia that was billed as a vehicle for developing the economy of the Palestinian state-to-be. PADICO—which stands for Palestinian Development and Investment Company—is the most important of a small number of conglomerates that control much of the Palestinian economy and in which Gulf Arab capital plays a dominant role.[141] PADICO's roughly seven hundred million dollars in assets are spread over investments in real estate, tourism and hotels, banking and financial services, energy, food manufacturing and distribution, and setting up industrial zones, as well as a large share in Paltel, the telephone and mobile-phone company that long held a monopoly in the Palestinian market. PADICO also owns 78 percent of the Palestinian Stock Exchange. Today Munib Masri is in the forefront of several economic peace initiatives, including one he headed with Israeli tycoon Rami Levy, who makes his money running supermarkets in the settlements.[142]

Palestinians criticized crony capitalism that conglomerates such as PADICO and the Palestine Investment Fund came to embody almost from the birth of the Palestinian Authority. In response, one PA minister declared in 1999, "Let those who criticize them come and compete with them."[143] But that would not have been possible. Samir Hulileh, a PA economic advisor, explained in 1998 that while the PA was committed from the start to "a free economy, free competition" and wanted to go "as much as we can into free trade agreements with other countries," in reality the game was rigged from the start. "In the first phase, our economic planning was completely determined by political reasoning," Hulileh acknowledged. "We had to be professional from a political point of view, not an economic point of view."[144] From the first days, the new elites used their proximity to Arafat to crowd out local competition. The indigenous business community was "infuriated by the visible preeminence of the *shatat* [diaspora] capitalists, and their overt influence on the PA's economic plans," observes Khalil Nakhleh, as well as these newcomers' ability to seize "privileged monopolies."[145] Hulileh justified the cronyism on the grounds that the PA's first priorities were to secure independent sources of financing, consolidate the new entity's power, and break Palestinian dependence on Israel and external donors. The close ties between the political and the economic realms are well illustrated by Hulileh's own career: he made the transitions from government economic advisor to PA cabinet secretary to CEO of PADICO and board member of numerous corporations. He chairs the Portland Trust in Ramallah, an investment firm founded by British Zionist businessman Sir Ronald Cohen, a leading advocate of economic peace.[146] Hulileh's counterpart in Tel Aviv, as Israel director of the Portland Trust, is Yossi Bachar, former director general of the Israeli finance ministry, in charge of privatization policy and "economic negotiations" with the Palestinian Authority.[147] Hulileh is also the chair of the Arab Hotels Company, the PADICO subsidiary that runs the five-star Mövenpick Hotel Ramallah, whose opening Hillary Clinton hailed as a milestone on the road to Palestinian statehood.

Today, the Palestinian elite that commands the economy and the PA apparatus still serves as a bridgehead for massive investment and increasing influence on the Palestinian economy from what School of Oriental and African Studies (SOAS) political economist Adam Hanieh terms "Khaleeji Capital."[148] Palestine, along with Egypt, Lebanon, Jordan, Syria, and much of North Africa, has experienced inflows of mind-boggling sums of oil and gas money from a handful of countries: Saudi Arabia, Bahrain, Qatar, the United Arab Emirates, and Kuwait. The Gulf-financed luxury real-estate projects—similar to Rawabi—that have sprung up all over the region and in some European countries are the most visible manifestations of this capital at work. This money can exert an even more profound impact through the influence its owners wield to impose free-market policies and distort the politics in the countries where they invest. After Israel's 2006 invasion of Lebanon, for instance, Gulf states conditioned their aid pledges on Lebanon implementing various neoliberal policies demanded by the IMF and the World Bank, including privatizing water, electricity, and other public services.[149]

One Hundred Sixty-Two Truckloads: The Economic Destruction of Gaza

Given what I knew about the effects of the siege and the economic situation in Gaza, I was struck when I visited at how supermarket shelves in the territory are stocked with Israeli goods, priced beyond the reach of many impoverished families. This is the result of a strategy more radical than anything seen in the West Bank to destroy Palestinians' economic self-sufficiency while directly benefitting Israel. Gaza is at the leading edge of what Harvard scholar Sara Roy calls Israel's "deliberate, considered and purposeful" effort to transform the Palestinian economy from "a captive economy restricted to fluctuating levels of growth (at best) but still possessed of the capacity to produce and innovate (within limitations), to an economy increasingly deprived of that capacity."[150] During Operation Cast Lead, for instance, the Israeli forces invading Gaza destroyed the chicken farms of Sameh Sawafeary and his family in the Zaytoun area. Over several days in early January 2009, the UN-commissioned Goldstone Report records that Sawafeary and other witnesses hid in terror as they watched "Israeli armoured bulldozers systematically destroy land, crops, chickens and farm infrastructure." In all, thirty-one thousand of Sawafeary's chickens were killed.[151] He estimated that a hundred thousand chickens had been killed at other farms. This widespread destruction was confirmed by UN satellite imagery. In discussing the army's assault on the farms in the Zaytoun area, the Goldstone Report states: "The systematic destruction along with the large numbers of killings of civilians suggest premeditation and a high level of planning."[152] It finds that "the Sawafeary chicken farms, the 31,000 chickens and the plant and material necessary for the business were systematically and deliberately destroyed, and that this constituted a deliberate act of wanton destruction not justified by any military necessity."[153]

The Israelis could offer no explanation that contradicted these factual findings. But where there was no "military necessity," there was certainly a commercial opportunity. Sawafeary told the UN investigators that he and his family had supplied approximately 35 percent of the eggs on the market in Gaza. Egg prices soared due to the large number of chickens Israel destroyed; Gaza's stores are now full of frozen chickens supplied by Israeli firms.

Israel has also repeatedly destroyed dairy processing plants (Israeli yogurt is a big seller in Gaza) and on January 4, 2009, bombed the El-Bader flour mill—the last one still operating—destroying it completely.[154] Again, UN investigators found no "military necessity," but as the Goldstone Report states, the "consequences of the strike on the flour mill were significant. . . . The population of Gaza is now more dependent on the Israeli authorities' granting permission for flour and bread to enter the Gaza Strip."[155] The family that owned the El-Bader mill also ran a tomato-canning factory and a diaper factory, both of which had closed down before the attack because Israel would not allow empty cans and other needed raw materials into Gaza.[156]

The fates of these and hundreds of other shuttered Gaza businesses illustrate that whatever economic destruction Israel could not achieve with the blockade, it finished off with air strikes. Indeed, such is the chilling meticulousness of Israeli planning that in January 2008, almost a year before the invasion of Gaza, the Israeli defense ministry prepared a document detailing the minimum number of calories that Gaza residents would be permitted to consume, according to demographic data such as sex and age. The defense ministry concluded that 106 truckloads of food per day would be just enough to meet a level of "nutrition that is sufficient for subsistence without the development of malnutrition."[157] The military's analysis, published after a three-and-a-half-year court battle waged by the Israeli monitoring group Gisha, includes detailed tables of how much domestic food production existed in Gaza before the invasion. Israeli military planners were very familiar with how many chickens laid how many eggs and recommended setting a "minimum bar" for the quantity of agricultural inputs, including eggs for breeding allowed into Gaza. The military planners were also fully aware of the damaging effects of Israel's restrictions on imports of supplies and of the prohibition on exporting goods out of Gaza. The defense ministry calculated, for instance, that Gaza's production of fruits and vegetables would decline from a thousand tons per day to five hundred tons within a few months, meeting only 30 percent of the territory's needs. Gisha calculated that between 2007 and 2010, the amount of food Israel allowed into Gaza often fell far short of the minimum the defense ministry had set.

While Israel eased restrictions on food imports in 2010, the main impact of the siege never disappeared: destruction of productive capacity, poverty, unemployment, isolation, and dependence. It should be recalled whenever Israel boasts, as it often does, about how many hundreds of truckloads of supplies it allows into Gaza on any given day that much of what comes in are Israeli consumer goods, profiting Israeli companies. Even the food supplies bought by UN agencies for the majority of Palestinians in Gaza who rely on humanitarian assistance are purchased predominantly from Israeli companies and paid for with international aid money—another direct benefit to Israel.[158] Overall, the value of Israeli exports to the "Palestinian Authority"—the West Bank and Gaza Strip—grew from just over two billion dollars in 2006 to $3.6 billion in 2011.[159] This puts the captive Palestinians among Israel's top ten export destinations, ahead of the United Kingdom, Germany, France, India, Japan, and China.[160] This bonanza, in the words of Shir Hever, allows Israel's government and various Israeli companies to "reap the profits, while the international community pays the bill. The Palestinians' desperate need is turned into a lever to promote the prosperity of their occupiers."[161]

Meanwhile, restrictions on raw materials and so-called "dual-use" items remain in place, leaving much of Gaza's productive capacity and workforce idle. A stark indicator of what Israel has done to Gaza's economy is the number of truckloads of exports it allows out from those farms or factories that can still produce even under siege. In 2000, before the Second Intifada, exports from Gaza peaked at more than fifteen thousand truckloads in a year, with hundreds of thousands of tons of fresh fruit and cut flowers being shipped to Israel, the West Bank, and markets across Europe. Exports declined as the economy plunged, hovering at just over 9,300 truckloads by 2005. In 2006 and 2007, the years of Hamas's election and the subsequent struggle with Abbas's Fatah faction, only five thousand trucks left Gaza each year. But that was still far more than what has been allowed since the tightened blockade began: from 2008 to 2012, Israel has permitted an average of just 162 truckloads of exports out of Gaza per year. That's about a dozen trucks per month.[162]

The destruction Israel has wrought on Gaza's economy is not incidental to its "security" policies; it has been a deliberate goal. As Sara Roy points out, Israel has "explicitly referred to its intensified closure (or siege) policy in Gaza as a form of 'economic warfare.'" Israeli officials even argued that "damaging the enemy's economy is in and of itself a legitimate means in warfare and a relevant consideration even while deciding to allow the entry of relief consignments."[163] "Israel's goal is no longer simply Gaza's isolation and disablement," Roy states, "but its abstraction and deletion. Israeli policy has shifted from addressing the economy in some manner (whether positively or negatively) to dispensing with the concept of an economy altogether." Israel now treats the economy in Gaza as "a dispensable luxury"; its impact has been the "near total collapse" of the private sector, the traditional engine of economic growth there.[164]

Palestinians in Gaza have found creative ways around the formidable obstacles. One of the more spectacular sites I've visited was the tunnels dug deep under the border between Egypt and Gaza. My companions and I stood on the wooden planks of a large, circular platform, big enough to park two cars. The operator pressed the button and a warning horn sounded. A few seconds later the platform began to descend down the deep cement-lined shaft, guided by steel rails, cables and motors on two sides. In less than a minute we were at the bottom of the shaft, some thirty meters below, the bright sky a mere circle high above. The air was cool and clammy and got cooler still as we walked off the platform into the tunnel mouth, which was wide enough for one car and felt perfectly secure, reinforced by steel I-beams and lit with electric lamps. This was only one of hundreds of tunnels serving as lifelines, although the vast majority were much smaller.

The goods I saw entering Gaza included gravel, steel rebar, bags of cement, and bricks for construction. Some tunnels brought in gasoline, pumped through hoses and then discharged into large plastic water tanks to be transported all over Gaza. Electric winches suspended over deep shafts hauled up large canvas baskets of gravel. Then workers slid the baskets sideways along an overhead rail and dumped the gravel into pits below. Trucks rolled down ramps into the pits to load up and take the cargo away. It was all cleverly engineered for maximum efficiency. Other essentials brought in through the tunnels include food, generators to help cope with the blackouts that still leave Gaza dark for eight to twelve hours per day, and the Chinese-made moto-taxis that are replacing many of Gaza's ubiquitous donkey carts to transport goods and people. This underground economy has helped Gaza remain resilient, but at a desperately high price: since 2006, at least 232 Palestinian workers have died in the tunnels and hundreds more have been injured in what some call "graveyards for the living."[165] Nine of the dead were children. At least twenty of the workers were killed as a result of Israeli airstrikes intended to collapse the tunnels, but the poverty and unemployment in Gaza ensure that the lure of paid work, even under such dangerous conditions, remains irresistible. I visited the mouth of a tunnel that had collapsed just a day earlier, killing nineteen-year-old Hamada Abu Shalouf from Rafah.[166]

Although Hamas-controlled authorities have regulated the tunnels to some extent on the Gaza side, including requiring tunnel owners to pay compensation for deaths and injuries, the long-term consequences of the move from a formal to an underground economy are likely to include further decay of Gaza's economy while significant parts of it shift into the hands of unaccountable, clandestine organizations. The political motivations of the siege are underscored by the tacit support the block-ade has always received from the Western-supported, Fatah-controlled Palestinian Authority leadership in Ramallah, who bet that misery would help bring down Hamas and return them to power in Gaza. In meetings with Israeli and American officials (the content of which was leaked as part of the Palestine Papers), PA officials repeatedly complained that not enough was being done to keep Gaza isolated. An exasperated PA chief negotiator Saeb Erekat reported in October 2009 to US presidential envoy George Mitchell how he had chided the Israelis for not doing enough to enforce the siege and complained that US aid to Egypt to build an underground steel wall to thwart the tunnels was having no effect: "It's business as usual in the tunnels—the Hamas economy."[167] But the tunnels still leave Gaza's economy vulnerable to political shocks: following the July 3, 2013, military coup in Egypt, the Egyptian army renewed with unprecedented ferocity its periodic campaign to destroy the tunnels to enforce the siege, including flooding them with sewage. Within weeks, the volume of building materials and affordable food entering Gaza through the tunnels had plummeted by 80 percent, leading to an immediate spike in prices and a sharp slowdown in construction, with an estimated loss of thirty thousand jobs.[168]

Outsourcing the Nation

During the First Intifada, the avant-garde Palestinian dance company El Funoun produced *Marj Ibn Amer*, a play that took its name from the vast fertile plain known in English as the Jezreel Valley. The valley runs northwest from the hills near Jenin in the northern West Bank almost to the city of Haifa in present-day Israel. Building on traditional dance and song styles, the performance told the story of a village's struggle against a feudal landlord "who conspired with the occupiers to grant them control over . . . Ibn Amer, in return for helping him to kidnap a local village woman called Khadra."[169] Khadra's lover, Kanaan, battles the landlord, defeats him and wins her back. Amid great celebrations, the two marry and bear a son who grows up to continue the fight to protect the valley and the village's freedom.

El Funoun's performance was an allegory for the struggle that Palestinians under occupation faced in the early years of the First Intifada. In 1989, when the play was produced, Israeli occupation forces had shut down all the schools, the universities, and many cultural institutions in an effort to suppress the unarmed uprising. And just as teachers taught children in secret makeshift classrooms in private living rooms, El Funoun had to produce the performance in "clandestine dance sessions." Several members of the troupe were even arrested. The play also had other historical echoes. Marj Ibn Amer was a major target of the Zionist settlement movement in the early twentieth century, which insisted that acquired land could only be occupied and worked by "Jewish labor." In 1910, Zionists purchased some nine thousand dunams (2,250 acres), including the village of Fulla, from Elias Sursock, an absentee landlord and banker in Beirut. Palestinian notables appealed to the Ottoman government in Istanbul to stop the sale, fearing it would facilitate the Zionist takeover of the country. A telegram from religious leaders in Nazareth apprised the authorities in Istanbul that "the press is unanimous in recognizing that the Zionists nourish the intention of expropriating our properties. For us these intentions are a question of life and death." Still, the sale was approved and the peasants of Fulla were forced off their land.[170]

Today, a century later, the fertile fields of Marj Ibn Amer are once again the subject of a struggle between local farmers and distant financial interests. This time the Palestinian Authority plays the role of the feudal lord, threatening the villagers' ancient but tenuous hold on their land. In 2012, one family took the PA to court to try to stop the seizure of their farmland to build an industrial zone near the village of Al-Jalameh, just north of Jenin on the boundary between the West Bank and Israel. Farmers in this area have already seen some of their land seized by Israel for its West Bank wall. Daoud Darawi, the lawyer representing the family, told the *Electronic Intifada*'s Charlotte Silver that his clients were among many families affected and that the struggle to save their land had implications for all Palestinians.[171] The Al-Jalameh Industrial Zone is one of several being developed in the West Bank. With roots in the 1993 Oslo Accords, the industrial zone policy was revived at the 2007 Paris Donors Conference meant to boost the Fayyad government. They have been marketed as a means to create jobs, improve infrastructure, and prepare for statehood. Each has its sponsors: the Al-Jalameh zone is a project of Turkey and Germany, France is sponsoring the Bethlehem industrial park, another planned zone in the southern West Bank is jointly sponsored by Turkey and the World Bank, and Japan has put its name on an agricultural zone near Jericho in the Jordan Valley.

Far from empowering Palestinians, the industrial zones risk leaving Palestinians far worse off, argues economic researcher Alaa Tartir, as they "make the Palestinians even more subservient to Israel given that the PA has to rely on the occupiers' good will for access, movement and for transfer of tax revenues." Moreover, the zones give Israeli companies yet another "legal way to penetrate the Palestinian economy."[172]

As part of Fayyad's "state-building" effort, the World Bank recommended that the Palestinians enter a regional free-trade agreement with Israel. "In this scenario," the World Bank wrote, "it could be imagined that Israeli firms establish plants in the Palestinian state to access cheaper labor and then export from there to the rest of the Arab world."[173] In other words, the Palestinian state would function as a permanent low-cost labor pool for Israeli exporters, while the "Made in Palestine" label would serve as a cover to help them penetrate Arab markets. The industrial zones are perfectly suited for this role and are already being set up so that even if the Palestinians do achieve independence, they will not be able to change the rules or apply labor, environmental, or other regulations. Palestinians might, without even realizing it, exchange Israeli occupation for occupation by multinational corporations. There are other models for these industrial parks across the world, such as the *maquiladoras* in the US–Mexico border zone.

The planned Al-Jalameh Industrial Zone, like the others in the occupied territories, had its genesis in the Oslo process. The PA originally assigned a Palestinian firm to run the project and purchased five hundred dunums of land. But five families refused to sell. So in 2000, just as it would do a few years later to the villagers who stood in the way of Rawabi, the PA expropriated the land—933 dunams in total—for "public use" and transferred it to the Palestinian Industrial Estate and Free Zone Authority (PIEFZA). Created under a 1998 law, PIEFZA has a mandate to set up and run industrial estates and "free zones." Soon, the Second Intifada broke out and the Al-Jalameh Industrial Zone was effectively frozen.

In 2007, with the advent of US-led "West Bank first" policies, the PA-controlled Palestine Investment Fund announced the revival of the project.[174] Germany chipped in ten million euros for infrastructure. Now, however, the Palestinian management company was pushed aside; PIEFZA gave the concession of running the park to a new Turkish partner, TOBB-BIS Industrial Parks Development and Management Company. Jointly owned by the Economic Policy Research Foundation of Turkey (TEPAV) and bodies representing Turkish industry, TOBB-BIS aims to transfer Turkish know-how in "developing and managing industrial and technology parks." A "major goal of TOBB-BIS is to act as a catalyst in private sector development, while opening new avenues of growth for Turkish companies."[175] TEPAV functions in close alignment with the Turkish government's economic and foreign policies. Turkey had signaled its intention to get more involved in Palestine when it brought together Shimon Peres and Mahmoud Abbas at the 2005 Ankara Forum for Economic Cooperation, and its involvement in the industrial zones in Gaza and the West Bank soon followed. Israel's siege of Gaza following its 2005 "redeployment" and the 2006 election of Hamas ended Turkey's role in the Gaza projects, but it remained deeply entrenched in the Al-Jalameh zone despite the souring of its ties with Israel after the 2010 attack on the *Mavi Marmara*. The Turkish initiative operates under the soothing title "Industry for Peace."

A secret agreement signed in 2010 between the PA and TOBB-BIS, leaked to the *Electronic Intifada*, grants the Turkish company almost-unlimited powers and, arguably, more sovereignty and functional control than the PA itself possesses in any part of Palestine. The contract's terms sideline the PA executive, legislature, and judiciary:

> The PNA [Palestinian National Authority] recognizes the inviolability of the Zone and its internal security which will be under the sole control of the [Development Company]. No official or agent of the PNA or other person exercising any public, municipal, judicial, administrative, executive or legislative authority shall enter the zone to perform any duty therein except PIEFZA employee [*sic*] . . . and other officials whose work is necessary for the smooth operation of the zone.[176]

Valid for forty-nine years, the agreement stipulates that TOBB-BIS may "determine and implement procedures and regulations within the zone that will promote and secure the efficient operations" for the investors, including establishing its own security force.[177] The logic of giving up such total control to a foreign corporation, according to TEPAV, "is to create a secure, predictable and safe atmosphere." But for whom?

The agreement is silent on workers' health and safety and other rights, including the right to organize. The Turkish company makes no commitment to protecting the environment, except for a vague clause that "environment issues should be considered in accordance with the Palestinian laws and regulations." And while providing jobs has been a main justification for the industrial zones, the agreement commits the Turkish developer only to "give preference to local Palestinians subject to availability of the necessary skills, abilities and willingness to perform the relevant work within desired time periods and costs." At the same time, the agreement also stipulates that "all non-Palestinian personnel" of TOBB-BIS and any firms in the zone "are exempt from taxation with respect to their salaries and other benefits." This puts Palestinian workers and any firm that would employ them at a major competitive disadvantage. Goods imported and exported from the industrial zones are exempted from taxes and duties, another way that local companies already hobbled by Israeli restrictions are left at a major competitive disadvantage. As for the local farmers, not only do they face the loss of their land, but, according to Bisan Center researcher Ayat Hamdan, they "will not have the necessary skills to work in the industrial zones." The Bisan Center has been a leading critic of the zones, to the point where its leaders say they have received threats from the Palestinian Authority.[178] Darawi argues that the Al-Jalameh industrial estate serves no "public good." No one in Palestine will benefit: "only the businessmen and private investors will."[179]

It is instructive to understand how these kinds of extraterritorial zones have functioned in neighboring Jordan. After Jordan signed its 1994 peace treaty with Israel, it set up several so-called Qualifying Industrial Zones where Israeli–Jordanian joint ventures and other foreign firms can export goods duty-free to the United States. They have become notorious for horrifying abuses of human rights, including human trafficking and forced labor.[180] By 2006, fifty-four thousand people worked in the zones, a full two-thirds of whom were migrant workers, primarily from Sri Lanka, China, India, and Bangladesh. Jordan's labor ministry acknowledges that the proportion of Jordanian workers had been falling steadily and is now even lower. Despite the country's high unemployment rate, the ministry says that few Jordanians are prepared to put up with the "difficult working conditions and low wages" prevalent in the zones.[181] Workers are not allowed to join unions and are excluded from Jordan's social security system. Widespread abuses in the zones, acknowledged by the Jordanian government, include ninety-six-hour work weeks for wages of less than forty-four cents per hour, lack of medical care, confiscation of passports, persistent sexual harassment and rape by managers, and housing in jail-like conditions, for which workers' wages were illegally docked.[182] Workers who went on strike over these appalling abuses were routinely beaten, threatened, and deported. Despite promises by the Jordanian ministry to increase inspections and enforcement as far back as 2006, the abuses have continued.[183]

The point is not to accuse any particular firm or country of intending to operate the Palestinian industrial zones in the same way, but the fact is that there are simply no protections that prevent such abuses. The rights of the companies that operate in the zones are cast in iron, while those of workers and local communities are not even mentioned. Before they turned into a nightmare, the Jordanian zones, just like the nascent Palestinian ones, were heavily marketed with soothing rhetoric about peace, jobs, and development. It is therefore a fair and urgent question to ask how Palestinian industrial zones could compete with others around the world, including next door in Jordan, unless they offer companies similarly low costs in a race to the bottom.

For Whose Benefit?

Each of the current projects highlights troubling issues related to the PA's industrial zones policy. Although Japanese officials pitch their vision as part of a "Corridor for

Peace and Prosperity," many Palestinians fear the planned Japanese-run agro-industrial zone in the Jordan Valley will become a processor for produce grown in Israeli settlements, actually helping Israel consolidate its control over the fertile area.[184] The lack of trust is compounded by secrecy and a top-down approach surrounding the project, its investors, and its ultimate beneficiaries.[185] Feasibility studies and other plans were produced only in English and Japanese, not in Arabic—one example of the lack of real engagement and accountability.[186]

I found a similar lack of transparency around the French-managed project to create the Bethlehem Multidisciplinary Industrial Park (BMIP), which bills itself as an "eco-park" and regional model. The idea supposedly surfaced at an "intimate" dinner at the Élysée Palace hosted by French president Nicolas Sarkozy for Israeli president Shimon Peres in 2008. Peres rehearsed his well-worn slogans about how building up the Palestinian economy would help bring peace. Valérie Hoffenberg, one of the dinner guests and Paris director of the American Jewish Committee (AJC), was there too. Hoffenberg's relationship to Sarkozy dated back several years: she had arranged for him to receive the AJC's Light Unto Nations award at a gala dinner in Washington in 2007 and, as a member of his party, had worked on his presidential campaign.[187] "Go there and examine the feasibility of the idea," Sarkozy told Hoffenberg. Later, Sarkozy appointed Hoffenberg as his special envoy with responsibility for bringing the Bethlehem park from the drawing board to reality, making her in effect the French equivalent of Tony Blair.

Hoffenberg's main qualification for the task appears to be that she was well connected, as well as an ideologically committed Zionist who had said she would "consider it an achievement if one of my children will live in Israel and do army service there."[188] During the June 2012 French parliamentary election, Hoffenberg ran unsuccessfully for one of the eleven seats representing French citizens living abroad —the Southern Europe constituency that includes Italy, Turkey, Greece, and Israel. In a campaign video, Hoffenberg boasted about links she had forged between French and Israeli universities as an example of how she was "struggling against those who call for the boycott of Israel." In another video Hoffenberg stood smiling next to Israel's then–deputy foreign minister Danny Ayalon of the racist Yisrael Beitenu party, who offered a warm endorsement of her as a "personal friend."[189] Her official campaign blog was titled "Valérie Hoffenberg—Your member of parliament for Israel."[190] Hoffenberg has consistently expressed anti-Palestinian positions. She insisted that there is no blockade of Gaza and no need for solidarity flotillas because Palestinian farmers could easily import and export their goods through Israel, a flatly false assertion. She suggested that the activists should set sail instead for Libya and

Syria.[191] Hoffenberg, also a member of the Paris city council, led efforts to get that body to condemn the Gaza flotilla. She was so intransigent in her support of Israeli government positions that she was ultimately sacked for publicly opposing the Palestinian Authority's September 2011 bid to upgrade its status at the United Nations, a symbolic but toothless initiative France had decided to back.[192] This was the French official put in charge of helping Salam Fayyad build up the economy of a future Palestinian state.

After Sarkozy appointed her, Hoffenberg got down to business right away. "I spoke with Salam Fayyad and asked him for land. He gave me 500 dunams [125 acres] of public property and we started to work fast," she recalled. Hoffenberg didn't mention any sort of planning process involving Palestinians in momentous decisions about how to use scarce land. There was no time for that. "I created a Franco-Palestinian company—50-50," she said. "Fayyad agreed to change the law for me, because before that it was impossible to establish a company unless the Palestinians had 51 percent. I started to work with the private sector."[193] The French government contributed ten million euros for infrastructure. The Bethlehem zone was inaugurated in April 2010, with dozens of French businessmen and the French minister of industry in attendance. Before the ceremony, Hoffenberg arranged a meeting between the French delegation and Israeli businessmen "in the hope that they too will become part of this Franco-Palestinian venture in the future." On its website, BMIP is indeed described as "a 50/50 French–Palestinian company, registered in Ramallah with Palestinian partners." But there's no explanation for how any of these partners were chosen, what qualifications they have, what their responsibilities are, or what guarantees they may have received.

The holder of a 40 percent stake in the park is a French real-estate company called Deska, owned by the Belgian businesswoman, diamond heiress, and philanthropist Corinne Evens. Evens is a major donor to Tel Aviv University and Ben-Gurion University and a member of both of their boards of governors. Yet I could find no published accounts for Deska, nor even a website revealing what it invests in and where it makes its money. Through a search of French, British, and Luxembourgian public records, I learned that Deska paid $127,000 to two companies, Bold Rock Management and Zercon, to carry out feasibility studies and help implement the Bethlehem park. UK-registered Bold Rock Management, previously called Gold and Diamond Mining Projects (Ghana) Limited, is also owned by Evens. One of its three directors (the other two are Evens and a Luxembourg-based company she also owns) is an Israeli national named Gil Erez. Erez manages the real-estate business and financial and venture-capital investments of "a European family" and sits on the boards of several Israeli investment and real-estate firms.[194] He also personally represented Evens at a 2012 Ben-Gurion University ceremony recognizing her financial donations.[195] How Evens and her companies were chosen for such an important role in Palestinian "state-building" and to whom she is accountable were mysteries. Why, for example, wouldn't Palestinian institutions, researchers, and communities be given the leading role in determining the need for and feasibility of a project like BMIP? I wrote to Evens seeking more information on how and why she became involved in BMIP, asking her to disclose her business interests in Israel, the findings of the feasibility studies, the role of Erez, and whether she had taken into account any concerns of the Palestinian public before making her investment. Two letters went unanswered, but months after I wrote to her, she told *Haaretz* that BMIP had been her idea to "create a way for Israeli and Palestinian businessmen to meet and provide as many jobs as possible for local Palestinians." She is the one who "contacted Valérie Hoffenberg, a politician with connections at the Élysée Palace, and President Nicolas Sarkozy gave the project his blessing."[196]

Georges Evens, Corinne's father, was a Polish Jew who survived the Nazi concentration camps and eventually settled in Antwerp, where he prospered in the diamond trade and where his daughter was born. In recent years, Corinne Evens has sponsored memorial projects in Poland through the family foundation, even buying an apartment in the Warsaw building from which her family was expelled by the Nazis in 1939. Yet whatever good intentions she might profess; her own family's experience of dispossession, horrifying persecution, and flight; and the fact that she has funded "conflict resolution" programs at Israeli and European universities, these experiences have not endowed her with much empathy or insight. What we do know of Evens's views about Arabs in general, and about Palestinians in particular, is disturbing. "The Palestinians are totally unprepared for a process of peace. Nor are they ready to manage a state of their own," she told *Haaretz*.[197] "If they have a state, they will not know how to run it." Why? Not as a consequence of decades of crushing occupation and exploitation by Israel but, according to Evens, "because they are still a tribal society that does not know how to manage itself as a nation." She has, moreover, flirted with Nakba denial, accusing Palestinians of effectively creating refugee camps themselves just to embarrass Israel and win support: "They still hide under the rubric of refugee camps, supposedly, but I don't think one can call them that. Most of them do not live in those places. They only place a few people from their tribe in them in order to preserve them, like the Indians on the reservations. They are artificially keeping refugees in Jordan, Lebanon and Syria. But this is a matter of culture and it looks good internationally." Evens has echoed right-wing European anti-immigrant and Islamophobic rhetoric, claiming that "anti-Semitism is on the rise in Europe because of the Arabs who are flooding the continent and inundating it with anti-Israeli ideology." Due to the fear this "flood" induced in her, she told *Haaretz,* she was looking for an apartment in Israel.[198]

The specific problems with the Jenin, Jericho, and Bethlehem zones, including control by opaque foreign entities, individuals openly hostile to Palestinians, and unaccountable elite Palestinian beneficiaries as well as disregard and contempt for local people and their needs, underscore the basic contradiction in the nationalist rhetoric used to justify these projects. How can Palestinian "independence," "self-determination," and "sovereignty" have any real meaning when key decisions affecting the entire economy have already been set in stone with no public input or democratic oversight? These problems, as well as the horrifying abuses documented in the zones in Jordan, environmental degradation, and siphoning away resources from local and national economies are, Alaa Tartir notes, endemic to extraterritorial industrial export zones around the world. These critical concerns "should be the subject of public debate" in Palestine, Tartir says.[199] Instead, without the knowledge, input, or consent of the Palestinian people, powerful external actors and their local agents are planning to give industrial zones a central place in the economy of the would-be state, ensuring that Israeli economic domination is irreversible.

From Economic Peace to Economic Resistance

My goal has been to lay bare some of the realities hiding behind nationalist Palestinian rhetoric about "statehood." The harsh realities of Palestinian and Israeli economic interdependence under conditions of Israeli domination and colonial rule should lead us to conclude that "independence" and "statehood" by themselves cannot offer Palestinians real economic sovereignty, democratic control of resources, and dignified, sustainable livelihoods. The kind of state Israel, the Palestinian Authority, and their backers envisage would entrench a neoliberal system in which Israeli and Palestinian elites continue to collaborate in enriching themselves while millions of Palestinians, and indeed poorer Israelis, are left in misery. Sadly, there are still immense opportunities for profiteering and looting, particularly the large natural-gas deposits in the territorial waters of Gaza. For years, Israel has blocked their development and a credible analysis suggests that Israel's ultimate goal is to seize the gas fields. But in 2007, when there were still hopes that the gas would flow within a few years, Mahmoud Abbas concluded a secret deal with the Israeli government for the revenues to be channeled into an international account that would be inaccessible to the elected PA government, another example of the opacity and collusion with the occupation that rob Palestinians of any control over their resources.[200]

A political agenda that talks only about idealized notions of statehood, sovereignty, and borders neatly defining a national territory ignores and often deliberately conceals how exploitative capitalism cannot be restrained by national boundaries. Indeed, as the emerging industrial zones show, the "national boundaries" of a future Palestinian state could serve to create lawless zones where Israeli and other corporations operate in exploitative ways forbidden on their home territories. In the long run, it is clear that Palestinians must bring an agenda for economic justice and democratic economic sovereignty into the heart of their struggle. Obviously Palestinians are not alone in facing the formidable enemies of democracy, workers' rights, and self-determination represented by institutions like the IMF, the World Bank, politically manipulative Western and Arab "aid," and borderless corporations. Formulating the strategies that can tie Palestinians into other struggles around the world for economic sovereignty is a task that is beyond the scope of this chapter.

But Palestinians are not powerless. The obstacles are formidable, but some Palestinians are already engaged in creating a resistance economy. In a recent article, Sam Bahour and London School of Economics scholars Alaa Tartir and Samer Abdelnour have identified practical measures Palestinians can take toward ending aid dependency, such as ending the legal immunities and exemptions that the Palestinian Authority has granted to many large agencies and foreign nongovernmental organizations, including USAID.[201] Instead of exempting foreign experts and consultants from taxes—as the industrial zones also do—they propose a tax on foreign consultancies as a way to favor local expertise. These and other practical proposals to shift the balance of power back to Palestinians must be framed by a change in thinking away from the "technocratic and apolitical understanding of the development process toward recognizing the asymmetry of power and colonial dominance."[202] Nora Lester Murad, founder of the Dalia Association, a Palestinian foundation that raises money from Palestinians and promotes local community control over how donor resources are used, has also been involved in efforts to reform aid. The Dalia Association's consultations with Palestinians found that they "don't want 'aid' at all. They want political intervention and the financial support they are entitled to in order to pursue their own development." They want no more "false development projects that are, at best, distractions, and at worst, harmful to Palestinian dignity, independence and sustainability."[203] Palestinians want international donors to stop funding schools and other infrastructure while remaining silent and doing nothing when Israel bombs them. They want support to pursue remedies for the violations they experience, instead of being punished for trying to pursue their rights through the United Nations.

Murad goes even further, proposing that the tactics of the BDS movement should be expanded to include donor agencies. Her frustration with failed aid-reform efforts showed her that Palestinians can do little to influence the agendas of international donors, whose policies are tied to those of sponsoring states strongly supportive of Israel. But by using BDS and "focusing on what they can control—their own policy about what aid they will accept or reject—Palestinians can take control of their development." This suggests a role for the international solidarity movement as well: following the lead of Palestinians, citizens in the major donor countries could mount campaigns for transparency and accountability to ensure that aid is given for priorities set by Palestinians themselves, not to fit the agenda of their occupiers.

Palestinians can also take steps to promote economic self-sufficiency and domestic production rather than relying on expensive imports through Israel. "The first priority must be self-reliance in terms of basic foods," Tartir, Bahour, and Abdelnour argue.[204] Palestinians have already shown that such strategies work on a small scale, with experiments in permaculture, rooftop gardening, and promoting local biodiversity in crops.[205] Such efforts can also tie Palestinians into a broader global movement for sustainable local and urban farming. In the United States, for instance, grassroots initiatives in cities left devastated by capital flight and deindustrialization, such as the Detroit Black Community Food Security Network, may offer valuable experience.[206] Since the collapse of the Soviet Union, Cuba has demonstrated that transformation at such a scale is possible. With the end of generous Soviet subsidies, Cuba's oil imports, production, and malnutrition rose. By necessity Cuba adopted ecological and organic farming techniques, biological pest control, and animal traction on a large scale, all while improving yields and increasing biodiversity.[207] Palestinians could learn from such experiences and insist that international aid be redirected to support such efforts.

Palestinians in the countryside have a long history of domestic agricultural production, deeply rooted and celebrated in their culture, that can support locally controlled efforts to meet community needs or to produce sustainable exports. One of the more moving experiences of my life was seeing farmers harvest wheat in Khuza'a village, near Gaza's eastern boundary, in May 2013. This area's rich citrus and olive groves had been bulldozed by the Israeli army during its regular incursions. Yet even growing wheat was a life-threatening challenge: farmers have been frequently injured and killed by random Israeli fire from the watchtowers along the border. The women and men working the red soil under this constant threat might labor for weeks clearing, plowing, planting, and watching the shoots grow, only for their crops to be bulldozed or torched in a single night. The burning of a field of wheat by bored or vindictive Israeli soldiers does not make international headlines, but it is a costly and frustrating setback for a single family. The joy I saw on the faces of the farmers, and of the French and Spanish solidarity volunteers who stood daily as witnesses in an effort to deter Israeli fire, reflected relief and celebration that sweat, tears, and, too often, blood had not stopped them filling sacks with golden grain that would feed their families and communities.

In the West Bank, Canaan Fair Trade, an initiative founded by Nasser Abufarha in 2005, has enabled hundreds of small Palestinian farms and women's cooperatives to produce and market high-quality certified organic olive oil and other products internationally, at higher prices than they could obtain previously. Canaan works closely with the Palestine Fair Trade Association, whose general assembly is elected by its two thousand member farmers. According to an impact study supported by the Belgian government, farmers themselves "have initiated the inclusion of other crops such as almonds, chick peas, fennel seeds, and sesame seeds . . . crops that have a market [and] can actually be turned into products" that Canaan Fair Trade sells.[208] Olive-oil sales have grown from 23,000 kilograms in 2005 to 440,000 in 2011. With sales of $4.8 million in 2011, Canaan exports to fifteen countries, with 60 percent going to the United States. In 2008, the project opened a processing facility in Burqin village, near Jenin, that serves as its headquarters and includes a visitors' center. What sets this initiative apart from other internationally supported projects is its commitment to grassroots accountability and its fair-trade principles, including fair wages, healthy and safe working conditions, environmental stewardship, and "a broad social program that impacts the discourse on development itself," as well as supporting "national identity, political expression, farmers' rights, and community empowerment programs." These features, the study concludes, distinguish this initiative "from development efforts initiated and implemented by Western governments or other industrialized nations such as Japan."[209]

Israel's "economic peace" and Fayyadism will not, as their sponsors hope, extinguish the Palestinian struggle. Neither is economic resistance alone likely to liberate Palestine. But it must be part of the strategy. Even under occupation, some Palestinians are striving for alternatives that can help them stay on their land and strengthen their communities in the struggle for all their rights. They are doing this despite a lack of support from the official Palestinian leadership. In formulating their future visions, Palestinians must also break the neoliberal ideological shackles of the World Bank and IMF and take their place in a global community committed to economic democracy and to ending the overconsumption and environmental degradation that threaten to make life in many countries, Palestine included, unsustainable. The first step is to abandon the illusion that the formal recognition of a Bantustan-like Palestinian state alongside Israel would do anything to free Palestinians from an exploitative economic system that is already deeply entrenched.

Chapter 5

Israel Fights Back against BDS

"When there are efforts to boycott or divest from Israel, we will stand against them. And whenever an effort is made to delegitimize the state of Israel, my administration has opposed them." That vow by President Barack Obama, made to generous applause at AIPAC's 2012 policy conference in Washington, DC, offered proof that the Palestinian-led movement for boycott, divestment, and sanctions (BDS) toward Israel had come of age. Here was the president of the United States pushing back against an effort that just a few years earlier was easily dismissed as irrelevant. It was only in 2004 that the Palestinian Campaign for the Academic and Cultural Boycott of Israel (PACBI) was launched, and a year later that 170 Palestinian civil society groups issued what has come to be known as the BDS call. Inspired by the international campaign that helped isolate apartheid South Africa in the 1970s, 1980s, and early 1990s, it is an appeal to global civil society to launch broad-based campaigns to boycott, divest from, and sanction Israel until Israel respects the human rights and the right to self-determination of Palestinians by ending its occupation and colonization of all the territories occupied in 1967, ending systematic discrimination against Palestinian citizens of Israel, and respecting and promoting the rights of Palestinian refugees, including the right of return.

In his important book *BDS: The Global Struggle for Palestinian Rights,* human-rights activist and campaign cofounder Omar Barghouti traces the origins and spectacular growth of this movement through fits, starts, and setbacks, explains its principles, and refutes its critics. Boosted in the wake of Operation Cast Lead, which killed 1,400 people, and Israel's May 2010 assault on the Gaza flotilla, which killed nine activists aboard the *Mavi Marmara,* the BDS movement has emerged, in Barghouti's words, as a "qualitatively new stage in the century-old Palestinian resistance to the Zionist settler-colonial conquest and, later, Israel's regime of occupation, dispossession, and apartheid against the indigenous people of Palestine."[1] But while Obama uttered the Palestine solidarity movement's terms "boycott" and "divest"—albeit to pledge his opposition to them—by referring to "delegitimization," he expressed that opposition using the terminology prescribed for him by Israel and its lobby. It was a sign of just how seriously Israel's high-powered sponsors had begun to take the threat from grassroots activism.

In early 2010, the Reut Institute, an Israeli think tank founded in 2004 by Gidi Grinstein, an advisor in the office of Israeli prime minister Ehud Barak in the late 1990s and a head of strategic planning in Israel's navy, recast Israel's war against its enemies away from actual battlefields. Instead, it shifted the focus to college campuses, union halls, churches, and other civil society venues around the world, but especially in the United States. Israel's traditional strategic doctrine, which viewed threats to the state's existence in primarily military terms, to be met with a military response, was badly out of date, Reut argued.[2] What Israel now faced was a combined threat from a "Resistance Network" and a "Delegitimization Network." The Resistance Network, it posited, is made up of groups, including Hamas and Hizbullah, that wage asymmetrical armed struggle against Israel and whose goal is not military victory but to bring about Israel's political "implosion," like apartheid South Africa, East Germany, or the Soviet Union. In what Grinstein termed an "unholy alliance" with the Resistance Network was the "Delegitimization Network"—the whole panoply of Palestine solidarity and human-rights groups and activities, especially the BDS movement. The "hubs" of this Delegitimization Network were in global cities such as London, Madrid, Toronto, and San Francisco.

The rising tide of "delegitimization," the Reut Institute warned, formed a significant strategic and even "existential threat" to Israel. A "harbinger" of how imminent the threat might be, Reut estimated, would be "the collapse of the two-state solution as an agreed framework for resolving the Israeli-Palestinian conflict, and the coalescence behind a 'one-state solution' as a new alternative framework." If that coalescence has not yet occurred, it is plainly the case that doubt about the viability of a two-state solution, and interest in and support for a single state, are even more commonplace today than when the Reut Institute published its warning. Nowadays, it is sincere defenders of the "two-state solution" who feel like outsiders and dissidents. The Reut Institute even saw a warning in my words, quoting a speech I gave to the 2009 student conference on BDS at Hampshire College explaining that the apartheid regime in South Africa was never defeated militarily. The regime had retained its unassailable military advantage to the very end. Rather, something else did apartheid in: "The loss of legitimacy in the practices of the [South African] apartheid regime is what changed, and when a system loses its legitimacy, all the weapons in the world cannot protect it [and] we're beginning to see a similar loss of legitimacy for Zionism."[3]

This, in sum, was the new danger Israel faced; it required new weaponry, combat techniques, and orders of battle. The theater of war had become the whole world. In a presentation at Israel's annual Herzliya Conference, attended by the country's top political and military leaders, Grinstein called on Israel's "intelligence agencies" to focus on "attacking catalysts" of the "delegitimization network," especially in the so-called hubs. In its report, titled *The Delegitimization Challenge: Creating a Political Firewall*, Reut also recommended that "Israel should sabotage network catalysts." After an article I published pointed out that such language looked like a call on Israeli spy agencies to engage in possibly criminal interference with citizens and organizations exercising their democratic rights in other countries, the Reut Institute altered its online document to remove references to "sabotage," but not before we had made copies of the original that were later published by the *Electronic Intifada*.[4] Nonetheless, despite this effort at concealment, *Haaretz* revealed in 2011 that Israeli military intelligence had created a special department to monitor and collect "information about left-wing organizations abroad that the army sees as aiming to delegitimize Israel."[5]

It is difficult to overstate the influence of the report from the Reut Institute, which *New York Times* columnist Thomas Friedman has admiringly dubbed "one of the premier Israeli policy research centers."[6] The Israeli Ministry of Foreign Affairs declared that alongside "the nuclear threat posed by Iran and the missile threat posed by Hamas and Hizbullah," a "no less worrying threat posed to Israel is that of delegitimization, which attempts to negate the legitimacy of the Israeli state, its policies and its right to self-defense." Aiming at nothing less than the "liquidation of Israel as a Jewish state," the foreign ministry warned, the delegitimizers "seek to cause Israel's collapse by undermining the moral legitimacy of Israel, constraining its military activities, destroying Israel's image and isolating it as a pariah state."[7] Fighting delegitimization has become the top priority of major Zionist organizations in Europe and North America. In November 2010—amid futile efforts by the Obama administration to bribe Israel to agree to a short-term, partial "freeze" on building settlements in occupied Palestinian land—the White House reportedly committed itself for the first time to "fighting delegitimization of Israel."[8] Weeks later, a delegation from the

World Jewish Congress set off for Rome to ask Pope Benedict XVI to "speak out against the 'delegitimization' of Israel."[9] Israeli officials and diplomats fanned out all over the world singing the same song. Jewish Agency chairman Natan Sharansky and Minister of Public Diplomacy (*hasbara*) Yuli Edelstein, for instance, were dispatched to tell the Conference of Presidents of Major American Jewish Organizations of the need to fight delegitimization and especially to "combat anti-Israel activity on university campuses."[10]

Faced with a network of such dangerous enemies, the Reut Institute exhorted Israel's defenders to create their own counternetworks as part of a "systemic response." The broadest, best-funded, and most ambitious has been the Israel Action Network, launched jointly by the Jewish Federations of North America and the Jewish Council for Public Affairs in 2010 with an initial investment of six million dollars. "In fighting back against anti-Israel forces, the network will seek to capitalize on the reach of North America's 157 federations, 125 local Jewish community relations councils and nearly 400 communities under the federation system," the Jewish Telegraphic Agency (JTA) reported.[11] The network would "serve as a rapid-response team charged with countering the growing campaign to isolate Israel as a rogue state akin to apartheid-era South Africa." While the Reut Institute's Grinstein favored military analogies, leaders of this effort turned to biological ones. "The delegitimization and BDS movement is nationally coordinated, and it requires a national response," said William Daroff, a Jewish Federations of North America official involved in creating the Israel Action Network, adding that "we need to move forward as a community to counter this cancerous growth."[12] His words recalled a statement by Israeli army chief of staff Moshe Ya'alon, who in 2002 called the Palestinians a "cancer" and an "existential threat." Ya'alon, appointed as defense minister in Israel's new government in 2013, described the destructive and lethal invasions of Palestinian cities that he was commanding at the time as "chemotherapy."[13] In the UK, an analogous effort to the Israel Action Network was convened under the name Big Tent for Israel.[14]

One of the goals of the anti-delegitimization network called for by the Reut Institute is to "orchestrate the outing-naming-shaming campaign against key delegitimizers, based on detailed information"—in other words, to mount aggressive smear campaigns.[15] I was personally the target of these tactics on several occasions. In 2010, when I was invited to speak at the University of New Mexico, the directors of the Jewish Federation of New Mexico and the campus Jewish student organization Hillel wrote privately to several university departments urging them to withdraw their sponsorship of my lecture. "The department's endorsement sends a chilling message to the Jewish students and faculty of this public institution that the legitimacy of Israel within your department is questioned," the letter charged. Sam Sokolove, the executive director of the Jewish Federation of New Mexico who cosigned the letter, told the *Albuquerque Journal* that "a Jewish conversation" with me would be like a "debate between the NAACP and the Ku Klux Klan."[16] The vilification tactics did not work. None of the faculty or departments backed down, and the publicity generated by the attempted "naming and shaming" brought out hundreds of people who might not otherwise have known about the event.

In August 2010, just before I was due to travel to Port Townsend, Washington, for a lecture addressing an ultimately unsuccessful initiative in the local food co-op to boycott Israeli products, I discovered that the Pacific Northwest chapter of StandWithUs, an anti-Palestinian organization that works closely with the Israeli government, had been privately circulating a dossier about me to Zionist activists. Along with a mishmash of biographical information, the twelve-page document offered advice on how to "counter" and "expose" me. "When Ali Abunimah comes to your campus, be prepared for a sophisticated, smooth advocate of radical Palestinian positions," it began. "Though Abunimah seems calm and even reasonable, he is extremely radical," it warned. "When countering him, maintain your own composure and be as rational as he is. . . . Use his own words to expose and challenge him." In an all-too-predictable tactic drawing on racist stereotypes, the document sought to portray me as a secret "terrorist" sympathizer: "Despite the fact that he overtly condemns suicide bombing, he provides a rationale and justification for terrorism."[17]

The *Electronic Intifada* also found itself the target of a major smear campaign by NGO Monitor, another group that works closely with the Israeli government and whose goal has been to target sources of funding, especially from the European Union, for Palestinian, Israeli, and other groups that address Palestinian rights and Israeli human-rights abuses. NGO Monitor's campaign focused on a grant the *Electronic Intifada* had received from ICCO, a Dutch human-rights and development organization with a long history of working in Palestine. It alleged, without offering a single example, that the *Electronic Intifada* was a hotbed of anti-Semitism, and it claimed—again, completely falsely—that I had used funds from the *Electronic Intifada* to finance speaking tours. We stood firm and exposed these lies for what they were.[18] But NGO Monitor managed to engineer baseless public criticism of us by the Dutch foreign minister at the time, Uri Rosenthal, who promised to investigate our funding. Although ICCO's support was valuable, we were confident that our grassroots backing would see us through no matter what happened, since most of our funding comes from readers. Ultimately, the attack served to rally support around us and, I believe, offered a useful warning to the Palestine solidarity community of what was coming.

But for Dutch nongovernmental organizations—who were almost certainly NGO Monitor's real target—it was more than a distraction. It was a major crisis and a threat to their independence. ICCO director Marinus Verweij was summoned to the foreign ministry in The Hague, where he and officials had what a government statement termed a "frank" discussion "prompted by ICCO's funding of the website *Electronic Intifada*, which has published calls for the boycott of Israel." The foreign ministry declared that "Rosenthal considers this to be directly contrary to Dutch government policy and has urged ICCO to remedy the situation." He warned ICCO, which received seventy-five million euros a year from taxpayers—though ICCO said that its grant to us came from private sources—"that continuing activities that are in conflict with the government's position could affect funding."[19] Patros, the umbrella organization for more than one hundred Dutch civil society and international cooperation organizations, condemned Rosenthal's threats as a "dangerous precedent" and accused him of using methods similar to those of "restrictive regimes" to attempt to blackmail civil society groups into toeing the government line.[20] With such broad support behind it, ICCO did not cave in, but it was a bruising battle.

The Palestinian Return Centre (PRC), a London-based advocacy group, was the target of an even more sinister attack in which Israeli authorities participated openly. On December 27, 2010, an Israeli army communiqué solemnly declared that "Minister of Defense Ehud Barak signed a decree . . . affirming that a Hamas affiliated organization, the Palestinian Return Center [*sic*] in England, is an association illegal in Israel." The army labeled PRC a "European Hamas Affiliate" and claimed, without presenting a shred of evidence, that PRC "is involved in initiating and organizing radical and violent activity against Israel in Europe, while delegitimizing Israel's status as a nation among the European community." PRC, the army statement concluded, "is only one affiliate out of many global Hamas associations which supports and recruits for Hamas terror activities inside the Gaza Strip."[21] All of this was based on secret information supposedly obtained by the Israel Security Agency, Shin Bet. PRC's director Majed al-Zeer dismissed the Israeli accusations as "nonsense." He pointed to "hundreds of activities which were organized by PRC publicly and openly; it's all there on our website with photos and everything," and noted that the Israeli allegations had not "named any single incident or activity which refer[red] to violence." PRC's goal, explained al-Zeer, who is himself a Palestinian refugee, was to try to make the right of return a "mainstream theme for the British public and British officials."[22]

Despite the dramatic accusations, a UK Foreign Office spokesperson told the *Jerusalem Post* that "the Israeli government has not raised with the Foreign Office any concerns regarding the Palestinian Returns [*sic*] Centre."[23] If Israel were to "pass any evidence to us of illegal activity, we would of course look into the issue, working with the relevant authorities in the UK," the Foreign Office promised. Similarly, a statement from the School of Oriental and African Studies (SOAS), University of London, which was due to host a PRC conference, confirmed that "SOAS has spoken with the Foreign Office about the PRC, and we understand that the Israeli government has not raised any concerns with them regarding this organization, nor is it listed as a proscribed organization by the Home Office." More than two years after the Israeli army made its allegations and declared the PRC "illegal," there was no evidence that Israel had made such a complaint; the organization continued to operate with no apparent interference from British authorities. But a clue as to what was behind the attack came from Eran Shayshon, a senior analyst at the Reut Institute, who told the *Jerusalem Post* that "the PRC's activity in London contributed dramatically to London's status as a key delegitimization hub."[24] In Canada, too, Israel-lobby groups have worked with the Conservative government to strong-arm civil society groups into silence by pressuring and curtailing the funding of several organizations that openly supported Palestinian rights or gave grants to Palestinian and Israeli human-rights groups.[25]

While such attacks and smear tactics were certainly not new, Zionist groups pursued them with much greater ferocity and breadth in the battle against delegitimization. The Anti-Defamation League (ADL) published a list of the "Top 10 Anti-Israel Groups in America," which included Act Now to Stop War and End Racism (ANSWER), Jewish Voice for Peace, Students for Justice in Palestine, US Campaign to End the Israeli Occupation, the Christian ecumenical group Friends of Sabeel–North America, and the Muslim American Society. "We want Americans to know who these groups are and what it is they really stand for which is to delegitimize the Jewish state," explained ADL national director Abraham Foxman.[26] In the run-up to the February 2012 BDS conference at the University of Pennsylvania, another ADL list named the top five "anti-Israel individuals." Wesleyan University professor J. Kehaulani Kauanui, an activist with the US Campaign for the Academic and Cultural Boycott of Israel; author and publisher Helena Cobban; and Chicago-based journalist and media coordinator for American Muslims for Palestine, Kristin Szremski, were on the list. I was in the number-two spot, just behind journalist and *Mondoweiss* founder Philip Weiss.

No battle has seemingly been too insignificant or too local for Israel and its US-based surrogates to get directly and aggressively involved. Perhaps no case illustrates their zeal better than the assault on the Olympia Food Co-op (OFC). On July 15, 2010, the grocery cooperative's board adopted a boycott of Israeli goods, making it the first grocery store in the United States to remove Israeli products from its shelves in response to the Palestinian BDS call. Palestinians welcomed the decision, which also had a strong symbolic resonance: Olympia was the hometown of Rachel Corrie, the solidarity activist run over and killed by the driver of an Israeli army bulldozer as she tried to stop the demolition of a Palestinian family home in the Gaza Strip in March 2003. It seemed fitting that campaigners in Olympia should be pioneers. The OFC is a well-loved institution in the Washington state capital, a leafy city of fifty thousand, but with just two stores, both smaller than a typical American supermarket, the boycott would not likely have any discernible economic impact on Israeli exports. Still, in the battle against delegitimization, Israel's backers were taking no chances lest the BDS "cancer" spread.

In September 2011, five individuals identifying themselves as members of OFC filed a lawsuit in the Thurston County Superior Court in Washington State and named every individual OFC board member as a defendant, alleging that the boycott had only been imposed after "members of an organization calling itself Boycott, Divestment and Sanctions (BDS)—an international alliance of anti-Israel political organizations" had made a presentation to the OFC board and the board had violated its established procedures. Although OFC had in place a long-established policy to honor "nationally recognized" boycotts, the lawsuit alleged that the boycott of Israel did not fit this definition. Unless the court declared the OFC's boycott of Israeli goods "null and void," the lawsuit asserted, the plaintiffs would "continue to sustain irreparable injury insofar as the Israel Boycott and Divestment policies are fracturing the OFC community; sowing division and mistrust among OFC members, staff members and Board members, alienating numerous OFC members and staff members from OFC and the Board and causing numerous OFC members to either resign their membership or otherwise cease shopping at OFC."[27] In addition to overturning the boycott, the lawsuit demanded financial damages and court costs from each of the OFC board members.

The lawsuit presented the plaintiffs as concerned local people aggrieved about alleged violations of OFC's democratic procedures and seeking only to restore the sense of harmony that the international BDS conspiracy had shattered in their close-knit community. But this was far from the truth. I had been tipped off that a lawsuit was being planned, and began to investigate for the *Electronic Intifada*. I discovered that the lawsuit had been carefully stage-managed with the assistance of the Pacific Northwest chapter of StandWithUs. Days before the lawsuit was filed, I spoke with

Rob Jacobs, the Seattle-based director of StandWithUs Northwest. He told me he knew some Olympia residents were considering filing suit but claimed his organization's role was largely limited to providing printed materials for handouts, helping bring in speakers, and offering general advice. "Since we're not actually a party to anything down there, frankly we're not in any of the loop regarding the legal matters," he claimed. "Just from an attorney-client privilege standpoint, anything we would do with anybody would be violating some kind of potential privilege. So, we know that they're doing some stuff. I know they've been working with an attorney. I know which firm it is but beyond that we have not in any way participated in the legal discussion." Jacobs also acknowledged keeping the San Francisco–based Israeli consul general Akiva Tor informed about "what's happening in the community here," but denied that the Israeli diplomatic mission played any "active role" in opposing the OFC boycott. This too was misleading, to say the least.

Jacobs was unaware when I spoke with him that we had already obtained copies of messages sent to a private email list of StandWithUs organizers that were accidentally left publicly accessible on a website. The emails—records and agendas of meetings—revealed that Jacobs and his deputy had met in Olympia in March 2011 with the plaintiffs in the lawsuit, along with Israeli consul general Tor and Seattle attorney Avi Lipman. The meeting notes included "presentation of legal case" and "discussion of Evergreen strategy." The latter was a reference to StandWithUs efforts to suppress Palestine solidarity activism at Rachel Corrie's alma mater, Evergreen State College, whose student body had voted in June 2010 to support divestment. The record showed that, at the very least, Tor, an Israeli government official, had sat in on a meeting to formulate legal strategies to strike back at Americans freely advocating their opinions. Moreover, an agenda for an upcoming meeting of the StandWithUs Northwest executive committee listed several items under the heading of "Project Status," including "the law suit [sic] against the Olympia Food Co-op"— a clear indication that, contrary to Jacobs's claims, StandWithUs was fully aware of the details of the legal case and was effectively managing the whole show. Months before they filed suit, the five plaintiffs had written a warning letter to OFC board members urging them to reverse course or face "expensive" legal action. Neither Jacobs nor Lipman—to whom I also spoke in the course of my reporting—were able to tell me where five ordinary community members would obtain the considerable financial resources to pursue such "expensive" litigation against more than a dozen individuals. I had no doubt that the goal of the lawsuit was to punish the OFC financially and to send a clear warning to other American businesses and organizations that they would pay a similar price if they answered the BDS call.

The behind-the-scenes efforts of StandWithUs and the Israeli consulate were accompanied by an aggressive public campaign to smear the Olympia community. In a striking example, four of the five plaintiffs had appeared in a June 2011 video posted on YouTube entitled "Why BDS Scars Don't Heal: A StandWithUs Production." It portrayed sleepy and famously progressive Olympia as something akin to 1930s Berlin.[28] "I really don't think it's comfortable for Jews to live in the city of Olympia and be outwardly expressing Jews," plaintiff Kent Davis claimed. "You know, you can be a closet Jew and that's fine. I just don't feel comfortable discussing my religion or my beliefs in a mixed-group environment anymore." Tibor Breuer, identified in the video as an OFC member but not a party to the lawsuit, claimed, "It's amazing that I've been pushed aside as a Jew in this town because of the BDS." A woman from Port Townsend, Washington, where there had been an unsuccessful but equally contentious boycott effort at the local co-op, charged that BDS had generated a "climate of fear and terror for Jews."

At one point, an image of a Nazi swastika superimposed onto a Star of David appeared in the video, with a caption above it stating "actual image from handout." But there was no information on where or when the handout was supposedly distributed or any evidence that it had anything at all to do with the OFC or any BDS campaign anywhere. All the other grave claims of Jewish persecution in Olympia were similarly presented without a shred of evidence to back them up. Even the ADL did not mention a single anti-Semitic incident in Olympia—or for that matter in Port Townsend—in its 2009, 2010, and 2011 annual audits and generally found that Washington State had few reports of harassment of Jews.[29] The video also repeated the claims that the OFC boycott had been instigated by outsiders, even though it was always spearheaded and defended by local activists and co-op members. But the truth did not matter. The StandWithUs propaganda aimed to reflexively associate BDS—which one speaker called a "dark organization"—with anti-Semitism and even Nazism. "BDS activities have no impact on the Arab/Israeli conflict," the video claimed, "they only instigate anti-Semitism and leave communities divided and scarred for years."

The Olympia community's fightback is a model for all who face such assaults. It included a video featuring Rachel Corrie's mother Cindy Corrie and other activists challenging the plaintiffs to use the existing democratic procedure to try to overturn the boycott. A solidarity petition declared that the lawsuit was an "attack" on the co-op's "commitment to social justice, and, by extension, on all of us who raise our voices against injustice and in the hope of creating a better world." The statement concluded, "We . . . stand in solidarity with Olympia Food Co-op, and say to those who have brought this lawsuit: we will not be intimidated or silenced!"[30] This community response was crowned by a major legal victory in February 2012 in a countersuit brought by the Center for Constitutional Rights and local lawyers on behalf of the OFC and its board members. As supporters of the boycott rallied outside the Olympia courthouse, Thurston County Superior Court judge Thomas McPhee ruled that the StandWithUs-backed legal action violated a state law against malicious lawsuits being used to prevent people from exercising their constitutional rights on matters of public concern. The legal victory set a precedent that boycotting is a form of constitutionally protected free speech and, according to observers in court, the judge refuted the claim that the BDS movement was not "nationally recognized."[31] The judge awarded ten thousand dollars in damages to each of the sixteen OFC board members, to be paid by the plaintiffs.[32] With this total defeat, StandWithUs had fallen into its own trap.

There have also been efforts to use the courts to suppress BDS activism in other countries. Campaigners in France have faced a string of prosecutions under the country's laws restricting incitement to racial or religious discrimination for protests in supermarkets calling on shoppers not to buy Israeli produce. French activists have developed a distinctive form of protest in which a group of protestors enters a supermarket and loads Israeli goods into shopping carts before abandoning them in the middle of the store while handing out flyers, singing, chanting and explaining their action to passersby. Such "deshelving" protests had also been part of the campaign against goods from apartheid South Africa a generation earlier, except now the protests are filmed and uploaded online, where they quickly reach thousands of people.

The prosecutions of activists taking part in these protests often followed complaints by Zionist groups, including a European affiliate of the Simon Wiesenthal Center.[33] CRIF, the main umbrella group for Jewish communal groups in France and the country's leading Israel-lobby organization, has published legal studies claiming that the boycott is illegal and amounts to anti-Semitism.[34] The judicial crackdown received a boost from François Hollande, the Socialist candidate who later won the French presidency. Hollande told the Jewish communal publication *Tribune Juive* in May 2012, "I am totally opposed to the boycott of Israeli goods, which is illegal and does not serve the cause of peace." But just days later, a court in the Paris suburb of Bobigny disagreed, acquitting four activists over a protest they had staged in a supermarket in 2009. The court ruled that the charge of incitement to discrimination could only apply to calls for boycott of a population or population group, not to calls for boycott of a country.[35] Prosecutors have brought charges against activists in cities across France, including Paris, Perpignan, Mulhouse, Bordeaux, and Pontoise, many resulting in acquittals. But several convictions resulting in stiff fines have raised the price of public protest and advocacy for Palestinian rights in France.

The Israel Action Network had to wage an even longer campaign to score a razor-thin victory against church divestment. At the Presbyterian Church USA General Assembly in July 2012, a proposal to divest some seventeen million dollars in church assets from companies complicit in Israeli occupation of Palestinian land failed by 331 votes in favor to 333 votes against. Despite this, the Presbyterians and later other denominations, including the Methodists, voted to recommend a boycott of settlement goods, something the Israel advocates had also opposed. The narrow defeat of the Presbyterian divestment initiative obscured how much progress had been made in building support for Palestinian rights. The depth of that support could be heard in the days of debate, especially from members of the study committee, who had taken two years to consider their overwhelming recommendation for divestment. There was little public celebration by the Israel Action Network, not only because of the narrow margin of the vote, but because just days before the Presbyterian vote divestment campaigners had celebrated their own victory: Caterpillar was removed from a benchmark social investment index by the firm MSCI explicitly because of concerns about the Israeli army's use of the company's bulldozers in home demolitions, among other ethical problems, including labor practices.[36] The index is used by many other investment funds, including TIAA-CREF, the largest teachers' and university pension fund, to decide which companies to include in their socially responsible investment products. With its high profile on campuses, TIAA-CREF has been the target of a coordinated national divestment campaign by a coalition of groups under the umbrella name We Divest.[37] It particularly worries the Israel Action Network that, after several unsuccessful church divestment initiatives in the early 2000s, such efforts were re-emerging in response to the 2009 Kairos Palestine statement, an ecumenical call by Palestinian Christian leaders on the churches of the world to go beyond lip service to "peace" and to take action for justice, especially through BDS initiatives.[38] Whatever comfort the Israel Action Network took from its narrow victory in 2012 must have been dampened by the knowledge that the divestment activists began gearing up right away to bring the issue back again at the next General Assembly in 2014.

There is no doubt that accusations that voting for divestment from companies like Caterpillar, Boeing, or Hewlett-Packard is somehow anti-Semitic or anti-peace still had a hold on some church delegates and that this was a factor in the narrow defeat of the Presbyterian divestment initiative. The Israel Action Network's messaging to Christian clergy and laity overtly stressed that there had been a "dramatic increase" in "anti-Jewish rhetoric from groups promoting anti-Israel boycotts, divestment and sanctions" and that the "programs, websites, and social media of church groups supporting BDS" have included "rhetoric focused on Jews and money, denial of Jewish national identity, and anti-Jewish theology."[39] While ostensibly denouncing boycotts, Abraham Cooper, associate dean of the Simon Wiesenthal Center, warned that if the votes went the wrong way, it would "leave Jews little choice but to end all ties with Presbyterian leadership."[40] The Wiesenthal Center—notorious for its project to build a "Museum of Tolerance" on top of an ancient Palestinian Muslim cemetery in Jerusalem—was still enraged that, even though the Presbyterian Church narrowly rejected divestment, it nonetheless adopted a call to boycott AHAVA Dead Sea cosmetics and other products manufactured in Israeli settlements in the occupied West Bank. That resolution, the Wiesenthal Center fulminated, "shows how the world-wide BDS . . . movement that seeks nothing less than the destruction of Israel has infiltrated the leadership of the Church." Another measure of the Wiesenthal Center's extremism could be taken from its objection that the resolution "refers to 'Palestinian land.'" This was illogical, the Wiesenthal Center claimed: "As there is no Palestinian state with defined borders, what exactly is 'Palestinian land'?"[41] Presumably, extending this logic and pointing out that, since Israel has no borders, there is therefore no "Israeli land" would hardly have assuaged them. Such "one-sidedness" by church leaders, the Wiesenthal Center asserted, "will continue to be an obstacle in the interfaith relationship with the Jewish community."[42] The claim that deviating from Israeli government policy or in any way questioning Israeli actions or US policies that support those actions is an attack on "interfaith relations" or on the Jewish community, if it is not outright anti-Semitism, has become an all-too-common tactic of establishment Zionist groups. Don Wagner, the national program director of Friends of Sabeel–North America, the ecumenical Palestine solidarity organization that has borne the brunt of many such attacks, terms this tactic "interfaith bullying."[43] A danger of such cynical and indiscriminate accusations deployed to shield Israel from criticism is that they may desensitize some people to genuine instances of anti-Jewish bigotry. Nonetheless, we must always be vigilant against anti-Jewish bigotry, whether it comes from supporters or critics of Israel, as we must against any other form of racism or discrimination.[44]

Rebranding Israel: Pinkwashing

The "naming and shaming" attacks, smears against individuals and organizations, attempts to target and sabotage funding, and legal assaults on BDS activists represent the sharper edges of the Israeli campaign against the global movement for

Palestinian rights. The Reut Institute also recommended a "softer side" to "rebrand" the Zionist state and alter the all-too-accurate "perception of Israel as a violent country that violates international law."[45] This isn't entirely new, and such efforts, in one form or another, stretch back decades. In 2005, the Israeli government launched a major "Brand Israel" initiative to "reinvent the country's image in the eyes of both Jews and non-Jews" and showcase Israel "beyond the conflict."[46] Underlying the effort was the idea that "Israel will win supporters only if it is seen as relevant and modern rather than only as a place of fighting and religion." This was to include such things as "making Israeli products, such as medical devices, more identifiably Israeli," among other efforts coordinated by ad agencies and public relations consultants.[47]

"We will send novelists and writers overseas, theater companies, exhibits. This way you show Israel's prettier face, so we are not thought of purely in the context of war," Arye Mekel, the foreign ministry's deputy director general for cultural affairs, told the *New York Times* in 2009, as Israel faced a new public relations crisis in the wake of its attack on the Gaza Strip.[48] Israeli artists and performers engaged in such activities have been routinely made to sign a contract—which they must also keep secret—to assist the state's official messaging.[49] It is precisely such calculated and political use of culture for state propaganda, among other things, that justifies the Palestinian call for the boycott of such events, Barghouti argues.[50] Now, Reut called for an Israeli charm offensive to become part of the comprehensive strategy of the counter-delegitimization network. Israel would, for example, engage in international aid in poor countries to improve its image. Working directly through its diplomats and indirectly through diasporic Jewish communities, it would "aspire to maintain thousands of personal relationships with political, financial, cultural, media, and security-related elites and influentials."[51]

"It takes 'all instruments of the orchestra' to win this fight—from the political right and left," Reut argued, but it was the political left in particular that it identified as a main concern and target: "The more critical a voice against Israeli politics, the more credible its stance against delegitimization. Simply put, the most effective voices against Israel's delegitimization come from the progressive left." Thus, the think tank argued, "there is a need to substantively engage liberal and progressive circles—mobilizing this constituency to stand against delegitimization requires substantively responding to their concerns and building personal relationships."[52] In effect, this meant focusing on strategies to market Israel to progressive constituencies seen as both left-wing and receptive to the Palestinian struggle, in an attempt to split them and realign segments of them with traditional right-wing politics. This charm offensive would presumably go on while Israeli military intelligence was monitoring the same target communities.

Perhaps the most discussed example of this maneuver has been "pinkwashing." Sarah Schulman, a professor of humanities at the College of Staten Island, defines pinkwashing as "the co-opting of white gay people by anti-immigrant and anti-Muslim political forces in Western Europe and Israel."[53] Pinkwashing typically includes intensely marketing Israel as a destination for gay (male) sex tourism, depicting Israel as a haven for gay life, and financing film screenings at LGBTQ (lesbian, gay, bisexual, transgender, and queer) film festivals around the world.[54] These efforts, Schulman says, amount to "a deliberate strategy to conceal the continuing violations of Palestinians' human rights behind an image of modernity signified by Israeli gay life." At its core, says *Electronic Intifada* writer Benjamin Doherty, "pinkwashing is an attempt to change the subject: 'Don't look at Gaza where we're besieging 1.6 million people, look over here where we're having a gay pride parade!'"[55]

Just as important has been the depiction of Palestinians in particular, but also "Arabs" and "Muslims" in vague and general terms, as unusually hostile and threatening to gay life. Netanyahu, for instance, told the US Congress that the Middle East was "a region where women are stoned, gays are hanged, Christians are persecuted." Another typically overheated claim, made in this case by a pro-Israel activist in the *Toronto Sun*, is that the "Hamas-controlled Gaza Strip has declared homosexuality punishable by death. Hamas justifies beheadings, beatings, torture and killings of gays with Islamic law or simply declares that homosexuals are collaborators of the enemy."[56] StandWithUs published an open letter from a "gay Israeli" responding to what the writer termed Queers Against Israeli Apartheid's attempt to "hijack" the Toronto Pride parade.[57] Echoing the sensational claims about Palestinian society, the letter asserted that "Israel is a safe haven for Palestinian homosexuals. Israel grants refugee status to LGBT Palestinians who face severe persecution from the Palestinian Authority's security forces and from terrorists who demand that they become suicide 'martyrs' to overcome moral guilt about their homosexuality."[58]

In fact, in the West Bank, where Jordanian law is still applied, there is no legal prohibition on sexual acts between persons of the same sex. In the Gaza Strip, the British Mandate–era Criminal Code of 1936, which outlaws sexual acts between men, remains in effect with a penalty of up to ten years' imprisonment. The law does not cover women, meaning, in effect, that sex between women in Gaza is not illegal.[59] Since its creation in 1994, the Palestinian Authority has made no effort to legislate for or against same-sex practices, and there are no known cases of the law in Gaza being enforced to punish same-sex relationships. The absence of such cases is why pinkwashing claims are seldom accompanied by specifics and are often illustrated with shocking, misrepresented images that are not even from Palestine.[60]

What about the frequent claim that gay Palestinian men can find safety in Israel when they flee the kinds of societal persecution, violence, and taboos around sexual practices that can be found all over the world, including in Israeli Jewish society? In 2008, Michael Kagan and Anat Ben-Dor of the Refugee Rights Clinic at Tel Aviv University published a report titled *Nowhere to Run* based on their work "assisting a small number of gay Palestinians since 2002."[61] Observing that the plight of such men—as they all were—is "easily politicized," Ben-Dor and Kagan noted that their clients find no "safe haven" in Israel, where they are seen as a "security and demographic threat." Although Israel had a "nascent asylum system," the Palestinian men were singled out for especially harsh treatment by Israeli authorities. "Palestinians are excluded by virtue of their nationality from applying for asylum." In some cases, the men had reported interrogations and mistreatment by Palestinian security forces, which suspected them of collaborating with Israel, and feared going back to areas under Palestinian Authority control. Yet even when the men faced danger, Ben-Dor and Kagan said, Israel treated them "as undocumented migrants, and thus [they were] constantly exposed to arrest and deportation back to the occupied territories. Because they are Palestinians, they have been subject to more rapid deportation with fewer procedural safeguards than other migrants in Israel." If such "practices with regard to Palestinian asylum-seekers do not change," the report stated, "Israel will be in breach of several bodies of international law."

In at least one case, in 2011, an Arab citizen of Israel who identified as gay was granted asylum in the United States because of the "lack of adequate action by Israeli police" to protect him from a well-founded fear of violence.[62] Meanwhile, a small number of Palestinians in Palestine are publicly organizing as gay or queer—identities that many who engage in same-sex practices would not necessarily choose—and have done so for several years.[63] Despite the facts, pro-Israel campaigners continue to spread misinformation and baseless or grossly exaggerated atrocity stories while deceptively painting Israel as a welcoming refuge. Pinkwashing, like much other contemporary pro-Israel advocacy, has shown little regard for accuracy and often merges seamlessly with a broader Islamophobic agenda that aims to vilify its targets and build on longstanding portrayals of Israel as the region's "only democracy."[64]

Yet these campaigns have met with considerable criticism and resistance from the very constituencies they are supposed to engage. Organizers of the 2010 Madrid Pride Parade disinvited a delegation sponsored by the Tel Aviv city government because municipal officials had failed to condemn the Israeli army's attack on the Gaza flotilla weeks earlier. "After what has happened, and as human rights campaigners, it seemed barbaric to us to have them taking part," Antonio Poveda, of Spain's Federation of Lesbians, Gays, Transsexuals and Bisexuals, told the *Guardian*. "We don't just defend our own little patch."[65] What the *Guardian* did *not* report—but which was revealed in the Israeli press—was that the Tel Aviv delegation was also directly sponsored by the Israeli foreign ministry. "Israel is the only country in the Middle East that holds pride parades, hangs pride flags on the streets and respects the gay and lesbian community's rights," protested foreign ministry official Yossi Levy. With considerable chutzpah, Levy asserted, "The primitive politicization and the blatant capitulation to the terror and violence of anti-Israeli elements go against the Pride Parade's principle of preventing discrimination." Shunning the Tel Aviv delegation had, in Levy's view, turned the Madrid event into a "shame parade."[66] A municipal spokesman for Tel Aviv said the city government planned, as a response, to invite a Spanish LGBTQ delegation to Israel and to take them to Gaza (which Israel claims not to control) to witness a place "that is controlled by the fundamentalists of Hamas, who do not respect any human rights and believe that homosexuals should be killed."[67] Those who have defended Israel in such terms miss Schulman's point: "Gay soldiers and the relative openness of Tel Aviv are incomplete indicators of human rights—just as in America, the expansion of gay rights in some states does not offset human rights violations like mass incarceration."[68] Emmaia Gelman of Queers Against Israeli Apartheid, which protested at the New York City "Salute to Israel" parade, accused Israel of trying to sell a "twisted message": Israel "supports gay rights, so you must support Israel—you can't oppose Israeli violence against Palestinians. What a disgusting abuse of the LGBT community!"[69]

Rather than neutralize Israel as an issue in LGBTQ communities, Israeli and Zionist interventions accentuated it. Under threat of a donor boycott orchestrated by Michael Lucas, a pornographer whose oeuvre includes *Men of Israel*, a film featuring men having sex against the backdrop of the ruins of ethnically cleansed Palestinian villages, the New York City's Lesbian, Gay, Bisexual, and Transgender Community Center banned meetings of Siege Busters, a Palestine solidarity group. Siege Busters had met in the facility regularly for more than a year and was planning an Israeli Apartheid Week event in early 2011.[70] Local activists continued to struggle against the effort to silence them. At a protest organized by Queers Against Israeli Apartheid marking the first anniversary of the ban, philosopher and academic Judith Butler charged that the center had "forgotten its commitment to social justice" and "sold out."[71] In February 2013, *Gay City News* revealed that the LGBT Center had refused a request for space for Sarah Schulman to read from her book *Israel/Palestine and the Queer International.*[72] Schulman accused the center's managers of a "weird kind of anti-Semitism," where they held "cliched and stereotyped beliefs about punitive rich Jews who will pull out their Jew-money if anyone criticizes Israel."[73] In the face of persistent protests and growing outrage over what now amounted to book banning, the LGBT Community Center relented. Two years after it was imposed, the ban was lifted.[74]

Israel's effort to promote itself among LGBTQ communities suffered another setback when IGLYO, the International Lesbian, Gay, Bisexual, Transgender, Queer Youth and Student Organization, reversed a decision to hold its 2011 general assembly in Israel, following a campaign spearheaded by Palestinian Queers for Boycott, Divestment, and Sanctions.[75] And in the Pacific Northwest, three events in Seattle, Tacoma, and Olympia sponsored by StandWithUs and the Israeli consulate were canceled in early 2012, "following actions by anti-pinkwashing activists."[76] The hardest blow was certainly the Seattle LGBT Commission's cancelation of a planned reception at City Hall for the Israeli LGBT delegation. The decision followed an hours-long hearing at which Palestinians and allied activists made their case.

Some pinkwashing schemes have been bizarre and farcical. In June 2011, the *Electronic Intifada* exposed as a hoax a YouTube video featuring and purporting to be the creation of a gay-rights activist in the United States who complained that he had wanted to join a new solidarity flotilla to Gaza but had been rebuffed by organizers in London on the grounds of his homosexuality. In fact, the man in the video was an Israeli actor named Omer Gershon, a minor celebrity on the Tel Aviv club circuit, and there was no truth to his story. The first people to share the video on social media were staffers in the Israeli prime minister's office and the Government Press Office as well as Neil Lazarus, a former communications consultant to the Israeli government. While subsequent investigations, including by the UK journalist Jon Ronson, indicated that the video may have been part of an elaborate propaganda effort indirectly supported by the Israeli government, the people ultimately behind it have yet to be exposed.[77]

At other times pinkwashing efforts sponsored by pro-Israel groups have veered into open and crude homophobia and even anti-Semitism. During the 2011 San Francisco Pride Parade, one of the floats featured a man wearing a giant papier-mâché head meant to depict Iranian president Mahmoud Ahmadinejad. Grotesque and hook-nosed, it was reminiscent of anti-Semitic caricatures of Jews. As the float went by, participants raped and sodomized the Ahmadinejad character with a nuclear bomb and forced it to simulate fellatio on another whip-wielding figure wearing a leather mask. The float was sponsored by a group called Iran180, ostensibly a human-rights organization concerned about gay rights in Iran. Rather than expressing any solidarity, "the sexual depictions of Ahmadinejad are designed to humiliate and ridicule the Iranian president by associating him with gay identity and homosexuality and even in some instances—Judaism," Benjamin Doherty observed.[78] Another piece of Iran180 street theater in New York enacted a same-sex wedding of two men, dressed as Ahmadinejad and Syrian president Bashar al-Assad, standing under a chuppah—a traditional Jewish wedding canopy. This mocked them not only as gay, but also as Jews—echoing persistent anti-Semitic rumors that Ahmadinejad is of Jewish ancestry. Scott Long, who formerly headed Human Rights Watch's division on international LGBTQ issues, observed that Iran180's performances seemed "torn from the discredited writings of Raphael Patai," the Israeli-American Orientalist whose 1973 book *The Arab Mind* dissected Middle Eastern masculinity and became the "ür-text" underpinning the torture and sexual humiliation techniques US occupation forces applied against Iraqis at Abu Ghraib prison. US military planners were great fans of Patai's book, which posited the idea that fear of sexual humiliation is the key vulnerability of Arab or Muslim men that can be exploited in order to control them.[79]

Iran180 was no grassroots human-rights campaign. It was created by the New York Jewish Community Relations Council to generate a spectacle because rallies against Ahmadinejad's annual visits to the UN headquarters in New York had been attracting few attendees and little media attention.[80] The fake grassroots "coalition" included key members of the Israel Action Network, such as the New York Jewish Federation, and, in order to give a veneer of interethnic credibility, groups representing Latino, African American, Korean, and other communities. Several of these ostensible members, however, including the Coalition of 100 Black Women and the Coalition of 100 Hispanic Women, had never even heard of Iran180. The NAACP had heard of it but its spokesperson, Thomasetta Waters, said, "We don't deal with Iran180," and explained that the venerable Black civil rights organization's name had been used without its permission.[81] The mastermind of Iran180 was Marco Greenberg, director of the public relations consultancy Thunder 11, a veteran of various "Brand Israel" initiatives, and a former Israeli army officer who helped revise the army's "strategic media infrastructure."[82] Greenberg also gained valuable experience in his previous role as a managing director of public relations giant Burson-Marsteller, notoriously the first choice of human-rights-abusing regimes, tobacco companies, and other corporations with image problems.[83] While not directly related to the Palestinian issue, the Iran180 initiative was a clear example of pinkwashing. In this case, even the brains behind Iran180 recognized they had gone too far when Doherty's reporting on the group drew broader media attention to the grotesque San Francisco Pride float. The group issued a statement acknowledging "there were elements of the performance that unfortunately crossed the line and were clearly inappropriate. For that we sincerely apologize and have taken steps to ensure that this will not happen again."[84]

Doherty emphasizes that pinkwashing and other strategies used by Israel "rely on attacking and dehumanizing the people who stand in the way of Zionism's fulfillment. They rely on a culturalist discourse in which Israelis are supposedly morally superior—and therefore worthy of support and empathy—and Palestinians, Arabs and Muslims are uncivilized, thus justifying Israel's violence against them." But what the strategy fails to do, Doherty observes, is to offer "any affirmative arguments for why [Israel] should be allowed to carry on as it does" in its mistreatment of Palestinians.[85] He also highlights a serious inherent contradiction: Israel's most reliable, organized, and vocal base of support in North America has increasingly become the Christian far right, which has also traditionally been staunchly opposed to LGBTQ causes and advocacy. "It's hard to see how Israel can simultaneously promote itself as LGBTQ-friendly while enjoying financial and political support from these powerful friends . . . who are so notoriously LGBTQ-hostile."[86]

These contradictions came into stark relief when B'nai B'rith Canada, a leading Jewish communal and pro-Israel advocacy group, acknowledged that it had teamed up with Charles McVety of the fundamentalist Canada Christian College to lobby city councilors against Toronto Pride's inclusion of Queers Against Israeli Apartheid (QuAIA—a separate group from its New York namesake). "Fundamentalist Christians recognize that Israel is not an apartheid state," B'nai B'rith Canada CEO Frank Dimant explained. "They recognize that this is part of the propaganda machine against the Jewish state, and therefore they are concerned."[87] But this is how Canada's leading LGBTQ publication, *Daily Xtra*, described Dimant's partner: "In recent years, McVety has opposed every piece of human-rights legislation for queer people, including the Accepting Schools Act and gay-straight alliances, sexual health education in high schools and trans human rights" at both the provincial and federal levels.[88] Indeed, it was opposition to same-sex marriage "that propelled [McVety] to organize what became the Christian right in Canada," notes Marci McDonald, author of *The Armageddon Factor: The Rise of Christian Nationalism in Canada.*[89] Toronto city councilor Joe Mihevc objected to the alliance between Canada's Israel lobby and anti-gay groups. "That's a very disconcerting alliance that has formed," he told *Daily Xtra*. If pinkwashing was intended simply to change the subject from Palestinian rights, all the indications are that it has backfired spectacularly.

Rebranding Israel: Greenwashing

Coinciding with the UN's Rio+20 Summit on Sustainable Development in June 2012, the Israeli government began sponsoring the world weather bulletins on CNN International. "Live weather update, in association with Israel. Pioneering green technology for a better world," the TV spots intoned as images of solar panels, fields of wheat, and green shoots emerging from rich soil flashed onto the screen. The Israeli prime minister's office announced on its official YouTube channel that it had created the spot in collaboration with the National Information Directorate, the Environmental Protection Ministry, and the Foreign Ministry. The advertising blitz represented "the first time that the State of Israel has launched an international campaign of this kind," the prime minister's office said.[90] Other ads stressed that 40 percent of Israel's drinking water is desalinated and that 70 percent of sewage is reprocessed for use in agriculture.[91] A "green travel" feature in the influential conservationist magazine *Audubon* described Israel—and Syria's occupied Golan Heights, which the magazine failed to mention are not part of Israel by any internationally recognized definition—as "a blessed oasis in the desert" for hundreds of species "in a region roiled by military conflict." It linked budding birders to the Israeli Ministry of Tourism website.[92]

These are examples of what has been dubbed "greenwashing," the companion strategy to pinkwashing—all part of Israel's effort to appeal to progressive constituencies and open up new markets. It consists of portraying Israel as an advanced, technological, and environmentally concerned country that, in the words of AIPAC executive director Howard Kohr, "draws energy from the sun, water from air."[93] President Obama reinforced this branding message in his March 2013 speech in Jerusalem when he claimed that Israel's inventive "spirit" had led to "human progress" in solar power, electric cars, and other advanced technologies. But a stark examination of Israel's record reveals not a clean, green country of solar power, wind energy, and pristine landscapes as much as a propaganda campaign of smoke and mirrors to conceal some of Israel's most troubling, environmentally destructive, and criminal activities, many directly linked to military occupation and colonization.

International business consulting firm Ernst & Young ranked Israel an unimpressive thirty-seventh out of forty countries in its 2011 index of a country's "attractiveness" for investors in renewable energy. Far down on the list, Israel was well behind Morocco (27), Egypt (26), South Africa (23), Ireland (14), and India (4), with China, the United States, and Germany at the top.[94] Yet Israel's Ministry of Industry, Trade and Labor boasts that the country has two hundred renewable energy companies, 30 percent of which are startups.[95] While some might do useful work on green technologies, other companies listed in the ministry's online "Cleantech" directory have close ties to military industries and West Bank settlements and little or nothing to do with renewable energy or good ecological stewardship.[96] One, Beth-El Industries, makes nuclear, biological, and chemical protection equipment as well as high-efficiency fuel pumps for military vehicles.[97] Tahal Group, a civil engineering contractor, advertises its role in major government projects such as building the Zikim military base near the Gaza Strip.[98] Wave Worldwide financed and built a twenty-six-thousand-square-foot industrial building in the Barkan Industrial Park, a settlement in the occupied West Bank.[99] Other "Cleantech" companies in the government list include Mekorot, the Israeli national water company, which has been directly responsible for overexploitation and destruction of water sources in the occupied territories, and Shikun ve Binui, Israel's largest real-estate development firm. Norway's national pension fund divested from Shikun ve Binui in 2012 due to the company's involvement "in the building of settlements in breach of international humanitarian law in East Jerusalem."[100]

If Israel is the showcase for its green technologies and environmental management, it has little to boast about. The OECD's "Better Life Index" ranked satisfaction with water quality in Israel at thirty-fifth out of thirty-six countries, worse than Brazil, Mexico, Poland, and Turkey and better only than the Russian Federation. And Israel placed twenty-seventh out of thirty-six for harmful particulate matter in the air, with the OECD noting that "particulate matter and ground-level ozone concentrations frequently exceed limit values for the protection of human health."[101] Between 1990 and 2010, some rapidly industrializing countries saw large increases in their emissions of carbon dioxide, a major contributor to climate change produced by burning fossil fuels. Israel, which experienced no rapid spurt of industrialization in the same period, saw its carbon dioxide emissions shoot up by 103 percent—three times the OECD average in its region and about the same increase as in nearby Jordan, Iraq, and Saudi Arabia.[102] Israel's per-capita emissions have dropped from their peak in recent years but remain more than twice the regional average at nine tons per capita, 20 percent above the EU average of 7.5 tons, according to the World Bank.[103] Israel can still boast that it is well below the seventeen tons per capita emitted by the United States. These numbers are not surprising given that fossil fuels amount to 97 percent of Israel's total energy consumption, equal to the figures each for Jordan, Iraq, and Egypt, all carbon-dependent countries with no nuclear electricity generation or significant hydroelectric power.[104]

REN21, the Renewable Energy Policy Network, ranked Germany, Spain, Italy, the United States, and Japan as the world's top per-capita producers of renewable energy from wind, solar for electricity (photovoltaic), solar for domestic hot water, geothermal, and biomass in its 2012 report. In only one subcategory does Israel appear in the top five: per-capita energy production from solar systems for domestic hot water, a useful but decidedly low-tech application. Even here it came a distant second to world leader Cyprus and only slightly ahead of Austria, neither of which promotes itself in the aggressive manner that Israel does.[105] Israel does have ambitious plans for solar electricity generation, but these have suffered big setbacks. In 2012, Germany's Siemens, the major partner and investor, pulled out of a significant solar project in the Negev. The Israeli plant was based on the technology of concentrating solar power, in which Israeli firms claim to specialize. But Michael Suess, a Siemens board member, explained that "the global market for concentrated solar power has shrunk from four gigawatts to slightly more than one gigawatt today."[106] As of 2010, renewable energy projects planned in Israel totaled just over 1,300 megawatts, modestly more than the 950 megawatts planned in much-poorer neighboring Jordan.[107]

Solar Mirage

In his weekly video address on October 2, 2010, President Obama had some good news:

> I want to share with you one new development, made possible by the clean energy incentives we have launched. This month, in the Mojave Desert, a company called BrightSource plans to break ground on a revolutionary new type of solar power plant. It's going to put about a thousand people to work building a state-of-the-art facility. And when it's complete, it will turn sunlight into the energy that will power up to 140,000 homes—the largest such plant in the world. Not in China. Not in India. But in California.[108]

According to Obama, the project was an example of the United States "staking our claim to continued leadership in the new global economy" and demonstrated how his administration's policies were "putting Americans to work producing clean, home-grown American energy." Technically, the president was correct; BrightSource had relocated its official headquarters to California—but its roots and main operations are in Israel, and it is promoted as an Israeli company in the Israeli government's Cleantech directory. The firm is the reincarnation of Luz, a solar-energy company that declared bankruptcy in 1991. Luz was founded by an American emigrant to Israel named Arnold Goldman, a recipient of the "Builder of Jerusalem" Award from the extreme Zionist and pro-settlement organization Aish HaTorah. Goldman is also a board member of the Jerusalem College of Technology, which bills itself as "vital to the State of Israel & the IDF."[109]

Months before Obama's announcement, *Israel21c*, a website established to disseminate positive, technology-related, stories about Israel, reported that "Israel's BrightSource" had received $1.37 billion in subsidized loan guarantees from the US Department of Energy to build the California plant. It was a "well-planned process that took three years to roll out," said CEO Israel Kroizer, and it would put "US and Israeli solar energy entrepreneurs on the solar energy map."[110] At the time of Obama's announcement, the center of BrightSource's activities was in Israel and the lion's share of the high-tech career opportunities BrightSource was advertising were located in Jerusalem. The jobs boom Obama anticipated in the United States, by contrast, was mostly limited to temporary construction work.[111] All the technological development had been done at a test site in the Rotem industrial park near Israel's Dimona nuclear reactor and, in 2013, three hundred of BrightSource's four hundred employees were engineers and development staff employed in its Israeli operation.[112]

Notwithstanding Obama's misleading portrayal of the company, could BrightSource be the real success story of cutting-edge Israeli-developed technology brought to scale in the United States, with the potential to bring cheap, renewable energy to hundreds of thousands of homes and plentiful jobs to Americans? Unfortunately for the company—and US taxpayers—BrightSource's US ventures have been beset by problems from the start. Native Americans protested that the BrightSource solar plant Obama had announced, to be built on public land at Ivanpah in the Mojave Desert, would destroy their cultural heritage and ancestral lands, a "habitat shared by federally protected desert tortoises, bighorn sheep, mountain lions, hawks, snakes, and many sensitive and medicinal plants."[113] BrightSource dismissed the concerns, saying its studies had found very little wildlife in the area, but the Native American group La Cuna de Aztlan Sacred Sites Protection Circle Advisory Committee filed a lawsuit to stop construction of five planned solar plants on public lands, including BrightSource's Ivanpah plant. "There's no good reason to go into these pristine wilderness areas and build huge solar farms, and less reason for the taxpayers to be subsidizing it," Cory Briggs, a lawyer representing the group, told the *New York Times*. "The impacts to Native American culture and the environment are extraordinary."[114] A second lawsuit, filed by the environmental nonprofit Western Watsheds Project in January 2011, sought to halt work on the Ivanpah plant, charging that the Endangered Species Act and other laws had been violated and that the US government had "relied upon the project proponent's self-serving science that woefully underestimated the number of desert tortoise that would be impacted by the development."[115] These were two examples of what the *New York Times* described as a "storm of lawsuits" by environmental, labor, and American Indian groups, most still winding their way through the courts, accusing the government of cutting corners and violating laws and regulations to fast-track the government-subsidized solar projects.

A troubling aspect of Obama's decision to boost BrightSource in a high-profile weekly presidential address is that, at the time, the company had been "quietly" preparing for an initial public offering (IPO)—a stock market flotation to raise perhaps billions more, a move that would have vastly enriched its owners.[116] Public backing from the president would have been a major selling point and the US government loan could only have helped reassure potential new investors. *Israel21c* celebrated Obama's "endorsement" of BrightSource and called it a "feather in its cap" in the run up to the IPO.[117] A more cautious president would have steered clear of making statements about a controversial company that was about to be listed on the stock exchange. Yet Obama's involvement with BrightSource received no attention whatsoever from Congress or the media, unlike the intense scrutiny and atmosphere of scandal that swirled around the subsidies given to another solar firm, Solyndra, by the same US Department of Energy program.

In April 2012, BrightSource canceled the IPO just hours before trading in its shares was supposed to begin, due to what the company called "adverse" market conditions.[118] Chris Clarke—director of the nonprofit group Desert Biodiversity, a critic of the solar projects, and a commentator for KCET public radio in Southern California—called the failed IPO a "conclusive sign that the desert solar gold rush is grinding to a halt."[119] In Clarke's view, smart investors had been driven off because BrightSource "is using nineteenth-century technology to compete against tech from the twenty-first century, and basing its business plan on assumptions about the power industry that will soon be just as obsolete." BrightSource's "core technology is antiquated," Clarke asserted, "hundreds of mirrors focusing light and heat on a boiler, the chief concession to modernity being computers helping the mirrors track the sun." This is the same "concentrating solar power" technology whose market Siemens saw dramatically shrinking when it decided to pull out of the solar business altogether, including its investments in Israel.[120] All over the world, concentrating solar power is being eclipsed by photovoltaic cells—which convert sunlight directly into electricity. A major factor is that prices for the newer technology, in which China leads, have plummeted.

Confirmation that Clarke's skepticism was well-founded came in early 2013 when BrightSource announced that it had abandoned a major five-hundred-megawatt concentrating solar project at another desert site in Rio Mesa, California. Complying with demands for studies on environmental and economic impacts had made the project, composed of two solar fields, unviable, especially after the California Public

Utilities Commission had approved only two of five contracts for power utility Southern California Edison to buy electricity generated by BrightSource. "The [Rio Mesa 1 and 2] projects compare poorly on price and value relative to other solar thermal projects," the commission ruled.[121] Although the body did approve one of the two planned Rio Mesa solar fields, that wasn't enough to rescue the project, and BrightSource and Edison canceled their contract.[122] But these failures have not stopped Obama and others from promoting the myth of Israel's solar successes.

Electric Dreams

Just a few years ago, Shai Agassi, one of the World Economic Forum's Young Global Leaders, was fêted around the world as a visionary and a shining example of Israeli innovation and entrepreneurship. With the support of the Israeli government and especially the enthusiastic boosterism of President Shimon Peres, Agassi started Better Place, a company that was finally going to take electric cars mainstream with a revolutionary new concept. The company would solve the problem of the short range that limited the adoption of electric vehicles by setting up a national network of high-tech battery-switching stations. The customer buys or leases her own car (made by French–Japanese automaker Renault-Nissan), pays Better Place a subscription—rather like for a mobile phone—to use the network of switching and charging stations, and is then billed based on mileage driven. A driver running low on charge and far from home could simply drive into a battery-switching station that looks something like a car wash and have a depleted battery swapped out for a fully charged one in minutes, without leaving her seat. "We use the same technology that F-16 fighters use to load their bombs," explained Agassi.[123] Before a single car hit the road, the hype went into overdrive; the company was the subject of dozens of glowing media profiles highlighting Israel's pioneering green technologies. Reut Institute director Gidi Grinstein even featured images of the Better Place logo in his PowerPoint presentation at the Herzliya Conference laying out his strategy to combat "delegitimization."[124] The company also set up partnerships and demonstrations in Australia, Denmark, and the Netherlands. In September 2012, it opened a battery-switching station for a fleet of ten taxis at Amsterdam's Schipol airport with the public support and backing of the Dutch government and the European Union.[125] Agassi promised that four thousand electric cars would be on the road by 2012 and a hundred thousand by 2016. But the customers did not come. Better Place sold only five hundred cars in Israel and just a few dozen in Denmark, as customers balked at the higher-than-expected cost amid persistent skepticism about the concept. Agassi was forced out as CEO of the company he founded; the firm's prospects looked increasingly grim amid huge losses and layoffs. [126] In 2013, although it continued to operate, Better Place declared bankruptcy and was sold for just five million dollars, after losing almost a billion dollars.[127]

The greenwashing in this case is not just that Better Place took a risk with a worthy environmental vision that ultimately proved too ambitious, but that the company was used from the outset to promote Israel. In their book *Start-Up Nation: The Story of Israel's Economic Miracle,* frequently used in pro-Israel advocacy, Dan Senor, a former senior official of the US occupation authority in Iraq after the 2003 invasion, and longtime *Jerusalem Post* editorial writer Saul Singer predicted that the "global impact of Better Place on economics, politics, and the environment might well transcend that of the most important technology companies in the world. And the idea will have spread from Israel."[128] Better Place also used its clean, green image to cover up its complicity with Israel's illegal colonization of the West Bank. An *Electronic Intifada* reporter who visited Better Place's headquarters incognito for a promotional tour in 2010 asked if home charging stations could be installed in West Bank settlements and was told the company would put them "anywhere . . . that you want to live."[129] On a map included in the video presentation shown to the reporter, charging stations were located in areas in the Jordan Valley and along major routes going east from Jerusalem—indicating that Better Place had or planned to extend its network inside the West Bank—effectively building a "greener" infrastructure of occupation and colonization. It was necessary for the reporter to go undercover because Better Place has been very coy about the locations of charging and battery-switching stations. I have never been able to find a detailed map of its network on its website. Further confirmation came from Israeli media reports that Better Place planned to install charging spots at existing Dor-Alon gas stations owned by Israeli oil tycoon Idan Ofer, a major investor in Better Place, along Highway 443, which runs through the occupied West Bank.[130] Israel laid this road in the 1980s, using fourteen kilometers of an existing route that runs through the West Bank and had "served for decades as the main Palestinian traffic artery in the southern Ramallah District, dating back to Mandatory times," according to the Israeli human-rights organization B'Tselem.[131] In 2002, using the pretext of attacks on Israelis during the Second Intifada, Israel closed the road to all Palestinian traffic "by vehicle or on foot, for whatever purpose, including transport of goods or for medical emergencies."[132] The Palestinians whose land was confiscated by Israel to build the road, ostensibly for their own benefit, could no longer use it. Israel has blocked off exits to nearby villages, which makes it impossible for many farmers to reach their fields. The Israeli seizure of the road also led to the closure of some one hundred Palestinian businesses.

Now this route, which B'Tselem calls a "road for Israelis only," serves as "the main road linking Jerusalem and the West Bank settlements with the bloc of Modi'in communities and the Tel Aviv area in central Israel." An Israeli journalist who took a Better Place Renault Fluence EZ electric car out for a test drive found that the vehicle's onboard energy management and navigation system, named Oscar, sent him along Highway 443 as the "quickest way" to the next battery-switching station.[133] No wonder it was so fast—there is no Palestinian traffic to slow an environmentally conscious Israeli driver down.

Better Place's complicity in Israeli occupation and settlement is hardly surprising given that the CEO of its Israeli division is former general Moshe Kaplinsky, who commanded Israeli occupation forces in the West Bank during the second Palestinian intifada, a period of widespread, well-documented Israeli violations of Palestinian human rights. Kaplinsky was also deputy chief of staff of Israel's army during its 2006 war on Lebanon, when Amnesty International and other human-rights groups charged that Israel committed numerous war crimes, including widespread use of cluster bombs in civilian residential neighborhoods.[134] Kaplinsky promoted Better Place explicitly as a way to cut US dependence on Middle Eastern oil and thus a weapon in the US-led "war on terror" against Muslims. "I was a general in the IDF," he told the BBC World Service's ecology program *One Planet* in 2009, "and I understand where the money from the oil is going and what it cause[s] to our society in the Western side of the globe [*sic*]." Yet when Kaplinsky stood beside Dutch deputy prime minister Maxime Verhagen and the European Union Transport Commissioner at the launch of the Schipol Airport battery-switching station, Better Place was the general's clean, green vehicle from the shadows of involvement in occupation and war crimes into the sunshine of international respectability. Ehud Olmert, prime minister during the 2006 assault on Lebanon and 2008–2009 attack on Gaza, has attempted a similar transformation, no doubt making a tidy profit along the way, by agreeing to chair the advisory board of Genesis Angels, a venture-capital fund seeking to invest in "the next big thing" in Israeli technology.[135]

Environmental Crimes

If Israel's most heavily promoted green technologies have miserably failed to live up to the hype when put to the real-world test, what does truly stand out is the record of ecological devastation in the region as a direct result of its occupation and colonization, often with the involvement of "green" firms like Mekorot. Because of discriminatory allocation by Israel, Palestinians face severe and chronic shortages of water, a 2009 report from Amnesty International found.[136] "Over more than 40 years of occupation, restrictions imposed by Israel on the Palestinians' access to water have prevented the development of water infrastructure and facilities in the [occupied Palestinian territories], consequently denying hundreds of thousands of Palestinians the right to live a normal life, to have adequate food, housing, or health, and to economic development," said Amnesty's Donatella Rovera.[137] Up to two hundred thousand rural Palestinians do not even have running water and "the Israeli army often prevents them from even collecting rainwater." By claiming ownership of all the water under the ground and even in the sky, Amnesty observed, Israel's systematic denial of access to water is a tactic to force Palestinian farmers off their land. Overall, Israel monopolizes 80 percent of the water from the West Bank's main aquifer, while allowing Palestinians a mere 20 percent. In the West Bank, some four hundred fifty thousand Israeli settlers use as much or more water than the Palestinian population of 2.3 million. In 2013, the UN Human Rights Council found that Mekorot and the agro-industrial firm Mehadrin had exploited wells on Palestinian land in the occupied West Bank's Jordan Valley to the point of exhaustion in order to supply Israel and its settlers. And while Palestinians are forced to buy water from Mekorot, the company does not supply Palestinian farmers with the recycled water available to settlers. Palestinian farmers must therefore use much more expensive drinking-water supplies to irrigate their crops.[138]

Stingy as it is with recycled water, Israel has nonetheless been exceptionally generous with raw sewage. As the Israeli government frenetically erected settlements in the occupied West Bank, it did not bother to build proper wastewater treatment facilities for many of them. In its 2009 study *Foul Play: Neglect of Wastewater Treatment in the West Bank*, B'Tselem reported that forty of 120 "recognized" settlements in the West Bank (excluding East Jerusalem) were not connected to wastewater treatment facilities; many others had inadequate or chronically defective or nonfunctional facilities due to poor maintenance and neglect. As a result, some 5.5 million cubic meters of untreated sewage from the settlements is dumped directly into West Bank streams and waterways each year.[139] Israel, moreover, "does not enforce the legal requirement that wastewater treatment be arranged prior to occupancy of buildings in settlements or operation of industrial areas in the West Bank."[140] As a consequence, more than half of the seventeen million cubic meters of sewage Jerusalem and the settlements around it produce flows directly into the occupied West Bank as well. B'Tselem highlighted the horrific ecological impact:

> Approximately 10.2 [million cubic meters] flow untreated into the Kidron Basin, in southeast Jerusalem, a nuisance that the Ministry of Environmental Protection defines as "the largest sewage nuisance in Israel." Some of this wastewater

undergoes preliminary treatment, after which the water is used for irrigation of date trees in settlements in the Jordan Valley and the remained [*sic*] waste continues to flow freely, seeping into the Mountain Aquifer in an area that is considered sensitive to pollution. The wastewater creates a horrible stench and severe sanitation and environmental nuisances, including pollution of groundwater and of the Dead Sea.[141]

Yet, B'Tselem observes, the lack of proper solutions for treating the waste did not stop Israel establishing new settlements in occupied East Jerusalem, whose ever-growing population continues to add to the eastward flow of sewage.

Some 90 to 95 percent of wastewater from Palestinian communities in the West Bank also flows into the environment untreated, a devastating reality that B'Tselem attributes to "prolonged and unreasonable delays" by Israeli occupation authorities, sometimes up to a decade, in approving plans for treatment facilities. Israel has tried to force Palestinians to build—presumably with international aid—"advanced facilities that are still not used in Israel, which increase the cost of plant construction and operation and maintenance costs, and are not required according to World Health Organization standards."[142] Israel has even tried to compel Palestinians to connect its illegal settlements to planned Palestinian treatment facilities. Because of the Israeli-imposed delays, donors, including the United States and Germany, have cut funding for such projects. To add insult to severe environmental injury, Israel treats some wastewater from Palestinian communities in the West Bank at plants inside Israel and uses it to irrigate its own crops and rehabilitate its own water resources. Yet it still bills the Palestinian Authority for the cost. Israel even charged the Palestinian Authority forty million shekels (eleven million dollars) to build one of the treatment plants it uses for this purpose—even though it only cost thirty million shekels and also serves Israeli communities.[143]

Since the settlers get their drinking water from Israel's water supply system, the neglect of wastewater treatment in the West Bank has almost no effect on them, according to B'Tselem. The settlements are generally perched high up on hilltops; their sewage flows down into the Palestinian fields, villages, and towns below. These Palestinian communities, which rely on natural water sources, suffer the direct damage, including making the chronic shortage of drinking water worse, contaminating crops, and long-term harm to the fertility of land. Indeed, from the perspective of Palestinians, the sewage flow into their communities is an additional weapon in the hands of the settlers.

Wadi Qana is a valley of renowned natural beauty near the West Bank village of Deir Istya and a place where local families go to picnic near its pristine stream and reservoir. About five years ago, the nearby Israeli settlements of Revava and Emanuel started dumping their raw sewage into the valley, contaminating the reservoir and damaging fields. Abu Nafez, a local man who has had his trees burned and cut in settler attacks, believes the sewage flow is just another tactic to force Palestinians out of the valley. All this damage has been done even though the Israeli occupation authorities declared Wadi Qana a "nature reserve" and then, bizarrely, ordered the destruction of 1,700 trees. Given their experience, local villagers understandably saw the Wadi Qana "reserve" as a threat and an excuse to eventually prevent them entering the area as settlers continue to encroach.[144] Abe Hayeem, a founder of Architects and Planners for Justice in Palestine, has pointed out how Israel uses the cover of nature protection for naked land grabs: "Areas owned by Palestinians are simply declared to be green areas, making their presence there 'illegal.'"[145] This is not mere greenwashing, it is green ethnic cleansing.

Israel's architecture of colonization and occupation, including its wall snaking through Palestinian land and surrounding and isolating villages and cities, compounds the environmental damage. In January 2013, the West Bank was hit with torrential rains. "Before the wall, the water used to drain fine, and flowed down to the sea easily," said Khaled Kandeel, a resident of the city of Qalqilya, which is completely encircled by the concrete barrier. Although the wall contains drainage channels, the automated gates were closed and clogged with debris—yet Israel prohibits Palestinians from clearing them or digging new drainage channels. The storms exacerbated the existing waste problem, spreading it further afield: "Driving rain could not mask the stench of raw sewage being unloaded from a tanker" outside Qalqilya, "its putrid contents mixing with the brown torrent pouring past olive trees clustered on the hills."[146] Further south, the village of Battir, recognized by the UN educational, cultural and scientific body UNESCO for its stewardship of a unique and ancient ecology of terraces and natural springs, is threatened by the wall Israel plans to build across its lands. Villagers have been fighting the plan and Friends of the Earth filed a court petition to stop it. Even Israel's nature and parks authority, which has shown little concern for Palestinians and their heritage in the past, urged the government to reconsider. In December 2012, Israel's high court ordered the government to reroute the planned wall. But even if the government complies and provides a partial reprieve for Battir, it would only treat a small symptom of a much bigger blight on the lives of Palestinians and their environment.[147]

The water situation in Gaza is even more catastrophic. Amnesty International reported that the Coastal Aquifer, Gaza's sole source of fresh water, is polluted by raw sewage from cesspits and sewage collection ponds and by infiltration of seawater that is itself already contaminated by raw sewage discharged into the sea. When I visited Gaza in 2013, I was told that the overpowering stench of untreated raw sewage flowing along the main east-west river, Wadi Ghazza, and in several other areas was a permanent feature of life. The underground aquifer has been severely degraded by Israel's overextraction on its eastern end, before the westward-flowing system even reaches Gaza. As a consequence, 90 to 95 percent of Gaza's water is polluted and unfit for human consumption, and waterborne diseases are widespread. Nitrates leaching into the water supply at levels far higher than the World Health Organization considers safe lead to "Blue Baby" syndrome—methemoglobinemia— a blood disorder that prevents infants from getting enough oxygen into their tissues. An outward sign is the development of blueness around the mouth and on the limbs; afflicted babies may suffer trouble breathing, vomiting, diarrhea, and, in severe cases, death. Earlier studies have found that methemoglobinemia prevalence reached as high as 48 percent in Gaza infants, prompting the United Nations Environment Programme to call in 2009 for a comprehensive study of the disease in Gaza in the wake of the most recent Israeli assault.[148]

Israel's tight blockade imposed since 2007 has denied or severely restricted the entry of equipment to develop the water infrastructure or to repair it after the extensive damage caused by Israel's bombing during Operation Cast Lead. In one incident, in January 2009, Israeli bombing destroyed the retaining wall of a sewage lagoon at Gaza City's main water-treatment facility, causing a huge outflow of untreated waste into surrounding agricultural land—a completely unjustifiable act the UN-commissioned Goldstone Report considered to be "premeditated and deliberate."[149] The report also found that eleven water wells providing water for human use were hit, three were completely destroyed, and thousands of meters of sewage pipes were damaged or destroyed, along with 5,700 rooftop water tanks destroyed and 2,900 more damaged.[150] During the assault, vast tracts of farmland were leveled by Israeli armored vehicles and "greenhouses, livestock shelters, irrigation channels, wells and pumps were bombed or bulldozed on a huge scale."[151] I saw this barren land myself along Gaza's eastern frontier: where productive orchards and olive groves once stood, the fertile ground is now bare and dry as far as the eye can see. Local farmers risk their lives when they enter the land to plant alternative crops such as wheat, since Israeli soldiers posted on watchtowers frequently shoot at them.

Amnesty International's 2009 report on the water crisis reminded Israel of the call by the UN Committee on Economic, Social and Cultural Rights for states to "refrain at all times from imposing embargoes or similar measures, that prevent the supply of water, as well as goods and services essential for securing the right to water.

Water should never be used as an instrument of political and economic pressure." But Israel has continued to use water as a weapon, first and foremost by denying Palestinians adequate access, damaging and exhausting their supplies, destroying and inhibiting the development of necessary and sustainable water management infrastructure, and more recently in its dishonest and cynical greenwashing propaganda.[152] In the summer of 2013, for instance, Israel's Consulate General to the Midwest in Chicago hosted its first "Israeli-Chicago Water Conference" jointly with Chicago's Department of Water Management. "Representing a country which is so poor in water resources and so rich in water technology, I am proud to cooperate with the City of Chicago, in this field, to the benefit of the Midwest region," Consul General Roey Gilad declared to an audience that included water management officials from as far away as Kansas.[153] Chicago mayor Rahm Emanuel, also in attendance, called the conference "a unique chance for Chicago to exchange ideas for improving water practices with the rest of the Midwest and with Israel."[154]

"Factories of Death"

In all Israeli propaganda and Zionist mythology, "Judea and Samaria"—the occupied West Bank—is described as the emotional cradle and heartland of Judaism. But rather than treat the area with the reverence such attachment might justify, Israel's use of the territory as a dumping ground for dirty industries bears the classic hallmarks of environmental racism. On September 5, 2013, a fire broke out at a nylon factory in the Nitzanei Shalom industrial zone, sending flames fifteen meters into the sky. "When people came outside after hearing the explosion to see what was happening, soldiers attacked them with tear gas," local resident Eyad al-Jallad told the *Electronic Intifada*'s Patrick Strickland.[155] As Israeli firefighters directed their efforts to protecting the other Israeli factories, Palestinian families living nearby were trapped in their homes. "With the smoke and the tear gas everywhere, we had to stay inside and seal the windows," al-Jallad said. Israeli forces also fired tear-gas canisters at Palestinian youths gathered at the junction nearby. Only later were Palestinian firefighters allowed to approach and protect Palestinian property. "If the fire had spread any further and caught my house on fire, we would have died," al-Jallad said.

Nitzanei Shalom is built on confiscated land near the occupied West Bank city of Tulkarem. The first of a dozen factories began moving into the area in the 1980s following complaints about pollution in Israeli cities. One of the factories, Geshuri Industries, makes pesticides and other chemical products. Another, Dixon Gas Industries, moved there after it was ordered to close its facility in the Israeli coastal city of Netanya. The fire, the third according to al-Jallad, was the worst so far. "After these fires, no one comes to clean up," he added. All the local residents Strickland spoke to reported chronic problems from respiratory inflammation and eye diseases to cancer, due to constant exposure to pollution from the factories. Their accounts were similar to those collected on video by the human rights group Al-Haq in 2010.[156] Local resident Imad Odeh told Al-Haq that on days when an easterly wind blew the pollution toward nearby Jewish settlements, the Geshuri factory would shut down. On days when the wind was northerly or westerly, pushing the pollution toward Palestinians, the smokestacks would operate. Other residents said that the chronic ill health caused by the pollution meant local workers were often absent from work and farmland had been left uncultivated and covered in thorns. One woman farmer showed her dying trees, their leaves shriveled and brown, standing amid puddles of poisonous water that flowed from the Israeli factory. She had given birth to four children on that farm, she said, "and this land is as dear to me as any of them."

Although there has been little research, a 2003 study from An-Najah National University concluded that Tulkarem, along with Jenin, had the highest rates of lung cancer in the West Bank, partly as a consequence of the pollution from the Israeli industrial zone and the presence of a large number of quarries.[157] Israel's Ministry of Industry, Trade, and Labor acknowledges that there are more than twenty such Israeli-run industrial zones in the occupied West Bank. In 2012 Israel's state comptroller slammed the ministry's "continued failure for years [to provide] substantial supervision and enforcement in the field of safety and hygiene in Israeli factories in Judea and Samaria, which has to point to ongoing disregard for human life."[158] The lawlessness with which Israeli companies can operate, without building permits, employment permits, or any environmental regulation, "places in real danger the well-being, health and lives of the workers in the industrial zones," the state comptroller found. "The fumes and the waste from the factories are killing us," Suheil Salman, another local resident near the Nitzanei Shalom zone, said. "We call them 'factories of death.'"[159]

Transplanting the Natives

Although it has always used tree-planting as a way to raise funds, in the era of greenwashing, the JNF, the state-sponsored Israeli agency that holds land confiscated from Palestinians and assists the government in "Judaizing" it, has actively tried to rebrand itself as an "environmental" group. Its website now speaks much less about "redeeming" Palestinian land for the use of Jews and emphasizes such topics as "water," "forestry," and "ecology." The JNF even held a "Green Sunday" fundraiser in the UK and other countries in 2012 and asked volunteers to "give two hours of your time to help turn the Negev green" and "make the Negev a livable place." Palestinians and Bedouins who live there point out that the Negev (Naqab in Arabic) is the place they have lived for generations—despite the fact that Israel has already forced them off much of their land. What the JNF was doing now was working hand in glove with the government to make the rest of the Negev an unlivable place for the Bedouins—who are nominally citizens of Israel, but lack essential rights because they are not Jews. Usama Uqbi, head of the Naqab Bedouin Committee, mocked Israeli claims that the area was empty as a "big lie."[160] It was a line reminiscent of the foundational Zionist myth of Palestine as a "land without a people" where pioneering settlers "made the desert bloom." Green Sunday became a focus for campaigners from the UK group Stop the JNF, which charged that the event was nothing more than a cover for continued ethnic cleansing. It also emerged that the JNF was accepting money from GOD TV to buy trees to plant on ancestral lands on which Bedouins were struggling to stay. GOD TV is a UK-based Christian Zionist channel whose founder said he had begun fundraising for the JNF forest after God had instructed him to "prepare the land for the return of my Son."[161]

The trees were intended for an area near the Bedouin village of al-Araqib, which Israeli forces had demolished dozens of times after the determined residents kept rebuilding. This is one of dozens of "unrecognized" Bedouin villages that are home to fifty thousand people on whose lands Israel—with the help of the JNF—has been encroaching for years. Bedouins faced an even more urgent threat of removal in 2013 as Israel's government approved the so-called "Prawer Plan," which, if not stopped, will force forty thousand more people off their land in order to create a string of Jewish settlements separating Arab communities in the eastern and western parts of the Negev.[162] An analysis by Human Rights Watch researcher Noga Malkin noted that the tactics Israel uses to seize Bedouin lands in the Negev "resemble its settlement policies in the West Bank." Yet many international actors who oppose the settlements—at least verbally—"appear unaware of the simultaneous land grab happening in the Negev." Malkin cited the example of diplomats from forty-nine countries, including Germany and Spain, attending the 2005 inauguration of the JNF's "Ambassador's Forest," planted on al-Araqib's lands.[163] Not only can a forest be used to cover up crimes against Palestinians, it can be done with celebration.

Even the trees that the JNF has planted around or over the ruins of Palestinian villages, including Ijzim, al-Manara, Jabaʿ and ʿAyn Hawd that are now within the JNF's "Ofer Forest," have exacerbated the risk of environmental catastrophe. This was the area just south of Haifa where a 2010 wildfire killed forty-four people and destroyed thousands of acres of trees, many of which had been paid for by JNF donors in the United States. Following the fire, even Israeli officials recognized that the JNF's habit of densely planting nonnative pines—a practice established by early Zionist settlers whose goal was to make Palestine's landscape look more like their Eastern European homelands—has made the region particularly vulnerable because these exotic trees are highly flammable in Palestine's arid Mediterranean climate.[164] This was by no means the first catastrophe attributable to the JNF's environmental mismanagement. In the 1950s, it drained some sixty square kilometers of natural wetlands—then viewed as useless "swamp"—in the Hula Valley in Palestine's north in order to use the land for agriculture, extract peat, and build roads. It was a disaster. Nitrates and sulfates released from decomposing peat, now no longer protected by wetlands, leached into Lake Tiberias, damaging the water quality. The peat itself, "once exposed, turned into highly flammable, infertile black dust. Strong winds sweeping the valley producing dust storms that in turn damaged agricultural crops and an entire area sunk some three meters."[165] In the 1990s, Israel reflooded about 10 percent of the area in an attempt to reverse the damage. But by that time it was too late for the estimated one hundred animal species that disappeared, as "numerous freshwater plant species became extinct, and many flocks of migratory birds found alternative areas to stop on their route between Africa and Europe."[166] Sadly, environmental catastrophe on such a vast scale due to Israel's mismanagement is not a thing of the past. The greatest disaster presently unfolding, the rapid evaporation of the Dead Sea, is directly attributable to Israel's diversion of the headwaters of the Jordan River into its "National Water Carrier." As a result, the legendary waterway in which Christians believe Jesus was baptized has been reduced, in the estimation of Tel Aviv University environmental sciences expert Professor Marcelo Sternberg, to a stream of little more than "sewage and effluent from fishponds."[167]

There are some hopeful signs that efforts to greenwash the JNF are not working. Prominent British politicians, including Prime Minister David Cameron, a former patron, have distanced themselves from the group, which has also seen its fundraising in the UK plummet.[168] Months before "Green Sunday," the Scottish Green Party passed a motion that condemned the "Jewish National Fund for its activities in excluding non-Jews from Israeli land," called for the JNF's charitable status to be revoked, and "denounce[d] the organization for claiming to be an ecological agency."[169] In 2011, more than a hundred Palestine solidarity organizations signed a letter urging the US Internal Revenue Service to revoke the JNF's charitable status on the grounds that its Israeli arm practices racial discrimination. While symbolic, the fact that the letter was signed by American Jewish activist groups, along with Palestinians, underlined the increasing difficulty major pro-Israel organizations have in claiming a monopoly in representing Jewish opinion.[170] Similar calls have been heard in Canada, where that country's JNF affiliate has in recent years stepped up "environmental" partnerships with provincial governments.[171] In 2013, the UK's Charity Commission finally began an investigation into whether the JNF's charitably funded activities fall afoul of British antiracism laws.[172]

Perhaps the most ominous environmental threat looming over millions of people in the region stems from Israel's nuclear reactor at Dimona, which sits in an active earthquake zone, as well as its other undisclosed chemical and biological weapons programs. Dozens of former workers at the Dimona reactor have alleged that the facility has suffered mishaps and radiation leaks repeatedly since it was built in the 1950s. The workers and their families made the claims in a 2011 lawsuit, alleging that they suffered from cancer and other diseases as a result.[173] Dr. Dan Litai, a radiation safety engineer at Dimona, confirmed in court the workers' allegation that results of their urine tests were systematically altered to indicate radiation levels of zero when they were in fact much higher.[174] Thelma Byrne, the former head of the radiation safety department at Israel's Soreq Nuclear Research Center, testified in court that "we would get contaminated each time," adding, "I worked with materials whose nature was unknown. They didn't tell us what we were exposed to."[175] There was, moreover, "no such thing as nuclear core safety. Safety concerns were insignificant," Byrne alleged. After an earlier court appearance in the case, Byrne claimed she had faced intimidation when a government official "called me, accused me of violating censorship laws, and threatened to take me to court."[176]

In 2011, Dr. Mahmoud Saadah, a radiation expert and head of the Palestine branch of International Physicians for the Prevention of Nuclear War, told Ma'an News Agency that he had detected elevated radiation levels around Hebron in the southern West Bank, the area closest to Dimona. "The recent period has seen an increase in the rate of uranium, caesium, and potassium radiation emanating from the southern region," Saadah claimed, citing specific measurements for uranium-238 in the area that were more than three times normal background levels. Saadah said his group had measured radioactive cesium in several areas, a compound that results from man-made nuclear reactions and explosions and does not occur naturally in the environment.[177] Israel admits that it has a "national radioactive waste disposal site" in the Negev, but the real threat level to human health and the environment from all its atomic activities is difficult to evaluate due to its secrecy and refusal to cooperate with international agencies.[178] Israel remains the only country in the region to refuse to sign the Nuclear Non-Proliferation Treaty and the Biological and Toxin Weapons Convention and, along with Egypt, the only one still to sign the Chemical Weapons Convention. Israel allows no inspections by the International Atomic Energy Agency and has not signed the Joint Convention on the Safety of Spent Fuel Management or the Joint Convention on the Safety of Radioactive Waste Management. Israel ranked a lowly twenty-fifth out of thirty-two countries in the Nuclear Threat Initiative's 2012 Nuclear Materials Security Index, largely due to its lack of transparency.[179] The 2011 Fukushima nuclear disaster in Japan is a stark reminder of the threat to millions of people posed by Israel's unregulated nuclear activities.

Is It Working?

When Israel launched its rebranding campaign in 2005, the central concept was that it would "win supporters only if it is seen as relevant and modern rather than only as a place of fighting and religion."[180] The more recent anti-delegitimization blitz spearheaded by the Reut Institute built on this idea and led to aggressive efforts to suppress and sabotage Palestinian solidarity groups around the world while promoting Israel as a progressive and technologically advanced "Western" nation in a region of Arab and Muslim backwardness. As we have seen, the Reut Institute emphasized that the highest-value targets were liberal and progressive constituencies.

Yet Israel, already one of the world's most negatively viewed countries, has seen its tattered reputation sink even lower. The 2012 Country Ratings Poll, conducted by GlobeScan/PIPA for the BBC World Service, asked more than twenty-four thousand people around the world to rate whether the influence of each of sixteen countries and the EU was "mostly positive" or "mostly negative." As in previous years, the most negatively rated countries were Iran, Pakistan, Israel, and North Korea. This is precisely *not* the company Israel's image strategists want it to keep. But the news got even worse, according to the report:

> Evaluations of Israel's influence in the world—already largely unfavorable in 2011—have worsened in 2012. On average, in the 22 tracking countries surveyed both in 2011 and 2012, 50 per cent of respondents have negative views of Israel's influence in the world, an increase of three points from 2011. The proportion of respondents giving Israel a favorable rating remains stable, at 21 per cent. Out of 22 countries polled in 2011, 17 lean negative, three lean positive, and two are divided.[181]

Apart from the US, in only two other countries, Kenya and Nigeria, did views of Israel lean positive. Everywhere else, the news was unremittingly bad. Negative views of Israel were 74 percent in Spain (up eight points) and 65 percent in France (up nine points), while positive ratings remained "low and steady." In Germany and the UK, negative ratings remained "very high and stable." Views of Israeli influence worsened significantly in Australia (65 percent, up seven points) and Canada (59 percent, up seven points)—a finding that indicates that public opinion is sharply out of step with official government policy. Both countries, especially Canada, have adopted ever more pro-Israel policies in recent years. Israel's image also made no headway among emerging powers, with negative attitudes recording increases among the Chinese, Indians, and Russians as well as across Latin America. Israel's global popularity sank even further in 2013, according to the following year's BBC survey, with favorability ratings in Germany and Spain plummeting, for the first time, into single digits.[182] "It doesn't matter what we do," Netanyahu declared in frustrated reaction to the poll. "Because it's not about the facts, it's about the defamation of Israel and our portrayal as peace rejecters, war mongers instead of an enlightened nation that is fighting against aims to destroy us."[183] The prime minister, like many other Israelis, continued to believe that all Israel had was an image problem, and that world publics were just stubbornly refusing to get the message.

Israel could take some comfort from results in the United States: half of Americans had a favorable view of Israel in 2012, up by seven points. Negative ratings dropped six points to 35 percent—the most positive views of Israel in the US since tracking began in 2005—though there was barely any improvement the following year. The United States remained the only Western country surveyed by the BBC with overall favorable attitudes toward Israel, underscoring why the Israel lobby sees it as the main battleground in securing long-term support for Israel. Indeed, surveys over many years have consistently shown that about half of Americans say they sympathize more with Israel, while only about 10 to 20 percent have expressed a stronger sympathy with Palestinians.[184] Those headline numbers should be reassuring to Israel, but some underlying trends less so. The 2012 US presidential election was characterized by politicians—especially President Obama—expressing ever more support for Israel in ever more abject and unconditional terms, with Obama boasting of how his administration had pledged more military aid to Israel than any before it. Yet here, too, elites appear increasingly out of step with significant segments of public opinion, particularly the coveted liberal-progressive constituencies identified by the Reut Institute.

On the eve of the 2012 election, 26 percent of Americans thought their government was too supportive of Israel, while 24 percent thought it not supportive enough, according to the Pew Research Center.[185] The number of those wanting to see more support for Israel rose to 46 percent among Republicans, while just

13 percent of Republicans thought the United States already gave Israel too much support. Among Democratic voters, the result was dramatically different: one-quarter thought the United States gave too much support to Israel, while just 9 percent thought it wasn't enough. Among "liberal" Democrats, only 33 percent said they were more sympathetic to Israel, while 22 percent said they sympathized more with the Palestinians—a much smaller gap than in the public at large. Almost one-third of liberal Democrats thought the United States gave too much support to Israel and just 3 percent said it was not enough. Given that the multiethnic, multicultural demographic that tends to vote Democratic is widely seen as ascendant, these are significant differences that may presage a long-term erosion of support for Israel. Notably, age differences matter more in how Israel is viewed: in the US population as a whole, 58 percent among those over age fifty sympathized more with Israel than the Palestinians. That figure dropped to just 38 percent of people under age thirty.[186]

Israel is viewed favorably among Americans compared to, say, Palestinians and some Arab and Muslim-majority nations that have been consistently demonized and defined as enemies, but its image is not spectacular when considered in the context of the ritual professions of unique and undying friendship and "shared values" spouted by American politicians. While just 10 percent of Americans had overall favorable views of Iran and 20 percent had favorable views of the Palestinian Authority (since "Palestine" is a forbidden concept), Israel enjoyed favorable ratings among 67 percent of Americans in 2010, according to Gallup.[187] But this was only slightly ahead of India and well behind Japan, Germany, Great Britain, and the most favorably viewed nation, Canada, at 90 percent. And while only 6 percent of Americans held unfavorable views of Canada, one-quarter viewed India and Israel unfavorably.[188]

A precedent that Israel-lobby officials may be eyeing nervously is the dramatic change in public attitudes toward same-sex marriage over a period of just a decade. A once-overwhelming majority against state recognition of such unions has melted since 2001; those supporting same-sex marriage outnumbered opponents by 49 to 44 percent by 2013. The rapid shift has been led by the "millennial generation" born after 1980.[189] Could similar, equally unthinkable changes transform how Israel is seen in the United States over the next decade? This is clearly what Israel advocacy organizations fear, which is why they are trying so hard to hitch Israel's image to progressive-identified causes such as LGBTQ rights.

The mediocre results of Israel's propaganda campaigns have caused disquiet among those leading them. Already in 2005, Jennifer Laszlo Mizrahi, founder of the Israel Project, an advocacy group with a twenty-million-dollar annual budget, presciently warned that trying to rebrand Israel and change the focus from the "conflict" with the Palestinians would not be enough. "Until there is peace we have to be dealing with the stories that the media is most interested in," Mizrahi had said. "There are still 400 permanently stationed reporters in Jerusalem. They didn't come to do a story about Israel beyond the conflict. You can't pretend that it's otherwise."[190] Although the Reut Institute strongly emphasizes "Brand Israel" strategies along with sabotage of the opposition, even it has paid lip service to the need for "an Israeli and Palestinian comprehensive Permanent Status Agreement that establishes a Palestinian state" and a "credible and persistent commitment for full integration and equality of Israel's Arab citizens" as part of a strategy to undermine the "delegitimizers."[191] Thus even the Reut Institute has tacitly conceded that resistance to Israel is based in genuine and justifiable grievances and the denial of Palestinian rights, not mere irrational hatred or insufficient knowledge about Israel's supposed achievements in gay rights and solar panels.

Kenneth Stern, the American Jewish Committee's "director on anti-Semitism and extremism," judged that the Israel lobby could be proud of its tactical successes in beating back church divestment and marshaling the support of university presidents against campus divestment initiatives. He dismissed Caterpillar's removal from the Social Investment Index as "isolated" and "near-meaningless."[192] Even in the face of the embarrassing legal defeat of the StandWithUs-backed lawsuit, he belittled the Olympia Food Co-op boycott as a decision by a single store to "remove Israeli ice cream cones, crackers, chocolate bars, baby wipes and hand sanitizers from its shelves." Yet Stern maintains that the BDS movement remains dangerous. The danger is not in economic damage to Israel but the potential of BDS to turn Israel into a "pariah" by allowing Palestinians to define the key issues. "BDS can change the perception of Israel by creating space for respectable people to have calm debates about the 'merits' of a world without a Jewish state," Stern warned. Put another way, the danger to Israel is that BDS is successfully shifting the focus of debate and action back to where it belongs: the urgent need to end Israel's systematic denial of Palestinian rights. Even worse from Stern's perspective, it is giving Palestinians a voice.

Israel's government also remains worried and is not giving up. Netanyahu announced in June 2013 that he had placed overall responsibility for the fight against "delegitimization" in the hands of the Ministry of Strategic Affairs, "including the coordination of efforts with [nongovernmental organizations] in Israel and all over the world."[193] Netanyahu's announcement came just weeks after the foreign ministry hosted a conference aimed at stepping up anti-BDS efforts. Calling for "enhanced intelligence capabilities," the conference action plan stated, "We need to have more information about the organizations promoting delegitimization, including their membership, funding and planned activities." The conference called for more intense lobbying, more "lawfare" (i.e., the use of courts or the legal system in an attempt to criminalize or repress legitimate advocacy), and stepped-up media campaigns. Returning to the Reut Institute's old favorite, the plan asserted, "Nations, foundations and other funders supporting BDS should be named and shamed."[194]

Israel's recent aggressive efforts to counter BDS have included "covert" efforts, revealed separately by the *Electronic Intifada* and *Haaretz*, to train and pay Israeli students to post favorable propaganda on social networks such as Facebook and Twitter as well as placing staff in its foreign embassies dedicated to countering Palestine solidarity activism. Some of these programs have been run directly out of the prime minister's office.[195] The National Union of Israeli Students and academic institutions have partnered in these government-led propaganda initiatives.[196] In one of the early versions of this tactic, during Operation Cast Lead, Israel raised what *Ynet* termed an "army of comment posters."[197] Based at a round-the-clock "war room" at the Interdisciplinary Center at Herzliya, a private university, "1,600 multilingual students, mostly foreign students who were studying in Israel at the time, commented on major news websites," countering what they perceived as unjustified criticism of Israel. "Three teams focused on posting comments to websites in 34 languages and 61 countries, and reached, they estimate, 20 million computer screens," *Ynet* reported. The Electronic Frontier Foundation's Jillian C. York, a well-known commentator on Internet freedom, said Israel's government-led farming of favorable opinion resembled online propaganda efforts by several repressive regimes. "When a state—be it Bahrain, Israel, Syria or China—needs to stoop to the level of paying citizens to fight its public relations wars, it has already lost," York observed.[198]

Indeed, for all the millions spent on promoting their cause, it has been impossible for Israel and its surrogates to hone a message that they are genuinely interested in peace or that the two-state solution they claim to want can win new supporters. Israel's clear priorities have been accelerating the colonization of the occupied West Bank and limiting the amount of space available to Palestinians, using whatever means are necessary to further these goals. High-profile support for the boycott, such as world-renowned physicist Stephen Hawking publicly pulling out of Israel's 2013 presidential conference, demonstrate that despite Israel's formidable counterattack, the arguments and strategies of the Palestinian campaign are resonating ever more widely. While Netanyahu and professional Israel advocates like Stern project the blame onto the BDS movement, Israel has succeeded in delegitimizing itself, especially with the liberal and progressive constituencies whose support it craves. As Omar

Barghouti put it, the BDS movement "has dragged Israel and its well-financed, bullying lobby groups into a confrontation on a battlefield where the moral superiority of the Palestinian quest for self-determination, justice, freedom, and equality neutralizes and outweighs Israel's military power and financial prowess."[199] In no theater has this battle been more fierce or have Israel advocates been more bullying and ruthless than on university campuses.

Chapter 6

The War on Campus

American public support for Israel remains strong, but the "growing cracks" in that support are most evident on campus, according to the David Project, and universities across America form "the leading venue for anti-Israel activity and the spread of anti-Israelism."[1] The case for working to stop this dangerous trend is clear: universities are not only "where the thinking of America's future political leadership is molded" but also "where the worldview of a large swath of influential people outside of the political class as well as the population at large is largely formed."[2] These warnings are contained in the David Project's 2012 white paper, *A Burning Campus? Rethinking Israel Advocacy at America's Universities and Colleges.* This document can be seen as the university-focused counterpart of the Reut Institute's blueprint for suppressing Palestine solidarity activism and criticism of Israel more broadly. The David Project, a four-million-dollar-per-year organization focusing on Zionist advocacy on campuses, was founded in 2002 and became notorious in the early 2000s for its witch hunt against Columbia University professor Joseph Massad as well as its aggressively Islamophobic rhetoric.[3] Under new leadership, the group has entered the mainstream of Israel advocacy in the United States and now boasts partners including AIPAC, the Hasbara Fellowships, Hillel, Scholars for Peace in the Middle East, the Jewish Federation of New York, and Taglit–Birthright Israel, the organization that sends thousands of young North American Jews on free trips to Israel and the occupied Palestinian territories.

The white paper criticizes earlier approaches to suppressing Palestine solidarity activism and academic inquiry related to Israel on campus, and lays out a new framework. The old approach involved confronting and debating. The new strategy, directly inspired by the Reut Institute, emphasizes making friends and influencing people. Surprisingly, the paper demolishes the notion, long promoted by Zionist groups, that American college campuses are rife with anti-Semitism. "Most American campuses are not hostile environments for most Jewish students," the paper acknowledges.[4] "Racial antisemitism of the kind most associated with the Nazis is not likely a serious problem on any American college campus." Claiming otherwise "does not jive with the lived experience of many Jewish students, who know they can identify as Jews and largely not suffer repercussions."[5] Consequently, "depicting campus as hostile to Jews has not to date proven to be an effective strategy for decreasing anti-Israelism."[6] For anyone committed to the struggle against racism in any form, the lack of anti-Semitism on campus can only be good news. But for Zionist organizations it makes the campus environment a more challenging, though no less central, battleground. To solve the problem posed by the absence of anti-Semitism, the David Project has promoted a new term, "anti-Israelism," which it describes as "a specific form of bigotry targeted against the modern state of Israel."[7] This redefinition—as we shall see—is a crucial element in the effort to restrict campus discussions of Israel's racist practices or its claim to have a right to exist as a Jewish state.

In the rest of the world, where Israel is generally unpopular, pro-Israel advocates are fighting to halt efforts to turn it into an "international pariah akin to apartheid South Africa."[8] But in the United States, where support for Israel is much broader, the David Project argues, the "battle" is to "maintain long-term two-party support. It's not good enough that we stop the US from becoming anti-Israel. We have to make sure the US remains pro-Israel."[9] Yet the analysis predicts "long-term bipartisan support for a strong relationship between Israel and the United States cannot be assured if the environments of key universities and colleges are largely negative toward the Jewish state." Simply put, allowing higher education to continue "in a milieu of pervasive negativity toward Israel by further generations of students may significantly weaken long-term American government support for the Jewish state." A related danger is that "anti-Israelism" would spread since the university "often serves as an incubator for social trends that go on to have a wide impact in society at large."[10] These are high stakes.

Among key reasons the David Project lists for why US campuses have become so dangerous for Israel is "financial support from Arab autocrats"—a claim taken from Zionist polemicist Martin Kramer's book *Ivory Towers on Sand*, published by the Washington Institute for Near East Studies, an AIPAC-affiliated think tank.[11] It is true that a number of Arab governments, including Kuwait, Saudi Arabia, the United Arab Emirates, Qatar, and Oman, have endowed chairs or made gifts to prestigious universities, but these are without exception conservative regimes closely allied with the United States, many of them hosting US military bases. Often the motive for such gifts is to improve the donor's standing with the US establishment. The assertion that such "Arab" money has promoted "anti-Israelism" ironically mirrors conspiracy theories about the outsized influence of "Jewish money." Money, however, is not the main target of the David Project, which identifies four "primary trends" that must be tackled if the dire situation is to be turned around. These are "a long-standing campus predilection toward relativism, postmodernism, and the views of the global left"; "the promotion of anti-Israelism by professors"; "Jewish student apathy and ignorance"; and "the unwillingness of administrators to treat anti-Israelism in the same manner as they treat other forms of bigotry."[12]

It would take several volumes to document all the instances of the Israel lobby attempting to suppress criticism of Israel on campus—something far beyond the scope of this chapter. Yet these supposed "trends" provide a useful framework to understand some of the tactics that have been used—some but not necessarily all practiced or advocated by the David Project itself—to cultivate and co-opt "influencers" and "campus celebrities" whom Israel lobby groups identify as key potential allies. These include witch hunts and attacks on individual professors; using criminal and civil legal proceedings to define protest and criticism of Israel as "bigotry" or hate speech; fostering Islamophobia and other forms of intimidation and bullying; and "positive" strategies—similar to pinkwashing and greenwashing. Yet despite all these tactics, which have at times taken a hard toll on individual students and faculty, campus Palestine solidarity movements continue to grow and forge promising new alliances.

Just like the Reut Institute's analysis, the David Project sees the war on critics of Israel as a war on the left more broadly. The white paper argues that campus has long been used by "a segment of ideologically committed faculty and graduate students to promote radical left politics, within which the Palestinian cause is increasingly popular."[13] The university is also the "most likely mainstream venue in American society to reflect the trends of the global left, absorbing the ethos of the United Nations and related international organizations, as well as human-rights organizations like Amnesty International and Human Rights Watch, all of which have long histories of undue focus" on Israel.[14] This dangerous receptivity to the human-rights values developed in the wake of the horrors of the Second World War and the Holocaust is only made worse by the ideological flaws of university faculties: "By overwhelming percentages, professors self-identify on the left of the political spectrum," the David Project asserts. It also faults "a bias against Western views of history and social progress, seeking to empower voices perceived to be on the margins of history." This assertion echoes the critique University of Chicago professor Alan Bloom made in his influential 1987 book *The Closing of the American Mind,* which faulted the abandonment of canonical "Western" thought for opening the universities to 1960s radicalism and cultural relativism. Bloom's thesis became the rallying cry for the Reagan-era conservative attack on universities that has continued to the present. Because "Israel defines itself and is defined as a part of the West," the David Project claims, "this kind of thinking also lends itself to a bias against Israel and Israeli perspectives."[15] In other words, universities that foster respect for human rights and international law, teach students to think critically, and encourage them to seek out marginalized voices and narratives, represent a grave danger to Israel. Although this threat might arise anywhere, the David Project singles out Columbia University and the University of California, Berkeley, as examples of universities that "can serve as the most important and influential node" in the "anti-Israel" network. These campuses have been targets of relentless attacks from various Zionist groups. While downplaying its broader influence, the David Project also gives special mention to Rachel Corrie's alma mater, Evergreen State College in Olympia, Washington, as a place where "anti-Israelism is intense and theatrical."[16]

Not all academic disciplines represent an equal threat to Israel in the eyes of the David Project. The most dangerous are the humanities and social sciences, alleged hotbeds of radicalism and leftism. The white paper predicts that a long-term decline in these disciplines and the rise of business and economics departments, whose faculty tend to be more politically "balanced," is likely to be beneficial to Israel.[17] The popularity of business schools also provides an opportunity for Israel to be marketed as a high-tech "startup nation," and the David Project notes that some business schools "offer special-themed courses and trips to Israel, sometimes after students take a longer course focusing on Israel's business history and climate."[18] The David Project also sees another promising development in the rise of for-profit colleges, which tend to offer majors focused on employment skills, especially among students of disadvantaged socioeconomic backgrounds. The fact that the for-profit education industry has offered poor education at high cost, often preying on financially vulnerable students, is not mentioned as a concern.[19] These "emerging campus trends" offer Israel advocates a strategic opportunity since narrowly vocational or business-focused majors "are not generally concerned with political issues, making the introduction of anti-Israel narratives into course work less likely, whatever the proclivity of individual professors."[20] If teaching critical thinking, fostering respect for human-rights values, and nurturing the humanities and social sciences are dangers to Israel, then dumbing down and privatizing education is good for the Jewish state.

Targeting Teachers

The David Project is explicit that university teachers must be a primary target of Israel-lobby campaigns: "In the long-term, efforts must be made to limit the ability of faculty members to use their positions to propagandize against the Jewish state."[21] But while longer-term strategies are formulated and take effect, the white paper is shockingly frank about what is to be done now:

> In the interim, accusing faculty members who propagandize against Israel of "academic malpractice" is likely to be a much more effective strategy than challenging specific allegations or invoking anti-Jewish bigotry. Rightly or wrongly, the current campus atmosphere is much more sympathetic to charges that teachers are not satisfactorily teaching their subject than to complaints of anti-Jewish bias and Israel supporters will likely have a greater practical impact by framing their concerns in this manner.[22]

It must be remembered that "propaganda" in the minds of the paper's authors includes any teaching that deviates from established "Western" narratives or "seek[s] to empower voices perceived to be on the margins of history." To make an analogy, anti-American propaganda by this standard would include encouraging students to hear and explore the voices of Tecumseh, Black Hawk, Sojourner Truth, Harriet Tubman, and Malcolm X alongside the words and deeds of white, slave-owning, land-conquering "Founding Fathers." "Propaganda" would also include allowing any criticism of Israel's 2008–2009 attack on Gaza, or as the David Project describes it, "Operation Cast Lead and other military efforts to combat terrorism"—and of course any discussion at all of Israel's claim to have a "right" to be a Jewish state. [23]

Alarmed by the United States government's post–September 11, 2001, antiterrorism crackdown and its effect on academic freedom, the Ad Hoc Committee to Defend the University warned:

> In recent years, universities across the country have been targeted by outside groups seeking to influence what is taught and who can teach. To achieve their political agendas, these groups have defamed scholars, pressured administrators, and tried to bypass or subvert established procedures of academic governance. As a consequence, faculty have been denied jobs or tenure, and scholars have been denied public platforms from which to share their viewpoints.[24]

One of the authors of this statement was Jonathan R. Cole, the former provost and dean of the faculty at Columbia University. In his magisterial book *The Great American University,* Cole recounts many of the efforts to curtail free speech and academic inquiry at universities across the country, especially Columbia, and notes that they have often been focused on silencing critical inquiry, teaching, and speech about Israel. Edward Said, who spent his career as one of Columbia's most recognized professors, was a frequent magnet for vilification campaigns, often goaded on by public officials and the media, demanding that he be fired whenever he made a statement in support of the Palestinian people. "Until Said's death in 2003, however, the university stood fast in defending his right to voice his opinions in his books and speeches," Cole observes.[25]

In the face of more sustained attacks over the decade after Said's death, the university has been less firm. Cole summarizes the battle over the tenure of Professor Joseph Massad:

> The tenure case of Joseph Massad at Columbia took years to be decided. He was finally granted tenure in June 2009. Massad, a professor of modern Arab politics and intellectual history, has published three books with highly reputable publishers and more than a score of peer-reviewed articles. His scholarship received overwhelmingly favorable evaluations by some twenty scholars in his field or in related fields who were asked to evaluate his work, and he has a stellar teaching record, at least as judged by the course evaluations of his students. Even when nobody loses his or her job, these assaults take a toll. As Massad explained on his website in 2005: "With this campaign against me going into its fourth year, I chose under the duress of coercion and intimidation not to teach my course [Palestinian and Israeli Politics and Societies] this year." Despite all of his accomplishments, Massad continues to be vilified and demonized in the press, where the quality of his work as judged by peers—and even an accurate account of its content—is never referenced.[26]

A major component of the vilification campaign against Columbia faculty was a 2004 documentary produced by the David Project, *Columbia Unbecoming,* in which students alleged that Massad and other faculty had intimidated and abused those who disagreed with their critical views on Israel and had made anti-Semitic remarks in class. The campaign had high-level support from Congressman Anthony Weiner, then still a rising star before his eventual fall from grace in a lewd-photo scandal. Weiner wrote to Columbia University president Lee Bollinger to demand that Massad be fired.[27] It could not have helped that the New York City Council also called for an "independent investigation" into the allegations made in *Columbia Unbecoming* at a time when the university was working to win its approval for a massive and controversial campus expansion into the Harlem neighborhood. "Columbia has reached the point that there really has to be some serious housecleaning," Michael Nelson, chairman of the council's Jewish Caucus, warned.[28] Faced with pressure on all fronts, Bollinger turned to the influential public relations firm Howard J. Rubenstein & Associates to assuage those accusing the university of coddling anti-Semites, as well as to lobby for approval of the campus expansion. Part of Bollinger's campaign included meeting "personally with dozens of Jewish and Israeli leaders in meetings arranged or facilitated" by Rubenstein.[29]

In response to the allegations in *Columbia Unbecoming*, Bollinger decided, after consultation with Nick Dirks, vice president for arts and sciences, to convene a faculty investigative committee.[30] As the three-month-long inquiry proceeded, so did the campaign of fearmongering and vilification. After *Columbia Unbecoming* was screened for Israeli audiences, Natan Sharansky, Israel's minister for "diaspora affairs" and intellectual guru to President George W. Bush, declared that Columbia and other US campuses were "islands of anti-Semitism." Sharansky said he feared "that the future leaders of American Jewry are becoming Jews of silence" as a result of the intimidation they supposedly faced.[31] When the investigative committee's report was released in March 2005, it concluded that the allegations were unsubstantiated and that there was no evidence of anti-Semitism. The committee nonetheless recommended that the university revamp its grievance procedures, an apparent concession to those who had leveled false and politically motivated charges. Even the *New York Times*, which was sympathetic to the view that alleged "anti-Israeli bias" at Columbia needed to be investigated, had to concede that "there is no evidence that anyone's grade suffered for challenging the pro-Palestinian views of any teacher or that any professors made anti-Semitic statements. The professors who were targeted have legitimate complaints themselves. Their classes were infiltrated by hecklers and surreptitious monitors, and they received hate mail and death threats."[32] Yet the results of the inquiry did not discourage those who made the accusations, and the campaign against Massad grinds on.

The controversy also had serious reverberations years later, when Columbia's Nick Dirks was named in November 2012 as chancellor-designate of the University of California, Berkeley. The UC Berkeley news office published a video interview with Dirks, "recorded shortly before the Regents approved his appointment," in which he attacked Columbia.[33] Singling out the Middle East studies department, Dirks claimed it had been "very difficult" for "some students to find safe spaces in which to talk about Israel where they didn't feel that the basic context in which they found themselves wasn't hugely not just anti-Israel, but by implication, anti-Jewish, and anti-Semitic." Dirks touted the role he played in the witch hunt against Massad. "It was my responsibility as the executive vice president for the arts and sciences" to convene "an unprecedented faculty committee to look into some of the allegations that had been made." He also repudiated a petition he had signed in 2002 calling for divestment from Boeing, Lockheed Martin, and other companies that supplied military hardware used by Israel against Palestinians. "Truth is, I do not support divestment as a strategy for the university. I don't support divestment with respect to Israel," Dirks affirmed. The implication was that Israel's most ardent supporters at UC Berkeley had nothing to fear from him, and that students advocating Palestinian rights—who have faced constant harassment and legal threats—would not be able to count on his protection any more than UC Irvine students would be able to count on their chancellor, as we shall see.

Dirks's comments stirred outrage among his former colleagues at Columbia. Fourteen members of the faculty of the Department of Middle Eastern, South Asian, and African Studies, including Massad, published a letter condemning him. "Our sense of outrage stems from Dirks' denial of the fact that the very committee set up by then–Vice President Dirks found no evidence whatever for concerns about the climate for Jewish students let alone about the nature of instruction in our department," the letter stated.[34] "We feel affronted by the fact that the Chancellor's defaming the department means that he now rejects the committee's finding and seems instead to accept as true the false accusations leveled against us by an external hate group that has since been exposed and discredited." But this kind of public declaration of fealty to Israel and denunciation of former colleagues as anti-Semites seemed, at least in Dirks's calculations, to be the price of admission to high office at the University of California. It also sent a message that faculty could not count on support from administrators should they come under attack.

In addition to Massad, other professors teaching Middle East studies have been subjected to "malicious attacks that are limited to their views on Middle East politics" rather than objections to their scholarship.[35] Norman Finkelstein was denied tenure at Chicago's DePaul University in 2007 after Harvard law professor and outspoken Israel advocate Alan Dershowitz conducted a high-profile campaign against him alleging various faults with his work.[36] Finkelstein had long been a lightning rod for pro-Israel groups due to his outspoken criticism of Israeli policies. Nevertheless, his department's faculty voted to give him tenure based on its evaluation of his scholarship and record, a decision unanimously endorsed by the college-level tenure committee. The university administration, however, took the unusual step of overruling those decisions, denying Finkelstein tenure not due to shortcomings in his scholarship but on vague grounds that he lacked collegiality.[37] The Illinois Conference of the American Association of University Professors (IL-AAUP) condemned DePaul's decision and the use of "collegiality" as a criterion in Finkelstein's and one other case as violating the association's standards as well as DePaul's own faculty handbook. "It appears likely that Professor Finkelstein was denied tenure," the IL-AAUP stated, "at least in part, due to the controversy generated by his publications and the extraordinary public-media blitz campaign that was waged by Professor Alan M. Dershowitz."[38] Finkelstein ultimately resigned under a settlement with the university, calling the decision to deny him tenure a "bitter blow." Although the university insisted it wasn't the case, Finkelstein concluded, "The only inference that I can draw is that I was denied tenure due to external pressures climaxing in a national hysteria that tainted the tenure process."[39]

As well as targeting individuals, Zionist advocates have also tried to dictate what students can and can't read or hear, often with the support of local politicians and media. In August 2010, Brooklyn College, of the City University of New York, assigned a book by one of its professors, Moustafa Bayoumi, to its incoming class—part of its effort to give students a wide range of perspectives on New York and immigrant-related experiences. "Everything was fine until about a week before classes began," Bayoumi recalled. "That's when the chair of my department called me to report that the college had received a small number of complaints from alumni and an emeritus faculty member about the selection. She assured me that the college was standing by its decision."[40] Bayoumi hoped the matter would fade, "but within days, tabloid news media had grabbed the issue from the right-wing blogosphere. Articles appeared in New York's *Daily News*, *The Jewish Week*, and *Gothamist* and were picked up by the *Huffington Post* and *New York Magazine*" among many others, frequently distorting and outright fabricating allegations about what was in the book. The volume, *How Does It Feel to Be a Problem? Being Young and Arab in America* (2008), tells the stories of seven young Arab American men and women living in Brooklyn and coping in a post–9/11 world.

The "tempest" began, Bayoumi says, "when Bruce Kesler, a conservative California-based blogger who is a Brooklyn College alumnus, labeled me a 'radical pro-Palestinian' professor in one of his posts and called the book's selection an 'official policy to inculcate students with a political point of view.'" Kesler had threatened to cut Brooklyn College out of his will. Bayoumi attributed the storm in part to the upsurge of Islamophobia, especially the manufactured controversy stoked by right-wing groups over a planned Islamic Center in downtown Manhattan. But it no doubt also stemmed from the fact that he had edited *Midnight on the Mavi Marmara*, a book that appeared just months after Israel's lethal May 2010 assault on the Gaza-bound flotilla.

Media-fueled uproar returned once again to Brooklyn College in early 2013 when the college hosted a presentation by Omar Barghouti and University of California, Berkeley, philosophy professor Judith Butler, sponsored by Students for

Justice in Palestine with the support of the political science department. The uproar was led by New York state assemblyman Dov Hikind, a former acolyte of Kach founder Meir Kahane and a former leader of the Jewish Defense League, the extreme anti-Arab organization implicated in bombings and a group that the FBI characterized as a "violent extremist Jewish organization."[41] Hikind demanded the resignation of Brooklyn College president Karen Gould over her institution's alleged support for "a racist, anti-Semitic" event.[42] Some two dozen elected officials, including some supposed "progressives" such as Congressman Jerry Nadler, Congressman Hakeem Jeffries, and City Council speaker Christine Quinn, threatened that Brooklyn College's public funding could be at risk if it didn't rescind its support. But this time it looked like the tide had started to turn against the familiar bully tactics. New York mayor Michael Bloomberg affirmed that he "violently" disagreed with the BDS movement, but nonetheless ridiculed those making the threats. "If you want to go to a university where the government decides what kind of subjects are fit for discussion, I suggest you apply to a school in North Korea," the mayor said in a stinging rebuke. "The last thing we need is for members of our City Council or State Legislature to be micromanaging the kinds of programs that our public universities run and base funding decisions on the political views of professors."[43] The uproar even prompted the *New York Times* editorial board to lament—ironically, given its own ideological blinders—that "too often in the United States, supporting Israel has come to mean meeting narrow ideological litmus tests."[44] Following these reactions, several officials backed off from their funding threats and the event went ahead.[45] After the event, Brooklyn College also rejected politically motivated charges of alleged anti-Semitism by the student organizers.[46] It was an important victory that publicly exposed the Israel lobby as being on the wrong side of the free-speech debate.

In 2011 Shurat HaDin, an Israeli legal advocacy group partially funded by American evangelical preacher John Hagee, founder of Christians United for Israel, sent "warning letters" to hundreds of presidents of colleges and universities in the United States "instructing them of their legal obligations to prevent anti-Semitism on campus."[47] The letters were supposedly prompted by "an alarming number of incidents of harassment and hate crimes against Jewish and Israeli students on US college campuses." Shurat HaDin founder and director Nitsana Darshan-Leitner claimed that "anti-Israel rallies and events frequently exceed legitimate criticism of Israel and cross the line into blatant anti-Semitism, resulting in hateful attacks against Jews." The letter also warned universities "of their legal obligation to monitor the funding and activities of all on-campus student groups" and "that by failing to do so, they could unwittingly fall foul of stringent US legislation." The *Jerusalem Post* report about Shurat HaDin's initiative cited as an example a decision by the student assembly of Rutgers University in New Jersey to make a donation to the Palestine Children's Relief Fund (PCRF), a well-respected, nonpolitical charity based in the United States that provides medical care to individual Palestinian children and supports the development of pediatric medical facilities in Palestine. Without providing any evidence, the *Jerusalem Post* cited claims that PCRF had "close ties to Islamic charity the Holy Land Foundation, which funds Hamas." Raising money for heart surgery for Palestinian children was apparently one of the dangerous "anti-Israel" campus activities that Shurat HaDin was determined to halt. But it also had faculty in its sights.

In April 2012, the Global Frontier Justice Center, an American front for Shurat HaDin, launched a public campaign against David Klein, a professor of mathematics at California State University, Northridge (CSUN), and wrote to the California attorney general demanding that Klein be investigated and prosecuted for misappropriating state funds and misusing the name of the university. His transgression was that his personal web page, hosted on a university server, included a list of links to organizations supporting the academic boycott of Israel.[48] Klein had already been a target of the AMCHA Initiative, a key player in the assault on academic freedom and freedom of speech in California, when he opposed the resumption of a study-in-Israel program. Klein argued that Israel's well-documented discrimination against American citizens of different ethnic backgrounds, including arbitrary denial of entry, would mean that the program could not be equally accessible to all students. Fortunately, the attorney general saw through the Global Frontier Justice Center's gambit, responding in a letter copied to Klein that "the evidence provided does not support a finding of misuse" of the university's "name and resources" and "we find no basis for any action on our part."[49]

It is reassuring that this assault was not successful from a legal standpoint, but there is no underestimating the personal stress such attacks cause to individuals or their broader chilling effect. Klein hopes his experience will encourage other faculty to overcome the fear of speaking out and praised the exceptionally strong support he received from his university's interim president, Harry Hellenbrand. In a public letter titled "*J'Accuse!* The New Anti-Semitism," Hellenbrand hit back at the campaign against Klein by the AMCHA Initiative and another Zionist group, Scholars for Middle East Peace, dismissing their accusations as "partisan and sectarian." "Invoking the apparatus of the state to proscribe broad categories of speech in hubs of innovation and disruption like public universities will have the paradoxical effect of chilling public exchange while heating up zealotry," Hellenbrand wrote.[50] If the AMCHA Initiative had its way, Hellenbrand feared, it would "eliminate nearly all political speech that had the slightest trace of public funding in higher education." Neither Hellenbrand nor Klein were aware, at the time those words were written, that Shurat HaDin's Darshan-Leitner had told US embassy officials in 2007 that her organization often decided who to go after based on tips and "evidence" passed on to her by Israeli intelligence. Originally founded in 2000 "to bankrupt Palestinian terrorist organizations as well as the PA" through aggressive legal action, Shurat HaDin has expanded its target list to go after college professors who voice opinions critical of Israel. The admission that Shurat HaDin acts, in effect, as a civilian front for the Israeli government was revealed in a US embassy cable released by WikiLeaks.[51]

The David Project claims to have moved away from its more confrontational and "shrill" approach since David Bernstein, previously the Washington director of the American Jewish Committee, became its director in 2010.[52] But in a surprisingly frank June 2011 article on the website *Israel Campus Beat* headlined "How to 'Name-And-Shame' Without Looking Like a Jerk," Bernstein revealed that under the new veneer of civility, the hard-nosed goals had not changed.[53] "While name-and-shame tactics can be put to positive effect, they can also easily backfire and do more harm than good," Bernstein warned. "We need to learn the art of being disagreeable in the most agreeable possible fashion." Among his tips for Israel advocates were such gems as: "Start every critique with supportive words for peace or free discourse or both" and "Don't accuse anti-Israel forces of anti-Semitism unless they openly vilify Jews; accuse them of being anti-peace for opposing Israel's right to exist." Foreshadowing what would appear in the David Project white paper, he advised, "In taking on an anti-Israel professor on campus, don't focus on the substantive arguments they make. That will make you look like you're trying to stifle discourse." Instead, Bernstein suggested, "accuse them . . . of 'academic malpractice' for propagandizing the classroom."

Intimidating Institutions

There is no place at any university for professors to physically or verbally assault students, to use epithets against them, or to coerce them into adopting particular viewpoints, former Columbia University provost Jonathan Cole sensibly observes. Students and employees alike should be protected from discrimination based on race, ethnicity, religion, sex, or sexual orientation. These prohibitions properly give rise to codes of conduct at universities and other places of work that allow victims to make grievances and to seek protection and redress. But, Cole warns, "the codes that place limits on conduct must never be directed at the content of ideas—however offensive they may be to students, faculty, alumni, benefactors or politicians." Cole accuses the David Project of doing precisely that by trying to "blur the distinction between speech and action" and accusing "professors of inappropriate action and intimidation when they are actually trying to attack the content of their ideas."[54] He also notes that most of the attacks have been leveled against social scientists and faculty in the humanities, the very disciplines singled out by the David Project's white paper as areas where most "anti-Israel" teaching allegedly takes place. The damage done by the assault on academic freedom will not be limited to those disciplines most targeted, he warns, but will harm everyone in the university community.[55]

There are disturbing parallels between the kinds of witch hunts against individuals suspected of anti-Israel views and the campaigns to root out alleged Communists during the 1940s and 1950s. Notwithstanding rare individuals like CSUN's Harry Hellenbrand, Cole laments that most universities then, as now, did not show great courage in standing up to intimidation by government and other outside groups, while some were actually complicit. The University of Washington's firing of three tenured professors accused of being Communists in 1949 had a devastating effect on academic freedom nationwide. The same year, the University of California began requiring professors to sign an "anticommunist disclaimer." When thirty-one professors refused to sign the oath, they were fired, even though it was acknowledged they were not Communists.[56] One of the rare exceptions to the complicity, a forceful defender of academic freedom and a public opponent of the anticommunist crusades, was Robert Maynard Hutchins, president of the University of Chicago from 1929 to 1951. "The question is not how many professors have been fired for their beliefs, but how many think they might be," Hutchins said in 1947. "The entire teaching profession is intimidated."[57] This can be updated: the question now is not how many professors have faced the Israel lobby's vilification campaigns, legal threats, and attempts to interfere with their careers and in what they can and can't teach inside the classroom and say or do outside it, but how many think they might be targeted if they don't self-censor when it comes to the topic of Palestine and the Israelis.

As noted, the David Project white paper is frank about the failure of Zionist groups' efforts to falsely portray US campuses as hotbeds of anti-Semitism and proposes the new term "anti-Israelism," which it defines in the following manner:

The key belief of anti-Israelism is that Israel is an illegitimate state with no moral claim to past, present, or continued existence under its own definition as a Jewish state. Anti-Israelism is usually, but not always, combined with longstanding anti-Jewish claims that the Jews are not a people, and therefore do not have the same rights (i.e. self-determination) as other peoples do. An "anti-Israelist" is a believer in anti-Israelism.[58]

As also noted earlier, the David Project defines "anti-Israelism" as "a specific form of bigotry targeted against the modern state of Israel." It follows, then, that any questioning of Zionism's political claims or the policies or practices of Israel necessary to maintain "its own definition as a Jewish state" is "bigotry" (see chapter 2). This would mean by extension that calling for full and equal rights for Palestinian citizens of Israel is bigotry; calling for Palestinian refugees to be allowed to exercise their right of return is bigotry; criticizing the Jewish National Fund's openly discriminatory land allocation policies is bigotry; and so on. "Jews are a people with a right to self-determination in their historic, ancestral homeland, a right expressed through the modern state of Israel," the white paper asserts. "Claims to the contrary, or that Israel cannot both define itself as a 'Jewish' state and a democracy that protects the rights of all of its citizens, are wrong and dangerous and therefore beyond the pale of reasonable debate."[59] The significance of this attempt to redefine substantive arguments and support for the rights of the Palestinian people as a form of hate speech should not be underestimated. In the absence of anti-Semitism, the David Project's goal is nothing less than to censor such discussions on campus by bringing them within the purview of disciplinary procedures normally reserved for cases of harassment, abuse, and discrimination.

The white paper faults university administrations, asserting that "currently many do not treat even the most shrill anti-Israelist rhetoric with the same seriousness as they treat other forms of bigotry." It concedes, "As with any form of bigotry, the precise boundaries between speech that represents fair if critical discourse about the Jewish state and unacceptable anti-Israel slander or unfair treatment of Israel supporters are difficult to precisely articulate. Nevertheless, a significant percentage of anti-Israel rhetoric does cross the line and would ideally be rendered socially unacceptable." There might be some comfort in recognizing that the David Project's insistence on redefining most debate about Zionism and Israel as bigotry—whether in the form of "anti-Israelism" or the more traditional and still widely deployed accusation of anti-Semitism—is a concession that Zionist advocates cannot win arguments. But irrespective of the term used, the goal remains the same: to stifle and censor discussion of Israel. These tactics have been aggressive and costly for students and faculty alike.

The attacks on speech and academic inquiry related to Israel should be seen in the broader context of the Bush administration's assault on the independence of universities in the years following the September 11, 2001, attacks. Cole notes two significant shifts: first, in contrast to the McCarthy period, the attacks are now spearheaded by private groups, albeit with strong government support; second, the primary target is increasingly the university as an institution, rather than an obsession with rooting out individual faculty suspected of disloyalty or thought crimes. Outside advocacy groups, Cole observes, "have long had the resources to lobby government figures, and to organize alumni and students, with the goal of generating public outrage and eventual pressure on the university to abandon some of its basic commitments." But during the Bush era, "they had a powerful voice in the White House and the ranks of their followers swelled, largely because of the 9/11 attacks and the fears of terrorism that came to the surface."[60] While McCarthy-style government-led witch hunts against faculty did not re-emerge in the Bush era, Cole argues that "if we shift our angle of vision from the individual to the institutional level, and focus on more subtle attacks on the structure of the university itself—and the principles of academic freedom and free inquiry—we can find a host of examples of attacks during the Bush years that may have been more harmful to the structure of universities than we found even in the McCarthy period."[61] The most damaging centered on the question of Palestine and often involved the collusion of members of Congress from both the Democratic and Republican parties, as well as targeting both public and private sources of support for academic research.

In 2002, the notorious anti-Palestinian, Islamophobic agitator Daniel Pipes and his group Middle East Forum set up the website Campus Watch, which encouraged students to act as "informants" on their professors. At one point Campus Watch published a "blacklist"—a term redolent of McCarthyism—of "professors who were purportedly supporters of Palestinian rights, were anti-Israel and against U.S. foreign policy in the Middle East."[62] The following year, Pipes, along with Martin Kramer, a former advisor to Israeli intelligence and the inspiration for much of the analysis in the David Project's white paper, and conservative commentator Stanley Kurtz convinced Congress to hold hearings into the content of the teaching at National Resource Centers funded by the federal government under Title VI of the Higher Education Act. These 125 multidisciplinary centers, linked with schools of public policy and international relations, exist at many of the country's leading private and public universities. The goal of the federal program supporting them, established after World War II, was to promote expertise about and knowledge of the languages of various regions of the world. Between 2011 and 2013, the federal government made grants to twenty such centers focusing on the Middle East. The congressional hearings Pipes, Kramer, and Kurtz instigated were prompted by allegations that the centers were "one-sided" and "biased" and that "they did not support US foreign policy objectives."[63] Kurtz went so far as to tell Congress that the centers were "anti-American."[64] At the time of the hearings, Zachary Lockman, then director of New York University's Hagop Kevorkian Center for Near Eastern Studies, one of the beneficiaries of Title VI funding, observed that the "priority of those behind this is defending Israel from any criticism. They understand that the universities are one of the few places where the debate and argument that take place cannot be heard in the media or anywhere else."[65] Kramer, Kurtz, and Pipes helped draft legislation that would have placed the curricula of the Title VI centers under the external control of a government-appointed board that would have included members of government "national security" agencies.[66] The legislation gained the support of Republicans and Democrats "attuned to anything that could be construed as anti-Israeli policy," but, amid pushback from the universities, the proposal for direct government control was dropped. Pipes, Kramer, and Kurtz did nevertheless succeed in influencing the reauthorization of the Higher Education Act, which now included a provision that international studies programs applying for federal funding must provide "an explanation of how the activities funded by the grant will reflect diverse perspectives and a wide range of views" and allow for "the systematic collection, analysis, and dissemination of data" to evaluate whether the former goal had been achieved.[67] In a context where these programs were accused of being "anti-Israel" and even "anti-American," words like "diversity" and "balance" are merely codes for inserting more pro-Israel content and imposing views less questioning of US foreign policy.

What Cole dubs "the most troubling case" of outside pressure to impose ideological positions on universities again focused on the question of Palestine. In 2003, the Jewish Telegraphic Agency published a series of articles by Edwin Black alleging that grants made by the Ford Foundation to support Palestinian nongovernmental organizations had been "misused" to fund "terrorism" and the distribution of "anti-Semitic" and "anti-Zionist" material. Some of the Palestinian organizations that had received funds participated in the 2001 United Nations conference on racism in Durban, South Africa, which was boycotted by the United States and Israel. But, Cole notes, Black's articles "did not present any evidence that the Ford Foundation had violated American laws or that its funds for Palestinian groups were being misused for support of 'terrorist' activities." Indeed, there was "not one piece of direct evidence that suggests that the flow of Ford dollars went to support 'terrorists,' unless [one] considers all Palestinian groups 'terrorist' supporters."[68] But the facts made no difference to the massive campaign that ensued as leaders of major Zionist organizations, including the American Jewish Committee, the Anti-Defamation

League, and the Conference of Presidents of Major American Jewish Organizations, denounced the Ford Foundation and demanded congressional investigations. This outcry triggered threats from Democratic congressman Jerrold Nadler, who circulated a petition signed by twenty colleagues demanding that the Ford Foundation stop funding "anti-Israel hate groups."[69]

The foundation, which had been "one of the few willing to endure criticism and still fund Palestinian groups," crumbled under pressure.[70] Ford admitted it had been wrong, even though the allegations were simply false, and "embraced 'advisors' from the Jewish organizations to help assess" its grants.[71] The fallout of the attack had a direct impact on universities because the Ford Foundation is also a major funder of their research. Capitulating to the Israel lobby groups, the foundation imposed a condition that universities receiving funding had to sign a letter including this statement: "By countersigning this grant letter, you agree that your organization will not promote or engage in violence, terrorism, bigotry or the destruction of any state, nor will it make sub-grants to any entity that engages in these activities."[72] The term "destruction of any state" is a clear indication that, even though it is not named, this policy is all about Israel. Zionist organizations routinely claim that any advocacy for Palestinian rights that calls for the implementation of international law on the right of return of refugees, or abolishing laws that privilege Jews at the expense of Palestinians, is tantamount to calling for the "destruction of Israel" or even, in the David Project's new definition, bigotry. Although nine universities objected and negotiated a separate deal with the Ford Foundation, Cole laments that the policy stood with little outcry overall.[73] Because of the Ford Foundation's size and influence, its imposition of content-related limitations on its grants was emulated by other major donors to university research, including the Rockefeller Foundation.[74]

In both the Higher Education Act and Ford Foundation cases, the freedom to engage in Palestine-related speech, research, and teaching came under direct, intense attack, but these attacks were also used as levers for a much broader assault on the independence of universities by individuals and organizations intent on curtailing dissent or critical inquiry related to US global power and hegemony. These incidents serve as warnings that any institution where uncensored speech about Palestine takes place may find itself at the center of a congressional and media storm accusing it of supporting anything ranging from "anti-Americanism" to "terrorism" and the "destruction of Israel."

Misusing Civil Rights Law to Censor Campus Activism

One of the celebrated achievements of the heroic people's struggle against Jim Crow and racism in the United States is the Civil Rights Act of 1964, abolishing official racial discrimination in the United States. Title VI of this landmark law (not to be confused with Title VI of the Higher Education Act, discussed above) prohibited discrimination in all federally funded programs on the basis of "race, color or national origin." The law imposes on responsible officials, including university and school administrators, the obligation to ensure that no such discrimination takes place on their campuses. In October 2010, after a concerted campaign by a dozen major communal Jewish organizations, including the Anti-Defamation League, the American Jewish Committee, Hillel, and the Zionist Organization of America, the Obama administration expanded its interpretation of Title VI to include the protection of religious groups.[75] The Office of Civil Rights (OCR) of the United States Department of Education, responsible for enforcing Title VI, announced the change in a public letter to educational institutions across the country.[76] On its face, this move might have been seen as a benefit not only for Jewish students but also Muslim students amid a rising crescendo of Islamophobia in the United States. It quickly became apparent, however, that the Civil Rights Act, born out of the struggle to end institutionalized racism, would now, perversely, be used as another weapon in the hands of anti-Palestinian bigots and would-be censors aiming to silence dissent against Israel's institutionalized racism against Palestinians.

In March 2011, the OCR announced its first official investigation of a complaint under the expanded definition of Title VI, lodged by Tammi Rossman-Benjamin, a lecturer in Hebrew, against her employer, the University of California, Santa Cruz (UC Santa Cruz). Oddly, the OCR investigation opened in 2011 was in response to a twenty-nine-page complaint Rossman-Benjamin, the cofounder of the AMCHA Initiative, had sent to the Department of Education in 2009, two years before the new Title VI policy was announced. American Muslims for Palestine, an advocacy group that organizes on campuses, challenged the OCR's retroactive application of the policy but received no replies to its requests for information.[77] Rossman-Benjamin's complaint made no bones about the fact that her concern was not really discrimination against Jews, but speech about Palestinian rights and criticism of Israel. As the *Chronicle of Higher Education* reported, the allegations included "several incidents in recent years in which [UC Santa Cruz] administrators rejected demands that the university drop its sponsorship of events focused on the Israeli-Palestinian conflict that she regarded as one-sided attacks on Israel and Zionism." Her 2009 complaint had asserted that "anti-Israel discourse and behavior in classrooms and at departmentally and college-sponsored events at [UC Santa Cruz] is tantamount to institutional discrimination against Jewish students, which has resulted in their intellectual and emotional harassment and intimidation." [78]

Among the first to welcome the UC Santa Cruz investigation was Kenneth L. Marcus, the director of the Institute for Jewish and Community Research's Initiative to Combat Anti-Semitism and Anti-Israelism in America's Educational Systems. The UC Santa Cruz investigation "is a really important signal from OCR that they may be taking their new approach to anti-Semitism as seriously as we wanted them to," he told the *Chronicle of Higher Education,* while cautioning, "There is still a big question as to how vigorously they will pursue cases that involve a mix of anti-Israelism and anti-Semitism." [79] Marcus, himself previously the head of OCR, has been the mastermind of and a major force in formulating the strategy of using the Civil Rights Act to suppress Palestine-related speech. He is also the head of the Legal Task Force for the pro-Israel group Scholars for Middle East Peace. The chilling effect of such assaults could also be felt at Rutgers University, the target of another Title VI complaint "alleging that the school fostered a hostile environment toward Jewish students." [80] University officials dismissed the complaints, but the attack on the university discouraged junior faculty from even discussing the Israeli-Palestinian conflict in class, according to Professor Charles G. Häberl, director of the Rutgers Center for Middle Eastern Studies from 2009 to 2012. "They are frightened to say anything about these issues, especially since they don't have the shield of tenure to hide behind. And I don't blame them." [81]

In July 2012, Jessica Felber and Brian Maissy, two former students at UC Berkeley, filed a Title VI complaint alleging that they had evidence of "a pervasive hostile environment towards Jews on the campus." The complaint asserted that Felber "was attacked and injured" by Husam Zakharia, the president of Students for Justice in Palestine (SJP), during Israeli Apartheid Week, when students had—as they had done on many other campuses—set up a mock checkpoint as a way to dramatize what life is like for Palestinians under Israeli occupation. Describing Israeli Apartheid Week "as a modern day version of the 'Passion Play,' the notorious anti-Semitic performance, initially performed at Oberammergau, Bavaria, which portrays Jews as bloodthirsty and treacherous villains," the complaint insisted that the "clear purpose of Apartheid Week is to delegitimize the existence of the State of Israel and to equate her with the system of government in place in South Africa between 1948 and 1993." [82] It also alleged that SJP "conspires and coordinates" with another Berkeley student organization, the Muslim Student Association (MSA), "which has a publicly documented history of affiliation with and support of organizations deemed 'terror organizations'" by the State Department. While offering no evidence of a physical assault on Felber or that the purported assault was motivated by her being Jewish, the complaint included a laundry list of inflammatory allegations against SJP. It claimed, for instance, that the MSA had "conducted a rally in support of Hamas, the Middle East extremist group," in 1995, when Felber and her alleged assailant would likely have been in kindergarten.

Felber's and Maissy's Title VI complaint was an almost-verbatim rehash of a 2011 lawsuit that the pair had filed in federal court, alleging that the University of California was responsible for the "anti-Semitic" environment supposedly created by the activities of SJP and the MSA because administrators had failed to act to curtail their activities. But as Palestine Legal Support, a project of the Center for Constitutional Rights, noted, the court dismissed the lawsuit in December 2011 during the earliest stage of the case, at which the judge "must assume that all allegations in the complaint are true."[83] The judge wrote that "a very substantial portion of the conduct to which [the complainants] object represents pure political speech and expressive conduct, in a public setting, regarding matters of public concern, which is entitled to special protection under the First Amendment."[84] In other words, the judge understood that Felber and Maissy were trying to sue the University of California for failing to crack down on free speech critical of Israel.

Felber's and Maissy's claims have also been publicly contradicted by Noah Stern, president in 2010–11 of the University of California Student Association (UCSA) and a member of the board of directors of Berkeley Hillel, a center of pro-Israel campus activism. In an article meant to "set the record straight," Stern ridiculed the portrayal of Berkeley in the "Jewish press" as "a dark, foreboding institution rife with anti-Semitism that is hostile to Jews and Israel while being the focal point for anti-Zionist agitation in the country, if not the world."[85] Berkeley had become a focus of attention for several weeks during the spring semester of 2010 after the student senate voted in favor of a resolution supporting divestment from companies selling weapons and equipment used by the Israeli occupation army. The senate president vetoed the bill, sparking a high-profile public debate that attracted global interest. Alice Walker, Archbishop Desmond Tutu, and Palestinian activists were among those who sent messages urging the student senators to vote to overturn the veto.[86] On the night of the vote, student senators deliberated in front of an audience of hundreds, which included Israeli consul general Akiva Tor. Ultimately, the effort to overturn the veto fell short by just two votes. As part of their strategy to defeat the divestment resolution, members of Hillel had convened a meeting with representatives of the ADL, AIPAC, the Jewish Community Relations Council, J Street, and Tor.[87] Yet, wrote Stern, "even in the midst of high-profile Israel-related political activity, and contrary to popular belief, Jewish students at UC Berkeley do not feel threatened, under attack or marginalized." Although the federal judge who dismissed their lawsuit gave Felber and Maissy a chance to resubmit, the pair eventually opted to withdraw their suit and pursue a civil rights complaint through the Department of Education instead.[88]

. Despite the aggressiveness with which Title VI complaints have been pursued and the fact that the Department of Education's 2010 policy change was the direct result of lobbying by pro-Israel groups, the strategy has been controversial even among ardent opponents of Palestinian rights. Kenneth Stern, the American Jewish Committee's "expert" on anti-Semitism, and Cary Nelson, president of the AAUP, issued a joint letter in April 2011 warning that some of the complaints "seek to silence anti-Israel discourse and speakers," an approach they termed "unwarranted" and "dangerous."[89] Stern's boss David Harris, executive director of the American Jewish Committee, publicly rebuked Stern, writing to AMCHA Initiative's Tammi Rossman-Benjamin that Stern's letter had been "ill-advised."[90] Harris apologized and dissociated the American Jewish Committee from the Stern-Nelson letter, which was subsequently removed even from the AAUP website—a disturbing example of self-censorship. The credibility of the Title VI complaints was also challenged by then–University of California president Mark Yudof, a self-described "strong defender of Israel." Yudof had blocked the University of California's Board of Regents from even discussing a divestment resolution on the grounds that "it was the board's policy to take up divestment only if America's government said that the regime in question was committing genocide"—a surrender of intellectual and moral independence to government authority.[91] Yudof has also accused his own students of calling for a boycott of Israel just for being a "Jewish state." Yet when asked about the Title VI complaints against UC Berkeley and UC Santa Cruz, Yudof said that the pervasive, hostile atmosphere claimed in the complaints was not supported by the facts. "I don't think in either of these cases these fact patterns exist," he told the *Forward*.[92]

The change in the government's interpretation of Title VI also provided an opportunity to renew the assault on Columbia University when Kenneth Marcus filed a complaint in October 2011 against its sister school, Barnard College, claiming that "a Jewish student from Barnard was discouraged from taking a class with Joseph Massad." The violation of the law, allegedly, was that Professor Rachel McDermott, chair of Barnard's Asian and Middle Eastern Cultures Department, "illegally 'steered' the student away from taking the class because Massad, a sharp critic of Israel, has often been accused of anti-Semitism."[93] The tactic also appeared to be a useful ploy to get Massad's name back in the media in a negative light, after those campaigning against him had lost the fight over his tenure. But this time, unlike during the grueling tenure battle, Columbia University president Lee Bollinger was quick to put his public support behind Massad, telling the *Columbia Spectator* that "the individual complaint appears to relate to academic advising at Barnard College and in no way involves Professor Joseph Massad. . . . It is extremely unfair for Professor Massad to be cited in a matter in which he played no part whatsoever."[94]

In January 2012, the Office of Civil Rights dismissed Marcus's complaint, writing in a letter to Barnard College president Deborah Spar that "neither the complainant nor the Student provided, and OCR did not find, any evidence other than the Student's assertions" to back up the allegations. Further, the letter added, "neither the complainant nor the Student provided, and OCR did not find, any other evidence to indicate that the Chair advised any other students of Jewish ancestry/ethnicity not to take a course with the Professor [Massad]." McDermott expressed her relief that the case was over and her gratitude for the "overwhelming support" she had received from colleagues as well as current and former students.[95]

This was only the first in a series of stinging defeats for Kenneth Marcus's strategy. In August 2013, OCR threw out complaints against the Berkeley, Irvine, and Santa Cruz campuses of the University of California. Just like the judge who threw out the Felber and Maissy lawsuit against Berkeley, the OCR ruled that the activity in question amounted to "expression on matters of public concern" and that "exposure to such robust and discordant expressions, even when personally offensive and hurtful, is a circumstance that a reasonable student in higher education may experience."[96] UC Berkeley chancellor Nick Dirks welcomed the ruling, noting, "The claim that there is a hostile environment for Jewish students at Berkeley is, on its face, entirely unfounded."[97]

This was a clear victory for free speech and a signal to students and faculty organizing for Palestinian rights, including supporting the boycott of Israeli academic institutions complicit with government abuses: their determination not to be intimidated and silenced had been vindicated. But despite his defeats, Marcus was undeterred, insisting that the Title VI strategy could still be used to intimidate students, faculty, and administrators whether or not civil rights complaints were eventually upheld. "These cases—even when rejected—expose administrators to bad publicity," Marcus wrote in the *Jerusalem Post* after the adverse OCR decisions.[98] He claimed he had only just heard from a university chancellor "eager to work" with him "to avert the possibility of a civil rights complaint." Marcus argued that the mere threat of litigation could achieve political goals: "If a university shows a failure to treat initial complaints seriously, it hurts them with donors, faculty, political leaders and prospective students. No university wants to be accused of creating an abusive environment." Marcus also celebrated the bullying effect tactics like his were having on students. "Israel-haters," as he called Palestine solidarity groups, "now publicly complain that these cases make it harder for them to recruit new adherents." Win or lose, accusations and threats of legal action could still be used to scare students or professors into silence. "Needless to say," Marcus advised, "getting caught up in a civil rights complaint is not a good way to build a resume or impress a future employer." Marcus knew what he was talking about.

Targeting Students

While bogus allegations about Jewish students being persecuted by the Palestine solidarity movement have abounded, a very real climate of fear, intimidation, and censorship has taken grip of many Muslim American, Arab American, and international students on campuses as a direct result of efforts to censor Palestine-related activism. Five civil rights organizations—the Center for Constitutional Rights, the Asian Law Caucus of San Francisco, American Muslims for Palestine, National Lawyers Guild, and the Council on American-Islamic Relations—wrote to University of California president Mark Yudof in December 2012 to "express our collective alarm about developments . . . that threaten students' civil rights and forsake the University's responsibility to make the campus welcoming for a range of political viewpoints on the Israeli-Palestinian conflict."[99] The letter, endorsed by twelve MSA and SJP chapters from across the UC system, was sent in advance of a meeting of the Advisory Council on Campus Climate, which Yudof created in response to the relentless complaints from Zionist groups. Yudof also commissioned a "campus climate" report prompted by this barrage of accusations. The letter pointed to "the rash of baseless legal complaints that have increased scrutiny of student activism on Palestine, to a UC-initiated 'campus climate' report that labels Palestinian rights advocacy as anti-Semitic and threatening to Jewish students, and to numerous public statements by UC officials that disparage such activism as 'bad speech' and compare it to truly anti-Semitic and racist incidents on campus, such as noose-hangings and graffiti disparaging Jews, Muslims and the LGBTQ community."

The civil rights groups detailed alarming examples of how the climate of fear tolerated or fostered by the UC administration and instigated by outside groups, had chilled many students' exercise of their First Amendment rights. These included examples of Arab, Muslim, and Palestinian rights activists on campus being subject to violent threats and racist language, as well as the bogus Title VI complaints. The letter charged, "While the UC administration is not behind the legal claims and violent threats targeting Arab, Muslim and pro-Palestine students at UC, it has an obligation to recognize the harm, and take steps to protect the targeted students where possible. Instead, the University has exacerbated the situation for these students." The letter, included the following specific examples, which I quote verbatim:

- PhD student active with Cal SJP was told by his adviser that his public status as a Palestinian rights activist would be detrimental to his career, as it has been to many academics that express pro-Palestinian views.
- Palestinian students often decline to join Cal SJP because they "don't want to risk anything." Although more than 20 students participate actively in Cal SJP, there are only two or three Palestinian members.
- Students frequently express anxiety about being falsely branded as anti-Semites at SJP meetings, in small group discussions and in private.
- A Cal SJP member sought advice from an immigration attorney, fearing that her participation in Cal SJP and the allegations in the Felber litigation would jeopardize her citizenship application.
- A Saudi international student declined his nomination for the Cal MSA board for fear that his student visa would be jeopardized if he were associated in any way with Cal MSA.
- Students understand that their liberty is at stake. They are aware that the FBI infiltrates and monitors Arab, Muslim and pro-Palestine student groups.
- Cal SJP students are routinely subject to video surveillance by Israel-aligned activists who attend Cal SJP events. Counter protestors from Israel-aligned organizations—both on and off-campus groups—frequently attend SJP events and take close-up videos. Students feel physically unsafe after being videoed at events because they do not know how Israel-aligned organizations will use data collected against them.[100]

Judging by his response to the OCR decisions, this kind of fear and intimidation is precisely what Kenneth Marcus hoped his legal assault would achieve. But Dalia Almarina, a Cal SJP alum from Berkeley, held Yudof personally responsible in part for fostering this climate. She pointed to an "open letter" the president had sent to the entire university in March 2012 condemning recent "incidents of intolerance" and asserting the "moral and ethical imperative for all of our University of California students, faculty and staff members to foster a climate of tolerance, civility and open-mindedness."[101] The incidents to which Yudof referred specifically included "the defacement of an Israeli flag at UC Riverside, a protest against a talk by former Israeli soldiers at UC Davis, a noose hung at UC San Diego two years ago [an act that made African American students feel especially targeted], vandalism of the LGBT Resource Center at UC Davis (also two years ago), and the drawing of swastikas on campus."[102] This was yet another example of the deliberate conflation of unmistakable expressions of bigotry, on the one hand, and protest of Israel and its policies, on the other.

Yet Yudof failed to mention a shocking incident that occurred just two weeks before he sent out his open letter, in which three people were attacked with pepper spray at a protest that included members of Jewish Voice for Peace and Cal SJP just outside the UC Berkeley campus. According to Lieutenant Dave Frankel of the Berkeley Police Department, "Two Israel supporters apparently had foreknowledge of the event and showed up at the intersection with pepper spray and began video-taping the protests and shouting counter chants." One of the pro-Israel supporters was armed with a stun gun.[103] When three bystanders not involved in either side of the protest intervened to try to de-escalate the situation, "the two pro-Israel supporters then pepper sprayed the three non-involved individuals," according to the police. Oddly, police decided not to charge the attack as a "hate crime" on the grounds that "neither the pro-Israel nor pro-Palestine supporters were pepper sprayed," even though the "Israel supporters" had come to a Palestine solidarity rally armed with pepper spray and Tasers, weapons they were clearly ready to use. Almarina cited Yudof's failure to mention this "egregious violation of campus safety," along with one other assault and numerous examples of vandalism targeting students expressing views sympathetic to Palestinian rights, as examples of his selective attitude to intolerance. Ray Hajduk, an SJP member who had taken part in the demonstration attacked by the "Israel supporters," expressed his dismay that "there was no statement from the administration at any level, no actions taken to ensure my own or other Jewish and non-Jewish students' safety."[104]

Two dozen California student groups also sent a joint letter to the US Commission on Civil Rights expressing their "alarm" at the threat to their freedoms from the "campus climate" report and California House Resolution 35 (HR 35)—cosponsored by sixty-six of the State Assembly's eighty members—passed in August 2012, which endorsed that report.[105] Both the campus climate report and HR 35 "define anti-Semitism to include a wide array of legitimate political speech that is not based in hate or bigotry, nor targeted at the Jewish people in any way," the student groups wrote. Perhaps one silver lining of these brazen attempts to stifle free speech is that they have sounded the alarm beyond groups traditionally involved in

Palestine activism. The executive of the UCSA, representing hundreds of thousands of students, passed a resolution 12-0, with two abstentions, condemning HR 35 "as one in a series of attempts to stifle legitimate speech by UC students by falsely conflating speech critical of Israeli policies with anti-Semitism."[106]

That so many students feel so vulnerable, so targeted, and so vilified by those orchestrating the crackdown on Palestine solidarity activism on campus is, as Marcus has acknowledged, no accident. It is part of a coherent strategy, as video of Tammi Rossman-Benjamin speaking at a synagogue in June 2012 revealed. Addressing what she may have thought was a private audience, Rossman-Benjamin, who has made campus Palestine-solidarity activism and criticism of Israel her main target, alleged that students "have become poisoned by the rhetoric they hear on campus. . . . And who are the primary sources of this?" she asked, before providing the answer:

> Primarily the MSA and the SJP students. . . . They are generally motivated by very strong religious and political convictions, they have a fire in their belly, they come to the university, many of them are foreign students who come from countries and cultures where anti-Semitism is how they think about the world. . . . These are not your ordinary student groups like College Republicans or Young Democrats. These are students who come with a serious agenda, who have ties to terrorist organizations.[107]

The comments caused outrage among students targeted by this attempt to criminalize and smear them. But when *Mondoweiss* reporter Alex Kane asked Yudof's office for its reaction, the president's spokesperson, Shelly Meron, wrote back, "We have no comment on this."[108] Students launched an Internet petition, gathering more than 1,500 signatures to demand that Yudof speak out against Rossman-Benjamin's "hateful attacks," recalling Yudof's own words that the UC administration had a "moral obligation" to condemn hateful speech.[109] But Yudof's silence indicated that any obligation he felt did not extend to students targeted by Zionist organizations.

This wasn't the only example of students at a university of national standing being vilified in racist terms for engaging in Palestine-related activism and a university president failing to defend them while pandering to their attackers. Jews as well Arab and Muslim students have been the victims. Zionist groups spewed intense inflammatory rhetoric in advance of the February 2012 conference on BDS organized by students at the University of Pennsylvania. The Israel Action Network, spearheaded in this instance by the Jewish Federation of Greater Philadelphia, led the effort, which included a joint statement with the Israeli consulate in Philadelphia asserting that the conference would promote "intolerance on campus."[110] The campus group Hillel of Greater Philadelphia accused the conference of "delegitimizing" Israel, claiming it "destroys the sophisticated civil discourse that is a core element of the mission" of the university. Hillel said it had "communicated its objections to the University about having this type of conference on Penn's campus."[111] Several major donors to the university reportedly threatened to withdraw their support if the conference were allowed to proceed.[112]

Feeling the pressure, university president Amy Gutmann sent a February 2, 2012, letter to the Jewish Federation of Greater Philadelphia saying she was "bound to recognize the right of any student or student group to freely express their opinions," but that she was dismayed that anyone would think this meant the university endorsed all opinions that were expressed. With regard to the BDS conference, Gutmann wrote, "that could not be further from the truth."[113] Gutmann assured her correspondents, "We are unwavering in our support of the Jewish state," adding for good measure that "we do not support the goals of BDS." She thanked the Jewish Federation for putting together a "thoughtful educational response" to the conference, which was to include a speech by Harvard law professor Alan Dershowitz, who led the witch hunt against Norman Finkelstein. "I have long admired Alan's intellect and passion," Gutmann wrote, "and know his words will inspire you all." This was the same Dershowitz who had been quoted in the *Philadelphia Inquirer* the day before Gutmann sent her letter making the accusation that advocates of boycotts—including, presumably, students at the University of Pennsylvania—"have blood on their hands" because the actions they urge "discourage the laying down of arms."[114]

By far the vilest and most disturbing attack on the students came from one of Gutmann's own faculty. A week before the BDS conference, the campus *Daily Pennsylvanian* published a column by Abbas Naqvi, Madeline Noteware, and Matt Berkman, three members of the recognized student group Penn BDS, calmly responding to the criticisms that had been leveled at the conference they were organizing.[115] To the claim that the conference would "delegitimize" Israel, they responded with the less-than-revolutionary nostrum that the "legitimacy of a state derives from the consent of the governed" and cited the undeniable fact that "Israel effectively rules over four million Palestinians in the Occupied Territories to whom it denies voting rights and other political and civil liberties due to their non-Jewish ethnicity." Mentioning the systematic discrimination against Palestinian citizens of Israel, the writers affirmed that the "goal of BDS is to use non-violent civil society action to bring those inequalities to an end. Should BDS achieve this goal, Israel would become more, not less, legitimate in the eyes of both the people it governs and of third parties." They patiently answered absurd accusations including of "anti-Semitism," pointing out that "our speakers are careful to distinguish between Jews and Judaism on the one hand, and Israel and Zionism on the other hand," and concluded with Martin Luther King Jr.'s dictum, "True peace is not merely the absence of tension; it is the presence of justice."

A few days later, Ruben Gur, a professor in the Departments of Psychiatry, Radiology, and Neurology, responded in a letter to the editor. "I could barely believe my eyes," Gur exclaimed. "It is bad enough that Penn has allowed itself to be associated with this hateful genocidal organization, but for you to give room for their 'explanation' and then dignify this outpouring of misinformation and anti-Semitism to the level of guest column without any kind of balancing opinion?"[116] Gur, a former Israeli soldier, wrote that Omar Barghouti's book *BDS: The Global Struggle for Palestinian Rights* was the student organizers' "version" of Hitler's *Mein Kampf* and asserted that the "aim of the hateful and discriminatory BDS rhetoric is to delegitimize Israel in preparation for the ultimate goal of its destruction." As ugly, false, and inflammatory as this rhetoric was, it was not unique among Zionist attacks on the BDS movement. What broke new ground was Gur's singling out Jewish students who were helping to organize and planning to participate in the conference: "A relevant precedent for such a movement is the groups organized by the Nazis in the 1930s to boycott, divest and sanction Jews and their businesses. Sadly, now as then, there are Jews among the posse in the assault on their own people. The macabre sight of the likes of Stella Kuebler, (arguably Hannah Arendt) and the Capos in the extermination camps is about to be replayed here at Penn." (Gur apparently meant to write *kapos*, the term used to describe Jewish collaborators who helped exterminate fellow Jews in Nazi death camps.) The conference organizers wrote to President Gutmann deploring Gur's shocking letter: "Statements like these by a tenured professor in a school newspaper are not only outrageous, deplorable, and frankly unprecedented, but they also incite against and endanger both the speakers and organizers of this weekend's conference."[117] As the keynote speaker at the conference, I recall clearly that the intensity of the attacks, particularly Gur's letter, had generated a palpable sense among many of us that the physical safety of those attending the conference could be at risk. If we were being likened to acolytes of Hitler preparing the ground for a second Holocaust, it would perhaps not take very much for an unbalanced individual hearing this rhetoric to feel he or she had a duty to stop us by any means. Students had planned a conference at a university in the United States to discuss a nonviolent movement to promote human rights, but in their final days they had to divert much of their time to thinking about how to raise money for extra security and planning escape routes for speakers in case they were assaulted.

Following Gur's letter, Gutmann and David L. Cohen, chairman of the university's board of trustees and a former vice-chair of the board of the Jewish Federation of Greater Philadelphia, published a joint letter in the *Daily Pennsylvanian* reiterating their opposition to calls for boycott, divestment, and sanctions on Israel, though they defended the right of the conference to proceed.[118] They made no mention of Gur's letter or any of the other attacks on the students or the conference by Zionist groups, but offered a paean to the university's 270-year "tradition" of "free exchange of ideas." I had also written to Gutmann asking her to condemn Gur's "inflammatory rhetoric." Two days later I received an email from Stephen MacCarthy, vice president for university communications.[119] "It is always unfortunate when people make personal or ad hominem attacks against others," MacCarthy wrote. "This kind of attack is counter to [Gutmann's] personal values and the goal of civility on campus. . . . It is, however, neither possible, nor consistent with the value of free expression, for me or the Administration to intervene in the exchange of words that will inevitably occur in the context of highly controversial and deeply emotional issues."

It is instructive to contrast this response with Gutmann's relentless and forceful denunciations of the views of the student group Penn BDS. That was apparently consistent with "the value of free expression," yet her administration refused to condemn the singling out of Jewish students by a member of faculty whose words had created fear for their safety. Although we cannot know, it seems unlikely that Gutmann would have remained quite so reserved if a professor had called Jewish students *supporting* Israel "Nazis." But it is a safe bet that the Jewish communal groups leading the Israel Action Network's campaign against the conference would have loudly clamored for the professor to lose his job. Yet none of them condemned Gur's anti-Semitic "*kapos*" slur. The conference itself went smoothly, with hundreds in attendance and far more press coverage than we could have hoped for if the Zionist groups had not made such a fuss. But even in the tensest moments before the conference, as the vilification campaign was in full swing, none of the students or organizers I interacted with wavered. They were courageous under enormous pressure, in the face of intimidation, and despite the denunciations and cowardice of the university administration.

Criminalizing Protest on Campus

On September 23, 2011, ten University of California students stood before Judge Peter J. Wilson in the Orange County Superior Court in Santa Ana, California, to await sentencing. The courtroom was packed with family members and well-wishers and many more waited outside. Mohamed Mohy-Eldeen Abdelgany, Khalid Gahgat

Akari, Aslam Abbasi Akhtar, Joseph Tamim Haider, Taher Mutaz Herzallah, Shaheen Waleed Nassar, Mohammad Uns Qureashi, Ali Mohammad Sayeed, Osama Ahmed Shabaik and, Asaad Mohamedidris Traina, seven from UC Irvine and three from UC Riverside, had just endured a two-week trial. Only two hours before, they had been convicted by a jury of offenses under Section 403 of the California Penal Code: conspiracy to disrupt a public meeting and disrupting a public meeting. Each student knew that he faced up to one year in prison on each charge. Dreading this possibility, the young men, their families, and supporters were relieved when the judge sentenced each of them to fifty-six hours of community service and up to three years of probation. But the formal sentence would be the least of their punishment. Before the trial, the students had already endured more than a year of investigations by Orange County prosecutors and had been vilified as extremists who wanted to take away free-speech rights. They and their families faced all the stress and uncertainty of being ensnared in America's system of mass incarceration. These were the Irvine 11 (only ten went to trial, as UC Irvine student Hakim Nasreddine Kebir had charges dropped earlier in exchange for accepting community service). Their prosecution represents perhaps the most severe use of state power to punish Palestine solidarity activists on campus for their opinions. It was a verdict publicly welcomed by the Jewish Federation of Orange County, an affiliate of the Israel Action Network.[120]

What crime had the Irvine 11 committed? On February 8, 2010—more than a year and a half before they were convicted and sentenced—the students attended a speech at UC Irvine by Michael Oren, the Israeli ambassador to the United States. The event was cosponsored by pro-Israel groups on and off campus, including Hillel, Anteaters for Israel, Chabad at UCI, the College Republicans, the Jewish Federation of Orange County, the Israeli consulate, and several academic departments.[121] Born in New York as Michael Scott Bornstein before changing his name at the urging of the Israeli foreign ministry, Oren is a former academic who has held posts at the Hebrew University and visiting professorships at several American institutions.[122] Oren renounced his American citizenship in 2009 in order to accept the appointment as Israeli envoy to the United States, but his romance with Israel had begun thirty years earlier when he enlisted in the Israeli army in 1979. He participated as a paratrooper in the 1982 invasion of Lebanon that killed tens of thousands of Lebanese and Palestinian civilians.[123] Oren also served as Israeli army spokesman during the 2006 invasion of Lebanon that left another 1,200 people, the vast majority of them civilians, dead.[124]

When Oren rose to speak that day at UC Irvine, it was at a lectern bearing not the seal of the University of California but the official emblem of the Israeli state, the seven-armed candlestick with the word "Yisrael" prominently emblazoned beneath it in Hebrew. As Oren began to recount being summoned to Jerusalem by Israeli prime minister Benjamin Netanyahu to be offered the ambassadorial post, a student rose and shouted, "Michael Oren, propagating murder is not an expression of free speech!" To jeers from some in the audience, the student was quickly led out by university police officers.[125] A forty-eight-minute video posted online captured much of what happened next as each of the students rose in succession and called out a brief statement objecting to Israel's actions, particularly those during the 2008–2009 attack on Gaza.[126] None of the students resisted the police officers and most can be seen voluntarily moving from their seats toward the officers to be led out after making their statements. While their lawyers later argued that the disruptions, including the jeers from the audience, cumulatively took up no more than about five minutes of an event scheduled to last an hour and a half, there is no doubt that the protest did disrupt the flow of Oren's lecture, enraging university officials.

Professor Mark Petracca, chair of the School of Social Sciences, came to the lectern and berated the audience several times over the protests. "Shame on all of you!" he shouted at the students. "You did nothing to enhance the reputation of this campus. All you did today is embarrass yourself and the university." Returning to the podium after Petracca's intervention, Oren told the audience that Irvine was "not Tehran," a nakedly Islamophobic jab at the protesting students and a particularly insensitive comment in a region of Southern California noted for its large Iranian American community. When Petracca's scolding failed to stop the protests, Oren suspended his lecture to consult offstage about whether he would continue or abandon the event. UC Irvine chancellor Michael Drake asked the audience for patience as Oren decided what to do. "We cannot, we will not, we do not tolerate disruptions of academic freedom of the type that have occurred here today," the chancellor said. As the audience waited, some audience members danced and sang "Am Yisrael Chai," the ultranationalist song associated with the West Bank settler movement and Israel's racist far right. Oren resumed his lecture, but when it was clear that Drake's intervention had also failed to stop the students standing up one at a time, making their brief statements, and walking out of the room, Petracca announced that the protesting students were being arrested. "I know that it is midterm week," he warned the audience, "and you might want to spend it in your dorm room instead of in jail." It was about this point that a large segment of the audience sympathetic to the protestors stood up and walked out. Oren completed his lecture, but the video shows that loud protests outside the building could be heard inside the ballroom where he spoke. Among the points Oren made about the strength of the US-Israeli relationship under the Obama administration was that "we are united in fighting the Goldstone Report," the UN investigation into the very crimes in Gaza that the students were protesting, "which seeks to deny Israel's right to defend itself and even its right to exist." After the lecture, Chancellor Drake returned to the lectern and praised "the "courage of the ambassador for what he did tonight to stand up for free speech."

The event's videographer interviewed Chief Henisey immediately after Oren had left the ballroom, asking what would happen to those arrested. "In this particular case, we've had twelve individuals that we've arrested for [a] penal code section which has to do with disrupting a public event on university grounds, which is a misdemeanor," Henisey explained. "We're going to be processing those arrests. We'll be submitting them to the District Attorney's office for consideration of filing charges." Although it is unclear if Henisey misspoke when he said twelve people, rather than eleven, had been arrested, his statement indicated that the university police and administration had done their research and already had a plan to deal with protests using the State of California's *penal* code in addition to university disciplinary procedures. Rabbi David Eliezrie, director of the North Orange County Chabad Center and a board member of the Jewish Federation of Orange County, told the videographer, "We as Jews have to stand up with pride and the idea of America was that we left the swords at the door . . . apparently the Muslim Student Union believes in violence as a political alternative." Eliezrie said this although the protest was entirely peaceful. He asserted that Oren had considered ending his lecture prematurely but, when university officials "agreed that they would also talk about possibly expelling students, then he was willing to come back." The university suspended the Muslim Student Union and imposed community service on the students.

Several months before the trial, defense attorneys won a court victory when the judge granted an order restraining the prosecution from using the media to inflame the jury pool. This came after Orange County district attorney spokesperson Susan Schroeder told the *Electronic Intifada*'s Nora Barrows-Friedman that, "whether you like the speaker or not, it doesn't matter . . . if the Ku Klux Klan disrupted a speech by Martin Luther King, Jr., that would be a law violation."[127] Schroeder had bluntly compared the students to white supremacists who lynch African Americans and likened the Israeli ambassador Michael Oren to the world's best-known American civil rights leader. In another example of misconduct, prosecutors used privileged attorney-client communications between the students and Reem Salahi, one of their lawyers, found among thousands of pages of emails and documents seized from the students with search warrants, to lay additional charges against at least one student.

As a result, the judge ordered the removal of the district attorney's top investigator, Paul Kelly, and three deputies from the case.[128] The district attorney responded by putting Dan Wagner, the head of Orange County's homicide unit, on the Irvine 11 case instead.

At the trial, each side argued that it was the party defending basic principles, including freedom of speech. Because of the interruptions, the prosecution charged, Oren had been unable to hold a question-and-answer session at the end of his lecture. "Who is the censor in this case?" Wagner asked jurors. "Right there—ten of them."[129] Lisa Holder, one of the six defense attorneys, explained that the students had modeled their protest on the actions of Martin Luther King Jr., Nelson Mandela, and Mohandas Gandhi and were speaking out against violence. Their actions, the defense argued, were in the best American tradition of speaking truth to power. As one of several witnesses brought by the defense to show that the university sanctions and prosecution were selective and discriminatory, former student Kareem Elsayed testified that he had witnessed College Republicans trying to shut down a speech by a Muslim activist in 2001, but the university had not intervened when the speaker was repeatedly drowned out and had made no prior rules dictating the conduct of the audience.[130] Evidence then came to light that Oren, who had arrived late in the first place, had rushed off not because protests had made a question-and-answer session impossible, but because he was in a hurry to make the tip-off for an LA Lakers game for which he had VIP tickets. A photo from later that evening showed star player Kobe Bryant with his arm around a smiling Oren.[131]

As the Irvine 11 students awaited the outcome of an appeal against the constitutionality of their conviction, one of them, Taher Herzallah, acknowledged that he is now "more cautious about the things I do"—but his determination remained intact.[132] Yet Herzallah noticed that the trial had a broad impact: "Many people ask the question—if we were to protest this way, would we get arrested, too? Would we be convicted, too?" Herzallah hoped that a successful appeal would send a message that perseverance can pay off. "It's going to be a struggle," he said. "This is part of what we do. Of course we would prefer it not to be this way, but . . . it's Palestine."

Hosting War Criminals and Hiding behind "Free Speech"

During the Irvine 11 trial, the prosecution showed the jury emails the students had sent each other in which they discussed holding a "Chicago-style protest" at Oren's lecture. The district attorney argued that these emails, which formed a key part of the prosecution's case, proved that the students had intended to prevent Oren from speaking altogether. This was a reference to a protest I participated in during a visit by former Israeli prime minister Ehud Olmert to the University of Chicago on October 15, 2009. Both the Irvine 11 prosecutors and defense attorneys showed a video of that protest, made and published by the *Electronic Intifada*, in court. Even though the University of Chicago did not pursue criminal proceedings against us, it did, like UC Irvine, accuse us of stifling free speech. Indeed, I have heard this question several times: How can you complain about pro-Israel organizations trying to shut down the free speech of the Palestine solidarity movement when you have participated in, or supported, protests that disrupt or shut down speeches by Israeli officials? Isn't this a double standard?

This is a fair question. It can only be answered with an understanding of what happened and why I, an alumnus of the university, along with students from that university and other campuses, decided to disrupt Olmert's speech and why I defend that action. The short answer is that we were protesting not against Olmert's ideas or his right to express them but against his *actions*. Olmert was prime minister, the top civilian official in charge of the military, when Israel invaded Lebanon in 2006 and repeatedly attacked Gaza, actions that killed some three thousand civilians during his term of office. Major international human-rights organizations repeatedly found strong evidence that many of the actions leading to these deaths amounted to war crimes and crimes against humanity. Yet there has still been no legal accountability, despite the findings of the UN-commissioned Goldstone Report. We felt that a disruptive protest was the only way to draw attention to these crimes and to the university's complicity in providing Olmert with a platform where they could not be addressed in any meaningful way but that would enhance his reputation and market him as a worthy statesman.

When students heard that Olmert had been invited to speak by the University of Chicago's prestigious Harris School of Public Policy as part of its King Abdullah II Annual Leadership Lecture, they began to tell the university about their concerns. Mere months had passed since Israel's attack on Gaza; the Goldstone Report had been published only weeks before Olmert's visit. "The Harris School seems terribly misinformed about Olmert," wrote Nadia Marie Ismail, then a third-year student, in the campus *Chicago Maroon*.[133] She expressed consternation that the university's publicity materials described Olmert as "one of the most respected leaders in Israel's history" when—even leaving aside his role in Gaza and Lebanon—he was at that moment the first Israeli prime minister ever to be on trial for corruption. He had resigned from office in disgrace over these charges. Even more ill-informed and insensitive, the Harris School claimed that "Ehud Olmert became Prime Minister with a courageous vision: achieving prosperity through peace." This was the same Olmert who had, even before the December 2008 attack, been responsible for the punishing siege that devastated Gaza's economy and pushed its people to the edge of starvation. The university's choice of Olmert for a prestigious lectureship for which he would receive a significant honorarium appeared to students to be an endorsement and a show of callous disregard for the innocent victims of Israeli violence in the occupied Palestinian territories and in Lebanon, including students whose families had been directly affected. Students who had communicated their concerns to the university told me the university was unresponsive and uninterested even in reformulating the event or the promotional materials in a way that addressed their serious objections. I booked myself a place for the lecture, as did many other people I knew.

Though it refused to engage meaningfully with students, the university was aware of the growing opposition to Olmert's planned appearance and began to impose measures to restrict free speech and to make any interaction that would allow for Olmert to be confronted about his actions impossible. The day before Olmert's lecture, the university announced airport-style security, informed attendees of a ban on bags and backpacks, and decreed via email that no one would be allowed to bring in signs. Even silent opposition to Olmert would not be tolerated. And instead of an open question-and-answer period, audience members would have to write their questions on cards to be distributed and collected by university officials who would select which ones to put to Olmert. Just as troubling, the email said, "At the request of the speaker, no independent photos or recordings will be allowed." This warning suggested that the university's real motive for complying with Olmert's demand was to spare him and the university the embarrassment of the prestigious Harris School event being protested by the very students who were supposed to be impressed by this paragon of "leadership." This was no empty threat: the university's ban was strictly enforced even on news media, as I saw firsthand.

Al Jazeera's senior correspondent Wajd Waqfi told me that university officials had informed her that Al Jazeera would not be allowed to cover the event from inside the hall. Instead, the journalists would only be allowed to shoot a few minutes of footage before the event started as people trickled in and took their seats but would then have to pack up their cameras.[134] I told my colleague Benjamin Doherty, who was also in the auditorium, what I had learned from Waqfi and asked him to do his best to evade this heavy-handed censorship and film as much as he could of Olmert's lecture using the pocket-sized Flip camera he had smuggled in. We later speculated that the Israeli guards screening people for cameras and other contraband as they entered the hall had mistaken the tiny Flip camera for an ordinary cell phone and allowed it to pass (in 2009 it was still not common for cell phones to contain video cameras). We were lucky: Doherty was eventually caught shooting video, threatened with arrest, and expelled from the auditorium by University of Chicago police, but not before he captured most of the protest. It was because of the University of Chicago's strictly enforced censorship that the footage of what happened at Olmert's lecture that Al Jazeera broadcast to its global audiences was not its own but Doherty's. Doherty and I rushed the video late that night to the editing facility in downtown Chicago where the Al Jazeera crew was putting together Waqfi's report. That footage would later be shown to the jury in the Irvine 11 trial.

It was only on the day of Olmert's speech that students from several campuses met at the University of Chicago and, exasperated by the university's shameless boosting of Olmert, its unresponsiveness to student concerns, and its measures to restrict free speech, decided to protest inside the auditorium. I decided to join them. Within seconds of Olmert opening his mouth, I stood up from my seat close to the front of the auditorium and shouted as loudly as I could, "War crimes are not free expression! Shame on my university for inviting a murderer who bombed a university in Gaza!" I had chosen my words carefully to make clear that it was Olmert's acts, not his views, we were protesting—acts the university refused to acknowledge and was seemingly ready to overlook or even, we felt, endorse with its prestigious invitation. As I saw two university police officers making their way toward me, I continued to call out that it was obscene to invite Olmert to the University of Chicago and demand that his freedom of expression be treated as sacrosanct above any other value of justice. The attack he had directed against Gaza had "killed students and teachers and professors," I called out. I had in mind the fact that schools and universities had been among Israel's primary targets during Operation Cast Lead. Eighteen schools were completely destroyed, and 280—almost half of all schools in Gaza—were damaged. From the government schools, 164 students and twelve teachers were killed and a further 454 injured, while from UNRWA schools, eighty-six children and three teachers were killed and another 402 injured.[135] The Goldstone Report commented on Israel's destruction of the American School and buildings from the Islamic University in Gaza: "These were civilian, educational buildings and the Mission did not find any information about their use as a military facility or their contribution to a military effort that might have made them a legitimate target in the eyes of the Israeli armed forces."[136] The University of Chicago, famous for its defense of academic freedom, had not uttered one word of solidarity for the right to education, and indeed life, of all those in Gaza whose places of learning had been bombed on the orders of their honored Leadership Lecturer.

After my protest, the two university police officers led me out to the street, where

I joined the demonstration outside. But inside the auditorium, as the video shows, students continued to stand up. "You're going to jail!" one shouted at Olmert as others read out names of Palestinian children killed in Gaza. As the protests continued, Harris School dean Colm O'Muircheartaigh came to the lectern and urged the audience to listen to Olmert with "civility," disingenuously adding that, after the lecture, there would be a chance "to ask him to justify what you think he should justify." A young woman responded by calling out, "He can give his views to an international court of justice," again bringing the issue back to Olmert's *acts*. As Olmert droned on about how Israel was part of the "free" and "democratic" world fighting against "the forces of blood and terror," a young woman from the University of Illinois stood up and made what I thought was the most poignant protest of the evening. "This is a list of the 1,400 people massacred in Gaza," she said, waving a thick sheaf of paper above her head. "It's 101 pages long!" As police led her out, she cried "Justice will be done!"

The *Electronic Intifada*'s video of the protest quickly went viral on YouTube, garnering tens of thousands of views within days; the footage was shown by global media, including Al Jazeera and most mainstream Israeli media. The University of Chicago, meanwhile, retreated into a defensive posture. The news office set up a special web page of "Frequently Asked Questions" about what had happened at the event.[137] According to the university, eighteen people in total were removed from Olmert's lecture. University president Robert J. Zimmer and Provost Thomas F. Rosenbaum released a public letter titled "Freedom of Expression and Protest," condemning the protests as "disturbing" and a "rupture" of the university's "long-standing position as an exemplar of academic freedom."[138] I countered the university's reasoning in an article in the *Chicago Maroon*: "The killings of more than 3,000 Palestinians and Lebanese during Olmert's three years in office are not mere differences of opinion to be challenged with a polite question written on a pre-screened note card. They are crimes for which Olmert is accountable before international law and public opinion."[139] Reminding the university officials that "crimes against humanity" are considered "crimes that shock the conscience," I argued,

> When the institutions with the moral and legal responsibility to punish and prevent the crimes choose complicit silence—or, worse, harbor a suspected war criminal, already on trial for corruption in Israel, and present him to students as a paragon of "leadership"— then disobedience, if that is what it takes to break the silence, is an ethical duty. Instead of condemning them, the University should be proud that its students were among those who had the courage to stand up.

As we have seen in the Irvine 11 and Olmert cases, universities always claim to be champions of free speech regardless of its content. But the point of these examples is to show that this has simply not been true. Universities have no qualms about sponsoring appearances by officials representing governments accused of atrocities or abuses as long as they are either from the United States or friendly to it. Israeli political and military leaders in particular are regularly received, honored, and praised by American university officials.

Double Standards

An academic conference at Harvard University on the one-state solution, scheduled just weeks after the Penn BDS conference in the winter of 2012, faced intense vilification from the ADL and other Zionist organizations. In response, David Ellwood, dean of Harvard's Kennedy School of Government, where the conference was taking place, denounced the conference in a public statement. "Harvard University and the Harvard Kennedy School in no way endorse or support the apparent position of the student organizers or any participants," Ellwood said. "We would never take a position on specific policy solutions to achieving peace in this region, and certainly would not endorse any policy that some argue could lead to the elimination of the Jewish State of Israel." Even more extraordinary, Ellwood criticized the makeup of the conference, calling for "balance" in a "one-sided" list of speakers.[140] Organizers were required to add a disclaimer to the official conference website that "students alone are responsible for all aspects of the program, including content and speakers, as with all student-run events. It does not represent the views of the Harvard Kennedy School, Harvard University, or any Harvard school or center."[141] Reflecting the outside pressure Ellwood was facing, the ADL praised the dean for "publicly rejecting odious ideas," but objected to the idea of any campus discussion of a one-state solution at all. Massachusetts senator Scott Brown condemned the conference in the "strongest possible terms" and demanded that the university "cancel" it outright.[142]

Meanwhile, Harvard's Kennedy School, especially its International Security Program, has operated as a revolving door for Israeli military officers and politicians, many granted comfortable fellowships or received as honored visitors despite being implicated in war crimes. In October 2012, for example, the Kennedy School's Institute of Politics sponsored a panel featuring Major-General Amos Yadlin, the former head of Israeli military intelligence, and a fighter pilot in the Israeli air force, and Tzipi Livni, former foreign minister and vice prime minister during Operation Cast Lead. Nicholas Burns, former State Department spokesman, introduced both "distinguished" speakers with no mention of the occupation or the crimes against Palestinians in which both are implicated, adding, "you're looking at a Kennedy

School graduate in Major-General Yadlin, so welcome back to the Kennedy School."[143] Neither Burns nor Dean Ellwood offered any disclaimer that the Harvard Kennedy School, Harvard University, or any Harvard school or center did not endorse Yadlin's or Livni's thoughts or actions. Nor did Burns, Ellwood, or any Kennedy School official complain that the panel, which also included two former US government officials, lacked "balance" for its total exclusion of any Palestinians or, say, lawyers on behalf of victims of Israeli military attacks seeking to bring officials like Livni and Yadlin to justice.

Only weeks after the one-state conference, another ostensibly student-run conference took place, the Israel Conference at Harvard. Hastily arranged, apparently in reaction to the one-state conference, it was subtitled "Small country. Big ideas." The conference promoted Israel as a technological "startup nation" and a haven for innovation—classic "Brand Israel" themes. It was, according to the organizers, "created by a group of Israeli students, who wanted to bring the Israeli spirit to campus the way they see it—as that of a vibrant, innovative and eternally optimistic state."[144] The conference was also sponsored by Hillel and several private, pro-Israel foundations. Not only did the conference website lack a disclaimer dissociating itself from Harvard University and the Kennedy School, but Harvard's provost Alan Garber, the university's second most senior administrator after the president, gave the opening address. Kennedy School Dean Ellwood himself spoke at the conference, introducing Dennis Ross, the former US diplomat and director of the AIPAC-founded think tank the Washington Institute for Near East Policy. Ellwood profusely thanked all the organizers of the Harvard Israel Conference before leading the audience in applause.[145] "Very well done," he gushed, praising the conference as a testament to "Israel's vibrant and innovative spirit."[146] And though he also hailed the "extraordinary" and "exceptional" speakers, Ellwood did not condemn the conference for its clear lack of "balance": while the Harvard Israel Conference was obviously intended to promote Israel, no speakers had been invited to make the case against Israel—unlike the much more "balanced" one-state conference, which did actually bring a prominent professor, Stephen Walt, to defend the two-state solution. At least two of the speakers, moreover, were directly involved in Israel's illegal colonization of occupied Palestinian and Syrian territories.[147] Just like UC Irvine chancellor Michael Drake, who was only too happy to stand at a lectern emblazoned with the official symbol of Israel to berate his students and praise the "courage" of the Israeli ambassador, Harvard administrators had no problem openly identifying themselves and their institution with Israel.

The visit of Iranian president Mahmoud Ahmadinejad to Columbia University in September 2007 represents one of the very rare occasions when the head of state of a country designated by the United States and Israel as an enemy was officially received on campus by a major American institution. Yet the visit showed that Columbia's commitment to free speech is also far from neutral about content or the identity of the speaker. True, Columbia did give Ahmadinejad a platform and provide its students an opportunity to question him. But one week before Ahmadinejad's appearance, Columbia president Lee Bollinger issued a public statement setting out his "conditions," including that "President Ahmadinejad agree to divide his time evenly between delivering remarks and responding to audience questions." Bollinger explained, "I also wanted to be sure the Iranians understood that I would myself introduce the event with a series of sharp challenges" on various issues, including Ahmadinejad's "public call for the destruction of the State of Israel." Justifying his plan to berate the Iranian president, Bollinger insisted, "It is a critical premise of freedom of speech that we do not honor the dishonorable when we open the public forum to their voices. To hold otherwise would make vigorous debate impossible."[148]

On the day of the event, Bollinger was true to his promise and introduced Ahmadinejad with a scathing lecture to his face. As some in the audience applauded, Bollinger condemned the university's guest as a "petty and cruel dictator," accused Ahmadinejad of Holocaust denial, and condemned Iran's "brutal crackdown" on dissidents. Several high-profile faculty members later denounced Bollinger for his introduction, accusing him of "preemptively shutting down an open exchange of ideas."[149] Many—perhaps all—of Bollinger's criticisms of Ahmadinejad might be defensible or justified. But there is no recorded occasion when a US university president introduced an Israeli leader by condemning Israel's routine and state-sponsored Nakba denial, or the leader of a US-aligned Arab state, where the human-rights criticisms might be just as valid, in a similar manner, even though one could cite all the same human-rights groups on Israel, Saudi Arabia, or Qatar as one could on Iran. The University of Chicago's Harris School named its "Leadership Lecture" after the king of Jordan, where basic democratic rights and academic freedoms are routinely violated by the intelligence services, and then invited Olmert, who had just been accused of war crimes by a UN panel, to give it. Columbia University has established its Middle East Research Center (CUMERC) in Amman, Jordan, headquartered in a building "made available for Columbia's use by Her Majesty Queen Rania Al Abdullah"—in effect, a major subsidy.[150] And Nicholas Burns, the Kennedy School's Sultan of Oman Professor of International Relations, has not hosted, as far as can be determined, any public forums or published any articles on the lack of basic freedoms in the country sponsoring his position.[151] There's simply no evidence to justify the David Project's and Martin Kramer's fears that funding from various Arab states makes Harvard or other leading institutions any less hospitable to Israeli military and political officials or more open to those advocating Palestinian rights.

Over the past decade, US institutions, including Harvard University, the University of Chicago, Cornell University, Carnegie Mellon University, New York University, Georgetown University and Northwestern University, have stampeded to open branches or programs in Gulf Arab states where basic freedoms are routinely trampled, often with funding from those governments, which seek the prestige of hosting brand-name American universities. In practice, the commitment of American institutions to providing an equally welcoming forum for all points of view, no matter how controversial, has been conditioned and constrained by these universities' institutional interests and practical alignment with US foreign policy and interstate alliances. The tendency we have seen time and again of university administrators to merely tolerate advocacy or academic inquiry critical of Israel or in support of Palestinian rights while loudly condemning it and publicly stigmatizing students and faculty who engage in it is a symptom of this phenomenon.

How Israel Attempts to Win (Ethnic) Friends and Influence People

One way that students all over the United States have adapted their tactics in the wake of the Irvine 11 trial is to stage walkouts, rather than audible protests, when Israeli officials, especially soldiers taken on tour by Israel advocacy groups, visit their campuses. In some cases, students have placed tape over their mouths to symbolize the chilling of protest or worn T-shirts expressing their protest message. Videos of such actions at many campuses have shown them to be highly effective: the visiting Israeli soldiers start lecturing before a full auditorium, then watch in consternation as most of the audience quietly gets up and files out, leaving the speaker standing before a largely empty room. By changing tactics, students have found a way to avoid the increasingly repressive atmosphere on campus. Northeastern University in Boston, however, even found a way to punish this kind of protest. In April 2013, the university's SJP group staged a walkout from a presentation by Israeli soldiers. "At the start of the event, 35 students stood, small signs taped to their shirts. One member called the soldiers war criminals. One or two chanted slogans. They were gone in a minute," wrote *Boston Globe* columnist Yvonne Abraham.[152] But for this, the SJP was placed on probation and threatened with permanent suspension for any future "transgressions." Northeastern administrators claimed SJP was "sanctioned purely because it failed to get a permit for its demonstration, which the school requires at least seven days in advance." But Abraham's column cast doubt on this: In

2010, SJP members pointed out, members of a campus pro-Israel group disrupted a speech by Norman Finkelstein but never faced any sanctions. "The university is concerned about its image," Tori Porell, an SJP leader, told Abraham. "Some people are trying to smear them as anti-Semitic, so they're attempting to stop anything seen as controversial." Just like the University of Chicago had before Olmert's speech, Northeastern administrators sent the students an email in advance of the Israeli soldiers' appearance "to urge 'respect and decorum,' directing them not to bring in signs, and to 'discourage vocal disruption.'" After the protest, the university required the SJP to "create a civility statement, laying down rules for future conduct."[153] For Abraham, the onerous "permit" requirements, the sanctions imposed on SJP, and the "civility statement" were indications that the university objected not to the form of the protest but its content. Sarah Wunsch, staff attorney for the American Civil Liberties Union of Massachusetts, which took up the students' case, observed, "All of it operates to squelch speech in a place that ought to be teaching students about the role of dissent and vigorous debate in a free society."[154]

The David Project has admitted that highly visible protests by Palestine solidarity activists have hurt the ability of Zionist groups to steer discourse on campus. "Provocative pro-Israel events, such as the popular 'Our Soldiers Speak' project of bringing former IDF soldiers to campus," can also "backfire by energizing anti-Israel groups and allowing them to hijack the event to promote an anti-Israel message," the white paper cautioned. It also asserted that "widely-attended events can be counterproductive" because "protests and controversies may lead the broad center of campus opinion (already prone to moral equivalence) to conclude that Israel advocates are as extreme as anti-Israelists."[155] This is undoubtedly a reaction to the growth of the solidarity movement and is as good an admission as any that high-profile Israeli government speakers, or "ordinary" soldiers with whom American youth are supposed to find a connection, just don't help Israel's cause on campus.

Instead, the David Project advises a quieter approach focusing on campus "influencers" and "celebrities"—a charm offensive to woo students who might later be influential members of society, such as star athletes and members of fraternities and sororities. One technique, "developed successfully on several campuses with the support of AIPAC," is convening "leadership dinners," bringing "a select group of influencers to a small event at which they are provided information on and/or a forum to discuss Israel-related issues of importance to them."[156] Other strategies involve Israel advocates seeking out so-called influencers for "personal dinners" and "one on one" lobbying. Perhaps preparing budding Israel lobbyists for life after college, the David Project also advises students that the best way to shape campus discourse is to "seek to become influencers themselves" by placing themselves in "key leadership roles" in student government and in the media: "Campus Israel advocates should work to achieve leadership roles on these publications themselves or at least develop relationships with those who do to positively impact their coverage of Israel."[157]

Of course there's nothing nefarious about students who are passionate about a cause seeking to advance it legitimately through existing mechanisms. In fact, advocates for Palestinian rights have sometimes pursued similar strategies. Shadi Matar, a member of SJP at the University of California, Riverside, was one of the students who helped push the student senate to pass a resolution supporting divestment in March 2013.[158] "Become part of your student government," Matar, who was himself running to be a student senator, advised students on other campuses. UC Riverside interim chancellor Jane Close Conoley immediately issued a statement reaffirming the university's subservience to US government policy regarding divestment from Israel. The UC Board of Regents "requires this action only when the US government deems it necessary," Conoley reassured Israel's supporters. "No such declaration has been made regarding Israel."[159] Tactics aside, the vote was another sign that the arguments for divestment were persuading an increasing number of students, including the "influencers" on student senates, even if university administrators remained adamantly determined to set aside any institutional or intellectual independence and to follow instructions from government officials in Washington.

There is another factor at work driving pro-Israel groups to try to seek new alliances: in California, many campuses reflect the state's, and the country's, increasing diversity. UC Riverside is one of the most diverse of all: In 2011, 40 percent of its twenty-one thousand students were Asian or Asian American, 29 percent Chicano or Latino, 8 percent African American, and 17 percent white, with others, including Native Americans and international students, making up about 6 percent.[160] In a context where "liberal" Zionists such as *The Crisis of Zionism* author Peter Beinart have sounded the alarm that the cause of Israel is failing to attract—and even repelling—young American Jews, this diversity presents an infinitely more challenging environment.[161] The ADL, for instance, has long been primarily an Israel advocacy organization, but it poses as a promoter of interracial and interethnic harmony. Its website offers trainings and lesson plans on such worthy topics as "religious diversity," "LGBT people and issues," "general anti-bias," and "immigrants and immigration."[162] Nothing, it would seem, pleases the ADL more than to see people of all backgrounds get together, except of course when the cause is Palestinian rights. In its 2011–12 annual review of "Anti-Israel Activity on Campus," the ADL fretted about new strategies appearing widely at universities.[163] The first was that the pinkwashing tactic had not worked and public debate had turned toward "the allegation that Israel exploits its progressive LGBT values as a way to distract attention from the occupation." The second was "intense outreach by anti-Israel groups to Hispanic student groups under the pretext of alleged similarities between the hardships faced by immigrants and Palestinians." Such developments "represent an effort by the anti-Israel movement to couch their agenda in terms that will appeal to a broader base of support."

For the ADL, Latino/a and LGBTQ individuals and groups are no more than passive recipients of Palestinian propaganda. The implication is that if any see a common interest, share similar experiences with Palestinians, or resist the use of their communities in Israeli propaganda, they have somehow been duped. What particularly worried the ADL was the growing alliance between SJP groups and Latino student organizations. Students for Justice in Palestine is often spoken about as a national organization but, in fact, the name "Students for Justice in Palestine"—usually shortened to SJP—is used independently by dozens of individual campus organizations whose status is no different from other campus groups that have used various names, such as "Students Against Israeli Apartheid" or "Students for Palestinian Equal Rights." In 2011, delegates from dozens of these campus Palestine solidarity organizations came together at Columbia University for the first-ever National Students for Justice in Palestine conference, with the goal to build up their networks and democratic structures and improve coordination across their movement.

On César Chávez Day, which coincided with Palestine's Land Day in 2012, Movimiento Estudiantil Chican@ de Aztlán (MEChA), a major national Chicano/a student organization, officially endorsed the Palestinian BDS call during its own national conference.[164] Emerging from the upsurge of Chicano activism in the 1960s, MEChA was founded by students at the University of California, Santa Barbara, in 1969. Now with hundreds of chapters, MEChA has played a crucial role in helping to establish Chicano/a studies programs and defending Hispanic culture, which has come under systematic attack from English-only and other nativist movements. I saw a poignant reminder of this ugly history in the remote West Texas town of Marfa, where I spent two months while working on this book. There, at the corner of Abbot and Waco Streets, sits an austere adobe building with a gabled roof. It is the last remaining structure from the Blackwell School, a segregated school. The school's alumni association has curated artifacts and photographs documenting the history of the school and its community as part of an ongoing preservation effort. Outside, an official Texas historical marker now stands: "Education for local children of Mexican descent dates from 1889, when the former Methodist Church became a schoolhouse. The school, named for longtime principal Jesse Blackwell, served hundreds of children up to ninth grade. Students were told to speak only English on campus; Spanish words written on slips of paper were buried on the grounds in a mock funeral ceremony. The school closed in 1965 with the integration of Marfa schools."

Yanely Rivas, a MEChA representative, explained at the second National SJP conference (held at the University of Michigan in November 2012) how MEChA's adoption of BDS came about: "It all started in the sun-filled state of Arizona, where the heat isn't the only thing burning, but also, the fire ignited in the souls of those fighting for the rights of people who are being explicitly exploited by unjust government policies and corporate interest."[165] The vote to endorse BDS was "not only because of the brutal abuse of power executed by military occupation and the application of settlements" against Palestinians, "but because our Raza can relate to the concept of invasion, dispossession, occupation, exploitation, and discrimination." Rivas reminded her fellow students that in the United States, "land was accumulated through forceful removal of the native people based on the premise of racial class difference. Under the law, native people and African Americans were not citizens of the US and therefore could not own land." In 1848, when the United States occupied half of Mexico—what is now the southwestern United States including Colorado, California, Nevada, New Mexico, Arizona, and Utah—the same racial land expropriation practices were applied to Mexican natives, those from whom Chicano/as are descended genealogically or culturally, who remained behind in these newly conquered territories, as well as in Texas, which the US annexed in 1845. "Anglo settlers," Rivas said, acquired the "lawful right" to "challenge property titles of Mexican landowners." Rivas drew a direct comparison between the "accumulation by the oppressors" in the former Mexican lands and in present-day Palestine, where the peoples present before the conquest "are being treated as disposable commodities."

The cooperation between student activists with SJP and MEChA was forged in the heat of the renewed assault on Latino/as in Arizona under the banner of fighting undocumented immigration. In April 2010, the Arizona legislature passed Senate Bill 1070 (SB 1070), the most draconian anti-immigration law in the United States, empowering police to stop and interrogate any person regarding his or her citizenship status and making it a criminal offense to be an undocumented person. Human-rights campaigners feared that the law would lead to a dramatic increase in racial profiling by police.[166] A protracted court battle led the US Supreme Court to strike down parts of the law in 2012, but the justices kept some of the most repressive provisions intact, particularly those that could lead to racial profiling. At the same time, Arizona became a focus of international scorn and national immigrant rights and anti-racist activism, as the National Council of La Raza and other leading Latino/a, immigrant, and labor-rights organizations called for a boycott of the state reminiscent of the Palestinian call for boycott, divestment, and sanctions on Israel. "If you're dark-skinned; if you sport a big Zapata mustache; if you're a woman and cover yourself with a shawl—then don't even think of living or even visiting the North American state of Arizona, which has officially declared itself racist," legendary Mexican novelist Carlos Fuentes wrote in a scathing editorial.[167] A wave of city councils and municipalities, including Los Angeles, Oakland, San Francisco, Seattle, and Cook County, Illinois, where Chicago is located, all voted for bans on doing business with companies in Arizona. "We're making a statement—equal justice and equal protection under the law for all human beings, notwithstanding their race or their ethnicity," said Cook County Commissioner Earleen Collins, explaining her vote in favor of the boycott.[168] Kanye West, Sonic Youth, Cypress Hill, and Rage Against the Machine were among musicians who signed a "Sound Strike" pledge that they would not play in Arizona.[169] The high school women's basketball team from Highland Park, Illinois, a suburb of Chicago, made headlines and caused controversy when local education officials canceled the team's long-planned participation in a tournament in Arizona, in part to protest the new law and because the officials said they could not guarantee that some team members would not be vulnerable to discrimination if it were enforced.[170]

In the first months of the boycott, Arizona lost $140 million in business, according to a study by the Center for American Progress, a think tank close to the Obama administration. The administration's own crackdown on immigrants in its first term included 1.5 million deportations—a record far outpacing the Bush administration; vast numbers of those sent out of the country were the breadwinners for families with children who had been living in the United States for years.[171] Obama's machinery was working so fast that University of California, Merced, sociologist Tanya Golash-Boza, author of *Immigration Nation: Raids, Detentions, and Deportations in Post-9/11 America* (2012), projected that deportation numbers during Obama's presidency would by 2014 exceed all the deportations from the United States carried out from 1892 to 1997. Obama oversaw a tenfold increase in the deportations of parents of US citizen children; from 1994 to 2012 there was a sixfold increase in detention rates of immigrants to an average of thirty thousand per day, with many detainees ending up in privately run prisons.[172] In 1992, there were only 3,500 border patrol agents on the US-Mexico border. By 2010, the number had risen to more than twenty thousand.[173]

While the main targets of border militarization have been migrants and border communities, members of Congress and the think tanks that provide their expertise have relied on lurid, fanciful, and unsubstantiated or even debunked tales of Middle Eastern "terrorists" crossing into the United States from Mexico. Government officials even claimed, conveniently for those seeking ever-greater border "security," that "people with Middle Eastern names have adopted Hispanic last names before trying to get into the United States"—though without providing examples of this phenomenon or evidence that it was related to "terrorism."[174] Demagogues embellish these claims, often with barely disguised racism, in whatever way suits their agendas. During an interview on C-SPAN in April 2013, for instance, Texas Republican congressman Louie Gohmert, who has insistently pushed for more funding for border militarization, called for the United States to build a wall the full length of its border with Mexico, modeled on Israel's West Bank wall. Gohmert argued, "Finally the Israeli people said, 'You know what? Enough,'" and as a result, "they finally stopped the . . . violence from people that wanted to destroy them. . . . And I'm concerned we need to do that as well," the congressman insisted. "We know that al Qaeda has camps with the drug cartels on the other side of the Mexican border. We know that people are now being trained to come in and act like Hispanics when they're radical Islamists," he claimed. Yet no shred of evidence has been produced to support these frightening assertions. "We know these things are happening, and it's just insane to not protect ourselves."[175] In post–9/11 America, every brown person was now potentially a criminal, a suspected "illegal alien," or a closeted Muslim terrorist. With the federal government spending more on immigration, customs and border enforcement agencies, and the US Coast Guard than on any other category of law enforcement, Obama's new system of mass deportation had merged into the already existing mass-incarceration industry and the endless "War on Terror."[176]

For centuries, the US-Mexico border had been largely unmarked, undemarcated in places, and unfortified, interfering little in the lives of the communities and families whose existence straddled it. After the September 11, 2001, attacks, the US began building hundreds of miles of walls and fences—projects in which the Israeli arms company Elbit participated—now on the pretext of preventing terrorism as well as to control immigration.[177] Whereas the dramatic militarization of the border region did little to slow the movement of people and increased financial incentives for human trafficking and other illicit activities, it has had devastating effects on border communities. Like Palestinians assaulted by Israel's walls and fences, people on the border saw their lives and land increasingly divided and controlled. In some cases, where the actual border line ran through the middle of the Rio Grande (known in Mexico as the Río Bravo), the US fortifications were built north of the river, "slicing off part of a nature reserve here, a few holes of a golf course there and cutting a university campus in two." US citizens stranded on the "Mexican side" of the barriers have been left to "wonder if they now live in Mexico."[178] When I visited the Arizona-Mexico border a few years ago with activists from the human-rights group No Más Muertes/No More Deaths, whose name reflects anguish and outrage against the numbers of people who have died crossing the desert, I often heard the saying "we didn't cross the border, the border crossed us." Nowhere was this more starkly apparent than in the border city of Nogales, which now has a high wall dividing its American and Mexican sides.

Amid the struggle against this federal and state war on immigrants and their children, and on American and Mexican border communities, Palestinian and Chicano/a activists have found common ground and built ties between their movements. Yusi El Boujami, Gabriel Schivone, and Ryan Velasquez, three Arizona students and organizers, saw even more similarities in Israel's and Arizona's efforts as settler-colonial regimes to "deny native peoples access to their cultural institutions which preserve and enrich their heritage, memory and future generations."[179] Specifically, Arizona had passed another law in May 2010, House Bill 2281 (HB 2281), listing "prohibited courses and classes," effectively outlawing Chicano/a and other ethnic studies.[180] In compliance with the law, the Tucson Unified School District, serving a city whose population is 42 percent of Hispanic or Latino/a origin, released a list of titles that would be removed from classrooms, including Shakespeare's *The Tempest,* Paolo Freire's *Pedagogy of the Oppressed,* pioneer Chicano historian Rodolfo Acuña's *Occupied America: A History of Chicanos,* and *Rethinking Columbus: The Next 500 Years*—a textbook that had sold hundreds of thousands of copies around the country and included pieces by Native American authors Suzan Shown Harjo, Buffy Sainte-Marie, Joseph Bruchac, Leslie Marmon Silko, and Winona LaDuke.[181] Two dozen civil society and education organizations, including the American Association of University Professors, PEN, the American Civil Liberties Union, and the Arizona English Teachers' Association, released a joint statement condemning "book-banning and thought control" in Arizona.[182]

Recalling Israeli prime minister Ariel Sharon's 2004 statement that "Palestinian education and propaganda are more dangerous to Israel than Palestinian weapons," El Boujami, Schivone, and Velasquez accused Arizona governor Jan Brewer and Attorney General Tom Horne of trying to stamp out ethnic studies "because it enables our people to retain our education on our terms rather than simply accept imposed history."[183] Here, too, there was an unmistakable parallel with Israel's 2011 "Nakba Law," which allows the government to withhold funding from institutions and municipalities that commemorate the 1948 ethnic cleansing of Palestine. Adalah, a legal advocacy group for Palestinians in Israel, warned that the law would "cause major harm to the principle of equality and to the rights of Arab citizens to preserve their history and culture."[184] Thus there is also a strong similarity not only between Israeli and Arizona laws, but also in the coercive methods and criminalization used to limit free speech and education on these issues within American institutions.

Supporters of the ban on ethnic studies defended it on the grounds that such teaching encouraged "racial resentment" and disharmony. They have seized on the use by Latino/as of the Spanish term *la raza*, which appeared in the early twentieth century, to identify their communities and culture. The word literally translates into English as "race," but has very different connotations from the meaning of "race" in the American context, in which European pseudoscientific biological racialism has been used to justify the oppression of African Americans. The National Council of La Raza (NCLR) explains that the term is better translated as "the people" and, far from promoting separatism or exclusivity, "was coined by Mexican scholar José Vasconcelos to reflect the fact that the people of Latin America are a mixture of many of the world's races, cultures, and religions."[185] Calling the English rendering "race" a "mistranslation," NCLR emphasizes that *la raza* is an "inclusive concept, meaning that Hispanics share with all other peoples of the world a common heritage and destiny." In spirit, the Arizona law was a twenty-first-century version of the mock funerals students at the segregated Blackwell School in Marfa, Texas, were once forced to hold for the Spanish language and for their culture and identity.

Governor Brewer also attacked the use of the term *la raza* in her justification of both the anti-immigrant and anti-ethnic studies laws as necessary defenses against an assault from "multiculturalism," which, she claimed, "encourages its followers to put racial and ethnic identity above all."[186] Calling ethnic studies the "teaching of race hatred," she approvingly quoted French president Nicolas Sarkozy's pithy line, "We have been too concerned about the identity of the person who was arriving and not enough about the identity of the country that was receiving him."[187] In a revealing statement, Brewer argued, "In the end, the illegal immigration debate isn't about the identity of those coming to America; it's about preserving the identity of America itself."[188] Those who wanted to teach ethnic studies were the same people who "don't believe in protecting America's borders" and who denied "American exceptionalism," the governor claimed.[189] Brewer, a transplant to Arizona, born in California to parents of Norwegian ancestry who had previously lived in Minnesota, could apparently not see the irony of lecturing Hispanic communities whose ancestors had been on that land long before it was part of the United States that *they* were the ones seeking to undermine the country's identity and culture.[190] "They don't care about our identity—in fact, they see a strong, cohesive American identity as something people cling to out of fear and bigotry," Brewer charged.[191]

Brewer's anxiety about controlling the influx of unwanted people into the state and her determination to defend Anglo settler-colonial monoculturalism from the dangers of "multiculturalism" provide a clue to her real concerns—what she calls "preserving the identity of America." The battles over immigration in the United States have been waged amid profound demographic change. In 2005, Texas joined Hawaii, New Mexico, and California, as well as the partially disenfranchised District of Columbia, to become a "majority minority" state. Just over half of the state's population was comprised of Hispanics, African Americans, Asian Americans, and others, leaving whites—still the largest single group—as a minority. The *Houston Chronicle* predicted profound political shifts in coming years, turning Texas from a solidly "red state" controlled by Republicans, the party overwhelmingly supported by white voters, into a "blue state" where Democrats would take back power.[192] The changes in southwestern states, including Texas, foreshadow a transformation that is happening nationwide. In 2012, for the first time in recorded United States history, white births were no longer the majority, "a milestone for a nation whose government was founded by white Europeans and has wrestled mightily with issues of race, from the days of slavery, through a civil war, bitter civil rights battles and, most recently, highly charged debates over efforts to restrict immigration."[193] William H. Frey, a demographer at the Brookings Institution, described the shift as an "important tipping point," marking the "transformation from a mostly white baby boomer culture to the more globalized multiethnic country that we are becoming."[194] While whites are still 63 percent of the US population, their median age is much older than that of the other groups that are likely to outnumber them during the next thirty years. These changes are happening rapidly in Arizona, where the non-Hispanic white population fell from 72 percent in 1990, according to the United States census, to 58 percent in 2010. Most white Americans may not care and few would be as explicit as Israelis in talking about a "demographic threat," yet there is increasingly pervasive right-wing and white supremacist agitation about Mexican women allegedly crossing the border to give birth to "anchor babies" who could then supposedly, decades later, confer their US citizenship on their parents.[195] Such dehumanizing claims are thin on facts, but are redolent of the same demographic anxieties manipulated by Israeli politicians to pass a law to prohibit Palestinian and other Arab spouses from living in the country with their Israeli-citizen wives or husbands (see chapter 2) and prompted Israel's interior minister Eli Yishai to declare that "this country belongs to us, to the white man."[196]

Racist beliefs of this kind are perhaps some of the less frequently trumpeted "shared values" of the United States and Israel as states founded through settler-colonialism and where the political order that has kept the descendants of the settlers in power looks increasingly shaky. Those committed to human rights, equality, and antiracism should welcome, deepen, and support the developing solidarity between Palestinian activists and Latino communities. This solidarity must be more than a transactional "we'll support your cause if you support ours" arrangement, but must be founded on a deep analysis that the political forces, power centers, and white supremacist ideologies that advance racist laws and practices in states such as Arizona are the same ones that support and sponsor Israel and propagate the rhetoric and global violence of the "War on Terror." It is the same racialized order—embodied in the endless parade of admiring US police officials visiting Israel—that has created and maintained America's atrocious system of mass incarceration. The important work SJP and MEChA do to build understanding that they are a generation working in a common cause offers a promising beginning for what needs to become a much broader and more sustained mobilization.

The ADL's unbridled horror at the cooperation between SJP and MEChA is one indicator of the transformative potential such alliances could have in reshaping the political balance of power on campus and in US politics more broadly. It is no wonder then that Zionist organizations are determined to disrupt or divert this kind of campus coalition-building. The David Project advises campus Israel advocates to seek out groups with which they have "a potential for a natural affinity." It singles out Indian Americans, whose "leaders," the white paper alleges, "see American Jews as a model for minority success in the United States, and have a natural desire to work with Jewish groups."[197] Among the key "affinities" that the David Project sees driving Indian Americans into alliance with Zionist groups is that both India and Israel "are primary targets and victims of Islamist terrorism [and] suffer from protracted border disputes with majority Muslim populations." Both countries market themselves as high-tech pioneers and "see themselves as the modern political manifestations of ancient civilizations."[198]

The view that Israel and India are "natural" partners has grown in recent years in parallel with Hindutva, a Hindu nationalist and chauvinist movement which claims India, officially a secular state, as the true patrimony and homeland of Hindus, with Indian Muslims viewed as interlopers and invaders and Muslims more generally as the antagonistic other.[199] It was this chauvinist ideology that in 1992 motivated Hindu nationalists to destroy the four-hundred-year-old Babri Mosque in the northern Indian city of Ayodhya, which they claimed was built over the ruins of a Hindu temple marking the birthplace of the god Lord Ram. The ensuing riots killed thousands of people, exacerbating sectarianism and communalism in India to this day, and offer an ominous warning of what could happen, almost certainly on a much larger scale, if Jewish nationalists attempt to fulfill their desire to build a Jewish Third Temple in Jerusalem on the site where the Al-Aqsa Mosque now stands. The fact that 180 million Indians are Muslims—more than 10 percent of the world's Muslim population, and as many as live in Pakistan—does not register in the David Project's understanding of India. The implication is that India should be seen as the "Hindu state," analogous to Israel as the "Jewish state." Thus the alliance the David Project promotes is one based on ethno-religious chauvinism and more-or-less-explicit Islamophobia. San Francisco Bay area activist Yasmin Qureshi has seen this alliance materialize in efforts by Zionist and Hindutva groups to scuttle events that discuss India's human-rights abuses in Kashmir, India's military cooperation with Israel, and Israel's treatment of Palestinians. "Zionists and Hindutva advocates," Qureshi observes, "have adopted a similar Islamophobic language and worldview that considers any grievances or struggles by Muslims to be simply a cover for 'jihadism' or 'wahhabism' and thus justifies treating all such movements for justice—however they are conducted—as 'terrorist.'"[200]

Religion can also be the basis of alliances with other ethnic diasporas identified by the David Project: "South Korea has a large and growing evangelical population and there is evidence of increasing affinity for Israel and Jews in that country." In China, too, "there is also some evidence of Chinese affinity for Jewish culture and Israel."[201] What all these appeals have in common is a basis in supposed cultural characteristics, not any principled agenda about universal rights. As for Latino/a student groups, the David Project, like the ADL, laments that many are "susceptible to partnership in an anti-Israel coalition." "Convincing them not to publicly affiliate with or otherwise support anti-Israelism would itself be a significant victory for Israel supporters on many campuses," the white paper states.[202] Yet it offers no advice at all on how this is to be done, other than attempting to co-opt individual "influencers."

While seeking to take advantage of right-wing chauvinism and religious fervor to shore up support for Israel, the David Project believes that Zionist groups should not be seen to be doing so, for fear that this could dent efforts to market Israel as a progressive and liberal cause. Christian evangelical students, in particular, are another group with a "natural" affinity toward Israel due to the popularity of Christian Zionist dispensationalist theology—an implicitly anti-Semitic belief system that requires the ingathering of Jews to Israel, where they will be converted to Christianity or die as the world is consumed during Armageddon, as a necessary condition for the return of Jesus Christ. Thus, the David Project recommends that Israel supporters should work with this "important demographic" without alienating other target groups or entering into a "permanent coalition" that "associates Israel's 'brand' too closely with unpopular 'social' issues."[203] In other words, pro-Israel messaging has to be able to appeal simultaneously for the support of LGBTQ communities and of the Christian Zionists who consider same-sex relationships an abomination.

Perhaps the most cynical of all such "outreach" efforts has been AIPAC's recruitment and training of Black students on American campuses as spokespersons for Israel.[204] AIPAC saw the tactic as particularly useful to combat the perception of Israel as an apartheid state, attempting to stir outrage that Palestinians should compare their own suffering to that of Black people in South Africa. What made it more than usually hypocritical is that AIPAC, along with most other major American Jewish organizations, remained conspicuously silent about the rampant and alarming racism and mob protests against Africans in Israel, often fueled and led by politicians like Interior Minister Eli Yishai. Yishai ordered the construction of special desert camps to hold Africans and continued to threaten, harass, and deport African refugees and asylum seekers to countries where they would be at risk of persecution. Israel even began to threaten asylum seekers from Sudan and Eritrea with long prison sentences unless they agreed to leave.[205] In a shocking example of Israel's dehumanization of Africans, Israeli media reported in July 2013 that the government was ready to sign deals to use asylum seekers as a form of currency. "African countries who will accept tens of thousands of African migrants currently residing in Israel" would receive "a benefits package" that "will include Israeli arms and military knowledge and training," senior officials told Israel's *Ynet*.[206]

The Zionist strategy of seeking inter-community alliances and trying to disrupt those formed by the Palestine solidarity movement depends on an implicit understanding that Palestinians, Arabs, and Muslims can remain marginalized from mainstream American civic life, as they have been for so many years. An encouraging sign that this is a miscalculation came when Sadia Saifuddin, a member of the UC Berkeley student government, became the first Muslim to be named student representative to the Board of Regents, the University of California's highest governing body. When her nomination came up for discussion, "she was opposed by a number of pro-Israel groups, including StandWithUs and the Simon Wiesenthal Center, and by conservative activist David Horowitz, who wrote in an open letter: 'If she were confirmed, it would set a dangerous precedent to encourage anti-Semitism on campus, which is already a big problem in the UC system.'"[207] In a remarkable editorial, the *Los Angeles Times* gave short shrift to this all too common calumny: "Oh, for goodness' sake, will this never stop?" Saifuddin's real transgression, the editorial noted, is that she is "a critic of Israel" who, "like many people . . . opposes the occupation of the West Bank, the continued building of settlements and what she sees as the mistreatment of Palestinians." She had also cosponsored the UC Berkeley divestment resolution. "There's no indication that Saifuddin is an anti-Semite, despite her criticism of Israel, her involvement with the Muslim Students Assn. or her condemnation of anti-Islamic 'hate speech,'" the editorial said.[208] The newspaper's high-profile support for Saifuddin, as well as its sharp rebuke of her critics, is an important sign that the efforts to delegitimize and marginalize those who criticize Israel no longer carry the weight they once did. Even more significant, Saifuddin received the votes of all the regents except for one, Richard Blum, who claimed she was too "divisive."[209] Yet, while Saifuddin's election was a step forward, the same Regents meeting that approved her also confirmed Janet Napolitano, the former US secretary of homeland security, to succeed Mark Yudof as president of the University of California. The nomination of Napolitano, who oversaw the Obama administration's "War on Terror" and mass deportations, generated immediate protest from a coalition of student groups, including SJP, concerned about her commitment to human rights and free speech.[210]

Failed Pacification

Much of the emphasis of Israel-lobby organizations has been on demonizing, suppressing, or criminalizing the Palestine solidarity movement on campus, very much in line with the Reut Institute's calls for "sabotage" and "attack." But some Israel-lobby leaders have begun to understand that this approach alone cannot turn things around. "We must give people reasons to support Israel, not to dislike the other side," argues Elliot Mathias, founder and director of Hasbara Fellowships, a group that trains students to advocate for Israel.[211] One campus in particular was to become a showcase for more positive strategies. UC Irvine "has become a hotbed of pro-Israel activity, only two years after an anti-Israeli attack on former envoy Michael Oren during a speech on campus," Israel's *Ynet* reported on November 5, 2012, under the sunny headline "Israel shines in California campus." It was of course at Irvine that the Israel lobby, in collusion with university administrators and judicial authorities, scored one of its biggest hits on the Palestine solidarity movement with the convictions of the Irvine 11. The Reut Institute itself celebrated the trial as an "achievement," along with the attacks on the *Electronic Intifada* and the Palestinian

Return Centre in London, calling these examples of putting a "price tag" on the "delegitimization" of Israel (see chapter 5).[212] The use of the term "price tag" cannot have been an unconscious choice: it is the same term often spray-painted by Israeli settlers on mosques, homes, and other Palestinian property they vandalize or set fire to in the West Bank. There could be no clearer indication that the Reut Institute proudly identified with and sought to emulate, on an international scale, this type of intimidation. Now, however, according to *Ynet*, there was a "drastic change" in the atmosphere at UC Irvine.

Having been pacified by the heavy artillery of the Irvine 11 trial, the campus was now seen as defenseless against Israel's soft cultural power. A university conference hosted digital media experts from Tel Aviv and "a recent campus concert by leading Israeli singer Idan Raichel, which hundreds of students attended, was enjoyed by all—uninterrupted," *Ynet* reported. Raichel and his group, the Idan Raichel Project, had been traveling to college campuses in the United States on Israeli government-sponsored tours for years. In 2005, the musician embarked on the first such propaganda trip financed by the foreign ministry "to give the African-American population a new perspective" on Israel. "I'm not black," the dreadlocked Raichel explained at the time, "yet the Ethiopians in the project and I work together."[213] His deployment to UC Irvine was an indicator of how seriously the turnaround campaign was being taken. *Ynet* revealed that Los Angeles–based Israeli consul general David Segal had "contributed greatly to the change," among other things by bringing UC Irvine chancellor Michael Drake on a tour of Israel, where he was received by President Shimon Peres, "met with academic leaders and agreed on future collaboration with the Israel Institute of Technology, as well as the Tel Aviv, Beersheba and Hebrew universities." It must have been a quite a shock to Segal when, just one week after the self-congratulatory *Ynet* report appeared, the UC Irvine student government passed a resolution calling for divestment from companies that profit from Israeli "apartheid" by 16 to 0.[214] This was a sweet victory for all the students involved in the divestment effort, especially those who just a year earlier had stood awaiting their fate in the Santa Ana courthouse.

In early 2013, the student government at UC San Diego passed a similar bill after a hard-fought battle. Zionist groups had waged a fierce campaign before the vote, bringing in some big guns. "As a member of Congress who sits on the Foreign Affairs Committee, there has been no credible proof that defines Israel as an 'apartheid' state," wrote Representative Juan Vargas, the Democratic member for California's fifty-first district, in a letter to student senators. "In fact, Israel is the only country in the Middle East with protection for free speech, free press, religious freedom, women's rights and gay rights." Representative Susan Davis, also a Democrat and member of Congress for the fifty-third district, sent a similar letter, including some passages that were identical to those in Vargas's letter.[215] Despite such high-level, and apparently coordinated, intervention in campus affairs, the student legislators kept their own counsel, debating the matter seriously for hours before passing the divestment resolution by 20 to 12.[216]

Israel lobby groups have demonstrated that even after they lose a vote, they will keep working against divestment. Despite the fact that some forty campus organizations supported the divestment resolution approved at UC Riverside in March 2013, the student senate voted to overturn it less than a month later after an intense campaign by Zionist advocates, including what student senator Ahlam Jadallah called "scare tactics."[217] After the reverse, Amal Ali of UC Riverside SJP conceded that the negative campaign had had an impact. "It was definitely a stark difference from the last time," she said. "But I'm ready to come back next week, and come back fighting."[218] Israel-lobby groups have suffered setbacks of their own, such as when Brown University's official Advisory Committee on Corporate Responsibility in Investment Policies wrote to the university's president urging consideration of calls for divestment from companies involved in Israeli occupation. These developments underscore that the effort to suppress divestment will be a long, grueling and nationwide struggle.[219] The Brown initiative is also a sign that divestment is starting to move beyond mere recommendations from student legislatures. Outgoing University of California president Mark Yudof conceded, at a June 2013 conference in Israel, that heavy-handed efforts to suppress divestment campaigns were unlikely to succeed. "It seems that every six months, I'm reading about another vote of some sort of student organization on this issue, or some sort of academic organization, and too often, that vote is lost," Yudof lamented.[220] Malcolm Hoenlein, executive vice chairman of the Conference of Presidents of Major American Jewish Organizations, revealed that his organization was planning a major counteroffensive against the BDS movement following the string of setbacks: "It will be a major Internet and social media campaign, in which we hope to reach every single college student in America. The goal is to educate in creative ways and win the public back."[221]

The David Project identified college campuses as a key theater in the Israel lobby's battle to shore up American support for Israel in the future, and well-funded Zionist organizations are concentrating their resources and efforts to suppress Palestine solidarity on campus, targeting teachers, students, and the institutions themselves. No matter how much Zionist groups belittle this or that student-council divestment resolution as merely a nonbinding or insignificant recommendation, the intensity of Zionist and Israeli efforts belies an understanding that the BDS movement and the struggle for Palestinian rights more broadly have the potential to score much bigger victories in years to come. The David Project is correct when it predicts that what happens on campus can also shape broader views about Palestine and ultimately shift US support away from Israel. It is already happening. But this shift cannot and will not take place, much less bear fruit, in isolation. The Palestine solidarity movement must become an integral part of a bigger movement, especially in the United States, of the fight to bring an end to mass incarceration and the struggle against racist anti-immigration policies.

The United States will turn away from an imperialist and interventionist role around the world, the role that sustains support for Israeli occupation and apartheid, only to the extent that the transformation toward a just and democratic society is also under way at home. SJP put it best in the closing statement of its second national conference: "We believe that no struggle against oppression is divorced from one another, that in order to resist structural oppression we must embody the principles and ideals we envision for a just society, and that we must be vigilant about upholding ethical positions against homophobia, sexism, racism, bigotry, classism, colonialism, and discrimination of any form."[222] These values are the polar opposites of the demonstrated approach of the Israel lobby on campus, which has tried to use LGBTQ people as a wedge to divide the solidarity movement, attempted to co-opt people of color to put a rainbow face on racism, worked to shut down and punish free speech, celebrated and supported US and Israeli militarism, and sought to build alliances based on shared bigotries against Muslims and others. But despite all these generously financed reactionary efforts, the Palestine solidarity movement on campus continues to move forward.

Chapter 7

Reclaiming
Self-Determination

I n his iconic 1974 "gun and olive branch" speech to the United Nations General Assembly, Palestine Liberation Organization chairman Yasser Arafat addressed "the roots of the Palestine question," declaring, "Its causes do not stem from any conflict between two religions or two nationalisms. Neither is it a border conflict between neighboring states. It is the cause of a people deprived of its homeland, dispersed and uprooted, and living mostly in exile and in refugee camps."[1] How ironic, then, that the endless "peace process" that began more than two decades ago has reconceived the Palestine question as little more than a border dispute between Israel and a putative Palestinian state. The "roots" were first reduced to a laconic list of "final status issues"—borders, settlements, Jerusalem, and refugees—and then gradually buried. Any commitment to self-determination, in principle or in practice, has been lost.[2]

Although they have rarely been formally discussed, it has long been conventional wisdom in peace-process circles that the "final status" issues have already been effectively settled, largely according to Israel's requirements (we have heard *ad nauseam* the refrain "everyone knows what a final settlement will look like"). The United States and its handpicked Palestinian leaders have accepted, for instance, that the large Israeli "settlement blocs" housing most of the settlers will remain where they are in the West Bank, often on land violently seized from Palestinian communities. The same formula has been adopted for Jerusalem, as per the so-called "Clinton parameters" set out by the former president just before he left office: Israel would get

"Jewish neighborhoods" and the Palestinian state would get "Arab neighborhoods." What this would mean in practice is that Israel would keep everything it has illegally annexed and colonized since 1967, and Palestinians might get some form of self-rule in whatever is left—which is shrinking daily as Israel aggressively escalates its Judaization of eastern occupied Jerusalem. While everything east of the 1967 line is divisible and "disputed," the same does not apply to the west. Palestinians are never entitled, for example, to seek the return of the West Jerusalem neighborhoods Israel ethnically cleansed and colonized in 1948.[3] The "peace process" has actually created an incentive for Israel to accelerate its colonization of the West Bank, including Jerusalem, because it knows that whatever is left uncolonized automatically becomes the new maximum ceiling of what the United States and other peace-process sponsors would contemplate as Palestinian demands. Thus there was no contradiction between Secretary of State Kerry's "breakthrough" announcement of the resumption of direct negotiations between Israel and the Palestinian Authority "without preconditions" in July 2013, on the one hand, and, on the other, Israel announcing a few days later a massive increase in the number of settlements eligible for special government funding, a policy aimed at attracting more settlers.[4]

Similarly, the refugee question has been virtually "settled" as well. Palestinian Authority–appointed chief negotiator Saeb Erekat revealed in a paper he circulated in late 2009 that Fatah leader and acting Palestinian Authority president Mahmoud Abbas had proposed to Israel that no more than fifteen thousand Palestinian refugees per year, for ten years, return to their original lands in present-day Israel.[5] According to Erekat, then–Israeli prime minister Ehud Olmert had countered with an offer of one thousand refugees per year for a period of five years. In other words, the parties had already agreed to abrogate the fundamental rights of millions of Palestinian refugees and were haggling only over the difference between five thousand and one hundred and fifty thousand, or less than 3 percent of the Palestinian refugees registered to receive services from UNRWA. These concessions were confirmed by the Palestine Papers.[6] So what is left to negotiate?

Yet, despite these concessions, even now one still hears arguments that a two-state solution can still provide Palestinians with "sovereignty" in a state—and therefore "self-determination." So let us imagine, for the sake of argument, the remote scenario that Israel would agree to a Palestinian state in the West Bank, including East Jerusalem and the Gaza Strip, that satisfies official Palestinian positions and provides for a state no more or less sovereign than any other. The question that then arises is: Does this sovereign state provide for the self-determination of the Palestinian people? Does it restore and guarantee their fundamental rights? As I argue in this chapter, the answer is no. And this underscores the need to distinguish the limited goals of sovereignty and statehood from that of self-determination. Sovereignty is exercised by a state through the fulfillment of commonly agreed-upon functions: effective control of territory, borders, and resources and maintenance of political independence, among others. Self-determination is exercised by a people legitimately inhabiting a given territory. Self-determination might result in a sovereign state, but it might not. It is fundamental to understand this difference and to recognize that self-determination remains at the heart of the Palestinian struggle.

Understanding the Principle of Self-Determination

The principle of self-determination as it is understood today was enunciated by US president Woodrow Wilson toward the end of World War I. In Wilson's words, "the settlement of every question, whether of territory, of sovereignty, of economic arrangement, or of political relationship" is to be made "upon the basis of the free acceptance of that settlement by the people immediately concerned and not on the basis of the material interest or advantage of any other nation or people which may desire a different settlement for sake of its own exterior influence or mastery."[7] Put simply, territories and people could no longer be shifted around between empires and sovereigns like pieces on a chessboard. Any political arrangements—particularly in territories undergoing decolonization—had to enjoy the freely given consent of those who would have to live under them. The principle was no sooner enunciated than it was effectively violated in many cases after World War I, particularly in Palestine. It would be decades before Wilson's conception was extended to include lands and peoples colonized by Europeans, among others. However, the principle of self-determination gained ground and was later enshrined in Article 1 of the United Nations Charter and other instruments, assuming particular importance in post–World War II decolonization.

Tomis Kapitan, a philosophy professor at Northern Illinois University, provides an excellent summary of the history and application of this principle. He argues persuasively that, as conceived and practiced, the right of self-determination belongs not to national groups as national groups, but to the legitimate residents of any region whose status is unsettled, for example because it was previously colonized or recently liberated from foreign domination, or which is endangered because the current sovereign has persistently failed to protect or has itself consistently violated the fundamental rights of the legitimate residents. The residents of regions meeting these criteria "have a right to determine their political future either by constituting themselves as an autonomous political unit, or by merging with another state, or by dissolving into smaller states."[8]

Palestine, as Kapitan observes, "is the only territory placed under a League of Nations mandate in which the established inhabitants were not granted this privilege."[9] Instead, Great Britain, the mandatory power, agreed to partition the country over the unified opposition of the overwhelming indigenous-Arab majority and aided and abetted the buildup of settler-colonial Zionists from other parts of the world, who eventually carried out a violent takeover of much of the country. British officials from Balfour to Churchill explicitly understood and articulated that in order to support and fulfill the Zionist program, as they were committed to doing, the principle of self-determination, as even they understood it, could not be applied to Palestine.[10] Arafat noted in his 1974 speech that, by endorsing partition with Resolution 181 of 1947, "the [UN] General Assembly partitioned what it had no right to divide—an indivisible homeland" and thus contributed to the denial of the right of self-determination. No form of consultation through referendum, plebiscite, or any other democratic process was ever carried out or even contemplated.

Today, Kapitan argues, the legitimate residents of historic Palestine include, at minimum, all Palestinians living in any part of the country, as well as all refugees outside the country. "Because expulsion does not remove one's right of residency, then these Palestinians also retain residency rights in those territories from which they were expelled."[11] The establishment and maintenance of Israel as an exclusionary state over much of historic Palestine does not extinguish these rights. Thus, the Palestinian people collectively retain "an entitlement to being self-determining in [historic Palestine] . . . not *qua* Palestinians, but *qua* legitimate residents. That force was used against them has not erased the fact that they are, and are recognized as being, a legitimate unit entitled to participate in their own self-determination."[12] The peace process that began with the 1991 Madrid Conference, by contrast, has gradually excluded the majority of Palestinians from any role in determining the future of their country. In the eyes of peace-process sponsors, the "Palestinian people" now constitutes, at most, residents of the West Bank and Gaza Strip, though even Gaza now finds itself as marginalized as the Palestinian diaspora. Along with sidelining most Palestinians, peace-process discourse has also redefined and limited Palestinian horizons in a manner compatible with Israeli demands. In his famous June 2009 speech at Cairo University addressing Muslims around the world, for instance, President Obama declared, "America will not turn our backs on the legitimate Palestinian aspiration for dignity, opportunity, and a state of their own." This formula garnered applause for mentioning a "state," but what it notably lacked was any mention of Palestinian rights, particularly those of refugees. In the speeches of Obama and other international officials, vague terms such as "dignity," "aspirations," and "opportunity" have replaced any talk of enforceable rights, international law, or justice. These exclusions and obfuscations have allowed a cause of liberation, decolonization, and self-determination to be reduced to little more than a "border dispute."

Palestinian Self-Determination and the Rights of Israeli Jews

Could Palestinians exercising the right to self-determination throughout historic Palestine be compatible with eventual cohabitation between Palestinians and Israeli Jews? If so, on what terms? Omar Barghouti, a founder of the international Palestinian BDS campaign, has argued strongly against recognizing Israeli Jews as forming a national community in Palestine. Barghouti warns that "recognizing *national* rights of Jewish settlers in Palestine cannot but imply accepting their right to self-determination."[13] This would, he argues, contradict "the very letter, spirit and purpose of the universal principle of self-determination primarily as a means for 'peoples under colonial or alien domination or foreign occupation,' to realize their rights." Such recognition, he predicts, "may, at one extreme, lead to claims for secession or Jewish 'national' sovereignty on part of the land of Palestine." There can, Barghouti argues, be no "inherent or acquired Jewish right to self-determination in Palestine that is equivalent, even morally symmetric, to the Palestinian right to self-determination" as this would blur "the essential differences between the inalienable rights of the indigenous population and the acquired rights of the colonial-settler population."

This is an important point: Israel insists that an entity called "the Jewish people" has the right to "self-determination" in Palestine and the right to express that self-determination by creating and maintaining a state that discriminates against Palestinian citizens and other non-Jews living in it, as well as Palestinians living outside it, by denying their return solely on the grounds that they are not Jews. This is a clear violation of the rights of Palestinians, whose citizenship was recognized as a matter of international law in the 1924 Treaty of Lausanne and in the 1925 Palestinian Citizenship Order issued by the British Mandate authorities. As Susan Akram, a professor of international law at Boston University, noted in her speech at the One-State Conference at Harvard University in March 2012:

> Jewish claims of nationality and self-determination must be clearly distinguished from the claims of Israeli Jews to nationality and self-determination as a matter of international law. Israel proclaimed her state on behalf of "the Jewish people,"

a concept and definition that grants rights to and within the state on an extra-territorial basis. Israel enacted its citizenship law of 1950 to grant "nationality" to Jews only, repealing the Palestine citizenship law [of 1925]. Israel's claim of a state on the basis of exclusive and discriminatory rights to Jews has never been juridically recognized—in other words, the concept of "the Jewish people" as a national entity with extraterritorial claims has never been recognized in international law. The people entitled to national status in the "Jewish state" defined under [the 1947 United Nations partition resolution] 181 included both Jews and Palestinians already residing in the territory, all of whom were to be granted equal rights under a constitution to be in force in both new states (the "Jewish" and "Arab" states contemplated in the resolution) prior to UN recognition. The United Nations, including its treaty bodies and the International Court of Justice, has repeatedly called Jewish-preferencing under Israeli citizenship, property, and other laws, a violation of the UN Charter and human rights treaties. In other words, there has been no recognition of the "Jewish people" as a nationality concept that grants self-determination. Nor is there legal consensus that Israel has a right to maintain a legal-preferencing system that grants superior rights to Jews as against other citizens.[14]

In chapter 2, I argued that Israel has no "right" to exist as a "Jewish state" because that "right" can only be exercised by violating the fundamental individual rights of Palestinians. The additional point to be made here is that Israel's claim of self-determination for "the Jewish people" is not only unsupported in international law, but violates the well-established collective self-determination rights of the Palestinian people as a whole.

Yet the concept that a community established through settler-colonialism is entitled, under specific conditions, to participate in self-determination—not as a distinct national group but as legitimate residents—accords with precedents and international law in other decolonizing countries, including South Africa, Namibia, Northern Ireland, and Mozambique. Under Kapitan's formulation, Israeli Jews could be entitled to participate in self-determination not as a distinct national group, but only to the extent that they become legitimate residents in the context of complete decolonization. Barghouti spells out conditions under which colonial settlers could be accepted by the indigenous population as legitimate residents, as citizens in a society "free from all colonial subjugation and discrimination." It would require the settler-colonial community, in this case Israeli Jews, to relinquish their colonial character and settler privileges and accept "unmitigated equality," including the right of return and reparations for Palestinian refugees. This is, moreover, "the most magnanimous offer any indigenous population, oppressed for decades, can present to its oppressors."[15] From a legal and a political standpoint, Israeli Jews would have to relinquish their legally enshrined and socially normalized privileges, the way whites did in South Africa. It must be emphasized—especially in light of the incomplete process of decolonization in South Africa and the New Jim Crow in the United States—that decolonization must include comprehensive programs to redistribute wealth, income, and power while offering protection to all and working to build new political coalitions, so that the existing caste system does not persist in pernicious ways even under the guise of liberal democracy.

It is possible to begin to lay out principles that can guide such an approach. Inspired by the South African Freedom Charter and the 1998 Belfast Agreement, a group of intellectuals that included Palestinians and Israelis set out similar principles in the 2007 One State Declaration:

> The historic land of Palestine belongs to all who live in it and to those who were expelled or exiled from it since 1948, regardless of religion, ethnicity, national origin or current citizenship status;
>
> Any system of government must be founded on the principle of equality in civil, political, social and cultural rights for all citizens. Power must be exercised with rigorous impartiality on behalf of all people in the diversity of their identities.[16]

Mindful that decolonization extends far beyond notions of formal equality and representation, the declaration insists that "there must be just redress for the devastating effects of decades of Zionist colonization." Finally, the notion that Israeli Jews can be legitimate residents on the condition that they shed their colonial character and privileges derives directly from the traditional conception of Palestinian self-determination, which is inclusive and rights-based, not ethnic or religious. Indeed, Arafat embodied this in his 1974 UN speech, declaring that "when we speak of our common hopes for the Palestine of tomorrow we include in our perspective all Jews now living in Palestine who choose to live with us there in peace and without discrimination."

Focusing on Self-Determination

Placing self-determination back at the center of the Palestine question compels us to formulate a strategy that addresses the rights of all segments of the Palestinian community, inside and outside historic Palestine, and which ensures their right to participate in the struggle for and enjoy the fruits of self-determination. It requires setting out an agenda that addresses the three historic and current sources of injustice, the "roots" of the conflict. Such an agenda, as stated in the widely endorsed 2005 Palestinian call for BDS, demands that Israel recognize the Palestinian people's inalienable right to self-determination and uphold international law by ending its occupation and colonization of all Arab lands; dismantling the apartheid wall in the West Bank; recognizing the fundamental rights of the Arab-Palestinian citizens of present-day Israel to full equality; and respecting, protecting, and promoting the rights of Palestinian refugees to return to their homes and properties, as stipulated in UN Resolution 194.[17]

These three demands do not dictate a specific political outcome, but it is clear that the limited sovereignty that a West Bank–Gaza state would achieve addresses at best only the first point and cannot possibly meet the minimum requirements of Palestinian self-determination. Therefore, the formula "everyone knows" is the answer—a state on a fraction of Palestine for a fraction of the Palestinian people—would only perpetuate the denial of self-determination for the vast majority of Palestinians, no matter how "sovereign" that state. Once we accept nonracial equality as a principle, it becomes easier and more logical to conceive of an outcome involving a single democratic state encompassing Palestinians and decolonized Israeli Jews.

After six and a half decades, Israel is no closer to quieting the challenges to its legitimacy, nor could an agreement with an unrepresentative Palestinian leadership ever do so. Neither the passage of time nor declarations cajoled, bullied, or bought out of successive leaders of the Palestinian national movement have settled the questions of Israel's creation or its demand to be recognized as a "Jewish state" with the right to discriminate against Palestinians. Palestinian claims for self-determination have not been extinguished, nor have Palestinians generally pursued them with any less vigor. Indeed, Netanyahu's demand that Palestinians must accept Israel's "right to exist as a Jewish state," is an implicit recognition that the Zionist project can never enjoy legitimacy or stability without the active consent of the Palestinian people. Palestinians have steadfastly resisted granting such recognition because to do so would negate their rights and indeed threaten their very existence. There has never been a more opportune moment for Palestinians to put forward their demands for decolonization, equality, and justice in clear, principled, visionary, and inclusive terms. The tenacious resistance on the ground, in all its legitimate forms, and the growing global BDS solidarity movement need to be complemented by a program worthy of such efforts and sacrifices. Our energy should be invested in developing support for such a program rather than worrying about the minutiae of moribund negotiations which, long experience has shown, cannot result in the restoration of Palestinian rights. It is onto this new territory that the battle for justice in Palestine is now decisively shifting.

Notes

Introduction

1. John Kerry, "Remarks at the Saban Forum," news release, US Department of State, December 7, 2013, http://www.state.gov/secretary/remarks/2013/12/218506.htm.

2. Nadim Nashef, "Palestinian Youth Assert Right of Return with Direct Action," September 11, 2013, *Electronic Intifada*, http://electronicintifada.net/content/palestinian-youth-assert-right -return-direct-action/12760.

3. Adalah, "The Government's Decision to Cancel the Prawer Plan Bill Is a Major Achievement," news release, December 12, 2013, http://adalah.org/eng/Articles/2227/Adalah:-The-government's -decision-to-cancel-the.

4. Judith Butler, "Academic Freedom and the ASA's Boycott of Israel: A Response to Michelle Goldberg," *Nation*, December 8, 2013, http://www.thenation.com/article/177512/academic -freedom-and-asas-boycott-israel-response-michelle-goldberg.

5. Cecilia Dalla Negra, "'I Can't Dictate Methods of Palestinian Struggle': Israeli Boycott Activist Interviewed,' *Electronic Intifada*, August 8, 2012, http://electronicintifada.net/content/i-cant -dictate-methods-palestinian-struggle-israeli-boycott-activist-interviewed/11561.

6. Peter Fabricius, "Palestinian Head Rejects Boycott of Israel," *The Star* (South Africa), December 11, 2013.

Chapter 1: Shared Values, Shared Struggle

1. CRIF, "François Hollande Reçoit le CRIF," news release, January 30, 2013, http://www .crif.org/fr/lecrifenaction/françois-hollande-reçoit-le-crif.

2. Matthew Gould, "United against Terror," *Ynet*, August 24, 2013.

3. NPR, "Transcript: Obama's Speech at AIPAC," June 4, 2008, http://www.npr.org/templates /story/story.php?storyId=91150432.

4. White House, "Remarks by the President at AIPAC Policy Conference," news release, March 4, 2012, http://www.whitehouse.gov/the-press-office/2012/03/04/remarks-president-aipac -policy-conference-0.

5. On parallels between US and Zionist settler-colonialism, see, for example, Mahmoud Mamdani,

Good Muslim, Bad Muslim (New York: Random House, 2004).

6. For US condemnation of "targeted killings," see Associated Press, "Bush Urges Mideast Parties to End Violence," February 14, 2001. On Obama's "kill list," see Jo Becker and Scott Shane, "Secret 'Kill List' Proves a Test of Obama's Principles and Will," *New York Times*, May 29, 2012.

7. Associated Press, "AP Poll: Majority Harbor Prejudice against Blacks," October 27, 2012.

8. *Washington Post*, "Exit Polls 2012: How the Vote Has Shifted," November 6, 2012, http://www.washingtonpost.com/wp-srv/special/politics/2012-exit-polls/table.html; David Wilson, "The Elephant in the Exit Poll Results: Most White Women Supported Romney," *Huffington Post*, November 8, 2013, http://www.huffingtonpost.com/david-c-wilson/the-elephant-in-the -exit_b_2094354.html.

9. See Becky Pettit, *Invisible Men: Mass Incarceration and the Myth of Black Progress* (New York: Russell Sage, 2012).

10. Michelle Alexander, *The New Jim Crow: Mass Incarceration in the Age of Colorblindness*, revised edition (New York: New Press, 2012), 11.

11. Ibid., 4.

12. Ibid., 2.

13. Ibid., 8.

14. Ibid., 6.

15. Ibid., 6.

16. Ibid., 6–7.

17. Ibid., 98.

18. Ibid., 176.

19. Ibid., 99.

20. Ibid., 100.

21. Ibid., 60.

22. Ibid., 101.

23. Monica Davey, "Chicago Tactics Put Major Dent in Killing Trend," *New York Times*, June 11, 2013.

24. Glenn Greenwald, *With Liberty and Justice for Some* (New York: Metropolitan Books, 2011), 243.

25. Alexander, *New Jim Crow*, 12.

26. Ibid., 70.

27. Ibid., 71.

28. Ibid., 125.

29. Ibid., 256.

30. Ibid., 55.

31. Ibid., 44.

32. Alexander, *New Jim Crow*, chapter 1.

33. Elizabeth Tsurkov, *"Cancer in Our Body": On Racial Incitement, Discrimination and Hate Crimes against African Asylum Seekers in Israel* (Hotline for Migrant Workers, 2012), http://www .hotline.org.il/english/pdf/IncitementReport_English.pdf, accessed February 20, 2013. The lower crime rate was reported by the Knesset Research and Information Unit based on police data.

34. See Joseph Massad, *The Persistence of the Palestinian Question* (London: Routledge, 2006), 172, 213; and Joseph Massad, "Are Palestinian Children Less Worthy?" *Al Jazeera English*, May 30, 2011, http://www.aljazeera.com/indepth/opinion/2011/05/201152911579533291.html.

35. Alexander, *New Jim Crow*, 54.

36. Ibid., 9.

37. Ibid., 181.
38. See, for example, Louise Cainkar, *Homeland Insecurity: The Arab American and Muslim American Experience After 9/11* (New York: Russell Sage, 2009).
39. Naomi Klein, *The Shock Doctrine* (New York: Picador, 2007), 542, 551.
40. Yuval Azulai, "Arms Exports Hit Record $7.5b in 2012," *Globes*, July 23, 2013, http://www.globes.co.il/serveen/globes/docview.asp?did=1000864833&fid=1725; Gili Cohen, "Israel Ranks as the World's Sixth Largest Arms Exporter in 2012," *Haaretz*, June 25, 2013.
41. Klein, *Shock Doctrine*, 551.
42. Ibid., 542.
43. Jonathan Cook, "Israel's Booming Secretive Arms Trade," *Al Jazeera English*, August 16, 2013, http://www.aljazeera.com/indepth/features/2013/08/201381410565517125.html.
44. Ibid.
45. JUF News, "Chicago Law Enforcement Leaders Travel to Israel with JUF," news release, April 29, 2010, http://www.juf.org/news/israel.aspx?id=57594.
46. Alexander, *New Jim Crow*, 189.
47. Breaking the Silence, *Children and Youth: Soldiers' Testimonies 2005–2011* (Jerusalem: Breaking the Silence, 2012), http://www.breakingthesilence.org.il/wp-content/uploads/2012/08/Children_and_Youth_Soldiers_Testimonies_2005_2011_Eng.pdf.
48. Yesh Din, "Data Sheet, March 2012: Law Enforcement upon Israeli Civilians in the West Bank," news release, March 2012, http://www.yesh-din.org/userfiles/file/datasheets/LawEnforcement_datsheet_Eng_March_2012_Final.pdf.
49. Ali Abunimah, "Video Contradicts Israeli Occupation Soldier's Account of Hebron Teen's Killing," *Electronic Intifada*, December 18, 2012, http://electronicintifada.net/blogs/ali-abunimah/video-contradicts-israeli-soldiers-account-hebron-teens-killing.
50. Defence for Children International—Palestine Section, "Israeli Forces Paralyze Youth at Jalazoun Refugee Camp," news release, June 6, 2013, http://www.dci-palestine.org/documents/israeli-forces-paralyze-youth-jalazun-refugee-camp.
51. Benjamin Doherty, "Palestinian Boy Paralyzed by Israeli Bullet Expects No Justice," *Electronic Intifada*, August 8, 2013, http://electronicintifada.net/blogs/benjamin-doherty/palestinian-boy-paralyzed-israeli-bullet-expects-no-justice.
52. Yesh Din, *Alleged Investigation: The Failure of Investigations into Offenses Committed by IDF Soldiers against Palestinians* (Tel Aviv: Yesh Din, 2011), http://yesh-din.org/userfiles/file/Reports-English/Alleged%20Investigation%20%5BEnglish%5D.pdf.
53. Deborah Sussman Süsser, "Learning from the Experts," *Jewish News of Greater Phoenix*, November 21, 2008.
54. Ben Hartman, "US Police Visit Israel to Study Counterterrorism," *Jerusalem Post*, October 17, 2012. See also Project Interchange, "Senior NYPD, LAPD, Houston Police and Top Counterterror Experts to Visit Israel," news release, October 15, 2012, http://projectinterchange.org/?p=6794.
55. Amnesty International, "Israel: The Injustice and Secrecy Surrounding Administrative Detention," news release, June 6, 2012, http://www.amnesty.org/en/news/israel-injustice-and-secrecy-surrounding-administrative-detention-2012-06-01.
56. Ali Abunimah, "Alive and Victorious: Palestinian Footballer Mahmoud Sarsak Home after Epic 3-Month Hunger Strike," *Electronic Intifada*, July 10, 2010, http://electronicintifada.net/blogs/ali-abunimah/alive-and-victorious-palestinian-footballer-mahmoud-sarsak-home-after-epic-3.
57. Al-Haq, "14 Palestinian and Israeli Organisations Condemn Lack of Accountability for Torture of Palestinian Detainees," news release, March 1, 2013, http://www.alhaq.org/advocacy

/topics/right-to-life-and-body-integrity/677-14-palestinian-and-israeli-organisations-condemn-lack-of-accountability-for-torture-against-palestinian-detainees.

58. Defence for Children International—Palestine Section, "Palestinian Child Prisoners," written evidence submitted to European Parliament Sub-Committee on Human Rights, March 15, 2011, http://www.dci-pal.org/english/doc/press/EU_Parliament_Prisoners_MAR_2011.pdf.

59. Defense for Children International—Palestine Section, "Voices from the Occupation: Adham D.—Solitary Confinement," news release, December 5, 2012, http://www.dci-palestine.org/documents/voices-occupation-adham-d-solitary-confinement.

60. Ibid.

61. Defense for Children International—Palestine Section, "Voices from the Occupation: Jamal S.—Solitary Confinement," news release, December 5, 2012, http://www.dci-palestine.org/documents/voices-occupation-jamal-s-solitary-confinement.

62. Defense for Children International—Palestine Section, *Palestinian Child Prisoners: The Systematic and Institutionalised Ill-Treatment and Torture of Palestinian Children by Israeli Authorities* (Jerusalem: Defense for Children International, 2009), http://www.dci-pal.org/english/publ/research/CPReport.pdf.

63. Who Profits, *The Case of G4S: Private Security Companies and the Israeli Occupation* (Tel Aviv: Who Profits, 2011), http://whoprofits.org/sites/default/files/WhoProfits-PrivateSecurity-G4S.pdf.

64. According to the G4S corporate website, www.g4s.us.

65. Chaim Levinson, "Nearly 100% of All Military Court Cases in West Bank End in Conviction, *Haaretz* Learns," *Haaretz*, November 29, 2011, http://www.haaretz.com/print-edition/news/nearly-100-of-all-military-court-cases-in-west-bank-end-in-conviction-haaretz-learns-1.398369.

66. Ma'an News Agency, "Settler Firebomb Attack 'Turned Our Lives Upside Down,'" August 30, 2012, http://www.maannews.net/eng/ViewDetails.aspx?ID=515766.

67. Chaim Levinson, "Israel Police Link Fingerprints to Boys Suspected of Hurling Fire Bomb at Palestinian Taxi," *Haaretz*, August 27, 2012.

68. Chaim Levinson, "Case Dropped against Israeli Teen Suspected of Firebombing Palestinian Taxi," *Haaretz*, January 6, 2013.

69. Project Interchange, "Senior NYPD, LAPD, Houston Police and Top Counterterror Experts to Visit Israel," media release, October 17, 2012, http://projectinterchange.org/?p=6794.

70. JINSA, "World's Largest Police Organization Honors the Israel National Police at JINSA Event," news release, November 14, 2008, http://www.jinsa.org/events-programs/law-enforcement-exchange-program-leep/worlds-largest-police-organization-honors-isra.

71. Consultate General of Israel to the Midwest, "Israel Police Workshop Dealing with Counterterrorism Took Place in the Midwest in July," news release, June 29, 2012, http://embassies.gov.il/chicago/NewsAndEvents/Pages/The-Israeli-Ministry-of-Foreign-Affairs-sponsored-a-Mission-to-Israel-for-African-American-Academics,-which-took-place-June.aspx.

72. Bloomberg TV, "Sachs: Cyber Security, Safe Cities & Mega Events," video, November 12, 2012, http://www.bloomberg.com/video/sachs-cyber-security-safe-cities-mega-events-bfwRk-aaTrWdh_qUrHEj_g.html.

73. Israel Homeland Security 2012 website, http://israelhls2012.com, accessed January 27, 2012. See also Israel's Trade Administration Website: www.israeltradeca.org/events/israel-hls-2012.

74. Atlanta Police Department, "George N. Turner, Chief of Police," website, http://www.atlantapd.org/chiefofpolice-georgeturner.aspx.

75. Max Blumenthal, "From Occupation to 'Occupy': The Israelification of American Domestic Security," *Al-Akhbar English*, December 2, 2011, http://english.al-akhbar.com/content/occupation-"occupy"-israelification-american-domestic-security.

76. Matt Apuzzo and Adam Goldman, "The NYPD Division of Un-American Activities," *New York Magazine*, August 25, 2013, http://nymag.com/news/features/nypd-demographics-unit-2013-9/.

77. Associated Press, "NYPD: Muslim Spying Led to No Leads, Terror Cases," August 21, 2012.

78. Adam Goldman and Matt Apuzzo, "Informant: NYPD Paid Me to 'Bait' Muslims," Associated Press, October 23, 2012.

79. Apuzzo and Goldman, "NYPD Division of Un-American Activities."

80. Ibid.

81. Ibid.

82. Grace Rauh, "Warm Welcome in Boro Park for Police Commissioner," *New York Sun*, November 30, 2007.

83. Avi Ashkenazi, "NYPD Opens Branch in Israel," *Al-Monitor*, September 5, 2012, http://www.al-monitor.com/pulse/security/01/09/nypd-kfar-saba-branch-new-york-p.html. After the September 11, 2001 attacks, the NYPD established eleven overseas "intelligence" bureaus with private funds from undisclosed donors. These branches were heavily criticized for their total lack of transparency and oversight. See, for example, Jeff Stein, "NYPD Intelligence Detectives Go Their Own Way," *Washington Post*, November 10, 2010, http://blog.washingtonpost.com/spy-talk/2010/11/nypds_foreign_cops_play_outsid.html.

84. Apuzzo and Goldman, "NYPD Division of Un-American Activities."

85. Thomas Tracy, "Israel's Top Cop: My Guys Can Learn Manners from the NYPD," *New York Daily News*, April 19, 2013.

86. Israel Police, "Sukam: yuqmu tsvatay 'avodah 'im mishteret New York," news release (Hebrew), April 18, 2013, http://www.police.gov.il/articlePage.aspx?aid=1507.

87. Michael Schmidt and Eric Lichtblau, "Racial Profiling Rife at Airport, U.S. Officers Say," *New York Times*, August 11, 2012.

88. Interview with NPR *Morning Edition*, January 14, 2010.

89. Schmidt and Lichtblau, "Racial Profiling Rife."

90. AIPAC, "Homeland Security Monitor," newsletter, May 2009, http://www.aipac.org/learn/resources/aipac-publications/publication?pubpath=PolicyPolitics/AIPAC%20Periodicals/Homeland%20Security%20Monitor/2009/05/Homeland%20Security%20Monitor%20-%20May%202009; Joe Charlaff, "US Airport Security—Israeli Style," *Jerusalem Post*, April 2, 2009.

91. Michael Schmidt, "Report Says T.S.A. Screening Is Not Objective," *New York Times*, June 4, 2013.

92. Jonathan Cook, "South Africa Deports Israeli Airline Official Spying on Citizens," *Electronic Intifada*, November 22, 2009, http://electronicintifada.net/content/south-africa-deports-israeli-airline-official-spying-citizens/8549.

93. Itamar Eichner, "El Al Security Officer Deported from South Africa," *Ynet*, November 20, 2009, http://www.ynetnews.com/articles/0,7340,L-3808129,00.html.

94. Alexander, *New Jim Crow*, 69–72.

95. John Collins, *Global Palestine* (New York: Columbia University Press, 2011), x.

96. Ibid., 2.

97. Ibid., 2.

Chapter 2: Does Israel Have a Right to Exist as a Jewish State?

1. Ministry of Foreign Affairs, Israel, "Israel-PLO Mutual Recognition – Letters and Speeches – 10 September 1993," September 10, 1993, http://mfa.gov.il/MFA/ForeignPolicy/MFADocuments/Yearbook9/Pages/107%20Israel-PLO%20Mutual%20Recognition-%20Letters%20and%20Spe.aspx.

2. Yasser Arafat, "The Palestinian Vision of Peace," *New York Times*, February 3, 2002.

3. Israel Ministry of Foreign Affairs, "Israel's Response to the Roadmap," May 25, 2003, http://www.mfa.gov.il/MFA/Peace+Process/Reference+Documents/Israel+Response+to+the+Roadmap+25-May-2003.htm.

4. White House, "Remarks by President Obama and Prime Minister Netanyahu of Israel in Press Availability," news release, May 18, 2009, http://www.whitehouse.gov/the-press-office/remarks-president-obama-and-israeli-prime-minister-netanyahu-press-availability.

5. White House, "Remarks by the President at the AIPAC Policy Conference 2011," news release, May 22, 2011, http://www.whitehouse.gov/the-press-office/2011/05/22/remarks-president-aipac-policy-conference-2011.

6. Office of the Prime Minister of Canada, "Statement by the Prime Minister of Canada at a Joint News Conference with Benjamin Netanyahu, Prime Minister of the State of Israel," news release, March 2, 2012, http://pm.gc.ca/eng/media.asp?id=4675.

7. Ted Sampsell-Jones, "The Myth of Ashby v. White," *University of St. Thomas Law Journal* 8, no. 1 (2010), http://ir.stthomas.edu/ustlj/vol8/iss1/4. For a critical perspective on the relationship between rights and remedies see Daryl Levinson, "Rights Essentialism and Remedial Equilibration," *Columbia Law Review* 99, no. 4 (1999), 857–940. Levinson writes, "Rights are dependent on remedies not just for their application to the real world, but for their scope, shape, and very existence."

8. For numerous examples of the use of this term or similar expressions, see Ben White, *Palestinians in Israel* (London: Pluto Press, 2012), 51–54; see also Dan Perry, "Analysis: Israel Left Wing Sees Jewish State's End," Associated Press, January 11, 2013.

9. David Hirst, *The Gun and the Olive Branch* (New York: Thunder's Mouth Press/Nation Books, 2003), 369.

10. White, *Palestinians in Israel,* 13–14.

11. Adalah, "Israeli Supreme Court Upholds Ban on Family Unification," news release, January 12, 2012, http://www.adalah.org/eng/pressreleases/12_1_12.html.

12. Human Rights Watch, "Israel: High Court Rulings Undermine Human Rights," news release, January 20, 2012, http://www.hrw.org/news/2012/01/30/israel-high-court-rulings-undermine-human-rights.

13. Aluf Benn, "Legislation Seeks to Hinder Citizenship for Palestinians, Non-Jews," *Haaretz*, April 5, 2005, http://www.haaretz.com/print-edition/news/legislation-seeks-to-hinder-citizenship-for-palestinians-non-jews-1.155055.

14. Harrier Sherwood, "Court Upholds Law Banning Palestinian Spouses from Living in Israel," *Guardian*, January 12, 2012.

15. United Press, "White Supremacy at Stake, South Africa Warned," April 13, 1953, printed in *Lodi News-Sentinel*, April 14, 1953, http://news.google.com/newspapers?id=JYgzAAAAIBAJ&sjid=_e4HAAAAIBAJ&dq=must-inevitably-mean-to-white-south-africa-nothing-less-than-national-suicide&pg=4489%2C1382535.

16. Human Rights Watch, "Israel: High Court Rulings Undermine Human Rights," news release, January 20, 2012, http://www.hrw.org/news/2012/01/30/israel-high-court-rulings-undermine-human-rights.

17. This Basic Law was passed by the Knesset on July 30, 1980. On June 30, 1980, the United Nations Security Council had adopted Resolution 476, which stated that the council was "gravely concerned over the legislative steps initiated in the Israeli Knesset with the aim of changing the character and status of the Holy City of Jerusalem." The resolution also "reconfirms that all legislative and administrative measures and actions taken by Israel, the occupying

Power, which purport to alter the character and status of the Holy City of Jerusalem have no legal validity and constitute a flagrant violation of the Fourth Geneva Convention relative to the Protection of Civilian Persons in Time of War and also constitute a serious obstruction to achieving a comprehensive, just and lasting peace in the Middle East."

18. Basic Law: Human Dignity and Liberty, 1992, http://www.knesset.gov.il/laws/special/eng/basic3_eng.htm.

19. White, *Palestinians in Israel*, 15.

20. White, *Palestinians in Israel*, 12–13.

21. Associated Press, "Israeli Court Rejects Israeli Nationality, Saying It Could Undermine Jewish Character," October 4, 2013.

22. For the summary and definition of Palestinian citizenship, see United Nations Conciliation Commission For Palestine, "Definition of a 'Refugee' under Paragraph 11 of the General Assembly Resolution of 11 December 1948," April 9, 1951, http://unispal.un.org/UNISPAL.NSF/0/418E7BC6931616B485256CAF00647CC7.

23. Ilan Pappé, *The Forgotten Palestinians; A History of the Palestinians in Israel* (New Haven, CT: Yale University Press, 2011), 35–47.

24. See White, *Palestinians in Israel*, 22–50.

25. See for example: Benett Ruda, "Israel's Law of Return: One of Many Countries with Such a Law," *Daled Amos* (blog), February 27, 2012, http://daledamos.blogspot.com/2012/02/israels-law-of-return-one-of-many.html.

26. For the history of the idea of "the Jewish people" as a cohesive, transhistorical entity and its origins in the nineteenth century, see Shlomo Sand, *The Invention of the Jewish People* (London/New York: Verso, 2009).

27. Irish Naturalisation and Immigration Service, Department of Justice and Equality, "Citizenship through Descent," website, http://www.inis.gov.ie/en/INIS/Pages/WP11000024.

28. Tikva Honig-Parnass, *False Prophets of Peace: Liberal Zionism and the Struggle for Palestine* (Chicago: Haymarket, 2011), 54.

29. Ephraim Yaar and Tamar Hermann, "Peace Index: October 2012," Israel Democracy Institute, October 2012, http://en.idi.org.il/media/1838538/Peace%20Index-October%202012.pdf.

30. Nathan Jeffay, "Citing Disloyalty, Knesset Bans Main Arab Parties from Elections," *Jewish Daily Forward*, January 23, 2009.

31. Quoted in Sabri Jiryis, *The Arabs in Israel* (New York: Monthly Review Press, 1976), 53.

32. Quoted in Jiryis, *Arabs in Israel*, 53.

33. Pappé, *Forgotten Palestinians*, 126–34.

34. Steve Linde, "Editor's Notes: It's Now or the Negev," *Jerusalem Post*, October 25, 2012. Similarly, Yaron Ben Ezra, director-general of the Jewish Agency's settlement division, explained that the goal of Israeli development plans in the Negev "is to grab the last remaining piece of land and thereby prevent further Bedouin incursion into any more state land and the development of an Arab belt from the south of Mount Hebron toward Arad and approaching Dimona and Yeruham, and the area extending toward Be'er Sheva." See Ranit Nahum-Halevy, "Judaization of the Negev at Any Cost," *Haaretz*, January 9, 2012.

35. Guy Lieberman, "Housing Minister: Spread of Arab population Must Be Stopped," *Haaretz*, July 2, 2009.

36. Human Rights Watch, "Israel: New Laws Marginalize Palestinian Arab Citizens," news release, March 20, 2011, http://www.hrw.org/news/2011/03/30/israel-new-laws-marginalize-palestinian-arab-citizens; see also White, *Palestinians in Israel*, 48–50.

37. Jack Khoury, "Upper Nazareth Mayor: No Arab School Here as Long as I Am in Charge,"

Haaretz, January 17, 2013.

38. Pappé, *Forgotten Palestinians*, 74.

39. Eli Ashkenazi and Jackie Khoury, "Rosh Ha'ir Notzrat Illit Le Yishai: Lehakhriz 'Al Notzrat Ke'ir 'Oyenet," *Haaretz* (Hebrew), November 20, 2012, http://www.haaretz.co.il/news /education/1.1869948. Gapso's letter was published in Hebrew. For an English translation, see Ali Abunimah, "Israeli Mayor: Expel Palestinian Citizens of 'Hostile' Nazareth to Gaza for Opposing War," *Electronic Intifada*, November 21, 2012 http://electronicintifada.net/blogs/ali-abunimah /israeli-mayor-expel-palestinian-citizens-hostile-nazareth-gaza-opposing-war.

40. Shimon Gapso, "If You Think I'm a Racist, then Israel Is a Racist State," *Haaretz*, August 7, 2013.

41. Ali Abunimah, "Israel's Likud Hopes to Complete the Ethnic Cleansing of Jaffa," *Electronic Intifada*, October 9, 2013, http://electronicintifada.net/blogs/ali-abunimah/israels-likud-hopes -complete-ethnic-cleansing-jaffa.

42. Sami Abu Shehadeh and Fadi Shbaytah, "Jaffa: From Eminence to Ethnic Cleansing," *Electronic Intifada*, February 26, 2009, http://electronicintifada.net/content/jaffa-eminence-ethnic-cleansing /8088.

43. Israel Harel, "Kosovo Is Already Here," *Haaretz*, February 21, 2008.

44. Gideon Alon and Aluf Benn, "Netanyahu: Israel's Arabs Are the Real Demographic Threat," *Haaretz*, December 18, 2003.

45. The majority of the Israeli Jewish population is made up of Jews from Arab lands or their de-scendants. However, when Israeli organizations like Sikkuy use the term "Arabs" or "Israeli Arabs," they mean this to include only Palestinian citizens of Israel, not Arab Jews.

46. Ali Haider, Alaa Hamdan, and Yaser Awad, *The Equality Index of Jewish and Arab Citizens in Israel* (Jerusalem: Sikkuy, 2010), 9, http://www.sikkuy.org.il/english/en2009/r_sikkuy09.pdf.

47. Ibid., 26–27.

48. Ibid., 79.

49. Ibid., 75–77.

50. Pappé, *Forgotten Palestinians*, 99–100.

51. Sikkuy, *Equality Index*, 50.

52. Ibid., 61; OECD, "Israel: A Divided Society; Results of a Review of Labour-Market and Social Policy," news release, January 20, 2010, http://www.oecd.org/els/44394444.pdf.

53. Sikkuy, *Equality Index*, 69.

54. Ibid., 64. This was lower than in Egypt (24 percent) and Lebanon (22 percent), only slighter higher than in Saudi Arabia (17 percent), and Jordan, the West Bank, and the Gaza Strip (15 percent), and considerably lower than in Yemen (25 percent), Turkey (28 percent), the United Arab Emirates (44 percent), Qatar (52 percent), and Sudan (31 percent). See World Bank, "Labor Participation Rate, Female (% of Female Population Ages 15+)," table, in "World Development Indicators," online resource, http://data.worldbank.org/indicator/SL.TLF.CACT.FE.ZS.

55. OECD Better Life Index, online resource, http://www.oecdbetterlifeindex.org/countries/israel/.

56. Pappé, *Forgotten Palestinians*, 166.

57. Ibid.

58. Nadav Shemer, "Reversing the Brain Drain in Israel," *Jerusalem Post*, July 14, 2011. See also BioAbroad, an organization that works with the Israeli government to help Israeli scientists re-turn home and has partnerships with several major Israeli universities. Based on an examination of the organization's website (bioabroad.org.il), the staff and board do not include a single Pales-tinian citizen of Israel.

59. For the revival of Israeli interest in schemes to expel Palestinians, see my book *One Country*

(New York: Metropolitan Books, 2006), chapter 3.

60. Jewish Telegraphic Agency, "Feiglin Plan Would Pay Palestinians to Leave West Bank," January 2, 2013.

61. Moshe Feiglin, "Israel's Fifth Column," *Jewish Press*, November 5, 2008, http://www.jewishpress .com/indepth/columns/israels-fifth-column/2008/11/05/.

62. Martin Sherman, "Redefining the Palestinian Problem," Jerusalem Summit website, August 28, 2005, http://www.jerusalemsummit.org/eng/news.php?news=113. Sherman is identified as "the Academic Director to the Jerusalem Summit and lecture[r] in Political Science at Tel Aviv University."

63. Yoav Stern, "Poll: 50% of Israeli Jews Support State-Backed Arab Emigration," *Haaretz*, March 27, 2007.

64. Talila Nesher, "Israel Admits Ethiopian Women Were Given Birth Control Shots," *Haaretz*, January 27, 2013.

65. Talila Nesher, "Israeli Minister Appointing Team to Probe Ethiopian Birth Control Shot Controversy," *Haaretz*, February 28, 2013.

66. Asher Zeiger, "Comptroller to Probe Ethiopian Birth Control Claims," *Times of Israel*, July 14, 2013, http://www.timesofisrael.com/comptroller-to-probe-ethiopian-birth-control-claims/.

67. Len Lyons, "Last Ethiopian Jews Finally Make Exodus to Israel," *Jewish Daily Forward*, September 9, 2011, http://forward.com/articles/142154/last-ethiopian-jews-finally-make-exodus -to-israel.

68. Alistair Dawber, "Israel Gave Birth Control to Ethiopian Jews without Their Consent," *Independent*, January 27, 2013.

69. Dana Weiler-Polak, "Israel Enacts Law Allowing Authorities to Detain Illegal Migrants for Up to 3 Years," *Haaretz*, June 3, 2012. I have quoted *Haaretz's* translation of Yishai's statement. Yishai made his original statement in Hebrew in an interview with NRG, the website of the newspaper *Maariv*. Yishai stated: "*Rov ha anashim she ba'im hine hem muslemim she hoshvim she ha'aretz bikhlal lo shayekhet lanu, la adam halavan*" (Most of the people who come here are Muslims who don't think the country belongs to us, the white man). See Shalom Yerushalmi, "Eli Yishai b're'ayon meyuhad: 'Ze o anahnu o hem,'" *NRG* (Hebrew), June 1, 2012, http://www.nrg.co.il/online/1/ART2/373/346.html.

70. Peter Beinart, *Crisis of Zionism* (New York: Times Books, 2012), 25.

71. Barak Ravid, "Lieberman: Peace Talks Must Reassess Israeli-Arabs' Right to Citizenship," *Haaretz*, September 19, 2010.

72. Ronny Sofer, "Lieberman Demands Population Exchange," *Ynet*, October 28, 2007, http://www.ynetnews.com/Ext/Comp/ArticleLayout/CdaArticlePrintPreview/1,2506,L -3464689,00.html.

73. Barak Ravid, "Lieberman presents plans for population exchange at UN," *Haaretz*, September 28, 2010.

74. Gregg Carlstrom, "Expelling Israel's Arab population?" *Al Jazeera English*, January 24, 2011, http://www.aljazeera.com/palestinepapers/2011/01/2011124105622779946.html.

75. Ali Abunimah, "A Dangerous Shift on 1967 Lines," *Al Jazeera English*, January 24, 2011, http://www.aljazeera.com/palestinepapers/2011/01/201112411450358613.html.

76. White House, "Remarks of President Barack Obama to the People of Israel," news release, March 21, 2013.

77. Tamar Hermann, Nir Atmor, Ella Heller, and Yuval Lebel, *The Israel Democracy Index 2012* (Tel Aviv: Israel Democracy Institute, 2012), 64, 88.

78. Shmuel Rosner, "Children of Israel," *International Herald Tribune*, August 28, 2013.

79. I develop this argument more fully in two articles: Ali Abunimah, "A Curious Case of Exceptionalism: Non-Partitionist Approaches to Ethnic Conflict Regulation and the Question of Palestine," *Ethnopolitics* 10.3–4 (2011), 431–44, and Ali Abunimah, "Put Away the Partitionist's Knife and Think Anew: A Response to Bose, Adam and Oberschall," *Ethnopolitics* 10.3–4 (2011), 461–65.

80. National Committee for the Heads of the Arab Local Authorities in Israel, *The Future Vision of the Palestinian Arabs in Israel* (Nazareth: National Committee for the Heads of the Arab Local Authorities in Israel, 2006), http://www.adalah.org/newsletter/eng/dec06/tasawor -mostaqbali.pdf; Adalah, *The Democratic Constitution* (Shafa'amr: Adalah, 2007), http:// adalah.org/Public/files/democratic_constitution-english.pdf; Yousef T. Jabareen, *An Equal Constitution for All? On a Constitution and Collective Rights for Arab Citizens in Israel* (Haifa: Mossawa, 2007); Mada al-Carmel, *The Haifa Declaration* (Haifa: Mada al-Carmel, 2007), http://mada-research.org/en/files/2007/09/haifaenglish.pdf. The quotation is from the first document cited in this note.

81. Yoav Stern, "Arab Leaders Air Public Relations Campaign against Shin Bet," *Haaretz*, April 6, 2007.

82. See Ilan Peleg and Dov Waxman, *Israel's Palestinians: The Conflict Within* (Cambridge: Cambridge University Press, 2011), 19–47; and Pappé, *Forgotten Palestinians.*

83. Jeffrey Goldberg, "Goldblog vs. Peter Beinart, Part II," *Atlantic*, May 18, 2010, http://www .theatlantic.com/national/archive/2010/05/goldblog-vs-peter-beinart-part-ii/56934/.

84. Anne-Marie Slaughter, "A New-State Solution for Israel and Palestine," *Al Jazeera English*, March 26, 2013, http://www.aljazeera.com/indepth/opinion/2013/03/201332682321538283.html.

85. Barak Ravid, David Landau, Aluf Benn, and Shmuel Rosner, "Olmert to Haaretz: Two-State Solution, or Israel Is Done For," *Haaretz*, November 29, 2007.

86. Ephraim Yaar and Tamar Hermann, "Peace Index—January 2012," The Israel Democracy Institute, news release, January 2012, http://en.idi.org.il/media/599470/Peace%20Index-January %202012.pdf.

87. Ephraim Yaar and Tamar Hermann, "Peace Index—April 2012," Israel Democracy Institute, news release, April 2012, http://en.idi.org.il/media/602047/Peace%20Index-April%202012(1).pdf.

88. Max Blumenthal, "Why the Israeli Elections Were a Victory for the Right," *Nation*, January 23, 2013, http://www.thenation.com/article/172398/why-israeli-elections-were-victory-right.

89. Ali Abunimah, "Normal Racism: Election Over, 'Centrist' Kingmaker Yair Lapid Shuns Palestinian Citizens of Israel," *Electronic Intifada*, January 23, 2013, http://electronicintifada.net /blogs/ali-abunimah/normal-racism-election-over-centrist-kingmaker-yair-lapid-shuns-palestinian.

90. Karl Vick, "Yair Lapid: An Interview with Israel's New Power Broker," *TIME*, January 31, 2013.

91. David Remnick, "The Party Faithful," *New Yorker*, January 21, 2013, http://www.newyorker .com/reporting/2013/01/21/130121fa_fact_remnick.

92. Naftali Bennett, "The Israel Stability Initiative: A Practical Program for Managing the Israeli-Palestinian Conflict," onestateisrael.com, March 2012, http://www.onestateisrael.com/wp -content/uploads/2012/03/The-Israel-Stability-Initiative-Naftali-Bennett.pdf.

93. UN Office for the Coordination of Humanitarian Affairs—Occupied Palestinian Territories, "Area C Humanitarian Response Plan Fact Sheet," August 2010, http://unispal.un.org /UNISPAL.NSF/0/59AE27FDECB034BD85257793004D5541. This document includes an estimate of the population of Area C.

94. Ariel Ben Solomon, "Bennett Under Fire for Comments about Killing Arabs," *Jerusalem Post*, July 30, 2013.

95. Remnick, "Party Faithful."

96. Bennett, "Israel Stability Initiative."
97. Harriet Sherwood, "Binyamin Netanyahu Rejects Calls for Palestinian State within 1967 Lines," *Guardian*, January 20, 2013.
98. Yaar and Hermann, "Peace Index—April 2012."
99. Gideon Levy, "Survey: Most Israeli Jews Wouldn't Give Palestinians Vote if West Bank Was Annexed," *Haaretz*, October 23, 2012.
100. Ephraim Yaar and Tamar Hermann, "Peace Index—July 2013," news release, Israel Democracy Institute, August 6, 2013, http://peaceindex.org/indexMonthEng.aspx?num=254.
101. Joseph Massad, "The Rights of Israel," *Al Jazeera English*, May 6, 2011, http://www.aljazeera.com/indepth/opinion/2011/05/20115684218533873.html.
102. Susan Akram, "The Rights of Palestinian Refugees and Territorial Solutions in Historic Palestine" in *The Failure of the Two-State Solution: The Prospects of One State in the Israel-Palestine Conflict,* ed. Hani Faris (London/New York: I. B. Tauris, 2013), 171–84; Massad, "Rights of Israel."

Chapter 3: Israeli Jews and the One-State Solution

1. *Haaretz*, "Obama: Israel Won't Know Peace while Palestinians Are Gripped by Despair," November 7, 2009.
2. Anthony Bevins and Michael Streeter, "From 'Terrorist' to Tea with the Queen," *Independent*, July 9, 1996.
3. Phil Weiss, "A Debate about the Two-State Solution with Norman Finkelstein," *Mondoweiss*, June 12, 2012, http://mondoweiss.net/2012/06/a-debate-about-the-two-state-solution-with-norman-finkelstein.html.
4. United States Department of State, "Interview With Udi Segal of Israeli Channel 2 and Maher Shalabi of Palestinian Broadcasting Corporation," transcript, November 7, 2013, http://www.state.gov/secretary/remarks/2013/11/217314.htm.
5. This chapter is adapted and expanded from a paper I presented at a conference organized by the Afro-Middle East Centre in Pretoria, South Africa, in April 2010 and which was subsequently published as a chapter in *Pretending Democracy: Israel, an Ethnocratic State*, edited by Na'eem Jeenah (Johannesburg: Afro-Middle East Centre, 2012).
6. Ben Smith, "Obama-Era Goodwill for Rice at U.N.," *Politico*, April 4, 2009, http://www.politico.com/news/stories/0409/20881.html.
7. Palestinian Human Rights Organisations Council, "UN Resolution on Settlements: Another Missed Opportunity to Advance the Rights of the Palestinian People," news release, March 25, 2013, copy on Al-Haq website, http://www.alhaq.org/advocacy/targets/united-nations/685-un-resolution-on-settlements-another-missed-opportunity-to-advance-the-rights-of-the-palestinian-people-.
8. Jewish Telegraphic Agency, "U.S. Rips U.N. Human Rights Council for 'Disproportionate' Israel Focus," March 19, 2013.
9. Harriet Sherwood, "Kerry: Two Years Left to Reach Two-State Solution in Middle East Peace Process," *Guardian*, April 18, 2013.
10. For a clear explanation of the current, "durable" binational reality, see Meron Benvenisti, "United We Stand," *Haaretz,* January 19, 2010, http://www.haaretz.com/hasen/spages/1145896.html.
11. Omar Barghouti, "Re-Imagining Palestine: Self-Determination, Ethical De-Colonization and Equality," *Znet*, July 29, 2009, http://www.zcommunications.org/re-imagining-palestine-by-omar-barghouti.
12. Associated Press, "De Klerk Calls for Quick and Drastic Change," May 12, 1989.

13. Anthony Hazlitt Heard, "The Opportunity Is There, But Will De Klerk Grab It?" *Los Angeles Times*, August 18, 1989.
14. Pierre Hugo, "Towards Darkness and Death: Racial Demonology in South Africa," *Journal of Modern African Studies*, 26(4), 1988.
15. Ibid., 571.
16. Ibid., 571–76.
17. Ibid.
18. Ibid.
19. Ibid.
20. Peter Goodspeed, "Afrikaners Cling to Their All-White Dream," *Toronto Star*, October 5, 1986.
21. Kate Manzo and Pat McGowan, "Afrikaner Fears and the Politics of Despair: Understanding Change in South Africa," *International Studies Quarterly*, 36, 1992.
22. Ibid.
23. Ibid.
24. William Claiborne, "De Klerk Rejects Interim, Multiracial Rule," *Washington Post*, November 26, 1989.
25. Terry Coleman, "South Africa's Minister for Risk Management," *Independent*, March 13, 1990.
26. Hugo, "Towards Darkness," 567.
27. "South Africa's Blacks Want No Less than Equality," *San Diego Union-Tribune*, February 14, 1988.
28. Allister Sparks, "Backlash of the Boers: South Africa's Extreme Right Is Gathering Increasing Support," *Globe & Mail* (Canada), May 31, 1986.
29. Hugo, "Towards Darkness," 567.
30. Ibid., 583.
31. Allister Sparks, "No Hope for Peaceful Change," *Washington Post*, May 10, 1987.
32. *Economist*, "A Black South Africa?" February 1, 1986.
33. William Raspberry, "Is There a Way to End Apartheid?" *Washington Post*, March 27, 1985.
34. Michael Parks, "Soviets Urging ANC to Seek S. Africa Political Accord," *Los Angeles Times*, February 5, 1988.
35. Na'eem Jeenah and Salim Vally, "Beyond Ethnic Nationalism: Lessons from South Africa," in Jeenah (ed.), *Pretending Democracy*, 383.
36. Ali Abunimah, "Israel's New Strategy: 'Sabotage' and 'Attack' the Global Justice Movement," *Electronic Intifada*, February 16, 2010.
37. See Ali Abunimah, "Palestinians on the Verge of a Majority: Population and Politics in Palestine-Israel," Palestine Center Information Brief no. 162 (Washington, DC: Palestine Center), May 12, 2008, http://www.thejerusalemfund.org/ht/display/ContentDetails/i/2244.
38. Steven Friedman, "Jewish Identity and Minority Status in a Democratic Palestine," in Jeenah (ed.), *Pretending Democracy*, 313.
39. Ibid., 313–14.
40. Ibid., 315.
41. Goodspeed, "Afrikaners Cling."
42. *Economist*, "A Black South Africa?"
43. Friedman, "Jewish Identity and Minority Status," 315.
44. Ibid., 316.
45. Ibid.
46. Ibid., 323.
47. Ibid., 324.

48. Josh Nathan-Kazis, "AJC Turns towards Israel, Global Advocacy," *Jewish Daily Forward*, December 21, 2012.

49. Ibid., 321.

50. Conflict Archive on the Internet (University of Ulster), "Speech to DUP Annual Conference by Party Leader Rev. Ian Paisley, 28 November 1998," http://cain.ulst.ac.uk/events/peace /docs/ip281198.htm.

51. Ian Paisley spoke to Channel 4 television on March 14, 1984. His comments are partially quoted in a March 15, 1984, Associated Press report by Ed Blanche that appears in the Nexis database with no headline. His full comments can be heard in this video: "Ian Paisleys Reaction to an Attack on Gerry Adams - 1984," posted November 5, 2011, http://youtu.be/3hFM8qaRbK8.

52. Owen Bowcott, "Village Empties as Loyalists Revel in History," *Guardian*, July 13, 1991.

53. John Darnton, "Protestant and Paranoid in Northern Ireland," *New York Times*, January 15, 1995.

54. David McKittrick, "Orange Marches: Man Shot Dead before Peaceful 12th of July," *Independent*, July 13, 2000.

55. Michael MacDonald, *Children of Wrath: Political Violence in Northern Ireland* (Oxford: Polity Press, 1986), 61.

56. Joseph Ruane and Jennifer Todd, *The Dynamics of Conflict in Northern Ireland* (Cambridge: Cambridge University Press, 1996), 179.

57. Ibid.

58. See Joe Cleary, *Literature, Partition and the Nation-State* (Cambridge: Cambridge University Press, 2002), 70–72; and Ruane and Todd, *Dynamics of Conflict*, 180.

59. Ruane and Todd, *Dynamics of Conflict*, 182.

60. See, for example, Donald Harman Akenson, *God's People: Covenant and Land in South Africa, Israel and Ulster* (Ithaca, NY: Cornell University Press, 1992).

61. Ruane and Todd, *Dynamics of Conflict*, 178–84.

62. The formula "a Protestant state for a Protestant people" is widely attributed to Craig and became an iconic description of Northern Ireland's political regime both for supporters and detractors. Craig's actual words were: "In the South they boasted of a Catholic State. They still boast of Southern Ireland being a Catholic State. All I boast of is that we are a Protestant Parliament and a Protestant State." *Official Report of the Parliament of Northern Ireland*, Volume 16 (1933–34), 1095–96.

63. John McGarry and Brendan O'Leary, *Explaining Northern Ireland* (Oxford: Blackwell, 1995), 98.

64. Terence O'Neill, quoted in Joseph Lee, *Ireland, 1912–1985* (Cambridge: Cambridge University Press, 1989), 426.

65. MacDonald, *Children of Wrath*, 8.

66. See MacDonald, *Children of Wrath*, chapter 4, and Cleary, *Literature, Partition and the Nation-State*, 41.

67. See Yoav Stern, "Arab Leaders Air Public Relations Campaign against Shin Bet," *Haaretz*, April 6, 2007, http://www.haaretz.com/hasen/spages/846247.html.

68. Patrick Cockburn, "In Israel, Detachment from Reality Is Now the Norm," *Independent*, January 22, 2009.

69. John Newsinger, *British Counterinsurgency: From Palestine to Northern Ireland*, (New York: Palgrave Macmillan, 2002), 151; and Conflict Archive on the Internet (University of Ulster), http://cain.ulster.ac.uk/.

70. Ruane and Todd, *Dynamics of Conflict*, 116–78.

71. David Sharrock, "Orangemen on March Bring N. Ireland Back to the Boil," *Guardian Weekly*, July 16, 1995.

72. Conflict Archive on the Internet (University of Ulster), "Speech by Ian Paisley, Then Leader of the Democratic Unionist Party (DUP), to the Independent Orange Demonstration in Rasharkin, County Antrim (12 July 2004)," http://cain.ulst.ac.uk/issues/politics/docs/dup/ip120704.htm.

73. Conflict Archive on the Internet (University of Ulster), "Speech by Ian Paisley (DUP), Then First Minister, on the Resumption of Devolved Government in Northern Ireland, Stormont, Belfast, (8 May 2007)," http://cain.ulst.ac.uk/issues/politics/docs/dup/ip080507.htm.

74. Conflict Archive on the Internet (University of Ulster), "Extract from a Speech by Ian Paisley at the Site of the Battle of the Boyne, (11 May 2007)," http://cain.ulst.ac.uk/issues/politics/docs/dup/ip110507.htm.

75. Conflict Archive on the Internet (University of Ulster), "Speech by Ian Paisley, Then First Minister of Northern Ireland, at the Joint Official Opening of the Battle of the Boyne Site with Bertie Ahern, then Taoiseach (Irish Prime Minister), (Tuesday 6 May 2008)," http://cain.ulst.ac.uk/issues/politics/docs/dup/ip060508.htm.

76. Ibid.

77. Jeenah and Vally, "Beyond Ethnic Nationalism," 385.

78. Naomi Klein, *The Shock Doctrine* (New York: Picador, 2007), 245.

79. Ibid., 256–57.

80. Ibid., 264.

81. Michael Neumann, "The One-State Illusion: More Is Less—The Debate over Israel and Palestine," *CounterPunch*, March 10, 2008, http://www.counterpunch.org/2008/03/10/the-one-state-illusion-more-is-less-the-debate-over-israel-and-palestine/.

82. Liz Alderman, "More Children in Greece Are Going Hungry," *New York Times*, April 17, 2013.

83. Michael Scaturro, "Malaria and HIV Spike as Greece Cuts Healthcare Spending," *Atlantic*, May 15, 2013.

84. See Joseph Massad, "The Struggle for Egypt," *CounterPunch*, July 12, 2013; Ajamu Baraka, "Requiem for a Revolution that Never Was," *CounterPunch*, July 18, 2013.

85. Nora Barrows-Friedman, "Campaigners Strategize Refugee Return during South Africa Visit," *Electronic Intifada*, June 5, 2012, http://electronicintifada.net/content/campaigners-strategize-refugee-return-during-south-africa-visit/11366.

86. Badil, "Visions for a New State: Discussion Paper," February 2012, http://badil.org/comparative-study-visits/item/1807-3?lang=en; for more information about, and documents related to, the Badil-Zochrot study visit to South Africa, see the Badil website, http://badil.org/en/comparative-study-visits/itemlist/category/224-south-africa-1-10-february-2012.

87. Sumantra Bose, *Contested Lands* (Cambridge, MA: Harvard University Press, 2007), 296.

88. Ameer Makhoul, "A Palestinian Political Prisoner's Take on Israel's Protest Movement," *Electronic Intifada*, October 5, 2011, http://electronicintifada.net/content/palestinian-political-prisoners-take-israels-protest-movement/10455.

89. Alexander, *New Jim Crow*, 257.

90. Ibid., 259.

91. Ibid.

Chapter 4: Neoliberal Palestine

1. Thomas Friedman, "Green Shoots in Palestine," *New York Times,* August 5, 2009.

2. Palestinian National Authority, "Ending the Occupation, Establishing the State: Program of the Thirteenth Government," August 2009. This document was followed by several others, including "Homestretch to Freedom," August 2010, and "Establishing the State, Building Our

Future," April 2011.

3. Salim Tamari, Khalid Farraj, and Camille Mansour, "A Palestinian State in Two Years: Interview with Salam Fayyad, Palestinian Prime Minister," *Journal of Palestine Studies*, 39.1 (2009), 63.

4. Avi Issacharoff, "In the West Bank, New Cars Signal the Good Life," *Haaretz*, July 16, 2010, http://www.haaretz.com/print-edition/news/mess-report-in-the-west-bank-new-cars-signal -the-good-life-1.302237.

5. Juliane von Mittelstaedt, "Boom Times in the West Bank," *Spiegel Online*, April 27, 2011, http://www.spiegel.de/international/world/dream-of-a-palestinian-tiger-boom-times-in-the -west-bank-a-759046.html.

6. Roger Cohen, "Fayyad's Road to Palestine," *New York Times*, April 29, 2010.

7. Department of State, "Remarks to the American Task Force on Palestine: Hillary Rodham Clinton," news release, October 20, 2010, http://www.state.gov/secretary/rm/2010/10/149766.htm.

8. Kenneth Chasen, "A State of Palestine in the Making," *Los Angeles Times,* August 25, 2010, http://articles.latimes.com/2010/aug/25/opinion/la-oe-chasen-fayyad-2-20100825.

9. Thomas Friedman, "Real Palestinian Revolution," *New York Times,* June 29, 2010.

10. Z. Byron Wolf, "Israeli Prime Minister Gets 29 Standing Ovations in Congress, Sends Message to White House," ABC News, May 24, 2012, http://abcnews.go.com/blogs/politics/2011 /05/israeli-prime-minister-gets-20-standing-ovations-in-congress-sends-message-to-white-house/.

11. *Globe and Mail,* "Transcript of Prime Minister Netanyahu's Address to U.S. Congress," May 24, 2011, http://www.theglobeandmail.com/news/world/transcript-of-prime-minister-netanyahus -address-to-us-congress/article635191/.

12. Yezid Sayigh, "Policing the People, Building the State: Authoritarian Transformation in the West Bank and Gaza," paper, Carnegie Endowment for International Peace, February 2011, http:// carnegieendowment.org/2011/02/28/policing-people-building-state-authoritarian-transformation -in-west-bank-and-gaza/jke.

13. Alaa Tartir, "Why PA's New Prime Minister Heads a Papier-Mâché Government," *Electronic Intifada*, June 19, 2013.

14. Quartet, "Quartet Statement," January 30, 2006, http://www.un.org/news/dh/infocus/middle _east/quartet-30jan2006.htm.

15. Ahmed Yousef, "Pause for Peace," *New York Times*, November 1, 2006.

16. BBC, "Transcript: Khaled Meshaal Interview," February 8, 2006, http://news.bbc.co.uk/2 /hi/4693382.stm.

17. Ali Abunimah, "Hamas, the I.R.A. and Us," *New York Times*, August 28, 2010.

18. David Rose, "The Gaza Bombshell," *Vanity Fair*, April 2008.

19. Ibid.

20. Ibid.

21. Ibid.

22. Mark Perry, "Dayton's Mission: A Reader's Guide," *Al Jazeera English*, January 25, 2011, http:// www.aljazeera.com/palestinepapers/2011/01/2011125145732219555.html.

23. Rose, "Gaza Bombshell."

24. Ibid.

25. Ibid.

26. Ibid.

27. Ali Abunimah, "The Palestine Papers and the 'Gaza Coup,'" *Electronic Intifada*, January 27, 2011.

28. Rose, "Gaza Bombshell."

29. Ibid.

30. Ibid.
31. Ma'an News Agency, "Shtayyeh: PA 'Powerless' to Face Financial Commitments," September 6, 2012, http://www.maannews.net/eng/ViewDetails.aspx?ID=517849.
32. World Bank, *Towards Economic Sustainability of a Future Palestinian State: Promoting Private Sector-Led Growth* (Washington, DC: World Bank, 2012), 24, http://siteresources.worldbank.org /INTWESTBANKGAZA/Resources/GrowthStudyEngcorrected.pdf.
33. UNRWA, "Labour Market Briefing: West Bank; Second Half 2010," news release, April 2011, http://www.unrwa.org/userfiles/201106082849.pdf.
34. UNRWA, "Labour Market in the West Bank; Briefing on First-Half 2011," news release, December 2011, http://www.unrwa.org/userfiles/201112123454.pdf.
35. Reuters, "Palestinians Slipping Deeper into Poverty—UN," September 5, 2012.
36. World Bank, *Towards Economic Sustainability*, 49–50.
37. Ibid., 94.
38. Sam Bahour, "Analysis: Palestine's Economic Hallucination," Ma'an News Agency, December 29, 2011, http://www.maannews.net/eng/ViewDetails.aspx?ID=448743.
39. Palestinian Monetary Authority, "Monthly Statistical Bulletin," undated, http://www.pma.ps /Portals/1/Users/002/02/2/Monthly%20statistical%20Bulletin/Banking%20Data/table_23 _facilities_by_economic_sectors.xls. See Table 23, "Credit Distribution by Economic Sector."
40. Oxfam, "Palestinian Families Facing a $1bn Debt Burden, since Aid Embargo Started, Says Oxfam," news release, June 12, 2007, http://www.oxfam.org/en/grow/node/170.
41. Based on a representative geographic sample of 2,022 households. See Riyada Consulting and Training, "Financial Literacy and Consumer Awareness Survey in the West Bank and Gaza," July 2011, report commissioned by the World Bank and USAID, http://microdata .worldbank.org/index.php/catalog/1029/reports.
42. World Bank, *Towards Economic Sustainability*, 50, 66.
43. Jillian Kestler-D'Amours, "Palestinian Bubble Set to Burst," Inter Press Service, August 5, 2012, http://www.ipsnews.net/2012/08/palestinian-bubble-set-to-burst/.
44. Bisan Center for Research and Development, "Raghm irtifa' nisbat al-musa'adaat al-kharijiya, al-dayn al-'aama al-filistiniya tudaa'if 200%" (Arabic), media release, September 5, 2011.
45. UNCTAD, "Report on UNCTAD Assistance to the Palestinian People: Developments in the Economy of the Occupied Palestinian Territory," July 15, 2011, http://unispal.un.org /UNISPAL.NSF/0/63503F7B0AEDDFB4852578F5006780A6.
46. Reliefweb, "Children in West Bank Facing Worse Conditions than in Gaza," June 29, 2010, http://reliefweb.int/report/occupied-palestinian-territory/children-west-bank-facing-worse -conditions-gaza; See also Save the Children, *Life on the Edge: The Struggle to Survive and the Impact of Forced Displacement in High Risk Areas of the Occupied Palestinian Territory* (Jerusalem: Save the Children UK, 2009), http://www.savethechildren.org.uk/resources/online-library/life -edge-struggle-survive-and-impact-forced-displacement-high-risk-areas.
47. Nisreen Alyan, Ronit Sela, and Michal Pomerantz, "Policies of Neglect in East Jerusalem: The Policies that Created 78% Poverty Rates and a Frail Job Market," Association for Civil Rights in Israel, news release, May 2012, http://www.acri.org.il/en/wp-content/uploads/2012/05/The -Poverty-Policy-in-East-Jerusalem_ACRI_May-2012_ENG.pdf.
48. IRIN News, "Is Greater Food Security an Illusion?" August 2, 2012, http://www.irinnews.org /Report/96009/OPT-Is-greater-food-security-an-illusion.
49. Ibid.
50. UNCTAD, "Report on UNCTAD Assistance to the Palestinian People"; Palestinian Non-Governmental Organizations Network, Bisan Center for Research and Development, "Al-daf'a

al-musbiq fi qitaa'ay al-miyah wal-kahrabaa'" (Arabic), report, 2012, http://ar.bisan.org/sites /default/files/magazine_a5.pdf. The second cited report looks at the impact of the privatization and metering of electricity and water services.

51. Jillian Kestler-D'Amours, "In Peace, Palestinian Women under Attack," Inter Press Service, August 16, 2012, http://www.ipsnews.net/2012/08/in-peace-palestinian-women-under-attack.

52. Von Mittelstaedt, "Boom Times in the West Bank."

53. Harriet Sherwood, "Rawabi Rises: New West Bank City Symbolises Palestine's Potential," *Guardian*, August 8, 2013, http://www.theguardian.com/world/2013/aug/08/rawabi-west -bank-city-palestine.

54. Arwa Aburawa, "Interview: The Man Behind Palestine's Green City—Bashar Masri," *Green Prophet*, May 2, 2011, http://www.greenprophet.com/2011/05/rawabi-interview-bashar-masri.

55. Isabel Kershner, "Birth of a Palestinian City Is Punctuated by Struggles," *New York Times*, August 10, 2013.

56. *Witness*, "The Promised City," Al Jazeera English, May 16, 2013.

57. The official Rawabi website maintained live webcams showing the progress of construction: http://www.rawabi.ps.

58. Nathan Jeffay, "Palestinian-American Entrepreneur Re-Envisions West Bank Development," *Jewish Daily Forward*, March 4, 2011, http://forward.com/articles/135638/palestinian-american -entrepreneur-re-envisions-wes/.

59. Felice Friedson, "The First [Planned] Palestinian City," *Jerusalem Post*, November 30, 2009.

60. Emily Lawrence, "Transformation of Palestinian Landscape Focus of Designing Civic Encounter Project," *Electronic Intifada*, February 25, 2012, http://electronicintifada.net /content/transformation-palestinian-landscape-focus-designing-civic-encounter-project/10950.

61. Yousif Al-Shayib, "Sharika khaasa tuqim madina sakaniyya 'ala aradi fallahin qurb Ramallah bi qarar istimlak ri'asi" (Arabic), *Al-Ghad*, January 11, 2010, http://www.alghad.com /index.php/article/351771.html.

62. Uri Davis, "Rawabi: A National Project that Defeats Its Purpose," Ma'an News Agency, February 8, 2011, http://www.maannews.net/eng/ViewDetails.aspx?ID=358011; Uri Davis, "Rawabi Remains Settler-Colonial Sub-Contractor," Ma'an News Agency, March 30, 2011, http://www.maannews.net/eng/ViewDetails.aspx?ID=373702.

63. Al-Shayib, "Sharika khaasa."

64. *Al-Watan Voice*, "Munashada: istimlak aradi khasa min amlak aal al-husseini wa jam'a min ahali qaryat 'ajjul bikhusus mashrou' madinat Rawabi" (Arabic), August 5, 2009, http://www .alwatanvoice.com/arabic/news/2009/08/05/140248.html.

65. Al-Shayib, "Sharika khaasa."

66. Consulate General of the United States in Jerusalem, "Subject: Rawabi Land Title Resolved, On to the Next Challenge," diplomatic cable, November 20, 2009, released by WikiLeaks on August 30, 2012, http://wikileaks.org/cable/2009/11/09JERUSALEM2096.html.

67. Wattan TV, "Bil sawt wal sura . . . hikayat Rawabi min bidayatiha ila nihayatiha" (Arabic), *Sa'at Raml*, Wattan TV, video, posted January 15, 2011, http://vimeo.com/18814278. This hour-long program on Palestinian television features a long interview with Masri as well as interviews with landowners in the area of Rawabi.

68. Al-Shayib, "Sharika khaasa."

69. Al-Shayib, "Sharika khaasa"; Wattan TV, "Bil sawt wal sura."

70. Wattan TV, "Bil sawt wal sura."

71. Al-Shayib, "Sharika khaasa."

72. Ibid.

73. Consulate General of the United States in Jerusalem, "Subject: Rawabi."

74. Peace Now, "Methods of Confiscation – How Does Israel Justify and Legalize Confiscation of Lands?" web page, undated, http://peacenow.org.il/eng/content/methods-confiscation-how-does-israel-justify-and-legalize-confiscation-lands.

75. Wattan TV, "Bil sawt wal sura."

76. Ibid.

77. Al-Shayib, "Sharika khaasa."

78. Nathan Jeffay, "Palestinian-American Entrepreneur Re-Envisions West Bank Development," *Jewish Daily Forward*, March 4, 2011, http://forward.com/articles/135638/palestinian-american-entrepreneur-re-envisions-wes/.

79. Uri Davis, "Rawabi Implicates PA in Zionist Project," Ma'an News Agency, February 8, 2011, http://www.maannews.net/eng/ViewDetails.aspx?ID=358002.

80. Wattan TV, "Bil sawt wal sura."

81. Jeffay, "Palestinian-American Entrepreneur Re-Envisions West Bank Development."

82. Howard Schneider, "Palestinians Looking to American-Style Housing Developments, Financing," *Washington Post*, November 23, 2009.

83. Riyada Consulting and Training, "Financial Literacy and Consumer Awareness Survey in the West Bank and Gaza," July 2011, report commissioned by the World Bank and USAID, 22–23, http://microdata.worldbank.org/index.php/catalog/1029/reports.

84. Consulate General of the United States in Jerusalem, "West Bank Housing Projects: Financing on Track, But Hurdles Remain," diplomatic cable, July 27, 2009, released by Wikileaks on August 30, 2011, http://wikileaks.org/cable/2009/07/09JERUSALEM1282.html.

85. Ali Abunimah, "Role of Israeli Firms Raises Boycott Concerns about Rawabi," *Electronic Intifada*, December 30, 2010, http://electronicintifada.net/content/role-israeli-firms-raises-boycott-concerns-about-rawabi/9162. This article quotes a December 29, 2010, personal email from Bashar Masri.

86. Abunimah, "Role of Israeli Firms."

87. Rakesh Kochhar, Richard Fry, and Paul Taylor, *Wealth Gaps Rise to Record Highs Between Whites, Blacks, Hispanics* (Washington, DC: Pew Research Center, 2011), http://www.pewsocialtrends.org/2011/07/26/wealth-gaps-rise-to-record-highs-between-whites-blacks-hispanics/.

88. Khalil Nakhleh, *Globalized Palestine* (Trenton, NJ: Red Sea Press, 2012), 109.

89. Consulate General of the United States in Jerusalem, "Nablus Developer on Area C Constraints," diplomatic cable, February 12, 2010, released by WikiLeaks on August 30, 2011, http://wikileaks.org/cable/2010/02/10JERUSALEM279.html.

90. Ethan Bronner, "New Home-Buying Plan May Bolster Abbas," *New York Times*, April 15, 2008.

91. Human Rights Watch, *Razing Rafah: Mass Home Demolitions in the Gaza Strip*, October 2004.

92. Consulate General of the United States in Jerusalem, "OPIC's Affordable Mortgage, Risk Insurance," diplomatic cable, October 9, 2009, released by WikiLeaks on August 30, 2010, http://wikileaks.org/cable/2009/10/09JERUSALEM1800.html.

93. OPIC, "$500 Million Mortgage Facility Launched in Palestine," news release, June 2, 2010, http://www.opic.gov/node/288.

94. CHF International, "Palestinian Homebuyer Education Program (PHEP)," news release, March 7, 2012, http://www.chfinternational.org/node/37099.

95. CHF International, "Supporting Female-headed Households through Food Security Interventions in Gaza," news release, August 6, 2012, http://www.chfinternational.org/node/37322.

96. Consulate General of the United States in Jerusalem, "OPIC's Plan for Affordable Mortgages

in the West Bank," diplomatic cable, October 23, 2008, http://wikileaks.org/cable/2008
/10/08JERUSALEM1943.html.

97. World Bank, *Towards Economic Sustainability*, 101.

98. Consulate General of the United States in Jerusalem, "West Bank Housing Projects."

99. Consulate General of the United States in Jerusalem, "United States Trade and Development
Agency Awards Grants to Rawabi and PA Ministry of Finance," news release, March 15, 2010,
http://jerusalem.usconsulate.gov/pr031510.html; *Rawabi Home,* Spring 2011, http://www
.rawabi.ps/newsletter/2011/download/en/rawabi_spring_2011_en.pdf.

100. OPIC, "OPIC Completes Financing for First Private Equity Fund Investing in Palestinian Companies," news release, May 22, 2012, http://www.opic.gov/node/381.

101. Palestine Papers, "Meeting Minutes: Saeb Erekat and George Mitchell," October 2, 2009, http://
transparency.aljazeera.net/en/projects/thepalestinepapers/20121821919875390.html. In an October 2, 2009, meeting in Washington, Mitchell told Palestinian Authority chief negotiator Saeb
Erekat and other PA officials that Israeli permission for Rawabi and for the Qatari-financed mobile company Wataniya to use frequencies controlled by Israel were "issues we are working on."

102. *Rawabi Home,* Winter Edition 2012, http://www.rawabi.ps/newsletter/2012/download
/en/full.pdf.

103. Abunimah, "Role of Israeli Firms."

104. Boycott National Committee, "Palestinian Civil Society Denounces Bashar Masri's Normalization with Israel as Undermining the Struggle for Palestinian Rights," September 10, 2012,
http://www.bdsmovement.net/2012/bnc-denounces-bashar-masri-normalization-9500.

105. *Witness,* "Promised City."

106. Isabel Kershner, "Birth of a Palestinian City Is Punctuated by Struggles," *New York Times,* August 10, 2013.

107. Ali Abunimah, "Rawabi Developer Masri Helps Deepen Israel's Grip on West Bank," *Electronic
Intifada,* January 6, 2011, http://electronicintifada.net/content/rawabi-developer-masri-helps
-deepen-israels-grip-west-bank/9170.

108. Boycott National Committee, "Palestinian Civil Society."

109. Danny Rubinstein, "It's Not Politics—It's Just Business," *Ynet,* June 1, 2011.

110. Tani Goldstein, "'Big Step' for New Palestinian City," *Ynet,* January 26, 2012, http://www
.ynetnews.com/articles/0,7340,L-4181368,00.html.

111. Israel Ministry of Foreign Affairs, "PM Netanyahu and Quartet Rep Blair Announce Economic
Steps to Assist Palestinian Authority," news release, February 4, 2011, http://www.mfa
.gov.il/MFA/Government/Speeches+by+Israeli+leaders/2011/PM_Netanyahu_Quartet_Rep_Blair
_economic_steps_PA_4-Feb-2011.htm.

112. Lilach Weissman, "Idan Ofer Leads Peace Delegation to Ramallah," *Globes,* April 28, 2011,
http://www.globes.co.il/serveen/globes/docview.asp?did=1000641315&fid=1725.

113. Boycott National Committee, "Palestinian Civil Society."

114. Nakhleh, *Globalized Palestine,* 126.

115. Robert Danin, "A Third Way to Palestine: Fayyadism and Its Discontents," *Foreign Affairs,* January–
February 2011.

116. BBC, "Sharon Plan 'Blocked Peace Talks,'" October 6, 2004, http://news.bbc.co.uk/2/hi
/3720176.stm.

117. Klein, *Shock Doctrine,* 18.

118. Ibid.

119. Nathan J. Brown, "Are Palestinians Building a State?" Carnegie Endowment for International Peace,
July 1, 2013, http://carnegieendowment.org/2010/07/01/are-palestinians-buildingstate/2ynk.

120. Shir Hever, *The Political Economy of Israel's Occupation* (New York: Pluto Press, 2010), 9.

121. Ibid.

122. World Bank, *Towards Economic Sustainability*, 36.

123. Ibid.

124. Jordan ruled the West Bank from 1948 until Israel occupied it in 1967.

125. World Bank, *Towards Economic Sustainability*, 44.

126. Hever, *Political Economy of Israel's Occupation*, 10; Samer Abdelnour, Alaa Tartir, Rami Zurayk, "Farming Palestine for Freedom," policy brief, Al-Shabaka, July 2012, http://al-shabaka.org/sites/default/files/Abdelnour_et_al_PolicyBrief_Eng_July_2012.pdf.

127. Hever, *Political Economy of Israel's Occupation*, 11.

128. World Bank, *Towards Economic Sustainability*, 37.

129. Jonathan Cook, "Report: Israel Stole $2 Billion from Palestinian Workers," *Electronic Intifada*, February 4, 2010.

130. Leila Farsakh, "Palestinian Labor Flows to the Israeli Economy: A Finished Story?" *Journal of Palestine Studies,* 32.1 (Autumn 2002), 13–27.

131. Stephanie Westbrook, "SodaStream 'Treats Us like Slaves,' Says Palestinian Factory Worker," *Electronic Intifada*, May 9, 2013, http://electronicintifada.net/content/sodastream-treats-us-slaves-says-palestinian-factory-worker/12441.

132. Jillian Kestler-D'Amours, "For Palestinian Workers, the Enemy Is the Hope," Inter Press Service, September 25, 2012, http://www.ipsnews.net/2012/09/for-palestinian-workers-the-enemy-is-the-hope/.

133. Daniel Tepper, "In Photos: Palestinian Workers' Everyday Nightmare at Israeli Checkpoints," *Electronic Intifada*, July 9, 2013, http://electronicintifada.net/content/photos-palestinian-workers-everyday-nightmare-israeli-checkpoints/12597.

134. Palestinian Centre for Human Rights, "IOF Kills a Palestinian Worker and Wounds Another Three Workers at Al-Zaeem Checkpoint East of Jerusalem," news release, July 30, 2012.

135. Kestler-D'Amours, "For Palestinian Workers."

136. Caitlin Dewey, "Israel's Palestinian-Only Buses Draw Accusations of Segregation, Apartheid," *Washington Post*, March 4, 2013.

137. Joseph Massad, *The Persistence of the Palestinian Question* (Oxford: Routledge, 2006), 96–103.

138. Ibid., 103.

139. Nakhleh, *Globalized Palestine.*

140. Adam Hanieh, *Capitalism and Class in the Gulf Arab States* (New York: Palgrave Macmillan, 2011), 161.

141. Ibid., 162–3.

142. Jalal Abukhater, "BNC Condemns Palestinian Billionaire Munib Masri's Dealings with Israeli Settler Tycoon," *Electronic Intifada*, August 11, 2012; Max Blumenthal, "Kerry and Blair's $4 Billion Mystery Plan for Palestine: Crony Capitalism under the Guise of Peace?" *Mondoweiss*, May 31, 2013.

143. William Orme, "The Young Palestinian Giant: Holding Company Close to Arafat Casts Widest of Nets," *New York Times,* May 6, 1999.

144. Rabo Haje, "The Political Economy of Palestine: The Transformation of Economic Elites after Oslo," PASSIA, April 30, 1998, http://www.passia.org/meetings/98/meet03.htm.

145. Nakhleh, *Globalized Palestine,* 57.

146. "IsraelNewsAgency" (YouTube user), "Sir Ronald Cohen Israel Facing Tomorrow Portland Capital," YouTube video, May 17, 2008, http://youtu.be/HrBk84K1_BE. In this video interview with the Israel News Agency, Cohen explained that he believed economic growth in the

Palestinian economy would help "moderates" and "isolate" extremists and that "we can only arrive at a common goal of peace by a concerted effort to develop the Palestinian economy and the Palestinian private sector in particular."

147. Yossi Bachar, Portland Trust website, http://www.portlandtrust.org/senior-management/yossi -bachar.

148. See Hanieh, *Capitalism and Class.*

149. Hanieh, *Capitalism and Class,* 159–60.

150. Sara Roy, "2012 Edward Said Memorial Lecture," transcript, Palestine Center (Washington, DC), October 10, 2012, http://www.thejerusalemfund.org/ht/display/ContentDetails/i /36415/pid/897.

151. UN Human Rights Council, *Report of the United Nations Fact Finding Mission on the Gaza Conflict* (A/HRC/12/48), September 25, 2009, 263.

152. Ibid., 263.

153. Ibid., 264.

154. Rami Almeghari, "Israel Destroys Gaza Dairy for Second Time," *Electronic Intifada,* April 5, 2010, http://electronicintifada.net/content/israel-destroys-gaza-dairy-second-time/8766.

155. UN Human Rights Council, *Report,* 256.

156. Ibid., 254.

157. Gisha, "Reader: Food Consumption in the Gaza Strip—Red Lines," position paper, October 2012, http://www.gisha.org/UserFiles/File/publications/redlines/redlines-position-paper-eng.pdf.

158. Hever, *Political Economy of Israel's Occupation,* 36–37.

159. Central Bureau of Statistics (Israel), *Statistical Abstract of Israel 2012; No. 63* (Jerusalem: Central Bureau of Statistics), Table 15.4, "Current Account," 706.

160. Ibid., Table 16.12, "Exports, By Industry and Main Country of Destination," 752.

161. Hever, *Political Economy of Israel's Occupation,* 39.

162. Office for the Coordination of Humanitarian Affairs, Gaza Crossings Activities Database, http://www.ochaopt.org/dbs/Crossings/CommodityReports.aspx?id=1010003.

163. Amnesty International UK, Broederlijk Delen, Cafod, CCFD-Terre Solidaire, Christian Aid, Church of Sweden, et al., *Dashed Hopes: Continuation of the Gaza Blockade* (Amnesty International, 2010), 10n16, www.christianaid.org.uk/image/DashedHopesGazaNov2010.pdf.

164. Roy, "2012 Edward Said Memorial Lecture."

165. Al Mezan Center For Human Rights, "Death Toll in Tunnels Collapsing Rises to 232, Al Mezan Expresses Its Sorrow for the High Number of Victims and Demands Gaza Government Take Effective Steps to Protect Tunnel Workers," news release, January 17, 2013, http://www .mezan.org/en/details.php?id=16110; Mohammed Omer, "Gaza's Graveyards for the Living: Now Flooded With Sewage Water," *Vice,* March 17, 2013, http://www.vice.com/read/gazas -graveyards-for-the-living-now-flooded-with-sewage-water.

166. Ali Abunimah, "Yes, Gaza Is Still under Siege," *Electronic Intifada,* May 30, 2013. I spent a week in Gaza from May 23 to 28, 2013, as part of a delegation to the Palestine Festival of Literature.

167. Ali Abunimah, "Cutting Off a Vital Connection," *Al Jazeera English,* January 25, 2013, http://www.aljazeera.com/palestinepapers/2011/01/2011125144345427365.html.

168. UN Office for the Coordination of Humanitarian Affairs, "Humanitarian Bulletin Monthly Report, July 2013," news release, August 23, 2013, http://www.ochaopt.org/documents/ocha_opt _the_humanitarian_monitor_2013_08_23_english.pdf.

169. El Funoun, "Marj Ibn ʿAmer (The Plains of Ibn ʿAmer) 1989," undated website, http://www .el-funoun.org/productions/marj.html.

170. Gershom Shafir, *Land, Labor and the Origins of the Israeli-Palestinian Conflict, 1882–1914,*

updated edition (Berkeley: University of California Press, 1996), 205–206.

171. Charlotte Silver, "Leaked Documents Show PA Outsourced Palestinian Land and Rights to Turkish Firm," *Electronic Intifada,* September 19, 2012.

172. Alaa Tartir, "PA Industrial Zones: Cementing Statehood or Occupation?" *Al-Shabaka,* February 7, 2013, http://al-shabaka.org/node/572.

173. World Bank, *Towards Economic Sustainability,* 81.

174. Palestine Investment Fund, "PIF's Director General Confirms the Revival of Jenin Industrial Zone Project," news release, October 25, 2007, http://www.pif.ps/index.php?lang=en&page =1248093363276&sub=124861362702&news_item=12486904951129.

175. TOBB-BIS Industrial and Technology Parks Development and Management Company, "TOBB-BIS Industrial Parks Development and Management Company; Company Profile," brochure, March 2010, http://www.industryforpeace.org/TEPAV_brosur.pdf.

176. Silver, "Leaked Documents."

177. Ibid.

178. Bisan Center for Research and Development, "Taqrir warshat al-'amal 'hawla al-mantaqa al-sina'iyya fi sahli marj ibn 'amer" (Arabic), September 17, 2011.

179. Silver, "Leaked Documents."

180. Sam Bahour, "Economic Prison Zones," MERIP, November 19, 2010, http://www.merip.org /mero/mero111910.

181. Jordan Ministry of Labor, "Ministry of Labour Report on Status of Migrant Workers in the Qualified Industrial Zones," report, May 2006, http://www.carim.org/public/polsoctexts /PS2JOR005_EN.pdf.

182. Associated Press, "Rape Case Turns Focus to Jordan's Factory Problems," September 7, 2011.

183. See for example, Rebecca Whiting, "Abused Nepali Workers Flee Jordan," *Al-Akhbar English,* March 10, 2013, http://english.al-akhbar.com/node/15200.

184. Liz Ford, "Jericho Business Park Aims to Inch Palestine Towards Sustainability," *Guardian,* June 18, 2013.

185. Bahour, "Economic Prison Zones."

186. Alaa Tartir, "Jericho Agro-Industrial Park: A Corridor for Peace or Perpetuation of Occupation?," position paper, Bisan Center for Research and Development, December 2012, http:// al-shabaka.org/sites/default/files/Tartir_BCRD_Paper_EN.pdf.

187. Aviva Lori, "A Woman with a Mission," *Haaretz,* May 27, 2010, http://www.haaretz.com /weekend/magazine/a-woman-with-a-mission-1.292602.

188. Ibid.

189. Valérie Hoffenberg, "Mon programme pour les Français d'Israël," video, posted to YouTube, May 12, 2012, http://youtu.be/yKtixTpSCj4; and Valérie Hoffenberg, "D. Ayalon : Valérie Hoffenberg est une grande amie d'Israël," video, posted to YouTube, May 9, 2012, http:// youtu.be/65KlbAGEDFA.

190. Valérie Hoffenberg, *Valérie Hoffenberg – votre députée pour Israel* (blog), http:// valeriehoffenbergdepute2012.wordpress.com.

191. Valérie Hoffenberg, "Valérie Hoffenberg : Représenter les Français d'Israël à l'Assemblée Nationale," video, posted to YouTube, June 13, 2011, http://youtu.be/AcZ9Is8urUI.

192. Danna Harman, "French Mideast Envoy Fired for Opposing Palestinian UN Bid," *Haaretz,* September 7, 2011, http://www.haaretz.com/print-edition/news/french-mideast-envoy-fired -for-opposing-palestinian-un-bid-1.382960.

193. Lori, "Woman with a Mission."

194. Erez is a director of Mydas Investment Fund, Ltd. His personal information is contained in

the company's public filings made with the Tel Aviv Stock Exchange.

195. Ben-Gurion University of the Negev, *BGU & You: Newsletter of the Ben-Gurion University of the Negev*, Summer 2012, http://in.bgu.ac.il/en/BGU%20and%20You/BGU%20and%20You%20Summer%202012.pdf.

196. Aviva Lori, "The Archetype of the Wandering Jew: Corinne Evens' Globe-Spanning Empire of Business and Philanthropy," *Haaretz*, June 22, 2013.

197. Ibid.

198. Ibid.

199. Tartir, "PA Industrial Zones."

200. Anaïs Antreasyan, "Gas Finds in the Eastern Mediterranean: Gaza, Israel, and Other Conflicts," *Journal of Palestine Studies,* 17.3 (Spring 2013), 29–47.

201. Alaa Tartir, Sam Bahour, and Samer Abdelnour, "Defeating Dependency, Creating a Resistance Economy," *Al-Shabaka*, February 14, 2012, http://al-shabaha.org/policy-brief/economic-issues/defeating-dependency-creating-resistance-economy.

202. Ibid.

203. Nora Lester Murad, "Should Palestinians Boycott International Aid?" *Guardian*, October 18, 2012, http://www.theguardian.com/global-development/poverty-matters/2012/oct/18/should-palestinians-boycott-international-aid.

204. Tartir, Bahour, and Abdelnour, "Defeating Dependency."

205. Sarah Irving, "Palestinian Farmers Use Permaculture to Challenge Occupation," *Electronic Intifada*, June 3, 2009, http://electronicintifada.net/content/palestinian-farmers-use-permaculture-challenge-occupation/8275.

206. Megha Satyanarayana, "Urban Farming Invigorates Detroit Neighborhood," *Detroit Free Press*, May 20, 2013; Monica M. White, "Sisters of the Soil: Urban Gardening as Resistance in Detroit," *Race/Ethnicity: Multidisciplinary Global Contexts*, 5.1 (2011), 13–28. Also see the Detroit Black Community Food Security Network website, http://detroitblackfoodsecurity.org.

207. Miguel A. Altieri and Fernando R. Funes-Monzote, "The Paradox of Cuban Agriculture," *Monthly Review*, 63.1 (2008); Miguel Altieri, "Transforming Cuba's Agriculture," interview by Jerome McDonnell, *Worldview*, WBEZ, July 13, 2009. Also see Fernando Funes, Luis Garcia, Martin Bourque, Nilda Perez, and Peter Rosset, *Sustainable Agriculture and Resistance* (Food First Books: 2002).

208. Christa Bruhn, *Canaan Fair Trade Impact Study 2005–11* (Jenin: Canaan Fair Trade, 2013), http://www.canaanfairtrade.com/images/Canaan_Fair_Trade_Impact_Study.2012.pdf.

209. Ibid.

Chapter 5: Israel Fights Back against BDS

1. Omar Barghouti, *BDS: The Global Struggle for Palestinian Rights* (Chicago: Haymarket Books, 2011), 62.

2. Ali Abunimah, "Israel's New Strategy: 'Sabotage' and 'Attack' the Global Justice Movement," *Electronic Intifada*, February 16, 2010, http://electronicintifada.net/content/israels-new-strategy-sabotage-and-attack-global-justice-movement/8683.

3. Reut Institute, "Eroding Israel's Legitimacy in the International Arena," January 28, 2010, http://reut-institute.org/en/Publication.aspx?PublicationId=3766.

4. Abunimah, "Israel's New Strategy."

5. Barak Ravid, "Military Intelligence Monitoring Foreign Left-Wing Organizations," *Haaretz*, March 21, 2011.

6. Thomas Friedman, "Let's Fight Over a Big Plan," *New York Times*, March 16, 2010.

7. Israel Ministry of Foreign Affairs, "FAQ: The Campaign to Defame Israel," news release, November 10, 2011, http://www.mfa.gov.il/MFA/FAQ/FAQ_Attack_Israeli_Values.
8. Barak Ravid and Natasha Mozgovaya, "U.S. Offers Israel Warplanes in Return for New Settlement Freeze," *Haaretz*, November 13, 2010.
9. Shlomo Shamir, "Jewish Leaders ask Pope Benedict to Combat Delegitimization of Israel," *Haaretz*, December 10, 2010.
10. Conference of Presidents of Major American Jewish Organizations, "2011 Mission Sharansky Edelstein," web page, February 17, 2011, http://www.conferenceofpresidents.org/content.asp?id=132, accessed February 5, 2013.
11. Jacob Berkman, "Federations, JCPA Teaming to Fight Delegitimization of Israel," *Jewish Telegraphic Agency*, October 25, 2010.
12. Nathan Guttman, "Communal Groups Mobilize against 'Delegitimizers' of Jewish State," *Jewish Daily Forward*, March 31, 2010.
13. Ari Shavit, "The Enemy Within," *Haaretz*, August 30, 2002.
14. Asa Winstanley, "The *Electronic Intifada* Barred from Reporting inside UK 'Delegitimization' Conference," *Electronic Intifada*, November 26, 2011, http://electronicintifada.net/blogs/asa-winstanley/electronic-intifada-barred-reporting-inside-uk-delegitimization-conference.
15. Reut Institute, "The Assault on Israel's Legitimacy: London as a Case Study," December 19, 2010, http://reut-institute.org/en/Publication.aspx?PublicationId=3949.
16. James Monteleone, "UNM Jews Upset over Palestinian Speaker," *Albuquerque Journal*, November 2, 2010, http://www.abqjournal.com/news/metro/022318105083newsmetro11-02-10.htm.
17. I published a copy of the document on a personal blog. See "Zionist Dossier Exposed: 'How to Expose Ali Abunimah When He Comes to Your Campus,'" August 29, 2010, http://aliabunimah.posthaven.com/zionist-dossier-exposed-how-to-expose-ali-abu.
18. *Electronic Intifada*, "Why NGO Monitor Is Attacking the *Electronic Intifada*," November 30, 2010, http://electronicintifada.net/content/why-ngo-monitor-attacking-electronic-intifada/9125.
19. Ministry of Foreign Affairs, Netherlands, "Rosenthal Takes ICCO to Task," news release, January 13, 2011, http://www.government.nl/news/2011/01/13/rosenthal-takes-icco-to-task.html.
20. *Electronic Intifada*, "Democracy Under Threat over EI Funding, Dutch Groups Say," January 24, 2011, http://electronicintifada.net/content/democracy-under-threat-over-ei-funding-dutch-groups-say/9194.
21. Israel Defense Forces, "European Hamas Affiliate Deemed Illegal by Minister of Defense," news release, December 27, 2010, http://dover.idf.il/IDF/English/News/today/10/12/2703.htm. Also see Ali Abunimah, "Israel Army Uses Fabrications to Assert Flotilla Financial Links to Hamas," *Electronic Intifada*, June 30, 2011, http://electronicintifada.net/blogs/ali-abunimah/israel-army-uses-fabrications-assert-flotilla-financial-links-hamas.
22. Matthew Cassel, "Palestinian Return Centre Vows to Carry On Despite Israeli Attack," *Electronic Intifada*, January 11, 2011, http://electronicintifada.net/content/palestinian-return-centre-vows-carry-despite-israeli-attack/9176.
23. Jonny Paul, "UK to Israel: Ask for Probe of Palestine Return Centre, and We'll Launch One," *Jerusalem Post*, January 14, 2011.
24. Paul, "UK to Israel."
25. Yves Engler, "Canada's Neoconservative Turn," *Electronic Intifada*, February 26, 2010, http://electronicintifada.net/content/canadas-neoconservative-turn/8701.
26. Anti-Defamation League, "ADL Identifies Top 10 Anti-Israel Groups in America," news release, October 14, 2010, http://www.adl.org/press-center/press-releases/israel-middle-east/adl-identifies

-top-10-anti-israel-groups-in-america.html.

27. Ali Abunimah, "Lawsuit Filed against Olympia Food Co-op, Seeks to Force End to Israel Boy-cott," *Electronic Intifada*, September 10, 2011, http://electronicintifada.net/blogs/ali-abunimah /lawsuit-filed-against-olympia-food-co-op-seeks-force-end-israel-boycott.

28. "StandWithUs Northwest" (YouTube username), "Why BDS Scars Don't Heal: A Stand-WithUs Production," video, posted June 24, 2011, http://youtu.be/S6vnPTr_iCw.

29. Anti-Defamation League, *2011 Audit of Anti-Semitic Incidents*, October 29, 2012, http:// adl.org/assets/pdf/anti-semitism//united-states/2011-Audit-of-Anti-Semitic-Incidents.pdf; *2010 Audit of Anti-Semitic Incidents*, October 4, 2011, http://archive.adl.org/presrele/asus _12.html#.U+HNJp5dUqI; *2009 Audit of Anti-Semitic Incidents*, July 27, 2010, http://archive .adl.org/main_Anti_Semitism_Domestic/2009_Audit.html#U+HMiJ5dUqI.

30. Ali Abunimah, "Judge Throws Out Israel-Backed Lawsuit against Olympia Food Co-op, Up-holds Right to Boycott," *Electronic Intifada*, February 27, 2012, http://electronicintifada .net/blogs/ali-abunimah/judge-throws-out-israel-backed-lawsuit-against-olympia-food-co-op -upholds-right.

31. Ali Abunimah, "Anti-Boycott Group Forced to Pay $160,000 in Damages to Olympia Food Co-Op Board Members," *Electronic Intifada*, July 12, 2012, http://electronicintifada.net/blogs /nora/anti-boycott-group-forced-pay-160000-damages-olympia-food-co-op-board-members.

32. Jeremy Pawlowski, "5 Olympia Food Co-Op Members Who Sued to End Israeli Boycott Must Pay $160K," *Olympian*, July 12, 2012.

33. Ali Abunimah, "In Blow to Israel, French BDS Activists Acquitted of Crime in Calling for Boycott," *Electronic Intifada*, December 18, 2011, http://electronicintifada.net/blogs/ali -abunimah/blow-israel-french-bds-activists-acquitted-crime-calling-boycott.

34. See, for example, Michaël Ghnassia, *Le boycott d'Israël: que dit le droit* (Paris: Crif, 2011), http:// www.crif.org/fr/alireavoiraecouter/Le-boycott-d-Israel-que-dit-le-droit-Par-Michael-Ghnassia -(*)24639.

35. *Tribune Juive*, "François Hollande: 'Je serai intransigeant dans la lutte contre l'antisémitisme' interview exclusive à tribunejuive.info," May 1, 2012, http://www.tribunejuive.info/politique /intervieew-exclusif-de-francois-hollande-je-serai-intransigeant-dans-la-lutte-contre-lantisemitisme; Ali Abunimah, "New French President Says Boycott of Israeli Goods 'Illegal,' but Paris Court Ac-quits More BDS Activists," *Electronic Intifada*, May 7, 2012, http://electronicintifada.net/blogs/ali -abunimah/new-french-president-says-boycott-israeli-goods-illegal-paris-court-acquits-more.

36. Blake Sobczak, "Caterpillar Pulled from Social Indexes," *Associated Press*, June 27, 2012.

37. The National Coordinating Committee leading the "We Divest" campaign is made up of six or-ganizations: Jewish Voice for Peace, the US Campaign to End the Israeli Occupation, Adalah-NY, the US Palestinian Community Network, Grassroots International, and the American Friends Service Committee. As of early 2013, the campaign had been endorsed by more than fifty organ-izations, including the Palestinian Boycott National Committee. See http://wedivest.org.

38. See Kairos Palestine, http://www.kairospalestine.ps.

39. Israel Action Network, *IAN Facts 2*.

40. Abraham Cooper and Yitzchok Adlerstein, "PCUSA Could Mean End of Jewish-Presbyterian Dialogue," *Jerusalem Post*, July 2, 2012.

41. Simon Wiesenthal Center, "PCUSA Boycott Vote Helps No One in Middle East; Spate of Anti-Israel Initiatives Harm Interfaith Relations," news release, July 6, 2012, http://www.wiesenthal .com/site/apps/nlnet/content2.aspx?c=lsKWLbPJLnF.

42. Simon Wiesenthal Center, "PCUSA Boycott Vote Helps No One."

43. Donald Wagner, "FOSNA Encourages Peace, Cooperation between Faiths," *Albuquerque Jour-*

nal, September 21, 2012.

44. See the statement by more than a hundred Palestinian activists, intellectuals, and artists: "The Struggle for Palestinian Rights Is Incompatible with Any Form of Racism or Bigotry: A Statement by Palestinians," *Electronic Intifada*, October 12, 2012, http://electronicintifada.net/blogs/ali -abunimah/struggle-palestinian-rights-incompatible-any-form-racism-or-bigotry-statement.

45. Ali Abunimah, "Israel's New Strategy."

46. Nathaniel Popper, "Israel Aims to Improve Its Public Image," *Jewish Daily Forward*, October 14, 2005.

47. Ibid.

48. Ethan Bronner, "After Gaza, Israel Grapples with Crisis of Isolation," *New York Times*, March 18, 2009.

49. Barghouti, *BDS,* 123–24.

50. Barghouti, *BDS,* chapter 7.

51. Reut Institute, "Political Firewall: Strategy against the Assault against Israel's Legitimacy—Updated Executive Summary," news release, July 29, 2012, http://reut-institute.org/en/Publication .aspx?PublicationId=4155.

52. Reut Instite, "Political Firewall."

53. Sarah Schulman, "Israel and 'Pinkwashing,'" *New York Times*, November 22, 2011. In her book *Israel/Palestine and the Queer International* (Duke University Press, 2012), Schulman attributes the coining of the term "pinkwashing" to me in my 2009 speech at the Hampshire College BDS conference. While I did describe the Israeli strategy and concept, the term I applied to it was "gaywashing," which was not the term that ultimately caught on. For a transcript of my speech, see *Mondoweiss*, "Abunimah: There Is a Tremendous Struggle to Be Waged, to Force Israeli Introspection, and Change," December 4, 2009, http://mondoweiss.net/2009/12 /abunimah-there-is-a-tremendous-struggle-to-be-waged-that-will-force-israeli-introspection-and -change.html.

54. See, for example, Benjamin Doherty, "Tel Aviv Is the World's Gayest Apartheid Travel Destination," *Electronic Intifada*, January 12, 2012, http://electronicintifada.net/blogs/benjamin -doherty/tel-aviv-worlds-gayest-apartheid-travel-destination.

55. Benjamin Doherty, "Pinkwashing, 2008–2011: Obituary for a Hasbara Strategy," November 26, 2011, http://electronicintifada.net/blogs/benjamin-doherty/pinkwashing-2008-2011 -obituary-hasbara-strategy.

56. Martin Gladstone, "Gay Rights Are Human Rights," *Toronto Sun*, August 7, 2013.

57. Yossi Herzog, "An Open Letter to the Toronto Community from a Gay Israeli," StandWithUs website, undated, http://www.standwithus.com/news/article.asp?id=1871.

58. Herzog, "Open Letter."

59. Lucas Paolo Itaborahy and Jingshu Zhu, *State-Sponsored Homophobia: A World Survey of Laws: Criminalisation, Protection and Recognition of Same-Sex Love* (Brussels: International Lesbian and Gay Association, 2013), 68.

60. A widely circulated image is of two young men, Mahmoud Asgari and Ayaz Marhoni, blindfolded with nooses around their necks shortly before they were executed by hanging in the Iranian city of Mashhad on July 19, 2005, for, Iranian news media reported, raping a thirteen-year-old boy. International gay advocacy organizations claimed, based on mistranslations of such news reports, that the men, who were juveniles at the time of their alleged crime, were executed for being "gay." Right-wing blogger Andrew Sullivan, who did much to turn the case into a cause célèbre for gay internationalist activists, called the young men "two teenage gay lovers" (see Philip Kennicott, "Pictures from an Execution Come into Focus," *Washington Post*,

July 20, 2006). Scott Long, then executive director of the Lesbian, Gay, Bisexual, and Trans-gender Rights Program at Human Rights Watch, wrote in 2008 that "pictures of the horrific public hanging" of Asgari and Marhoni, "convicted, in all likelihood, of the rape of a 13-year-old boy while both were minors—spread virally round the world like a postmodern Pietà. Mon-strous, yes: but there is no conclusive evidence that they were gay or that consensual homosexual acts had anything to do with their judicial killing" (see Scott Long, "The Issue Is Torture," *Guardian*, March 31, 2008). The shocking image of Asgari and Marhoni at the gallows continues to spread virally, now more often associated with Israeli pinkwashing attacks on Palestinians, even though there is no doubt whatsoever that it has nothing to do with Palestine.

61. Michael Kagan and Anat Ben-Dor, *Nowhere to Run: Gay Palestinian Asylum-Seekers in Israel* (Tel Aviv: Tel Aviv University, Public Interest Law Program, 2008), 5–7.

62. Nathan Guttman, "Israelis Win Asylum in U.S.—But Mostly Not for Politics," *Jewish Daily Forward*, February 22, 2013.

63. Linah Alsaafin, "Though Small, Palestine's Queer Movement Has Big Vision," *Electronic Intifada*, July 12, 2013, http://electronicintifada.net/content/though-small-palestines-queer-movement -has-big-vision/12607. On issues related to the politics of "gay" identity in the Arab world, see Joseph Massad, *Desiring Arabs* (Chicago: University of Chicago Press, 2007), chapter 3.

64. Benjamin Doherty, "Sodomy for Jihad? Venerable LGBT Magazine *The Advocate* Spreads Vile Islamophobic Hoax," *Electronic Intifada*, July 12, 2012, http://electronicintifada.net/blogs /benjamin-doherty/sodomy-jihad-venerable-lgbt-magazine-advocate-spreads-vile-islamophobic -hoax. On false claims of execution of a "gay man" in Gaza, see Benjamin Doherty, "Reviving Pinkwashing and Zionist Fantasies of Violence against Queers and Transgender People," *Electronic Intifada*, February 27, 2013, http://electronicintifada.net/blogs/benjamin-doherty/reviving -pinkwashing-and-zionist-fantasies-violence-against-queers-and.

65. Giles Tremlett, "Madrid Gay Pride March Bans Israelis over Gaza Flotilla Raids," *Guardian*, June 9, 2010.

66. Yoav Zitun, "Sources Say Pro-Palestinian Groups Led Madrid to Cancel Invitation Extended to LGBT Delegation," *Ynet*, June 8, 2010, http://www.ynetnews.com/articles/0,7340,L -3901785,00.html.

67. Tremlett, "Madrid Gay Pride March Bans Israelis."

68. Schulman, "Israel and 'Pinkwashing.'"

69. Queers Against Israeli Apartheid, "At NYC Israel Parade, QAIA Challenges 'Gay Rights' Di-version from Apartheid Laws," news release, June 3, 2010, http://queersagainstisraeliapartheid .blogspot.com/2012/06/at-nyc-israel-parade-qaia-challenges.html.

70. Steven Thrasher, "Gay Center Axes Israeli Apartheid Week Event after Boycott Threat by Porn Activist," *Village Voice*, February 23, 2011, http://blogs.villagevoice.com/runninscared/2011 /02/apartheid_week.php. For information about Lucas's film see Max Blumenthal, "Money Talks, Desecration Walks: Nakba Porn Kingpin Michael Lucas Bullies LGBT Center against Anti-Apartheid Party," February 24, 2011, blog post, http://maxblumenthal.com/2011/02/money -talks-nakba-porn-kingpin-michael-lucas-bullies-the-lgbt-center.

71. Duncan Osborne, "Protest Hits Ongoing Ban on Israeli-Palestinian Debate at NYC LGBT Center," *Gay City News*, March 3, 2012, http://gaycitynews.com/protest-hits-ongoing-ban-on -israeli-palestinian-debate-at-nyc-lgbt-center.

72. Duncan Osborne, "LGBT Center Bars Sarah Schulman Reading," *Gay City News*, February 13, 2013, http://gaycitynews.com/lgbt-center-bars-sarah-schulman-reading/.

73. Saeed Jones, "Queer Activist Sarah Schulman Accuses LGBT Center of 'a Weird Kind of Anti-Semitism,'" *BuzzFeed*, February 14, 2013, http://www.buzzfeed.com/saeedjones/queer-activist

-sarah-schulman-accuses-lgbt-center-of-a-weird.

74. Josh Nathan-Kazis, "NY Gay Center Will Allow Israel-Related Events," *Jewish Daily Forward*, February 15, 2013, http://forward.com/articles/171351/ny-gay-center-will-allow-israel-related-events/.

75. Palestinian Queers for Boycott, Divestment and Sanctions, "Victory: IGLYO moves out of Israel!" news release, July 29, 2011, http://www.pqbds.com/2011/07/29/victory-iglyo-moves-out-of-israel.

76. Phan Nguyen, "Northwest Pinkwashing Events Cancelled, StandWithUs's Record of Queer Exploitation Exposed," *Mondoweiss*, March 19, 2012, http://mondoweiss.net/2012/03/northwest-pinkwashing-events-cancelled-standwithuss-record-of-queer-exploitation-exposed.html.

77. Max Blumenthal, "Anti-Flotilla Video Fraud Linked to PM Netanyahu's Office, Official Israeli Hasbara Agents (Updated)," June 24, 2011, http://maxblumenthal.com/2011/06/anti-flotilla-video-fraud-has-links-to-pm-netanyahus-office-official-government-hasbara-agents/; Benjamin Doherty, "Getting to the Bottom of marc3pax, Israel's Gay Flotilla Hoaxer," *Electronic Intifada*, May 5, 2012, http://electronicintifada.net/blogs/benjamin-doherty/getting-bottom-marc3pax-israels-gay-flotilla-hoaxer.

78. Benjamin Doherty, "Israel Lobby Group Iran180 'Sodomizes' Ahmadinejad Effigy with Nuke at San Francisco Pride," *Electronic Intifada*, June 11, 2013, http://electronicintifada.net/blogs/benjamin-doherty/israel-lobby-group-iran180-sodomizes-ahmadinejad-effigy-nuke-san-francisco.

79. Scott Long, "The Rape of the Jock: A-Jad, Manhood, and 'Iran 180'" *Paper Bird* (blog), June 13, 2013, http://paper-bird.net/2012/06/13/the-rape-of-the-jock-a-jad-manhood-and-iran-180/.

80. Jewish Council for Public Affairs, "Iran 180," March 24, 2011, http://engage.jewishpublicaffairs.org/p/salsa/web/blog/public/entries?blog_entry_KEY=1474.

81. Allison Deger, "Coalition Partners Don't Associate with Astroturfing 'Iran 180,'" *Mondoweiss*, June 29, 2012, http://mondoweiss.net/2012/06/coalition-partners-dont-associate-with-astroturfing-iran-180.html.

82. Benjamin Doherty, "Former Advisor to Israeli Army behind Iran180 Astroturf Project," *Electronic Intifada*, June 14, 2012, http://electronicintifada.net/blogs/benjamin-doherty/former-advisor-israeli-army-behind-iran180-astroturf-project.

83. Doherty, "Former Advisor"; Deger, "Coalition Partners."

84. Benjamin Doherty, "Israel Lobby Group Iran180,'" *Electronic Intifada*, June 11, 2013, http://electronicintifada.net/blogs/benjamin-doherty/israel-lobby-group-iran180-sodomizes-ahmadinejad-effigy-nuke-san-francisco.

85. Benjamin Doherty, "Pinkwashing, 2008–2011."

86. Benjamin Doherty, "Pinkwashing and the Gay International," *Electronic Intifada*, June 2, 2011, http://electronicintifada.net/blogs/benjamin-doherty/pinkwashing-and-gay-international.

87. Andrea Houston, "Strange Bedfellows Team Up to Fight QuAIA," *Daily Xtra*, July 4, 2013, http://dailyxtra.com/toronto/news/strange-bedfellows-team-fight-quaia?market=210.

88. Houston, "Strange Bedfellows."

89. Ibid.

90. "IsraeliPM" (YouTube user), "Green Israel Campaign on CNN," video, posted June 21 2012, http://youtu.be/-m4Fn3lT2eg.

91. Ali Abunimah, "New 'Green Israel' Ads on CNN Greenwash Sewage of Occupation and Apartheid," *Electronic Intifada*, June 22, 2012, http://electronicintifada.net/blogs/ali-abunimah/new-green-israel-ads-cnn-greenwash-sewage-occupation-and-apartheid.

92. See "Editor's Note," *Audubon*, September 2011, http://archive.audubonmagazine.org/editorial/editorial0911.html; Rene Ebersole, "Crossroads," *Audubon*, September 2011, http://archive.audubonmagazine.org/features0911/greentravel.html.

93. Howard Kohr, speech to AIPAC Policy Conference, May 3, 2009, http://aipac.org/-/media/publications-old/policy%20and%20politics/speeches%20and%20interviews/speeches%20by%20AIPAC%20leadership/2009/MESJune28(1).pdf.

94. Ernst & Young, "Renewable Energy Country Attractiveness Indices," Issue 31, November 2011, http://www.ey.com/Publication/vwLUAssets/Renewable_energy_country_attractiveness_indices_-_Issue_31/$FILE/EY_RECAI_issue_31.pdf.

95. Ministry of Industry, Trade and Labor, "Israel's Renewable Energy Sector," http://www.israelnewtech.gov.il/English/Energy/Pages/AboutUs.aspx.

96. Ministry of Industry, Trade and Labor, "National Sustainable Energy and Water Program, Company Directory," http://www.israelnewtech.gov.il/English/CompanyDirectory/Pages/default.aspx.

97. Beth-El Industries, website, http://www.beind.com.

98. Tahal Group, "Road and Infrastructural Works for Zikkim Military Base," http://www.tahal.com/projects_item.aspx?FolderID=96&docID=334, accessed February 11, 2013.

99. Wave Worldwide Ltd., website, http://www.waveworldwide.com/.

100. Ministry of Finance, Norway, "Exclusion of a Company from the Government Pension Fund," June 15, 2012, http://www.regjeringen.no/en/dep/fin/News/news/2012/exclusion-of-a-company-from-the-governme.html?id=685898.

101. OECD Better Life Index, online resource, http://www.oecdbetterlifeindex.org/countries/israel/.

102. International Energy Agency, *CO2 Emissions from Fuel Combustion: Highlights* (Paris: International Energy Agency, 2012), 48, http://www.iea.org/co2highlights/co2highlights.pdf.

103. For EU figure see European Commission Joint Research Centre, "Per Capita CO2 Emissions in China Reach EU Levels," news release, July 18, 2012, http://ec.europa.eu/dgs/jrc/index.cfm?id=1410&dt_code=NWS&obj_id=15150; for Israel see World Bank Data online, http://data.worldbank.org/indicator/EN.ATM.CO2E.PC.

104. World Bank, "Fossil Fuel Energy Consumption (% of Total)," http://data.worldbank.org/indicator/EG.USE.COMM.FO.ZS/countries.

105. REN21 (Renewable Energy Policy Network for the 21st Century), *Renewables 2012 Global Status Report* (Paris: REN21, 2012), 19, http://www.map.ren21.net/GSR/GSR2012.pdf.

106. Lior Gutman, "Siemens Pulls Plug on Solar Operations," *Ynet*, October 22, 2012, http://www.ynetnews.com/articles/0,7340,L-4295436,00.html.

107. International Renewable Energy Agency, "Renewable Energy Country Profile: Jordan," http://www.irena.org/REmaps/countryprofiles/middle/Jordan.pdf; "Renewable Energy Country Profile: Israel," http://www.irena.org/REmaps/countryprofiles/middle/Israel.pdf.

108. White House, "Weekly Address: President Obama Lauds Clean Energy Projects as Key to Creating Jobs and Building a Stronger Economy," news release, October 2, 2010, http://www.whitehouse.gov/the-press-office/2010/10/02/weekly-address-president-obama-lauds-clean-energy-projects-key-creating.

109. Jerusalem College of Technology, website, http://www.jct.ac.il/en/about.

110. Karin Kloosterman, "BrightSource Gets a Billion," *Israel21C*, March 1, 2010, http://israel21c.org/environment/brightsource-gets-a-billion/.

111. Ali Abunimah, "Obama Uses Weekly Address to Lobby for Israeli Firm BrightSource," blog, October 2, 2010, http://aliabunimah.posthaven.com/obama-uses-weekly-address-to-lobby-for-israel. At the time of Obama's weekly address, I counted thirteen jobs being advertised in Jerusalem and four in the United States on the BrightSource website and included this in the referenced blog post that provides additional background information on the company. In August 2012, BrightSource announced that it had reached "its peak construction workforce, with

more than 2,100 construction workers and project support staff on-site" and that all of these workers had been retained by the construction contractor Bechtel. See BrightSource, "Ivanpah Solar Project Reaches Halfway Mark and Peak of Construction Employment," news release, August 6, 2012, http://www.brightsourceenergy.com/ivanpah-solar-project-reaches-halfway -mark-and-peak-of-construction-employment.

112. Karin Kloosterman, "BrightSource Takes Solar Thermal Energy Home to Israel," *Israel21c*, October 9, 2013, http://israel21c.org/environment/brightsource-takes-solar-thermal-energy-home -to-israel.

113. Keith Rogers, "Tribes Join Protests of Ivanpah Solar Project," *Las Vegas Review-Journal*, September 14, 2010, http://www.lvrj.com/news/tribes-join-protests-of-ivanpah-solar-project-102926439 .html?ref=439.

114. Todd Woody, "Solar Energy Faces Tests On Greenness," *New York Times*, February 23, 2011.

115. John Marvel, "Energy Developers Underestimate by a Magnitude of Thousands the Number of ESA Listed Desert Tortoises Impacted by Ivanpah Solar Thermal Plant," Western Watersheds Project website, January 2011, http://hosted.verticalresponse.com/435877/1c6278f171 /1454001502/2094f66e48/; Chris Clarke, "Ninth Circuit Lets Ivanpah Solar Work Continue," KCET, August 15, 2012, http://www.kcet.org/news/rewire/solar/concentrating-solar/ninth -circuit-lets-ivanpah-solar-work-continue.html.

116. Iris Kuo, "BrightSource Energy Quietly Moves Toward IPO in 2011," Reuters, September 22, 2010.

117. "Obama's 'Bright' Spot for Israel," *Israel21c*, October 3, 2010, http://israelity.com/2010/10 /03/obamas-bright-spot-for-israel/.

118. David Baker, "Oakland's BrightSource Cancels IPO at 11th Hour," *San Francisco Chronicle*, April 13, 2012.

119. Chris Clarke, "Sun Crash: Solar Energy 'Green Rush' Slows Down in Desert," KCET, April 18, 2012, http://www.kcet.org/updaily/socal_focus/commentary/sun-crash-solar-energy-green -rush-slows-down-in-desert.html.

120. Chris Bryant, "Siemens to Sell Solar Power Business," *Financial Times*, October 22, 2013.

121. Chris Clarke, "BrightSource Walks Away from Rio Mesa 'For Now,'" KCET, January 14, 2013, http://www.kcet.org/news/rewire/solar/concentrating-solar/brightsource-walks-away-from-rio -mesa-for-now.html.

122. *San Francisco Chronicle*, "BrightSource, Edison Cancel Power Deal," January 18, 2013.

123. Joshua Hammer, "Charging Ahead with a New Electric Car," *Smithsonian*, July–August 2010, http://www.smithsonianmag.com/specialsections/40th-anniversary/Charging-Ahead-With-a -New-Electric-Car.html.

124. Ali Abunimah, "Quartet Ex-Envoy's Investment Helps Israel Greenwash Settlements," *Electronic Intifada*, May 6, 2010, http://electronicintifada.net/content/quartet-ex-envoys-investment -helps-israel-greenwash-settlements/8805.

125. Ali Abunimah "Israeli Occupation Profiteer Better Place Runs Taxis at Amsterdam Airport, with EU Backing," *Electronic Intifada*, September 3, 2012, http://www.smithsonianmag.com /specialsections/40th-anniversary/Charging-Ahead-With-a-New-Electric-Car.html.

126. Karl Vick, "A Smart Car Dream in Israel—Not So Smart, After All?" *Time*, November 9, 2012, http://world.time.com/2012/11/09/a-smart-car-dream-in-israel-not-so-smart-after-all.

127. Reuters, "Better Place's Israeli Assets Sold," July 10, 2013.

128. Dan Senor and Saul Singer, *Start-Up Nation: The Story of Israel's Economic Miracle* (New York: Hachette Books, 2009), 11.

129. Abunimah, "Quartet Ex-Envoy's Investment."

130. This was reported in the Israeli business publication *Globes* on February 3, 2010. Also see Abunimah, "Quartet Ex-Envoy's Investment."

131. B'Tselem, "Route 443—West Bank Road for Israelis Only," news release, January 1, 2011, http://www.btselem.org/freedom_of_movement/road_443.

132. B'Tselem, "Route 443."

133. Tomer Hadar, "Mivchan rechev: Harenault hachashmalit shel Better Place ola al hakvish" (Hebrew), *Calcalist*, February 9, 2012, http://www.calcalist.co.il/local/articles/0,7340,L-3561678,00.html.

134. Amnesty International, "Israel/Lebanon: Out of All Proportion—Civilians Bear the Brunt of the War," November 21, 2006, report, http://www.amnesty.org/en/library/info/MDE02/033 /2006/en.

135. Niv Elis, "Olmert to Chair Venture-Capital Fund," *Jerusalem Post*, April 18, 2013, http:// www.jpost.com/Business/Business-News/Olmert-to-chair-venture-capital-fund-310311.

136. Amnesty International, "Israel Rations Palestinians to Trickle of Water," news release, October 27, 2009, http://www.amnesty.org/en/news-and-updates/report/israel-rations-palestinians -trickle-water-20091027. Full report: Amnesty International, *Troubled Waters—Palestinians Denied Fair Access to Water in Israel-Occupied Palestinian Territories* (Amnesty International, 2009).

137. Amnesty International, "Israel Rations Palestinians."

138. UN Human Rights Council, *Report of the Independent International Fact-Finding Mission to Investigate the Implications of the Israeli Settlements on the Civil, Political, Economic, Social and Cultural Rights of the Palestinian People Throughout the Occupied Palestinian Territory, Including East Jerusalem (Advanced Unedited Version)*, January 2013, http://www.ohchr.org/EN/HRBodies/HRC /RegularSessions/Session19/Pages/IsraeliSettlementsInTheOPT.aspx.

139. B'Tselem, *Foul Play: Neglect of Wastewater Treatment in the West Bank* (Jerusalem: B'Tselem, 2009), http://www.btselem.org/download/200906_foul_play_eng.pdf. For a summary of the report, see B'Tselem, "Foul Play, Information Sheet," online resource, June 2009, http://www .btselem.org/node/48203.

140. B'Tselem, "Foul Play, Information Sheet."

141. Ibid.

142. Ibid.

143. B'Tselem, *Foul Play*, 25–26.

144. Charlotte Silver, "An Unnatural Thing: Israeli Occupation Plans to Cut Trees in the Name of Natural Preservation," *Electronic Intifada*, May 19, 2012, http://electronicintifada.net/blogs /charlotte-silver/unnatural-thing-israeli-occupation-plans-cut-trees-name-natural-preservation.

145. Abe Hayeem, "Architects Against Israeli Occupation," *Guardian*, October 4, 2010, http:// www.guardian.co.uk/commentisfree/2010/oct/04/architects-settlement-freeze-israel.

146. Noah Browning, "Walls and Winter Rains Afflict Palestinian Towns," Reuters, January 9, 2013.

147. Nir Hasson, "Israel's High Court Orders State to Find Alternative to Separation Fence at West Bank Village," *Haaretz*, December 14, 2012.

148. United Nations Environment Programme, *Environmental Assessment of the Gaza Strip Following the Escalation of Hostilities in December 2008–January 2009* (Nairobi: UNEP, 2009), 57.

149. UN Human Rights Council, *Report of the United Nations Fact Finding Mission*, 267.

150. Ibid., 346.

151. Amnesty International, UK Broederlijk Delen (Belgium), CAFOD (UK), CCFD Terre Solidaire (France), Christian Aid, Church of Sweden, Diakonia (Sweden), Finn Church Aid (Finland), Medical Aid for Palestinians, Medico International (Germany), Medico International Schweiz (Switzerland), Mercy Corps, MS ActionAid Denmark, Oxfam International, Trocaire (Ireland), United Civilians for Peace (a coalition of Dutch organizations—Oxfam

Novib, Cordaid, ICCO, and IKV Pax Christi), *Failing Gaza: No Rebuilding, No Recovery, No More Excuses* (London: Oxfam, 2009), http://www.oxfam.org/sites/www.oxfam.org/files/failing-gaza-no %20rebuilding-no-recovery-no-more-excuses.pdf.

152. Amnesty International, *Troubled Waters*, 29–32.

153. Consulate General of Israel to the Midwest, "First Israeli-Chicago Water Conference," media release, August 2, 2013, http://embassies.gov.il/chicago/NewsAndEvents/Pages/Consulate-hosts -first-Israeli-Chicago-Water-Conference.aspx.

154. City of Chicago, Mayor's Press Office, "Mayor Emanuel Joins Water Management Leaders at the First Israel-Chicago Water Technology Innovation Forum," news release, July 30, 2013, http://www.cityofchicago.org/city/en/depts/mayor/press_room/press_releases/2013/july_2013 /mayor_emanuel_joinswatermanagementleadersatthefirstisrael-chicag.html.

155. Patrick Strickland, "Palestinian Family Trapped in Home as Blaze Raged in Israeli Chemical Plant," *Electronic Intifada*, September 17, 2013, http://electronicintifada.net/content/palestinian -family-trapped-home-blaze-raged-israeli-chemical-plant/12776.

156. "Al-Haq" (YouTube user), "Geshuri Chemical Factories," YouTube video, posted on September 8, 2010, http://youtu.be/fvqwbxTM67s.

157. Samer Ahmad Soliman Diab, "Lung Cancer and Associated Risk Factors in the West Bank," An-Najah University, June 2003, http://scholar.najah.edu/sites/default/files/all-thesis/lung_cancer _and_associated_risk_factors_in_the_west_bank.pdf.

158. Ben White, "Israel's State Comptroller Slams West Bank Industrial Zones," *Electronic Intifada*, June 9, 2012, http://electronicintifada.net/blogs/ben-white/israels-state-comptroller-slams -west-bank-industrial-zones.

159. Strickland, "Palestinian Family Trapped."

160. Asa Winstanley, "Stop the JNF Campaign Makes Steady Gains as Israel Charity Goes 'On the Retreat' in UK," *Electronic Intifada*, February 22, 2012, http://electronicintifada.net/content /stop-jnf-campaign-makes-steady-gains-israel-charity-goes-retreat-uk/10974.

161. Jonathan Cook, "Christian Extremists Assist Israel in Displacing Negev Bedouin," *Electronic Intifada*, December 28, 2010, http://electronicintifada.net/content/christian-extremists-assist -israel-displacing-negev-bedouin/9159.

162. Ali Abunimah, "Video: Bedouins Resist Israeli Plan to Expel 40,000 and 'Judaize' their Land," *Electronic Intifada*, July 21, 2013, http://electronicintifada.net/blogs/ali-abunimah/video -bedouins-resist-israeli-plan-expel-40000-and-judaize-their-land.

163. Noga Malkin, "Erasing Links to the Land in the Negev," Human Rights Watch, March 11, 2011, http://www.hrw.org/news/2011/03/11/erasing-links-land-negev.

164. Joel Greenberg, "Forest Fire Fuels Review of Israel's Tree-Planting Tradition," *Washington Post*, December 26, 2010; Max Blumenthal, "The Carmel Wildfire Is Burning All Illusions in Israel," *Electronic Intifada*, December 6, 2010, http://electronicintifada.net/content/carmel-wildfire -burning-all-illusions-israel/9130.

165. Tamara Zieve, "This Week in History: Swamps, Birds, Water Wars," *Jerusalem Post*, October 28, 2012.

166. Ibid.

167. Ehud Zion Waldoks, "How Can the Rapidly Disappearing Dead Sea Be Salvaged?" *Jerusalem Post*, July 8, 2009.

168. Simon Rocker, "JNF Loses Half Its Revenue," *Jewish Chronicle*, October 11, 2012, http:// www.thejc.com/news/uk-news/85886/jnf-loses-half-its-revenue.

169. Stop the JNF, "Scottish Green Party Reject 'Green' Claims of Charity Involved in Ethnic Cleansing of Palestinians," news release, October 31, 2011, www.stopthejnf.org/scottish-green

-party-reject-claims-of-charity-involved-in-ethnic-cleansing-of-palestinians/.

170. Josh Nathan-Kazis, "JNF Challenged on Discrimination," *Jewish Daily Forward*, April 29, 2011.

171. Yves Engler, "Progressive Canadians Must Challenge JNF's Charitable Status," *Electronic Intifada*, November 1, 2010, http://electronicintifada.net/content/progressive-canadians-must-challenge-jnfs-charitable-status/9092.

172. Asa Winstanley, "Jewish National Fund UK Faces Official Questions over Racial Discrimination," *Electronic Intifada*, May 21, 2013, http://electronicintifada.net/blogs/asa-winstanley/jewish-national-fund-uk-faces-official-questions-over-racial-discrimination.

173. Gili Cohen, "Workers at Israel's Dimona Nuclear Reactor Say Leaks at Plant Gave Them Cancer," *Haaretz*, December 15, 2011, http://www.haaretz.com/print-edition/news/workers-at-israel-s-dimona-nuclear-reactor-say-leaks-at-plant-gave-them-cancer-1.401478.

174. Gilad Morag, "Radiation Levels Were Manipulated," *Ynet*, December 19, 2011, http://www.ynetnews.com/articles/0,7340,L-4164058,00.html.

175. Naama Cohen Friedman, "Nuke Plant Workers Exposed to High Radiation Levels," *Ynet*, December 8, 2011, http://www.ynetnews.com/articles/0,7340,L4158561,00.html.

176. *Jerusalem Post,* "Sorek Safety Head: Workers 'Highly Irradiated,'" December 8, 2011.

177. BBC Worldwide Monitoring, "Palestinian Expert Says Hebron Region Affected by Radiation," October 14, 2011.

178. Israel Atomic Energy Commission, "Nuclear Research Center NEGEV—NRCN," http://iaec.gov.il/English/NRCN/Pages/default.aspx.

179. Nuclear Threat Initiative, "Middle East and North Africa 1540 Reporting," news release, January 31, 2013, http://www.nti.org/analysis/reports/middle-east-and-north-africa-1540-reporting/; Amir Oren, "Israel Flunks Nuclear Safety Test, but Ranks Above Iran and North Korea," *Haaretz*, January 15, 2012, http://www.haaretz.com/print-edition/news/israel-flunks-nuclear-safety-test-but-ranks-above-iran-and-north-korea-1.407350.

180. Popper, "Israel Aims To Improve."

181. GlobeScan, "Views of Europe Slide Sharply in Global Poll, While Views of China Improve," news release, May 10, 2012, http://www.globescan.com/news-and-analysis/press-releases/press-releases-2012/84-press-releases-2012/186-views-of-europe-slide-sharply-in-global-poll-while-views-of-china-improve.html.

182. GlobeScan, "Views of China and India Slide in Global Poll, While UK's Ratings Climb," news release, May 22, 2013, http://www.globescan.com/commentary-and-analysis/press-releases/press-releases-2013/277-views-of-china-and-india-slide-while-uks-ratings-climb.html.

183. Noam Dvir, "Peres, Netanyahu Reject Idea of Bi-National State," *Ynet*, June 27, 2013.

184. Pew Research Center for the People and the Press, "As Hagel Fight Begins, Wide Partisan Differences in Support for Israel," news release, January 8, 2013, http://www.people-press.org/2013/01/08/as-hagel-fight-begins-wide-partisan-differences-in-support-for-israel/.

185. Pew Research Center for the People and the Press, "On Eve of Foreign Debate, Growing Pessimism about Arab Spring Aftermath," October 18, 2012, http://www.people-press.org/files/legacy-pdf/10-18-12%20Foreign%20Policy%20release.pdf.

186. Pew Research Center for the People and the Press, "Public Says U.S. Does Not Have Responsibility to Act in Syria," news release, December 14, 2012, http://www.people-press.org/2012/12/14/public-says-u-s-does-not-have-responsibility-to-act-in-syria/.

187. Lydia Saad, "In U.S., Canada Places First in Image Contest; Iran Last," Gallup, news release, February 19, 2010, http://www.gallup.com/poll/126116/Canada-Places-First-Image-Contest-Iran-Last.aspx.

188. Gallup, "Country Ratings," February 7–10, 2013, http://www.gallup.com/poll/1624/perceptions

-foreign-countries.aspx.

189. Pew Research Center for the People and the Press, "Growing Support for Gay Marriage: Changed Minds and Changing Demographics," news release, March 20, 2013, http://www .people-press.org/2013/03/20/growing-support-for-gay-marriage-changed-minds-and-changing -demographics/.

190. Popper, "Israel Aims To Improve."

191. Reut Institute, "Building a Political Firewall against Israel's Delegitimization Conceptual Frame-work," March 2010.

192. Kenneth Stern, "BDS Campaign Remains Dangerous, Despite Failures," Jewish Telegraphic Agency, August 15, 2012.

193. Ben White, "Israeli Government Ramps Up Anti-Boycott Fight," Electronic Intifada, June 27, 2013, http://electronicintifada.net/blogs/ben-white/israeli-government-ramps-anti-boycott-fight.

194. Ben White, "New Israeli Plan Calls for More 'Intelligence' Gathering to Disrupt BDS Move-ment," Electronic Intifada, June 1, 2013, http://electronicintifada.net/blogs/ben-white/new -israeli-plan-calls-more-intelligence-gathering-disrupt-bds-movement.

195. Ali Abunimah, "Israeli Students to Get $2,000 to Spread State Propaganda on Facebook," Elec-tronic Intifada, January 4, 2012; Ali Abunimah, "Israel Setting Up 'Covert Units' to Tweet, Facebook Government Propaganda," Electronic Intifada, August 13, 2013; Barak Ravid, "Prime Minister's Office Recruiting Students to Wage Online Hasbara Battles," Haaretz, August 13, 2013; Anshel Pfeffer, "BDS' Real Threat: Instilling Fear in Israelis," Haaretz, October 18, 2013.

196. Ali Abunimah, "Israel's 'Pretty Face': How National Union of Israeli Students Does Govern-ment's Propaganda Dirty Work," Electronic Intifada, January 5, 2013 http://electronicintifada .net/blogs/ali-abunimah/israels-pretty-face-how-national-union-israeli-students-does-governments.

197. Eyal Lehmann, "Comment Posted, Damage Done: Online Battle for Israel's Hasbara," Ynet, September 18, 2013.

198. Jillian C. York, "Dangerous Social Media Games," Al Jazeera English, January 13, 2013, http://www.aljazeera.com/indepth/opinion/2012/01/201211111642310699.html

199. Barghouti, BDS, 62.

Chapter 6: The War on Campus

1. David Project, A Burning Campus? Rethinking Israel Advocacy at America's Universities and Colleges (New York: David Project, 2012), 18, 15, http://www.davidproject.org/wp-content/uploads /2012524-ABurningCampus-RethinkingIsraelAdvocacyAmericasUniversitiesColleges.pdf.

2. Ibid., 15.

3. Naomi Zeveloff, "Hard-Nosed Campus Group Softens Tactics," Jewish Daily Forward, February 24, 2012, http://forward.com/articles/151479/hard-nosed-campus-group-softens-tactics.

4. David Project, A Burning Campus?, 21.

5. Ibid., 22.

6. Ibid., 35.

7. Ibid., 7.

8. Ibid., 1.

9. Ibid., 1.

10. Ibid., 15.

11. Ibid., 18.

12. Ibid., 37.

13. Ibid., 18.

14. Ibid., 19.

15. Ibid., 19.

16. Ibid., 20.

17. Ibid., 23.

18. Ibid., 24.

19. See, for example, Melissa Korn, "For-Profit Colleges Get Schooled," *Wall Street Journal*, October 24, 2012, http://online.wsj.com/article/SB10001424052970203937004578076942611172654.html.

20. David Project, *A Burning Campus?*, 23–24.

21. Ibid., 34.

22. Ibid., 34.

23. Ibid., 25.

24. Jonathan Cole, *The Great American University* (New York: Public Affairs, 2012), 369.

25. Ibid., 370.

26. Ibid., 371.

27. Jacob Gershman, "Rep. Weiner Asks Columbia to Fire Anti-Israel Prof," *New York Sun*, October 22, 2004.

28. Jacob Gershman, "Columbia Probe Eyed By Council," *New York Sun*, November 12, 2004.

29. Jacob Gershman, "P.R. Guru Quietly Guides Bollinger," *New York Sun*, March 14, 2005.

30. Columbia University, "Convening of Ad Hoc Faculty Committee," news release, December 8, 2004, http://www.columbia.edu/content/convening-ad-hoc-faculty-committee.html.

31. Chanan Weissman, "Film on 'Bias' at Columbia U. Sparks Fury among Israeli Alumni," *Jerusalem Post*, February 7, 2005.

32. Editorial, "Intimidation at Columbia," *New York Times*, April 7, 2005.

33. Transcript of Nick Dirks's interview: University of California, Berkeley, "Transcript Extra: Divestment," news release, November 27, 2012, http://newscenter.berkeley.edu/2012/11/27/transcript-extra-divestment/.

34. Wael Hallaq, Timothy Mitchell, Sudipta Kaviraj, Sheldon Pollock, Partha Chatterjee, Muhsin Al-Musawi, Mamadou Diouf, Mahmood Mamdani, Joseph Massad, Hamid Dabashi, Gil Anidjar, George Saliba, Frances Pritchett, and Brinkley Messick, "Letter to the Editor: Former Vice-President Dirks Defaming the Department," *Columbia Spectator*, December 19, 2012, http://www.columbiaspectator.com/2012/12/19/letter-editor-former-vice-president-dirks-defaming-department.

35. Cole, *Great American University*, 371–72.

36. Jennifer Howard, "Harvard Law Professor Works to Disrupt Tenure Bid of Longtime Nemesis at DePaul U.," *Chronicle of Higher Education*, April 5, 2007.

37. Scott Jaschik, "DePaul Rejects Finkelstein," *Inside Higher Ed*, June 11, 2007, http://www.insidehighered.com/news/2007/06/11/finkelstein.

38. American Association of University Professors, Illinois Conference, "Illinois AAUP Letter to DePaul University on Tenure Denials," news release, June 22, 2007, http://www.ilaaup.org/fall200710.asp.

39. DePaul University, "Joint Statement of Norman Finkelstein and DePaul University on Their Tenure Controversy and Its Resolution," news release, September 5, 2007, http://newsroom.depaul.edu/NewsReleases/showNews.aspx?NID=1655.

40. Moustafa Bayoumi, "My Arab Problem," *Chronicle of Higher Education*, October 24, 2010. All quotes from Bayoumi in this chapter are from this article.

41. Max Blumenthal, "The Former Terror Suspect Leading the Attack on the Brooklyn College BDS Panel," *Nation*, February 6, 2013, http://www.thenation.com/article/172699/former-terror-suspect-leading-attack-brooklyn-college-bds-panel.

42. Dov Hikind, "Hikind Calls for Brooklyn College President's Resignation," news release, January 30, 2013, http://dovhikind.blogspot.com/2013/01/hikind-calls-for-brooklyn-college.html.

43. Josh Nathan-Kazis, "Mayor Bloomberg Backs Brooklyn College in Flap over Boycott Israel Panel," *Jewish Daily Forward*, February 6, 2013, http://forward.com/articles/170665/mayor-bloomberg-backs-brooklyn-college-in-flap-ove/.

44. Editorial, "Litmus Tests," *New York Times*, February 4, 2013.

45. Alex Kane, "Bloomberg Backs Brooklyn College over BDS Event as Another Official Withdraws Funding Threat," *Mondoweiss*, February 6, 2013, http://mondoweiss.net/2013/02/bloomberg-official-withdraws.html.

46. Alex Kane, "Investigation of Brooklyn College BDS Event Rejects Charges of Anti-Semitism," *Mondoweiss*, April 16, 2013, http://mondoweiss.net/2013/04/investigation-brooklyn-semitism.html.

47. Joanna Paraszczuk, "US Colleges to Receive Warning Letters on Anti-Semitism," *Jerusalem Post*, September 8, 2011, http://www.jpost.com/JewishWorld/JewishNews/Article.aspx?id=237118; on Hagee's financial support for Shurat HaDin, see Max Blumenthal, "Netanyahu and Pastor Hagee's Lovefest on Eve of Biden's Arrival in Israel," *Max Blumenthal* (blog), March 9, 2010, http://maxblumenthal.com/2010/03/pastor-hagee-and-netanyahus-lovefest-on-eve-of-bidens-arrival-in-israel/.

48. Ali Abunimah, "In Blow to Zionist Censors, California Backs Professor's Right to Call for Israel Boycott on State University Website," *Electronic Intifada*, June 5, 2012, http://electronicintifada.net/blogs/ali-abunimah/blow-zionist-censors-california-backs-professors-right-call-israel-boycott-state.

49. Ali Abunimah, "In New Assault, Israel Group's US Front Asks City of Los Angeles to Sue Professor for Criticizing Israel," *Electronic Intifada*, June 12, 2012, http://electronicintifada.net/blogs/ali-abunimah/new-assault-israel-groups-us-front-asks-city-los-angeles-sue-professor.

50. Harry Hellenbrand, "*J'Accuse!* The New Anti-Anti-Semitism," personal website, April 2012, http://www.csun.edu/~hfaca002/new_anti_anti_semitism.pdf.

51. Tom Griffin and David Miller, "BDS Campaigner Targeted by Law Firm with Links to Israeli Intelligence," *Spinwatch*, October 5, 2013, http://www.spinwatch.org/index.php/issues/more/item/5550-bds-campaigner-targeted-by-law-firm-with-links-to-israeli-intelligence.

52. Naomi Zeveloff, "Hard-Nosed Campus Group Softens Tactics," *Jewish Daily Forward*, February 24, 2012.

53. The original David Bernstein article was published on June 14, 2011, at http://israelcampusbeat.org, but has since been deleted without explanation. For long extracts of the article, including the quoted passages, see Ali Abunimah, "Israel Lobby Group Outlines Dirty Tricks against Campus Palestine Activists," *Electronic Intifada*, June 24, 2011, http://electronicintifada.net/blogs/ali-abunimah/israel-lobby-group-outlines-dirty-tricks-against-campus-palestine-activists.

54. Cole, *Great American University*, 377.

55. Ibid., 377.

56. Ibid., 360.

57. Ibid., 367.

58. David Project, *A Burning Campus?*, 7.

59. Ibid., 25.

60. Cole, *Great American University*, 368–69.

61. Ibid., 382.

62. Ibid., 444.

63. Ibid., 445.

64. Ibid., 447.

65. Quoted by Cole, *Great American University*, 445; original source: Alissa Solomon, "Targeting

Middle East Studies, Zealots, 'Homeland Security' Creates Campus Insecurity," *Village Voice*, February 25–March 2, 2004.

66. Cole, *Great American University*, 445.

67. Higher Education Opportunity Act of 1965 (20 U.S.C. 1122), Section 602 (amended 2008); Cole, *Great American University*, 448; see also Doug Lederman, "Senate Higher Ed Bill Emerges (Slowly)," *Inside Higher Ed*, June 19, 2007, http://www.insidehighered.com/news/2007/06/19/hea.

68. Cole, *Great American University*, 415.

69. Ibid., 414.

70. Ibid., 415.

71. Ibid., 415.

72. Ibid., 416.

73. Ibid., 417.

74. Ibid., 416.

75. American Jewish Committee, "AJC Urges Protection of Jewish Students under 1964 Civil Rights Act," news release, March 17, 2010, http://www.ajc.org/site/apps/nlnet/content2.aspx?c=ijITI2PHKoG&b=849241&ct=8089065; Anti-Defamation League, "ADL Urges Education Secretary to Protect Jewish Students on Campus from Intimidation and Harassment," news release, March 17, 2010, http://archive.adl.org/PresRele/CvlRt_32/5720_32.htm; Zionist Organization of America, "ZOA Urges U.S. Education Department to Protect Jewish Students from Harassment Under Federal Law," news release, March 19, 2010, www.zoa.org/2010/03/02623-zoa-urges-u-s-education-education-department-to-protect-jewish-students-from-harassment-under-federal-law; Hillel, "Jewish Groups Urge Protection of Jewish Students under 1964 Civil Rights Act," March 19, 2010, http://www.hillel.org/about/blog/item?id=2125.

76. United States Department of Education, Office of Civil Rights, "Dear Colleague Letter: Harassment and Bullying," October 26, 2010, http://www2.ed.gov/about/offices/list/ocr/letters/colleague-201010.pdf.

77. Kristin Szremski, "New Moves to Curb Criticism of Israel in US and Canada," *Electronic Intifada*, July 29, 2011, http://electronicintifada.net/content/new-moves-curb-criticism-israel-us-and-canada/10219.

78. Peter Schmidt, "Education Dept. Investigates Complaint of Anti-Semitism at UC-Santa Cruz," *Chronicle of Higher Education*, March 15, 2011.

79. Ibid.

80. Jewish Telegraphic Agency, "ZOA Complaint Seeking Probe of Rutgers," July 27, 2011.

81. Ibid.

82. Joel Siegel and Neil Sher, "Title VI Complaint against the University of California–Berkeley," July 9, 2012. A PDF copy of the full complaint was posted in the public documents archive of the *Daily Californian*, the UC Berkeley student newspaper, http://s3.documentcloud.org/documents/399604/title-vi-complaint.pdf.

83. Palestine Legal Support, "Fact Sheet: Systematic Attempt to Shut Down Speech at the University of California—Asian Law Caucus," 2012, http://palestinelegalsupport.org/download/advocacy-documents/FACT%20SHEET%20Shutting%20Down%20Student%20Speech%20at%20U.C._fn_DISTRIBUTE.pdf.

84. *Felber v. Yudof*, 851 F.Supp.2d 1182, 1188 (2011), quoted in Palestine Legal Support, "Fact Sheet."

85. Noah Stern, "Debate among All Jewish Groups Belongs at U.C. Berkeley," *Jewish Weekly of Northern California*, January 12, 2012, http://www.jweekly.com/article/full/63918/debate

-among-all-jewish-groups-belongs-at-u.c.-berkeley/.

86. Dina Omar, "At Berkeley, Moral Victory Despite Divestment Vote Loss," *Electronic Intifada*, May 3, 2010, http://electronicintifada.net/content/berkeley-moral-victory-despite-divestment-vote-loss/8809.

87. Josh Nathan-Kazis, "How to Beat Back Israel Divestment Bill: Get Organized," *Jewish Daily Forward*, April 21, 2010, http://forward.com/articles/127439/how-to-beat-back-israel-divestment-bill-get-organ/.

88. Dan Pine, "Ex-Cal Students Drop Lawsuit, Lawyers File Federal Complaint," *Jewish News Weekly of Northern California*, July 19, 2012, http://www.jweekly.com/article/full/65805/ex-cal-students-drop-lawsuit-lawyers-file-federal-complaint.

89. Scott Jaschik, "Anti-Israel, Anti-Semitic or Both?" *Inside Higher Ed*, April 21, 2011, http://www.insidehighered.com/news/2011/04/21/statement_seeks_to_distinguish_between_anti_israel_activity_and_anti_semitic_activity_on_campus.

90. Rex Weiner, "Line between Anti-Israel and Anti-Semitic Protests Splits AJC," *Jewish Daily Forward*, August 26, 2011, http://forward.com/articles/141386/line-between-anti-israel-and-anti-semitic-protests.

91. Naomi Zeveloff, "College Leaders Balance Israel and Speech," *Jewish Daily Forward*, January 20, 2013, http://forward.com/articles/149684/college-leaders-balance-israel-and-speech.

92. Ibid.

93. Sammy Roth, "Federal Investigation Launched Following 'Steering' Complaint," *Columbia Spectator*, October 4, 2011, http://www.columbiaspectator.com/2011/10/04/office-civil-rights-launches-investigation-following-steering-complaint.

94. Ibid.

95. Sammy Roth and Jeremy Budd, "Investigation Finds No Discrimination at Barnard," *Columbia Spectator*, January 13, 2013, http://www.columbiaspectator.com/2012/01/13/federal-investigation-finds-no-discrimination-barnard.

96. Sara Grossman, "Department of Education Dismisses Complaint Alleging Campus Anti-Semitism," *Daily Californian*, August 29, 2013, http://www.dailycal.org/2013/08/27/department-of-education-dismisses-complaint-alleging-campus-anti-semitism/.

97. UC Berkeley, "Department of Education Dismisses Complaint Alleging Anti-Semitism at Berkeley," news release, August 27, 2013, http://newscenter.berkeley.edu/2013/08/27/doe-dismisses-anti-semitism-complaint/.

98. Kenneth Marcus, "Standing Up for Jewish Students," *Jerusalem Post*, September 9, 2013.

99. Center for Constitutional Rights, "Letter to University of California President Advising Him of Need to Protect Pro-Palestinian Speech on Campus," December 3, 2012, http://ccrjustice.org/update%3A-letter-university-of-california-president-advising-him-of-need-protect-protect-palestinian-s.

100. Ibid.

101. University of California, Office of the President, "Open Letter to UC Community from President Yudof," news release, March 8, 2012, http://www.universityofcalifornia.edu/news/article/27279.

102. Dalia Almarina, "How California Uni Chief Conflates Real Bigotry with Criticism of Israel," *Electronic Intifada*, April 18, 2012, http://electronicintifada.net/content/how-california-uni-chief-conflates-real-bigotry-criticism-israel/11163.

103. Sarah Burns, "Three Pepper-Sprayed South of UC Berkeley Campus Following Protest," *Daily Californian*, February 26, 2012, http://www.dailycal.org/2012/02/25/three-pepper-sprayed-south-of-uc-berkeley-campus-following-protest/.

104. Quoted in Almarina, "How California Uni Chief," April 18, 2012.

105. See University of California Students for Justice in Palestine, "UC SJP and MSA Groups' Letter to

US Commission on Civil Rights," November 7, 2012, http://sjpwest.org/2012/11/08/uc-sjp
-and-msa-groups-letter-to-us-commission/; California State Assembly, House Resolution 35,
August 29, 2012.

106. Nora Barrows-Friedman, "California Student Association Denounces CA Assembly Resolution
HR 35, Demands UC Stop Profiting from Israel's Occupation," *Electronic Intifada*, September
17, 2013, http://electronicintifada.net/blogs/nora/california-student-association-denounces-ca
-assembly-resolution-hr-35-demands-uc-stop.

107. Nora Barrows-Friedman, "US University Lecturer's Shocking Hate Speech against Arab, Muslim
Students Condemned," *Electronic Intifada*, February 12, 2013, http://electronicintifada.net/blogs
/nora/us-university-lecturers-shocking-hate-speech-against-arab-muslim-students-condemned.

108. Alex Kane, "Caught on Tape: California University Lecturer Smears Student Activists as Anti-
Semites with Ties to Terrorists," *Mondoweiss*, February 21, 2013, http://mondoweiss.net
/2013/02/california-university-terrorists.html.

109. Committee for Justice in Palestine at UCSC, "University of California President Mark Yudof:
Condemn UCSC Lecturer's Hateful Attacks on Muslim/Arab Student Groups," petition,
https://www.change.org/petitions/university-of-california-president-mark-yudof-condemn-ucsc
-lecturer-s-hateful-attacks-on-muslim-arab-student-groups.

110. Michael Matza, "BDS Conference Sparks Free-Speech Debate at Penn," *Philadelphia Inquirer*,
February 1, 2012.

111. Hillel of Greater Philadelphia, "Statement Regarding a National BDS Movement Conference
at the University of Pennsylvania," http://phillyhillel.org/node/46843.

112. Naomi Zeveloff, "BDS Movement Hopes to Go Mainstream," *Jewish Daily Forward*, February
10, 2013, http://forward.com/articles/151058/bds-movement-hopes-to-go-mainstream/.

113. Prameet Kumar, "Amy Gutmann's Remarks at the Dershowitz Talk," *Red and the Blue* (blog of the
Daily Pennsylvanian), February 3, 2013, http://redandblue.thedp.com/2012/02/amy-gutmanns
-remarks-at-the-dershowitz-talk/.

114. Matza, "BDS Conference."

115. Abbas Naqvi, Madeline Noteware, and Matt Berkman, "BDS Explained," *Daily Pennsylvanian*, January 26, 2013, http://www.thedp.com/index.php/article/2012/01/guest_column_bds_explained.

116. Ruben Gur, "BDS Is 'Hateful', 'Discriminatory,'" *Daily Pennsylvanian*, February 1, 2012,
http://www.thedp.com/index.php/article/2012/02/ruben_gur_bds_is_hateful_discriminatory/.

117. The students' February 1, 2012, letter to Gutmann was copied to me via email by one of the
signers and also published the next day on *Mondoweiss*. See Philip Weiss, "Penn's President Condemns Article Likening BDS Conference to Nazism as 'Counter to Her Personal Values and
Civility,'" *Mondoweiss*, February 2, 2012, http://mondoweiss.net/2012/02/penns-president
-condemns-article-likening-bds-conference-to-nazism-as-counter-to-her-personal-values.html.

118. Amy Gutmann and David L. Cohen, "Protecting Speech We May Not Like," *Daily Pennsylvanian*,
February 1, 2012, http://www.thedp.com/index.php/article/2012/02/your_voice_protecting
_speech_we_may_not_like. Like Gur's letter, the Gutmann/Cohen letter is dated February 1,
2012; however, the Gur letter was posted on the *Daily Pennsylvanian* website at 3:09 AM and
the Gutmann/Cohen letter was posted at 11:59 PM. In other words, the Gutmann/Cohen
letter effectively appeared almost twenty-four hours after Gur's.

119. Ali Abunimah, "BDS Is Nazism and Omar Barghouti is Hitler, Says UPenn Professor in Shocking Smear," *Electronic Intifada*, February 1, 2012, http://electronicintifada.net/blogs/ali
-abunimah/bds-nazism-and-omar-barghouti-hitler-says-upenn-professor-shocking-smear.

120. Nicole Santa Cruz, Mike Anton, and Lauren Williams, "10 of 'Irvine 11' Guilty," *Daily Pilot*,
September 23, 2011, http://www.dailypilot.com/news/columns/tn-dpt-0924-irvine-20110923

,0,1423432,full.story.

121. UC Irvine School of Social Sciences, "U.S. Israel Relations from a Political and Personal Perspective," http://www.socsci.uci.edu/node/921.

122. Joanna Ginsberg, "Former New Jerseyan to Be Israel's Envoy to U.S.," *New Jersey Jewish News*, May 7, 2009, http://njjewishnews.com/njjn.com/050709/njFormerNewJerseyan.html.

123. On renouncing US citizenship and joining the Israeli army in 1979, see Mark Landler, "Israeli Ambassador Draws on American Roots," *New York Times*, September 25, 2009; on service as a paratrooper participating in the 1982 Israeli invasion of Lebanon, see Ken Dilanian, "Israel's Envoy Steeped in History," *USA Today*, May 5, 2009.

124. Agence France Presse, "Netanyahu Taps Historian as US Envoy: Reports," May 3, 2009.

125. Stand with the Eleven Campaign, "What Happened?" http://www.irvine11.com/the-protest /what-happened/.

126. "DemoCast" (YouTube user), "Muslims Torpedo UC Irvine Invited Speaker, Israel's Ambassador," YouTube video, posted February 9, 2010, http://youtu.be/AfLs_ptJzQA.

127. Nora Barrows-Friedman, "Important Victory, Court Date in Case of the 'Irvine 11,'" *Electronic Intifada*, May 25, 2011, http://electronicintifada.net/blogs/nora/important-victory-court-date -case-irvine-11.

128. Mona Shadia, "Main Investigator, Deputies Removed from Irvine 11 Case," *Daily Pilot*, June 30, 2011, http://articles.dailypilot.com/2011-06-30/news/tn-dpt-0701-msu-20110630_1 _district-attorneys-privileged-documents-privileged-attorney-client-communications.

129. Michelle Woo, "Who's Gagging Whom in the Irvine 11 Case?" *OC Weekly*, September 22, 2011, http://www.ocweekly.com/2011-09-22/news/uv-irvine-eleven-first-amendment/.

130. Nora Barrows-Friedman, 'Eager for Closure': Nearing a Verdict in the Irvine 11 Trial," *Electronic Intifada*, September 16, 2011, http://electronicintifada.net/blogs/nora/eager-closure-nearing -verdict-irvine-11-trial.

131. Max Blumenthal, "How Kobe Bryant Blows a Hole in the Irvine 11 Prosecution's Case," *Electronic Intifada*, September 11, 2011, http://electronicintifada.net/content/how-kobe-bryant -blows-hole-irvine-11-prosecutions-case/10367.

132. Nora Barrows-Friedman, "Irvine 11 Appeals Filed: Defense Lawyers Say Convictions Were Unconstitutional, Cite Trial Errors," *Electronic Intifada*, January 24, 2013, http://electronicintifada .net/blogs/nora/irvine-11-appeals-filed-defense-lawyers-say-convictions-were-unconstitutional -cite-trial.

133. Nadia Marie Ismail, "The Harris School and Ehud Olmert," *Chicago Maroon*, October 13, 2009, http://chicagomaroon.com/2009/10/13/the-harris-school-and-ehud-olmert/.

134. In an Arabic-language report on its website, Al Jazeera confirms: "In the final minutes before the [Olmert] lecture, news media were prohibited from filming, as the university itself prohibited documenting the lecture pursuant to the desire of its guest" (my translation). See Al Jazeera, "Tulab yuqati'una Olmert bi Chicago" (Arabic), October 16, 2009, http://aljazeera.net/news /pages/4de96fcc-d575-4d7b-94fc-cc01b3a336f3.

135. Amnesty International et al., *Failing Gaza: No Rebuilding, No Recovery, No More Excuses* (London: Oxfam, December 22, 2009), http://www.oxfam.org/sites/www.oxfam.org/files/failing-gaza -no%20rebuilding-no-recovery-no-more-excuses.pdf.

136. UN Human Rights Council, *Report of the United Nations Fact-Finding Mission on the Gaza Conflict* (A/HRC/12/48), September 25, 2009, 353.

137. University of Chicago News Office, "Frequently Asked Questions about Oct. 15 Ehud Olmert Event," http://news.uchicago.edu/behind-the-news/free-expression/frequently-asked-questions -about-oct-15-ehud-olmert-event.

138. Robert J. Zimmer and Thomas F. Rosenbaum, "Freedom of Expression and Protest," University of Chicago News Office, news release, October 20, 2009, http://news.uchicago.edu/behind-the-news/free-expression/freedom-expression-and-protest.

139. Ali Abunimah, "Why I Disrupted Olmert," *Chicago Maroon*, October 23, 2009, http://chicagomaroon.com/2009/10/23/why-i-disrupted-olmert/.

140. Scott Jaschik, "Harvard and the 'One-State Solution,'" *Inside Higher Ed*, February 27, 2012, http://www.insidehighered.com/news/2012/02/27/harvard-distances-itself-student-conference-some-see-calling-elimination-israel.

141. Ibid.

142. Noah Bierman, "Scott Brown Calls on Harvard to Cancel 'One State' Conference," *Boston Globe*, March 2, 2012.

143. "Harvard University" (YouTube user), "The Middle East: U.S. and Israeli Perspectives," YouTube video, posted October 16, 2012, http://youtu.be/mOsw4G74AzA.

144. Israel Conference at Harvard website, http://israelconference2012.org.

145. "John F. Kennedy Jr. Forum" (YouTube user), "Paradigm Shift: How to Innovate the Peace Process," YouTube video, posted April 23, 2012, http://youtu.be/LJKo0Wwso_A. Ellwood introduced Dennis Ross on April 20, 2012.

146. Ibid.

147. Giacomo Bagarella, "Harvard Israel Conference Presents 'Innovation' to Hide Occupation," *Mondoweiss*, April 23, 2012, http://mondoweiss.net/2012/04/harvard-israel-conference-presents-innovation-to-hide-occupation.html.

148. Columbia University, Office of the President, "Statement about President Ahmadinejad's Scheduled Appearance," news release, September 19, 2007, http://www.columbia.edu/content/statement-about-president-ahmadinejads-scheduled-appearance.html.

149. Tom Faure, "Academic Freedom Still Issue at Columbia U.," *Columbia Spectator*, November 15, 2007.

150. Columbia University Middle East Research Center, "Annual Report 2009/2010," November 2010, http://www.globalcenters.columbia.edu/files/cgc/CUMERC_Annual_Report_2009_2010_2.pdf.

151. Amnesty International, "Oman Must End Assault on Freedoms of Expression and Assembly," news release, December 21, 2012, http://www.amnesty.org/en/library/asset/MDE20/006/2012/en/b2d479df-10b4-4026-8431-b0ecd8f4a6ca/mde200062012en.html.

152. Yvonne Abraham, "Stifling Student Voices," *Boston Globe*, June 13, 2013.

153. Ibid.

154. Ibid.

155. David Project, *Burning Campus?*, 30.

156. Ibid., 30.

157. Ibid., 28–32.

158. *Los Angeles Times*, "UC Riverside Student Senate Urges Divestment from Firms Working in West Bank," March 8, 2013, http://latimesblogs.latimes.com/lanow/2013/03/uc-riverside-student-senate-urges-divestment-from-firms-working-in-west-bank.html.

159. Kris Lovekin, "UCR Response to Student Government Resolution on Divestment," *UCR Today*, March 7, 2013, http://ucrtoday.ucr.edu/12619.

160. Source of statistics is the "Facts" page on the UC Riverside website, http://www.ucr.edu/about/facts.html.

161. See Peter Beinart, *The Crisis of Zionism* (New York: Times Books, 2012).

162. Anti-Defamation League, "Curriculum Connections," http://archive.adl.org/education/curriculum_connections/.

163. Anti-Defamation League, *Anti-Israel Activity on Campus, 2011–2012: An ADL Annual Review 2012* (New York: Anti-Defamation League, 2013), http://www.adl.org/israel-international/anti-israel-activity/c/anti-israel-activity-on-campus.html.

164. The organization recently began using "@" in its name to make it more inclusive and gender-neutral. "MEChA" is still a commonly used abbreviation.

165. Yanely Rivas, "National MEChA Representative Yanely Rivas' Address to National SJP Conference," *SJP Bruins* (blog), November 4, 2012, http://sjpbruins.com/2/category/mecha/1.html.

166. Sarnata Reynolds, "Tell Arizona's Governor to Veto SB1070," Amnesty International (blog), April 19, 2010, http://blog.amnestyusa.org/us/tell-arizonas-governor-to-veto-sb1070/.

167. Carlos Fuentes, "La frontera de cristal," *El Pais*, May 5, 2010. For translation see "Arizona's 'Glass Frontier,'" http://worldmeets.us/elpais000021.shtml.

168. *Huffington Post*, "Cook County Boycotts Arizona, Then Hires Arizona Firm," June 2, 2010, http://www.huffingtonpost.com/2010/06/02/cook-county-boycotts-ariz_n_597689.html.

169. Larry Rohter, "Musicians Differ in Responses to Arizona's New Immigration Law," *New York Times*, May 28, 2010.

170. Jeff Long, "Highland Park Basketball Team Trip to Arizona Scrapped," *Chicago Tribune*, May 12, 2010.

171. Tim Gaynor, "Immigration Law Boycott Cost Ariz. $140 Mln: Study," Reuters, November 18, 2010. On Obama's deportations, see, for example, Corey Dade, "Obama Administration Deported Record 1.5 Million People," National Public Radio (blog), December 24, 2012, http://www.npr.org/blogs/itsallpolitics/2012/12/24/167970002/obama-administration-deported-record-1-5-million-people.

172. Tanya Golash-Boza, "It Is Time to Stop Mass Deportation," *Al Jazeera English*, March 11, 2013, http://www.aljazeera.com/indepth/opinion/2013/03/2013368333991931.html.

173. Reece Jones, "Why Build a Border Wall?" *NACLA Report on the Americas* 4., No. 3, Fall 2012, 70–73, https://nacla.org/sites/default/files/21-Jones.pdf.

174. Mark Sherman, "People from Countries with Al-Qaida Ties Entering U.S. with False IDs, Mueller Says," Associated Press, March 8, 2005.

175. David Edwards, "Gohmert: Radical Muslims 'Being Trained to Come In and Act Like Hispanics,'" *Raw Story*, April 17, 2013, http://www.rawstory.com/rs/2013/04/17/gohmert-radical-muslims-being-trained-to-come-in-and-act-like-hispanics/.

176. Golash-Boza, "It Is Time."

177. Wendy Brown, *Walled States, Waning Sovereignty* (New York: Zone Books, 2010), 137.

178. Michael Dear, "Mr. President, Tear Down This Wall," *New York Times*, March 10, 2013.

179. Yusi El Boujami, Gabriel Schivone, and Ryan Velasquez, "From Palestine to Tucson, Solidifying the Bonds of Solidarity," *Electronic Intifada*, June 11, 2011, http://electronicintifada.net/content/palestine-tucson-solidifying-bonds-solidarity/10072.

180. Arizona House of Representatives, HB 2281 (2010), http://www.azleg.gov/legtext/49leg/2r/bills/hb2281p.pdf.

181. Tom Tolan, "Tucson's Removal of Ethnic Studies Book Sparks Controversy," *Milwaukee Journal Sentinel*, January 31, 2012; *Indian Country Today*, "Shakespeare and Native American Authors among Those Banned from Tucson Schools," January 16, 2012, http://indiancountrytodaymedianetwork.com/article/shakespeare-and-native-american-authors-among-those-banned-from-tucson-schools-72749.

182. American Association of Professors et al., "Joint Statement in Opposition to Book Censorship in Tucson Unified School District," January 30, 2012, American Booksellers Foundation for Free Expression (website), http://www.abffe.org/?AZKRRPStatement.

183. Sharon is quoted in Mazal Mualem and Aluf Benn, "Sharon: PA's Real Test Is Ending Incitement," *Haaretz*, November 19, 2004.

184. Adalah, "Nakba Law Violates Rights of Arab Minority to Preserve Its History and Culture," news release, March 27, 2011, http://www.adalah.org/eng/pressreleases/pr.php?file=27_03_11.

185. National Council of La Raza, "NCLR Q & A: What Is the National Council of La Raza?" undated, http://www.nclr.org/index.php/about_us/faqs/general_faqs_and_requested_resources/.

186. Jan Brewer, *Scorpions for Breakfast: My Fight against Special Interests, Liberal Media, and Cynical Politicos to Secure America's Border* (New York: Broadside Books, 2011), 188.

187. Ibid., 188, 192.

188. Ibid., 192.

189. Ibid., 192.

190. Brewer's "Minnesota-Norwegian" parents and other biographical facts are mentioned on her page at the website of the Republican Governors' Association, http://www.rga.org/homepage/governor-jan-brewer/.

191. Brewer, *Scorpions for Breakfast*, 192.

192. Hillary Sorin, "Today in Texas History: Texas Becomes a Minority-Majority State," *Texas on the Potomac* (*Houston Chronicle* blog), August 11, 2010, http://blog.chron.com/txpotomac/2010/08/today-in-texas-history-texas-becomes-a-minority-majority-state-2/.

193. Sabrina Tavernise, "Whites Account for Under Half of Births in U.S.," *New York Times*, May 17, 2012.

194. Ibid.

195. Politifact, "Fact-Checking the Claims about 'Anchor Babies' and Whether Illegal Immigrants 'Drop and Leave,'" August 6, 2010, http://www.politifact.com/truth-o-meter/statements/2010/aug/06/lindsey-graham/illegal-immigrants-anchor-babies-birthright/.

196. Dana Weiler-Polak, "Israel Enacts Law Allowing Authorities to Detain Illegal Migrants for Up to 3 Years," *Haaretz*, June 3, 2012.

197. David Project, *Burning Campus?*, 33.

198. Ibid.

199. For an excellent discussion of official secularism, Hinduism, and practice in India, see Perry Anderson, "After Nehru," *London Review of Books* 34, No. 15, August 2012, http://www.lrb.co.uk/v34/n15/perry-anderson/after-nehru.

200. Yasmin Qureshi, "Speaking Out on Kashmir and Palestine in the US," *Electronic Intifada*, November 9, 2010, http://electronicintifada.net/content/speaking-out-kashmir-and-palestine-us/9102.

201. David Project, *Burning Campus?*, 33.

202. Ibid., 34.

203. Ibid., 34.

204. Seth Freed Wessler, "The Israel Lobby Finds a New Face: Black College Students," *ColorLines*, January 18, 2012, http://colorlines.com/archives/2012/01/why_the_israel_lobby_looks_to_black_students_for_support.html.

205. Human Rights Watch, "Israel: Detained Asylum Seekers Pressured to Leave," news release, March 13, 2013, http://www.hrw.org/news/2013/03/13/israel-detained-asylum-seekers-pressured-leave.

206. Itamar Eichner, "Israel to Trade Arms for Migrants with African Countries," *Ynet*, July 9, 2013, http://www.ynetnews.com/articles/0,7340,L-4402834,00.html.

207. *Los Angeles Times*, "The Next UC Student Regent," editorial, July 19, 2013.

208. Ibid.

209. Larry Gordon, "UC Panel Names Activist as First Muslim Student Regent," *Los Angeles Times*,

July 17, 2013.

210. Nora Barrows-Friedman, "California Students Unite against 'Common Enemy' Janet Napolitano," *Electronic Intifada*, July 18, 2013, http://electronicintifada.net/blogs/nora-barrows-friedman /california-students-unite-against-common-enemy-janet-napolitano.

211. Elliott Mathias, "Advocacy 101: Give Reasons to Support Israel," *New Jersey Jewish News*, February 15, 2012, http://www.njjewishnews.com/article/8365/advocacy-101-give-reasons-to -support-israel.

212. Ali Abunimah, "Israel's Reut Institute Claims 'Price Tag' Attacks on EI, Irvine 11 and Palestine Return Centre," *Electronic Intifada*, December 15, 2011, http://electronicintifada.net/blogs/ali -abunimah/israels-reut-institute-claims-price-tag-attacks-ei-irvine-11-and-palestine-return.

213. Viva Sarah Press, "Bringing Israeli Soul to the US," *Jerusalem Post*, January 9, 2005.

214. Associated Students–UC Irvine, Resolution R48-15 (2012), "Divestment from Companies that Profit from Apartheid," http://www.asuci.uci.edu/legislative/legislations/print.php?cnum =R4815&gov_branch=ASUCI.

215. Vargas's letter, dated February 26, 2013, can be found at http://library.constantcontact.com /download/get/file/1109317602219239/Congressman+Juan+Vargas%27+letter+against +divestment.pdf; Davis's letter, dated February 27, 2013, can be found at http://library .constantcontact.com/download/get/file/1109317602219240/Congresswoman+Susan+Davis +letter+against+divestment.pdf. See also Miriam Raftery, "Local Congressional Members Oppose Students' Move to Divest UCSD from Companies Doing Business with Israel," *East County Magazine*, March 2, 2013,http://eastcountymagazine.org/node/12606.

216. Ali Abunimah, "After Hard-Fought Battle, Students Celebrate Divestment Vote Victory at UC San Diego," March 14, 2013, http://electronicintifada.net/blogs/ali-abunimah/after-hard -fought-battle-students-celebrate-divestment-vote-victory-uc-san-diego.

217. Nora Barrows-Friedman, "Zionist Groups Pressuring Student Government to Overturn UC Riverside Divestment Vote, Senator Says," *Electronic Intifada*, April 2, 2013, http://electronicintifada .net/blogs/nora/zionist-groups-pressuring-student-government-overturn-uc-riverside-divestment -vote.

218. Nora Barrows-Friedman, "Student Senate at UC Riverside Votes to Overturn Divestment Resolution after Zionist Pressure," *Electronic Intifada*, April 4, 2013, http://electronicintifada.net/blogs /nora-barrows-friedman/student-senate-uc-riverside-votes-overturn-divestment-resolution-after.

219. Monica Perez, "Committee Seeks Campus Discussion on Divestment," *Brown Daily Herald*, November 19, 2012.

220. Nora Barrows Friedman, "California University Chief Admits Failure to Curb Divestment Campaigns," *Electronic Intifada*, June 28, 2013, http://electronicintifada.net/blogs/nora /california-university-chief-admits-failure-curb-divestment-campaigns.

221. Judy Maltz, "'Attacking Israel Makes News, Supporting Israel Doesn't'—Hoenlein to *Haaretz*: World Jewry Must Say 'Enough' to Delegitimization of Israel," *Haaretz*, June 24, 2013.

222. National Students for Justice in Palestine, "National—Students for Justice in Palestine: Vision for Our Non-Hierarchical Movement," November 14, 2012, http://sjpnational.org/2012/11/14 /national-students-justice-palestine-vision-non-hierarchical-movement.

Chapter 7: Reclaiming Self-Determination

1.   Yasser Arafat, speech to the United Nations General Assembly, New York, November 13, 1974. See UN document A/PV.2282 and Corr. 1, http://unispal.un.org/UNISPAL.NSF/0 /A238EC7A3E13EED18525624A007697EC.

2.   This chapter is adapted from a paper first published by Al-Shabaka in May 2010.

3. See Salim Tamari (ed.), *Jerusalem 1948: The Arab Neighbourhoods and Their Fate in the War* (Jerusalem: Institute of Jerusalem Studies and Badil Resource Center, 1999).

4. Aron Heller, "Group: Israel Expands Subsidies to Settlements," Associated Press, August 4, 2013.

5. Ali Abunimah, "PLO Paper Reveals Leadership Bereft of Strategy, Legitimacy," *Electronic Intifada,* March 11, 2010, http://electronicintifada.net/v2/article11126.shtml.

6. Ian Black and Seumas Milne, "Papers Reveal How Palestinian Leaders Gave Up Fight over Refugees," *Guardian,* January 24, 2011.

7. Quoted in Tomis Kapitan, "Self-Determination," in Tomis Kapitan and Raja Halwani, *The Israeli-Palestinian Conflict: Philosophical Essays on Self-Determination, Terrorism and the One-State Solution* (New York: Palgrave Macmillan, 2008), 13–71.

8. Ibid., 27.

9. Ibid., 58.

10. Ibid., 37–38.

11. Ibid., 59.

12. Ibid., 58.

13. Omar Barghouti, "Re-Imagining Palestine: Self-Determination, Ethical Decolonization and Equality," *Znet,* July 29, 2009, http://www.zcommunications.org/re-imagining-palestine-by -omar-barghouti.

14. Susan Akram provided a copy of the speech she gave on March 3, 2012, at Harvard's Kennedy School. For additional legal background, see Susan Akram and Michael Lynk, "Arab-Israeli Conflict," in *The Max Planck Encyclopedia of Public International Law,* vol. 1, edited by Rudiger Wolfrum (Oxford: Oxford University Press, 2012), 499.

15. Barghouti, "Re-Imagining Palestine."

16. Ali Abunimah et al., "The One State Declaration," *Electronic Intifada,* November 29, 2007, http://electronicintifada.net/v2/article9134.shtml.

17. Palestinian Campaign for the Academic and Cultural Boycott of Israel (PACBI), "Palestinian Call for Boycott, Divestment, and Sanctions (BDS)," July 9, 2005, http://www.pacbi.org /etemplate.php?id=66.

Index

About the Author

Ali Abunimah is the author of *One Country: A Bold Proposal to End the Israeli-Palestinian Impasse* and is a contributor to *The Goldstone Report: The Legacy of the Landmark Investigation of the Gaza Conflict*. He has contributed to several other books and written hundreds of articles on the question of Palestine in a wide array of publications. He is the co-founder of the *Electronic Intifada* and the recipient of a 2013 Lannan Cultural Freedom Fellowship.